LANDMARK NEGOTIATIONS FROM AROUND THE WORLD

The publication of this book was supported by

 IRENE
Institute for Research and
Education on Negotiation

With sincere thanks to our translator Naomi Norberg who translated
several contributions from French.

LANDMARK NEGOTIATIONS FROM AROUND THE WORLD

Lessons for Modern Diplomacy

Edited by
Emmanuel VIVET

intersentia

Cambridge – Antwerp – Chicago

Intersentia Ltd
8 Wellington Mews
Wellington Street | Cambridge
CB1 1HW | United Kingdom
Tel.: +44 1223 736 170
Email: mail@intersentia.co.uk
www.intersentia.com | www.intersentia.co.uk

Distribution for the UK and Ireland:
NBN International
Airport Business Centre, 10 Thornbury Road
Plymouth, PL6 7PP
United Kingdom
Tel.: +44 1752 202 301 | Fax: +44 1752 202 331
Email: orders@nbninternational.com

Distribution for Europe and all other countries:
Intersentia Publishing nv
Groenstraat 31
2640 Mortsel
Belgium
Tel.: +32 3 680 15 50 | Fax: +32 3 658 71 21
Email: mail@intersentia.be

Distribution for the USA and Canada:
Independent Publishers Group
Order Department
814 North Franklin Street
Chicago, IL 60610
USA
Tel.: +1 800 888 4741 (toll free) | Fax: +1 312 337 5985
Email: orders@ipgbook.com

Landmark Negotiations from Around the World. Lessons for Modern Diplomacy

ISBN 978-1-78068-851-0
D/2019/7849/117
NUR 820

British Library Cataloguing in Publication Data. A catalogue record for this book is available from the British Library.

FOREWORD

Diplomats and History: A Return to Basics

The future belongs to those with the longest memory

Friedrich Nietzsche

At first sight, diplomacy and history should be considered a matter of fact. The intricacy of their relationship should make them natural-born partners, unlocking a path where both sides mutually benefit from each other. The two social actors which compose this tandem – the policy maker in charge of shaping the international order and the historian as the provider of useful explanations to tell us where we come from – should effortlessly be enticed by this complementarity and stir a fruitful collaboration. For any diplomat, history remains a companion both for acquiring the necessary knowledge to walk through the increasingly complex geo-political background and for helping furbish the toolkit of international negotiators. In a nutshell, the contribution of the study of history to the training of a young diplomat and to his following professional years sounds like an obvious choice, and a very logical one for that matter in the process of any successful diplomatic career.

How come, then, history seems to be fading away from diplomatic practice? Indeed as far as one can observe, this natural partnership has lost momentum and not much nowadays is heard of history in a meaningful way. Arguably it could be said that references to the Westphalia Treaty, for instance, have recently found a new lease of life in foreign policy discourses when doubts over the capacity of the present liberal order to survive the new multipolar world are emerging: nation-states would remain irreplaceable in this more chaotic and dangerous world. Yet the overuse of the Westphalia reference is far from implying a proper grasp of what precisely the Westphalian model means in the context of modern Europe, and even more so when applied to non-European reality. And an abusive exploitation of an undoubtedly major but somewhat outdated diplomatic achievement illustrates in its own way the contradictory relations that diplomats nourish today with history. While they acknowledge the invaluable contribution of historical references to their trade, they often misuse history for the purpose of a formatted narrative that misses the relevance of these references when attempting to understand the long-term changes in the making. Likewise, another impasse is to limit oneself to a simple examination of established precedents, essentially as a convenient safeguard against any major negotiating blunder. To say the least, this attitude seems far remote from a mutually beneficial cooperation, as one could expect from history and diplomacy. But it is more and more the reality of a relationship where both sides look as if they have progressively drifted apart.

What are the causes of this gradual disregard to history on behalf of professional diplomats? Common wisdom has it that history does not naturally come with a clear sense of its own destiny. True, the meaning of history in the making is rarely noticeable amidst an ongoing swirl of confused events, conflicts and crises that negotiators try if possible to anticipate but more generally only manage, at best to mitigate. "Men shape their history but they do not know the history they are shaping", French philosopher Raymond Aron once wrote in his *Leçons sur l'histoire* (Cours au Collège de France 1972–1974). Out of this reality stems the widely shared assumption that what is expected from diplomats is to constantly adapt and eventually transform the context in which they operate. When negotiators face at the conference table unprecedented positions or confront new colleagues dismissive of the "old school" diplomacy, they are seldom tempted to look back because they see the challenge as one of creativity and innovation. While they struggle to make sense of the ongoing global transformations and adapt to an ever morphing international landscape, they tend more and more to see history as of limited assistance. In their opinion, relying too much on the past can only deprive them of the agility required to adapt to modern times.

In truth, diplomacy has dramatically changed in recent years. Much as the contribution of history may have been in the past an indispensable resource for the tool box of any seasoned diplomat, its added value today is losing some of its relevance when it comes to grasping the ever changing nature of the international environment. With the new technological trends opening the way to the constant pressure of information input and social networks and with the new configuration of a multi-polar world in constant flux, the overall context of diplomatic activities seems to be facing a radical transformation. For diplomats, the priority then is to invent out of the box new answers to these multiple challenges. This quest for novelty may appear naïve, even shallow.

Yet diplomats cannot be entirely blamed for discarding historical references which bear so little resemblance to current reality. If this perception were not enough, the post-modern attitude of the US President Trump or the polarizing behavior of some of the populist leaders in power in Europe can only add to this impression of a profoundly transformed international scene where respect for facts, the protection of traditions, and a certain sense of decency are fading away. The intuitive notion that lessons learned may be an asset in diplomatic conversations seems to be evaporating at the same speed as populist pressure, high-tech innovation and social networks enter the daily life of foreign chanceries. Modern negotiators tend to presume there is not much relevance in looking for historical perspective while facing today in diplomatic gatherings new emerging countries which were absent or simply unnoticed a few years ago, and when issues involved bear little resemblance to the ones discussed in the past.

There may be an element of truth in this largely accepted assumption. Is there any relevance in dissecting the intricacies of the SALT negotiations (1969–1979) of the last century when today's threats involve cyber-attacks against nuclear systems and require new security concepts that were unheard of less than 20 years ago? Does the studious analysis of the Vienna Congress in 1815 offer any relevant key to practitioners dealing today with the unraveling of the world liberal order under pressure from an unprecedented combination of economic uncertainty, social anger, lack of a robust global governance, and an overall fear towards the future? However regrettable this new mindset may be, the lingering assumption that modern diplomacy does not require any substantial contribution from history becomes all the more compelling as policy makers and media call for rapidity and innovation and thrive on the notion of permanent creativity. For professional diplomats, history is overtaken by the speed of time and continuous adaptation is now the new brand.

This underlying current of unprecedented and permanent innovation is noticeable everywhere. It is a common feature of our societies and its impact on diplomacy operates in the same way as for the rest of the public action sphere. But the implications are not only affecting the backdrop in which diplomats operate. They also shape the rules and methods of the trade itself. The traditional setting of negotiations is increasingly giving way to more open formats where representatives from civil society sit and take the floor in multilateral meetings, as recently observed for climate change or migration talks. Inside the European institutions, commitments on transparency lead to the publication of negotiating mandates and a greater involvement of public opinion in the definition of an agreement and its eventual endorsement. Noticeably in recent years, the recourse to the referendum process is becoming a regular practice to conclude hazardous negotiations, which forces diplomats to pay more attention to popular demand. These novelties may look naïve, superficial, even irritating for many professional diplomats but are mostly perceived as lending reinvigorating legitimacy to international forums. Yet, irrespective of whether these more or less substantial innovations improve the negotiating processes, they are testimony to a changing mood at the national and international level that cannot be lightly dismissed. The substance of foreign policy has surreptitiously been transformed into a more complex pattern where previous boundaries nowadays are blurred. Today war and peace are confusingly intermingling on the ground; internal and external affairs are intricately intertwined leading to a more serious oversight from Parliaments and public opinion on all matters related to the foreign sphere; and professional diplomats work with civil society activists on common grounds with less and less separation between the two. The recent multiplication of track 2 mediations under the auspices of private diplomacy reinforces the necessity for public agencies to consider this new form of competition as a legitimate component of the diplomatic profession. Each one of these different features, in its own way, is reinventing the diplomatic trade.

This new reality leaves not much room for the dispensation of historical experience. History in the diplomatic world is being sidelined. The legacy of retired diplomats is parading nowadays in heavy volumes of memoirs which do not see great sales in bookshops. They may still attract the attention of historians but are seldom fit for professional use. As for direct contacts between old and young diplomats for the purpose of transferring experience and sharing some of the most cherished "tricks of the game", this tradition seems to be silently passing away. Time is too short for active diplomats to go through the reading of their seniors' thick volumes and the relentless pressure of their agenda does not allow much room for a meaningful dialogue of generations. Even when admitting such a practice was never deeply rooted amidst a diplomatic corps often handicapped by a solid tradition of individualism, it is nonetheless worth noting that valuable diplomatic experience looks like being increasingly lost in transition. The growing importance of the role played by Heads of State and Prime Ministers in the elaboration and management of national foreign policy coupled to the frequent changes of their staff leads more and more to the departure from the public service of high performing officials and the loss of an extensive expertise. In the new European Union department in charge of external action, the rule set up from the start to recruit seconded national diplomats only for a limited time has reduced the efficiency of the administration through this constant rotation of personnel. And the frequent lack of any serious orderly transmission of experience between diplomats when they rotate in their jobs (except for some superficial and often improvised meetings) speaks loudly for the depletion of resources frequently observed in diplomatic services.

More fundamentally, relations between policy-makers and policy-thinkers have never been an easy ride in modern diplomacy. Personalities like Henry Kissinger who ventured successfully into foreign policy out of their academic background have mostly been an exception in an otherwise complex cooperation, where both sides seem to largely ignore each other. When they step into the foreign policy world, representatives from the academic community are seldom immune from criticism coming from the professional diplomats, who complain over the lack of realism and experience of their input. Policy planning divisions, which are today commonly set up in most of the Foreign Affairs ministries, and where outsiders from the academic world are invited to come and share their thoughts, see their work frequently met with resistance and often sidelined inside their own administration. Conversely, historians have not always paid enough attention to the diplomatic dimension of their work nor tried to convert their historical knowledge into a concrete contribution for diplomatic practitioners. Historical studies on practical diplomacy remain scarce, thus forcing young generations of diplomats to search empirically after individual experiences or case studies for lack of theoretical work on the interaction between history and diplomacy in practice. For reasons inspired by the need to protect Academia's autonomy on one side, and the sense of irrelevance all too often shared by diplomats when considering a potential historical input, the two communities seem to struggle when they try to define some common ground between theory and action.

Should it then be definitely asserted that history and diplomacy henceforth form an incompatible couple doomed to divorce? It could be tempting to botch a conclusion of that sort, as today's professional diplomats, carried away by modernism and the irreversibility of the march of time, no longer find merit or relevance in lessons learned. This may well be the current state-of-play but is such a forthright conclusion the correct one? As diplomats struggle to grasp the causes behind the unraveling of the global order and face an ever-changing professional practice, the need for knowledge and experience paves the way for history to reemerge as a natural provider of the missing link between modernity and rationality.

To be efficient and reach breakthroughs in their negotiating efforts, diplomats often lack two important ingredients: the capacity to comprehend the outlines of the geopolitical situation they are facing and the proper attitude to drive a negotiation to a successful outcome. In both cases, historical experience provides useful elements to that end. Moreover a solid historical background can stir the kind of creative and original diplomacy that is desperately lacking nowadays. With a broad yet clear and precise perspective of the political, economic, and social strands involved in a complex diplomatic process, negotiators are protected from walking in a blind alley. A good link to history is also a way to avoid repeating the well-known mistakes of history. Diplomats can ascertain their options and deductions in the light of the lessons of history and be more assertive for that. More importantly, they can learn from experience some of the qualities that enhance the aptitude of a negotiator to engage discussions in the proper direction and eventually close a deal. They also can get a better grasp of the cultural specificities that shape the attitudes of their foreign interlocutors, thus avoiding the confusion that may arise from a behavior that was not perhaps understood at first sight. These are not unreachable peaks. They have more to do with elementary notions like the ability to listen to the other side and capture the genuine reasons behind the concerns expressed; the capacity to delineate the ground for a realistic compromise; and the propensity for any negotiating delegation to define the precise goals that can be reasonably reached. For all of these elements to find their appropriate place and compose a harmonious alignment, lessons learned from the past – the unknown negotiations just like the more prestigious ones – are the true reliable resources to achieve an optimal result.

At the European level for instance, many observers will indulge in the well-rehearsed argument that a Union of 28 members cannot greatly benefit from past lessons that operated a few years ago with a smaller number of nations. And there is some truth in that assessment. But what surfaces from this enlargement process are a few eternal lessons that apply whatever the size, format, or shape of the assembled convention, from the Holy Roman Germanic Empire to Westphalia to Vienna and the UN, and which should not be forgotten. They are about folding into the talks the difficulties of other delegations, finding the right tone of argumentation, manipulating one's own instructions to adapt to circumstances, showing empathy when it can help and firmness when required, never humiliating the defeated party. In short, it is about grasping a genuine understanding of the negotiating situation and making the best out of it. Much of the cause behind the current stalemate in many of the ongoing discussions in Brussels has to do with the ignorance of these simple guidelines.

This is definitely not rocket science. Nor perhaps is it the ground for ambitious academic research. Yet it is the substance that makes in the end the difference between a failed attempt at delivering a deal and a positive conclusion to a process that seemed at some point a desperate cause. The Iranian nuclear agreement, the peace plan in Columbia, or the outcome of the Brexit talks do not come out by chance or a peculiar stroke of genius. Each of these achievements is the outcome of a long and painstaking labor out of attention, steadiness, and humbleness. This is where history can teach today's diplomats the lessons of a long line of predecessors. And this is also how history patiently builds up a professional diplomatic expertise for the promotion of an international community still in the making.

Pierre Vimont
First Executive Secretary General of the European Union
External Action Service,
Former Ambassador to the USA, to the EU,
Former Chief of Staff of the French Minister of Foreign Affairs

PREFACE

Negotiation is a living thing. It is fact before theory, often a practice that is more or less clear before it is an art, and very likely an art before a science. The evolving, creative, and sometimes unforeseeable nature of the negotiation process is one of the features this book highlights. Each of its 30 chapters tells the tale of a noteworthy international negotiation chosen from across the centuries and around the world.

In these chapters, the reader will find brilliant negotiations, secret negotiations, calm negotiations, and chaotic negotiations. Some of the negotiators are in a strong position, but even more interesting are those that are in a weak position. Alliances are made; coalitions fall apart. The reader will also see how important individual determination, as well as organizational factors are in multilateral negotiations. Many peace treaties will be signed, while ambitious conferences will fail.

The same questions are raised every time. How can an improbable success be explained (such as, in 1513, when the governor of a city under siege managed to persuade the invading army to turn around and go home)? Is there a list of ingredients to achieve a resounding success (such as the 1787 Constitutional Convention in Philadelphia, or the 1998 Good Friday Agreement in Northern Ireland)? How can failures be explained (for example, why did the 1877 Constantinople conference get off to a good start but end in failure)? What makes reluctant parties eventually agree to come to the negotiating table (as the FARC and the Colombian government did in 2010)? Or, more simply, why didn't they think of negotiating at all (in late 1917 the German leaders were in an excellent position to negotiate)? How far can the negotiators' skill take them, and when must they admit that the conditions for success had not been met? Negotiation is not all there is to international relations, it can't explain everything, but it is the focal point – the place where a stable balance between nations is achieved – or not.

To answer these questions, each chapter contains both a summary account of a noteworthy case from the past (a bilateral or multilateral negotiation, an important treaty, a famous mediation, etc.) and a critical analysis of the events to see how they illustrate negotiation theories.

In each case, the author uses the most recent concepts developed in negotiation studies to analyze the events and arrive at a "lesson" that can be learned. Each chapter constitutes its own particular type of conversation between history and negotiation, and thus contributes to what Fernand Braudel called "the lowering of customs duties between the various disciplines". Negotiation studies essentially draw from neighboring disciplines, and with this book we hope to further the idea that history is one of the disciplines that has something to offer.

What contributions have these neighboring disciplines made? From about 1650, when ambassadors in residence were becoming the norm and started forming of professional category of their own, the French school of the 17th and 18th centuries[1] asked themselves what qualities were required to be a "negotiator" or "ambassador". The two terms were synonymous then, and the words "diplomat" and "diplomacy" did not exist yet – they were invented by Edmund Burke around 1790.[2] Authors such as Jean Hotman de Villiers;[3] Louis Rousseau de Chamoix;[4] François de Callières,[5] whose work was translated into five languages as soon as it was published; Antoine Pecquet;[6] and Fortuné Barthélémy de Felice[7] offered advice to professionalize the job of ambassador. They developed typologies and the first concepts (which would be rediscovered later) contrasting, for example "real interests" with "small passions", or highlighting "expedience" and stigmatizing "intrigue". As Pecquet wrote: "The qualities and talents of negotiator are the main causes that influence the fate of the largest affairs and also decide the greatest interests."[8]

---

1   See the two ESSEC IRENE colloquia held in Paris in 2002 and 2003: Aux sources de la négociation européenne. Les penseurs français de la diplomatie à l'âge classique, June 18, 2002, Paris; Talleyrand, Prince des négociateurs, February 1–4, 2004.

2   BERRIDGE, G.R., KEENS-SOPER, M., OTTE, T.G., Diplomatic Theory from Machiavelli to Kissinger, New York, Palgrave, 2001, p. 5.

3   HOTMAN DE VILLIERS, De la charge et de la dignité de l'ambassadeur, 1st ed., Paris-London, 1603; 2nd ed., Paris, 1604. Reprint: ESSEC IRENE, Paris-Cergy, 2003.

4   ROUSSEAU DE CHAMOIX, L., L'idée du parfait ambassadeur, Paris: 1692. Reprint: ESSEC IRENE, Paris-Cergy, 2003.

5   CALLIERES, F. de (1716/2002), De la manière de négocier avec les souverains. Published by LEMPEREUR, A., Geneva, Droz, 2002. Translated and published by Houghton Mifflin and by A.F. Withe, University of Notre Dame Press.

6   PECQUET, A., Discours sur l'Art de négocier, Paris, Nyon fils, 1737. Reprint: ESSEC IRENE, Paris-Cergy, 2003.

7   FELICE, F. B. de (1770–1778), "Négociations ou l'art de négocier", entry in L'Encyclopédie ou Dictionnaire raisonné des connaissances humaines, (Yverdon), in LEMPEREUR, A. and COLSON, A., (eds.), Négociations européennes. D'Henri IV à l'Europe des 27, Paris, A2C, 2008, pp. 87–121.

8   PECQUET, A., Discours sur l'Art de négocier, ESSEC IRENE, Paris-Cergy, 2003, p. 14.

Twenty-one centuries after Sun Tzu and one century after Machiavelli, in the context of European nation-states, the later authors would reply to each other and had begun to develop a model of how negotiators operate.

When research on negotiations started up again, in the mid-20th century in the United States, it was abundant and went in several directions simultaneously. At least five major disciplines have been contributing since then: game theory, which starting in the 1950s against the backdrop of the Cold War, made it possible to lay out the strategic dilemmas running through negotiations;[9] sociology, especially in the analysis of working relationships, which reminds us that negotiation is essentially an interaction between individuals or human groups;[10] political science, very apropos in the study of international relations;[11] psychology, which provides precious empirical results on negotiators' behavior;[12] and law, which helps us understand the rules that govern and increasingly shape negotiations. In his book on international negotiations Kremenyuk broadens the field even further, listing contributions from nine major disciplines: history, law, organizational theory, economics, game theory, analytics, psychology, cognitive science, and content analysis.[13]

This book is therefore a foray into history, a source of inspiration for research on negotiation.

Of course, famous studies have already been produced on major negotiations, from the Treaty of Westphalia to the Oslo Accords via the Congress of Vienna or the Yalta Conference. A whole segment of the university is producing remarkable work on the history of diplomacy, and some of those authors agreed to contribute to this book.

Systematic studies are rarer. In the introduction, I. William Zartman cites the well-known works of Theda Skocpol, Barbara Tuchman, and Bruce Jentleson. I would add Frederik Stanton's book, in which he explores eight fascinating historical cases, two of which are related to those in

---

[9]   See, e.g., SCHELLING, T.C. [1960], *The Strategy of Conflict*, 2nd ed., Cambridge, MA, Harvard University Press, 1980.

[10] See, e.g., WALTON, R. and MCKERSIE, R., *A Behavorial Theory of Labor Negotiations*, New York, McGraw Hill, New York, 1965; PRUITT, D.G. and CARNEVALE, P.J.D., *Negotiation in social conflict*, Pacific Grove, California, Brooks/Cole, 1993.

[11] See, e.g., IKLÉ, F.C. *How Nations Negotiate*, Harper Collins, 1964; NICOLSON, H., *Diplomacy*, Oxford University Press, 1963.

[12] See, e.g., PRUITT, D.G., *Negotiation Behavior*, Academic Press, 1981; KAHNEMAN, D., TVERSKY, A. and SLOVIC, P., *Judgement under Uncertainty: Heuristics and Biases*, Cambridge University Press, 1982.

[13] KREMENYUK, V. (ed.), *International Negotiation*, 1991, 2nd ed. 2002, PIN publications.

---

this book.[14] In the same vein, Graham Allison's successful *The Thucydides Trap*[15] is a sound analysis of 16 historical cases that speak very persuasively to the 21st-century observer interested in the relationship between the United States and China. Like those works, this book follows the case-study tradition. As Zartman says, case studies are the raw materials for understanding the past. Our modest hope is to take the path laid out by these major works and help make history a contributor to international negotiation studies.

The experience gained when the French book on the same subject was published in 2014[16] has helped me improve this version in various ways. Not only is the scope of this study broader (we cover every continent), it is also more structured (the book is divided into six sections). The first series of chapters addresses the sensitive question of the parties' desire to negotiate, i.e., how negotiations begin. With these premises laid, the second section deals with bilateral negotiations; the third looks at multilateral negotiations in all their complexity, from the angle of coalitions, or of the organizing process. The fourth section examines the issue of emotions and beliefs, as some international interactions cannot be explained solely by the rational interests of the parties. The fifth section discusses several negotiations that took place in the Near and Middle East, including with Iran. The book ends with three international mediations, which border on negotiation.

I. William Zartman has dealt in the introduction with the formidable theoretical question of the conditions under which lessons may be learned from historical cases. The goal is obviously not to draw lessons from the past without applying any filters. However, Zartman shows that this research is possible, using both an inductive and a deductive approach.

The concluding chapter contains a list of the negotiation lessons drawn from the various chapters, then picks up the conversation started by Zartman on the connection between the history of diplomacy and research on negotiation.

---

14   Stanton, F., *Great Negotiations; Agreements that Changed the Modern World*, Yardley Pennsylvania, Westholme Publishing, 2010.
15   Allison, G., *The Thucydides Trap: Are the US and China Headed for War?*, Atlantic, September 24, 2015.
16   Vivet E., *Négociations d'hier, leçons pour aujourd'hui*, Brussels, Larcier, 2014.

ACKNOWLEDGMENTS

This book is, first of all, the work of its 31 contributors. They are university professors, historians, researchers, diplomats, and practitioners. Each made a real effort in the direction of the subject matter they know the least, and I thank them for trusting me enough and play the game. Their willingness to listen patiently and be flexible given the constraints of the exercise made it possible to produce an organized, coherent book. Their varied bodies of knowledge, ways of thinking, and ways of stating problems are what make this collective adventure so enriching.

I especially thank I. William Zartman, a great author to whom negotiation studies owe so much, who did me the honor of writing the introduction; and Pierre Vimont, the author of a foreword that gives us a glimpse of the vast experience of one of the best French diplomats of his time.

This book is also the product of the encouragement it received from numerous people. I offer my particular thanks to Paul Meerts, former deputy director of the Clingendael Institute in the Netherlands, trainer of diplomats, and author of a doctoral dissertation on diplomatic negotiations throughout history who generously offered his support from the very beginning; Carrie Menkel-Meadow, from the University of California, whose enthusiasm and warm encouragements were so precious; and Guy Olivier Faure, who provided useful and wise counsel.

The book also owes much to the Institute for Research and Teaching on Negotiation (ESSEC IRENE) (*Institut de recherche et d'enseignement sur la négociation*, or IRENÉ – the word meaning "peace" in Greek), a center created in Paris by the business school ESSEC in 1996, where the French version of this project came to fruition in 2014. ESSEC IRENE's environment, which mixes researchers and practitioners interested in negotiation, be they academics, civil servants, managers in businesses, trade unionists or mediators, offers a fine setting for new enterprises. The threefold dedication of the institute to research (for instance on European negotiations), field work (for instance in contributing to the rapprochement of ex-combatants in the Horn of Africa) and training (for instance at the European Commission) helped to support this project. I especially thank Aurélien Colson, the Institute's director, who supported the initial idea in 2011 and helped me progress from scratching out a few notes to completing a much broader book. I must also thank Arnaud Stimec and Christian Thuderoz, the former and current editors-in-chief of the French-language review *Négociations*, who assuaged my every doubt and answered my every request for advice. My thanks also go to Naomi Norberg who carefully and accurately translated the chapters from the French version that are published here.

I would also like to acknowledge Ann-Christin Maak-Scherpe and Rebecca Moffat at Intersentia. With subtlety and generosity, they put their trust and professionalism to work for this project, enabling the authors, in turn, to give the best of themselves.

Finally, I would like to thank all the students and professionals in continuing education classes who are ultimately the people who gave me the idea for this book. Their questions and their desire to understand and learn are a constant source of challenge and inspiration. Because, like negotiation studies themselves, this book arose from a practice: the training sessions I have been giving for the past 15 years with ESSEC IRENE in Brussels and Paris, be it at the European Commission, the *Ecole de Guerre* [French School of War], the *Ecole Nationale d'Administration* [French School of Government] or the *Institut diplomatique* [French Diplomatic Institute]. Examples are needed to illustrate theoretical concepts; the anecdotes become stories; the stories lead to further verifications and research; and the research makes it possible to draw conclusions, then correct and refine the writing. All of that progressively became this book.

CONTENTS

LIST OF CONTRIBUTORS

William W. Baber has combined education with business throughout his career. His experience includes economic development in the State of Maryland, supporting business starters in Japan, and teaching business students in Japan and Europe. Currently he is teaching and researching negotiation and business models as an Associate Professor in the Graduate School of Management, Kyoto University. He is lead author of the 2015 textbook *Practical Business Negotiation* (Taylor and Francis, 2015). Recent publications include *Team Positions in Negotiation*, and *Identifying Macro Phases Across the Negotiation Lifecycle* (Group Decision and Negotiation, 2018), and negotiation simulations such as *Intellectual Property Negotiation Between Mukashi Games and Pixie*.

Marc Beretta is a Master Certified Coach (MCC) by the International Coach Federation (ICF). He is the CEO and the founder of *Inis alga* (www.inisalga.com), an international coaching company. He coaches CEOs, Management Committees, and Organizations to transform their rational, emotional and behavioral potential into life success. He is an Academic Faculty member of NYU-LSE-HEC TRIUM Global Executive MBA. He successfully trained top negotiators from international institutions (e.g. European Commission, European Parliament, AFD) and Vietnamese negotiators for WTO membership. He is Irish and French (dual citizenship) with Greek and Italian roots. He believes that small changes can make a big difference.

Yves Bruley is a lecturer in diplomatic history (19th century) at the *École Pratique des Hautes Études* (EPHE, PSL, Paris). His research focuses on the history of French diplomacy in the 19th century. He earned his doctorate from Sorbonne Université, the thesis thereof being published as *Le Quai d'Orsay impérial* (Paris: A. Pedone, 2012). Other books on the foreign policy of Napoléon III (1852–1870) include *La Diplomatie du Sphinx* (Paris: CLD, 2015). He also published with Thierry Lentz *Diplomaties au temps de Napoléon* (CNRS Ed., 2014). He is an adviser to the Chancellor of the *Institut de France*, an independent public commission founded in 1795 and dedicated to the progress of sciences and social sciences.

Nancy Caldwell, who unfortunately passed away in 2017, was an American trainer, consultant for international corporations and a lecturer. She was active in Paris in various French academic institutions and published regularly at the Paris *Biennale* on negotiation. She had been working notably on negotiation cultures and intercultural negotiations. Her emphasis was also on the use of applied creativity techniques in negotiation. Among other works, she had written the chapter "A Qualitative Interview with Thirteen Practitioners" in *Professional Cultures in International Negotiation: Bridge or Rift* (International Institute on Applied Systems Analysis / IIASA, 2003), where she examined the cultural components in the matrix of international negotiation dynamics.

Habib Chamoun has, over the past 25 years, conducted negotiation and business development activities in industrial sectors such as oil and gas, petrochemical, and chemical, for the sales and marketing of services and products. Among the companies he has worked for are ELF Aquitaine (Total), ICA Fluor Daniel, and Brown and Root. Dr. Chamoun has trained thousands business professionals on his "Business Development Approach" for sales and negotiation and has conducted research on negotiation. He is a visiting scholar and adjunct professor at the Cameron School of Business at St Thomas University in Houston, Texas. He received his PhD from the University of Texas in Austin.

Jean-Claude Cheynet is Emeritus Professor of Byzantine history at Sorbonne Université (1995–2015) and honorary member of the Institut universitaire de France (2008–2013). A former researcher at the French CNRS (1977–1995), he is also a member of the *Academia Europaea*. He edited the *Revue des études byzantines* from 1996 to 2005 and co-edited the *Studies in Sigillography* from 2003 to 2016. His main works are about Byzantine aristocracy (*Pouvoir et contestations à Byzance (963–1210)*, Paris 1990; *The Byzantine Aristocracy and its Military Function*, Aldershot, 2006) and the edition with a commentary of lead seals catalogues.

Aurélien Colson is Professor of Political Science at ESSEC Business School and Director of IRENE (Institute for Research and Education on Negotiation) since 2008. His research on international negotiation appears in peer-reviewed journals. He has authored or edited several books, translated into 10 languages. In 2008, his research was awarded a *Grand Prix* by the French *Académie des sciences morales et politiques*. He is co-director of the *Négociations* journal. He served as Adviser to the French Prime Minister (1998–2002). He has coordinated negotiation training curricula for several institutions, including the European Commission and the French Ministry of Foreign Affairs.

Larry Crump is Deputy Director of the APEC Study Centre at Griffith University (Brisbane, Australia) where he also teaches undergraduate and graduate courses on international negotiation. Larry has devoted over 25 years to the study of negotiation complexity by examining negotiations involving the G20, UN climate change negotiations, the WTO, negotiations involving regional associations (APEC, EU, Mercosur, Pacific Alliance, Union for the Mediterranean) and many bilateral trade negotiations to extend theory on negotiation strategy, linkage dynamics, closure, turning points, framing and coalition building. Larry provides negotiation training and consulting to business and government.

Julie d'Andurain is Professor in Contemporary History at the University of Lorraine, Metz (France). Her research focuses on the history of conflict, particularly colonial conflicts in the African and Arab worlds. She published, notably, the following books: *La Capture de Samory (1898), l'achèvement de la conquête de l'Afrique de l'Ouest* (SOTECA, 2012) and *Colonialisme ou impérialisme ? Le "parti colonial" en pensée et en action* (Hémisphères éditions/Zellige, Paris, 2017). She was the editor of issues of the *Outre-Mers. Revue d'histoire* journal (Nr. 390–391, Nr. 400–401). She received her doctorate in history from Sorbonne Université, Paris.

Isabelle Dasque is a lecturer at the Faculty of Arts in Sorbonne Université (Paris IV). Her research has focused on French diplomacy (19th–20th century) and on the renewal of its social, cultural and professional practices confronted with the changes in the international order and the emerging of parallel diplomacies. Her thesis is entitled "A la recherche de Monsieur de Norpois, les diplomates de la République 1871–1914" ["Looking for Mister de Norpois, the diplomats during the third republic"] and is to be published in 2019 with the Press University Publications of the Sorbonne. She received her doctorate from Sorbonne Université.

Stanislas de Laboulaye is a former French academic and diplomat. After having specialized in EU policies and negotiations for almost 10 years in Paris, in Brussels, and in Madrid, he was later appointed Consul General in Jerusalem (1996–1999), ambassador to Madagascar (2000–2002), to Moscow (2006–2009), and to the Holy See (2009–2012). As Political Director in Paris (2002–2006) he was the chief negotiator for

France in the negotiation between the EU3 (France, Germany, UK) and Iran on its nuclear program between 2003 and 2006.

Jean-Marc de la Sablière was French President Chirac's diplomatic advisor and sherpa. He also served as ambassador to Egypt and Italy and as France's permanent representative to the United Nations, in New-York, from 2002 to 2007, notably during the 2003 tense discussions on Iraq. He played a key role in the passing of Security Council resolutions on Lebanon, Iran, Darfur, Ivory Coast and protection of children in armed conflicts. After retiring in 2012 he taught for seven years at Sciences Po Paris School of International Affairs (PSIA). He is the author, among other books, of *Le Conseil de sécurité: Ambitions et limites* (Larcier, 2015, reissued in 2018).

Sami Faltas was born in Egypt and grew up in the Netherlands. During his career in universities and think tanks, he published widely on arms proliferation and control. Today he is an independent trainer and consultant on security governance and negotiation. His assignments on security governance take him all over Africa, Europe and Central Asia. He teaches negotiation at the College of Europe in Belgium and the University of Loughborough in the UK and designs simulation games. When discussing the culture and language of negotiation, he draws on his own multicultural and multilingual education.

Guy Olivier Faure is Visiting Professor at the CEIBS China-Europe International Business School, Shanghai, China, with an extensive experience in China or on Chinese issues since 1990, as well as a long-lasting experience in conflict resolution in the Middle East (2008–2012). A member of the editorial boards of three journals dealing with international negotiations, he has authored, co-authored and edited 19 books and over 120 articles, and his works have been published in 12 different languages. He is engaged in various consulting and training activities and is referenced in the Diplomat's Dictionary published by the United States Peace Press, Washington. He obtained his doctorate from Sorbonne Université, Paris.

Randy D. Hazlett holds the rank of Professor in the school of Mining and Geosciences at Nazarbayev University in the Republic of Kazakhstan. He obtained a PhD from the University of Texas in Austin. Dr. Hazlett's research spans a broad range of topics in reservoir engineering and asset management. He is a long-time business associate of Dr. Habib Chamoun and co-author on a number of negotiation and business-related projects.

Ariel Macaspac Hernandez is a researcher at the German Development Institute Bonn (Germany). He was a fellow at the Käte Hamburger Kolleg/ Centre for Global Cooperation Research (2016–2017) as well as a scientist at the Fraunhofer Centre for International Management and Knowledge Economy (2014–2017), Leipzig. In addition, he was a lecturer and researcher at the Universities of Leipzig, Cologne, Tartu (Estonia), Mexico and Ateneo de Manila, teaching climate change, environmental politics and negotiations. He was Coordinator of the Processes on International Negotiations (PIN) Program. He holds a doctoral degree in Philosophy (pol. science) from the University of Vienna and a doctoral degree in Economics and Social Sciences from the University of Cologne.

Kevin Homrighausen is a juris doctor candidate at the University of California, Irvine School of Law. Under the guidance of Professor Carrie Menkel-Meadow, his studies have focused on alternative dispute resolution and international legal analysis. As a member of UCI's International Justice Clinic, he also worked extensively on behalf of the United Nations Special Rapporteur on the promotion and protection of the right to freedom of opinion and expression. Upon graduation in May 2019, he carried his interest in negotiation and mediation into private practice.

R. Gerald Hughes is Reader in Military History and Director of the Centre for Intelligence and International Security Studies at Aberystwyth University (UK). He is the reviews editor of the journal *Intelligence & National Security* and his publications include *Britain, Germany and the Cold War: The Search for a European Détente, 1949–1967* (2007/2014) and *The Postwar Legacy of Appeasement: British Foreign Policy Since 1945* (2014). Hughes is the editor, with Len Scott, of *The Cuban Missile Crisis: A Critical Reappraisal* (2016). He is also a member of the Society for Historians of American Foreign Relations (SHAFR) and a Fellow of the Royal Historical Society (FRHistS).

Tobias W. Langenegger sadly and unexpectedly passed away in August 2019 after finishing his chapter in this book. He was a lecturer and a researcher at the Chair of Negotiation and Conflict Management at ETH Zurich with an academic background in natural sciences. He obtained his doctoral degree from ETH Zurich for his work on the mathematical modelling of conflicts. His research focused on negotiation and conflict dynamics in international politics, with publications in journals such as *Group Decision and Negotiation* and *Science*. Beside his activities in research, teaching, and training, Tobias had experience in negotiation consulting for administrations and governments on a national and international level.

Francesco Marchi is Adjunct Professor of Political Science and Director of the Research and Training program "Negotiators of Europe" at the Institute for Research and Education on Negotiation (ESSEC IRENE). He regularly delivers training on negotiation to European institutions' officials and diplomatic academies. He teaches negotiation courses at ESSEC Business School's MBA, and he is Visiting Professor at the ENA (Ecole Nationale d'Aministration), at the College of Europe (Bruges) and at the Paris School of International Affairs at the Institut d'etudes Politiques de Paris (Sciences Po). He is also actively involved in the research and application of innovative pedagogical tools for teaching negotiation. He holds a PhD in Political Science from the Institut d'études politiques of Paris (Sciences Po).

Paul Willem Meerts worked for 40 years as a trainer, manager and researcher at the Netherlands Institute of International Relations "Clingendael". Since 1989 he has been connected with the *Processes of International Negotiation* (PIN) research program, based in Austria, the Netherlands and Germany respectively. Paul published widely on negotiations between states. In 2014 he successfully defended his doctoral dissertation on "Diplomatic Negotiation, Essence and Evolution". He is the founder of the PIN *Program on International Negotiation Training* (POINT). Since 1989 he has been training diplomats and civil and military officials – as well as university students – in international negotiation processes in a hundred countries around the world.

Carrie Menkel-Meadow is Distinguished Professor of Law and Political Science at the University of California, Irvine and Professor Emerita at Georgetown University Law Center. She has published over 15 books and 200 articles on negotiation, mediation and dispute resolution, as well as on legal ethics, legal education and other subjects. She has been teaching negotiation and mediation in law schools in the United States and in over 25 countries since 1980 and is also a practicing mediator and facilitator in both public and private disputes. She also serves as a negotiation trainer to various audiences at governmental level. Among other books, she has published *Negotiation: Processes for Problem Solving*, 2nd ed. (Wolters Kluwer, 2014) and *Dispute Resolution: Beyond the Adversarial Model*, 3rd ed. (Wolters Kluwer, 2019).

Emmanuel Petit is Professor of Economics at the University of Bordeaux (France). He is a member of GREThA (Theoretical and Applied Economics: *Groupe de Recherches en Economie théorique et Appliquée*, UMR CNRS, 5113). His research and academic publications focus on the role of emotions in the emergence of cooperative or altruistic behaviors. He is the author of the *Economics of Emotions* (La Découverte, 2015) and the *Economics of Care* (PUF, 2013).

Lord Peter Ricketts was a British diplomat for 40 years. He was Ambassador to France 2012–2016, and before that served as Britain's first National Security Adviser from 2010–2012. He has held a range of other senior posts in the security policy field, including Chairman of the Joint Intelligence Committee in 2000, Political Director in the Foreign Office from 2001–2003 (dealing with policy on the Afghanistan and Iraq interventions, and the 9/11 terrorist attacks) and Permanent Representative to NATO from 2003–2006. After retirement, Peter became a cross-bench member of the House of Lords (non-political) and a Visiting Professor at King's College London.

Frans Schram is a Berlin-based independent trainer, consultant and researcher on EU negotiation, peace mediation and dialogue. He has been active at the intersection of diplomacy, negotiation and cross-cultural communication for almost 15 years and is a member of the *Program on International Negotiation Training* (POINT). Working with organizations such as the Berghof Foundation, ESSEC IRENE, the College of Europe, the Clingendael Institute, the European Commission and the Dutch MFA, Frans has trained and advised governments, non-state armed groups, private sector companies and diplomats at all levels of experience and in over 30 countries worldwide.

Arnaud Stimec is Professor of Management at Sciences Po Rennes. His research is focused on dialog and barriers to dialog in organizations including negotiation, conflict management, and participative management. Between 2008 and 2014 he was the editor-in-chief of the academic journal *Négociations*. He published over 40 chapters and articles in academic journals, as well as three books on negotiation, conflict management and mediation, notably *La médiation en entreprise* (Dunod, Paris, 2004) (three reprints). In addition to research and teaching, he serves as mediator in various contexts. He is also the director of a department dedicated to education in environmental transition with a focus on dialog.

Ghislaine Stouder is *agrégée* of Classical Literature, former fellow-member of the French School of Rome and Associate Professor of Roman History at Poitiers University. Her research has focused mostly on Roman diplomatic practices and international relations from the 5th to the

1st century BCE. In 2011 she obtained her PhD thesis entitled *History and representation of Roman diplomacy during the mid-Republic (396–264 B.C.)* from the University of Aix-Marseille. Since then, she has notably supervised the publication of a book, *The Roman Diplomacy under the Republic: a Practice under consideration*, published in 2015, and written several articles on Roman diplomacy.

Pierre Vimont was a French diplomat for 42 years. He was the first Executive Secretary General of the External Action Service of the European Union (newly installed EU diplomatic corps) 2010–2015, and before that served as Ambassador to the United States 2007–2010, as the Chief of Staff of three different French ministers of foreign affairs 2002–2007 and as the Permanent Representative of France to the EU 1999–2002. He has held a range of other senior posts in the development, science, and culture field. After retirement, Pierre became the first Mediator of the French MFA and a senior fellow at the foreign-policy think tank Carnegie Europe.

Laurent Vissière is Professor of Medieval History at Sorbonne Université, Paris. A specialist of the late Middle Ages (14th to early 16th century), he has written extensively on the Hundred Years War and the Italian Wars. He was the editor of and contributed to a book on the siege of Dijon (*1513 L'année terrible. Le siège de Dijon*, Dijon, 2013) He also edited a volume on the siege of Rhodes (*Tous les deables d'Enfer, Relations du siège de Rhodes par les Ottomans en 1480*, Geneva, 2014). He also co-managed with Bruno Dumézil a series of conferences focused on medieval political epistolary.

Emmanuel Vivet is a negotiation practitioner, a trainer and an associate research fellow at the Institute for Research and Education on Negotiation (ESSEC IRENE). He has spent 15 years specializing in international negotiations at governmental, European and UN levels (in international aviation, trade, postal and Asian issues). His research articles focus mainly on European negotiations, and his book *Négociations d'hier, leçons pour aujourd'hui* (Larcier, 2014) focuses notably on the relationship between history and negotiation studies. He authored two simulation exercises that are now used for EU diplomats in training at Brussels. In 2019, he was appointed chief negotiator for French civil aviation international agreements.

Mark Young is an independent consultant, trainer, writer and lecturer in the field of mediation and negotiation skills training and analysis;

his company, *Rational Games, Inc* (<www.rationalgames.com>), serves a variety of clients in the public and private sectors in the US, UK, and Germany, while also being registered as a nonprofit in the US and Germany. Mark has served as a corporate lending officer at Chase Manhattan Bank, a strategic consultant at McKinsey & Company, a partner at Price Waterhouse Corporate Finance and a trade negotiator in the US Department of Commerce. His PhD in Philosophy was earned at Humboldt-Universität zu Berlin with a philosophical treatise on game theory as applied to negotiations.

I. William Zartman is Jacob Blaustein Distinguished Professor Emeritus of International Organizations and Conflict Resolution at the Johns Hopkins University SAIS; and steering committee member of the Processes of International Negotiation (PIN) Program at GIGA-Hamburg. He was former faculty member at the University of South Carolina and Department Chair at New York University; served as Olin Professor at the US Naval Academy, Halevy Professor at Sciences Po in Paris, and Visiting Professor at the American University in Cairo; past president of the Tangier American Legation Institute for Moroccan Studies for 27 years, of the Middle East Studies Association, and of the American Institute for Maghrib Studies. He received his doctorate from Yale and honorary doctorates from the Catholic University of Louvain and Uppsala University.

INTRODUCTION

We Produce History;
We Might as Well Use it, Wisely

I. William ZARTMAN[*]

The relation between past events and present appreciation should not pose difficult questions: it is not a matter of whether but how the past is put to use. Simply, there are two reasons to look at history: the past and the future. Looking at history as the past is to read it as a story a historical novel, with an interesting – sad or happy – account that entertains. It is its own story, for its own sake. The future is what we really care about (unless we have none, then we fall back into the past, sharing our anecdotage). The past is, after all, all we have to study, and if negotiations analysts have any ideas about their subject, it is from observing practitioners when they are practicing best.

There are plenty of good stories in the collection, sewn here and there among other-minded accounts. St Malo in 1998 (Ricketts), Constantinople in 1096 (Cheynet), Paris in 1856 (Bruley), Pyrenees in 1659 (Vivet), Korea in 1950 (Petit), and Syria in 1920 (d'Andurain) are all intriguing tales with meaning for the train of events of the times. They seek no lessons; they tend to come from past eras and any possible lessons for later eras is hidden in the idiosyncrasies of the times, as the art of negotiation was developing. Indeed, the hidden lesson is that effective modern negotiations should

---

[*]   The Johns Hopkins University; Processes of International Negotiation (PIN-GIGA).

know how to handle those hallmarks of past eras that weakened diplomacy, such as negotiating for honor or face rather than interests – "egotiation" in a word (Meerts, 2010). But mainly, they are fascinating stories.

But the stories of history can also be used to enlighten the future. History is a collection of cases. This book is organized on case studies, and case study is a prime approach to drawing knowledge from the past (Mill, 1983/1967; George, 1993, 2005; George and McKeown, 1985; Ragin, 1997; Skocpol and Somers, 1980; Yin, 2003; Sambanis, 2004; Zartman, 2005a). If the case is just left there, each standing alone on its own, we are back in the enjoyment of the idiosyncratic past. If we are to learn from them anything beyond the details of their occurrence, cases have to be cases of something other than the unique event, with messages about that something that can illuminate understanding. Many chapters of this collection have a title alerting us to the case's desire to be read for something else that its idiosyncrasies. The story is merely the clothing on the body of a case of something, somehow, somewhere. It is the body that is important for the development of knowledge, the presentation of the event free of proper nouns that tells something about "events like this".

1. HISTORIC CASES AND THE INDUCTIVE APPROACH

That body can be studied for the larger lessons it conveys, or for the way others' larger lessons help in understanding it – inductively or deductively in a sense. Inductively, the analyst lets the case tell its story, looking for characteristics that stand out, internally or externally (contextually), usually causative characteristics that explain the or an outcome. The analysts may come with a hypothesis of their own or simply let the case speak for itself, a rather unguided fishing expedition. However approached, the results need to be encased in some identification of what this is a case of or what this case is like. The cases in this collection are presented in this fashion, not chronologically as history, but grouped by some typology that invites us to look for something beyond the story.

It may be objected that from the start this condition invalidates any attempt to draw historical lessons. As a well-placed American diplomat expressed recently: "All negotiations are sui generis." This attitude cannot use the word "negotiation", let alone "state", "diplomacy", or "democracy," because its composition of idiosyncratic events makes it impossible to use general terms. Relevant historical differences need to be discussed along with the case similarities if analysis is to distill out the useful and applicable lessons of the historical incident. After all, Thucydides ([-411], 1960) is frequently quoted (or at least referred to: Allison, 2017) despite his age and Hitler would have done well to read the account of Napoleon's trip to Moscow over a century earlier. The collection opens with a case from two millennia in the past that is centered on a contemporary abstract question about asymmetry with findings that are deemed to be relevant to present-day experience (Stouder); the same question is addressed from another angle in a contemporary setting (de la Sablière). Another case in this collection examines the Congress of Vienna – to bring out lessons that can fit at the UN Security Council today, overcoming the roughly two centuries that separate them (Meerts).

More specifically, the claim is frequently heard that everything is different these days and a new diplomacy is required to deal with the extra-modern world. The observation is incontrovertible but the conclusion is questionable. Vienna 1815 (Meerts) would have been different indeed if the countries present were democracies rather than royal personalities; Ludendorff (Vivet) would have made a different choice if the information sources of the 21st century were available a century earlier; the parties at Dijon (Vissière) six centuries ago might have acted differently if a mandate had arrived in time. But it is patently obvious that these experiences can help understanding of the Reagan-Gorbachev interaction at Reykjavik in 1989, the Nasser decision to go to war in 1967, or the successful effort by Kofi Annan to negotiate with Saddam Hussein without a mandate in 2000. The idea that modernizing changes in the conditions and subjects of diplomatic practice make all past lessons and comparisons outdated is mindless, a bit like saying that the shift from a coal stove to an electric oven makes the basic recipe for bread outmoded.

Thereafter, one has to establish the causative relations or terms of analysis that explain the relations or regularities illustrated in this particular case that the analyst seeks to convey. It is the move from proper to common nouns (and verbs and adjectives by extension) that turns the data into knowledge. The great works of history are great stories, bedside reading to keep you awake or put you to sleep, but they are also honored for the lessons they provide from salient events on how other "cases like this" can be understood and handled in the future (Thucydides, 1960; Gibbon, 1776–1788; Tuchman, 1984; Shiels, 1991; Parker, 1993; Crocker, 1992).

Even though the actions and characteristics of a historic case are turned into regularities and relations, nothing indicates that the findings will hold beyond the case itself. One case proves nothing; it only instructs and proposes. It offers a finding that is at least, arguably, supported by the case and that can therefore be used as a hypothesis to be examined elsewhere. Hypotheses and presumptive regularities are tested in two ways – by their internal logic and by their factual fit. Thus, the historical case study provides the factual base and the accompanying analysis offers an explanation of the logic of the relationships. Both ingredients can be tested – the logic challenged (internal validation) and the factual account verified (external validation). Even when facts of the action are verified, nothing establishes that the given account provides the only explanation for the outcome. Most events are multicaused and polycausal; the challenge of the analysis is to establish the lesson that it contains and leave it to others (or oneself later on) to use and test the results, again or elsewhere.

2. HISTORIC CASES AND THE DEDUCTIVE APPROACH

Thus, the historic events can also be studied deductively, drawing on generalities discovered elsewhere, either by logic or by historic induction, to test their validity and usefulness in explanation of events in other cases. To do so is to close the circle of knowledge and draw full meaning from history. Through the lessons historical events provide, they can be read to test the power of lessons drawn from other events and presented as general regularities, free of the idiosyncrasies of the events ("proper nouns") and formulated by the logic of other, similar events.

An example is the debate over the causes of revolution, which refers to the great instances of the phenomenon but it also then turns to further debate regarding whether less famous occurrences fit the label. While this debate can be focused on a few salient examples (Brinton, 1938), it is carried into the next level by references to cases studied comparatively (Moore, 1966; Skocpol, 1979), and then used to interrogate other instances for membership in the category. Such debates can only be carried out through concepts and conclusions, hypotheses and regularities – lifted above the historic events and then dropped on other historic events to try for size.

And again, the debate over the requirements for a coalition and the strategy and tactics (process) of assembling, blocking, or overcoming such a coalition has long occupied the minds and directed the actions of diplomats (but also legislators, stockholders, stakeholders, and families).

A series of improved concepts, such as minimum, minimum winning, minimum contiguous winning, and so on, has been derived from the juncture of situational logic and applied exercise for on-the-job testing. On their side, practitioners try to work on the fit of ideas in the context. As discussed in later chapters of this book, Talleyrand was a master of splitting the coalition assembled against his country into a series of coalitions around his country, whereas Wilson's purist insistence helped crystalize the formation of a coalition against him. On another dimension, the gathering of parties into a coalition of necessary size is paralleled by the combination of ideas and demands into a coalition of positions, often at the cost of their content. At Philadelphia (Menkel-Meadow) and also, two centuries later, in Brussels (Marchi), content was maintained in a tensile structure by crosscutting coalitions; at St Malo and later (1999) numbers were obtained at the cost of content; at Geneva (2005–2015) reformulated content brought in sufficient parties; at the UN in 1967 (Faltas), it was ambiguity on the positions that brought in the requisite number of parties.

Further, perhaps the most salient, and at the same time difficult, concept of relevance in analyzing and practicing negotiation is that of power – which is, at the same time, probably also the basic concept of political science. A great step in its use in negotiation analysis is the recognition of the importance of alternatives. Identified as reservation price, security point, or simply best alternative (BATNA), the interpersonal and extrapersonal position of the BATNA is probably the best measure of negotiating power. If a party can get nearly the same thing without negotiating as it could get with it (high BATNA) and if that level stands up well against the corresponding level of the other party, a negotiator is in a strong position. The problem of evaluating when the corresponding levels are equivalent (high vs high, low vs low) becomes more complex and leads to additional findings (Zartman and Rubin, 2002). Such calculations or, better yet, estimates are important to pursuing the negotiation, and producing its outcome, and then analyzing the process, as seen explicitly in the Republican Roman negotiations with which this book opens, but also seen in the Phoenician talks with the Hebrews (Chamoun and Hazlett), the Crusader-Orthodox negotiations, the Iranian non-proliferation negotiations (de Laboulaye and Langenegger), the FARC-Colombian negotiations (Schram), and even the US-Chile trade negotiations (Crump).

Moreover, in addressing the basic opening question of negotiation – when can negotiation begin? – ripeness theory has met broad acceptance and specific applicability. Like any theory, it is still open to further testing, correction and emendation, and application to discrete cases. Two cases (Vivet and Stimec) are examined in the light of this question.

Finally (illustratively, not exhaustively), one of the major questions that has always hung over the practice of negotiation is their transparency. De Callières (1716/2000, pp. 65, 70) and Richelieu, whom he cites, had no problem in admitting both secret and open negotiations, but they never indicated which was preferable when. History since then has seen a constructive evolution of the issue. Victor Hugo railed against the secrecy of negotiation by proclaiming, with further details, that "Diplomacy is darkness" (Bruley). Before him, Benjamin Franklin had managed to convince the delegates to the American Convention to keep the press away from the talks (Menkel-Meadow). The matter hung open until President Wilson (Colson) proclaimed "Open covenants, openly arrived at", in his attack on the secret treaties that led to World War I. But the antidote is as bad as the disease, since it would inhibit the kind of compromises (Meerts) and constructive ambiguities (Faltas) that make agreements possible. As a result, diplomats have generally made their own compromise between Wilson's two terms, i.e. "Open covenants, secretly arrived at," and on the second part have sought to handle the press so as to provide positive but no damaging information to the public.

3. HISTORIC CASES AND THE COUNTERFACTUAL APPROACH

Beyond induction and deduction, history offers a third way in which it can be used for learning about negotiation – counterfactually. It may sound odd to use what happened to study what *could* have happened, but that situation is precisely the one facing decision makers. History is authoritative on the first but only a part of the second, and policymakers face a range of possibilities when taking action. The range is not infinitely open, but it does include a number of alternatives discussed and available at the time. Careful selection criteria for decision analysis involves (1) an identifiable decision point; (2) a contextual opportunity, (3) a conceivable alternative following the minimum-rewrite rule; (4) specific alternatives that were discussed at the time; and (5) feasible actions relevant to the intended outcome (Tetlock and Belkin, 1996; George and Holl, 1997; Jentleson, 2000; Zartman, 2005b). An examination of that range allows an understanding of why a particular choice was made and also an evaluation of the roads not taken. History is used as a foil against which alternatives are played. The approach has been used insightfully (Tuchman, 1984; Parker, 1993). The analysis may draw on concepts and precedents drawn from other similar moments but it also examines the array of options open to authoritative figures, treating the decision point rather than the unique outcome as the historical scene.

In sum, it is hard to get away from history, and dangerous to try. There are plenty of wise sayings to recall, such as: "He who refuses to study the mistakes of the past is condemned to repeat them." The weight of the debate (if any were possible) leans in this direction, but it is also wise to recall that no past event ever repeats itself. One must pick carefully among its relevant parts to draw its real lesson.

REFERENCES

ALLISON, Graham (2017), *The Thucydides Trap: Are the US and China Headed for War?* Boston: Houghton Mifflin Harcourt.

BRINTON, C. Crane (1938/1965), *The Anatomy of Revolution*, New York: Vintage Books.

CALLIERES, Francois de (1716/2000), *De la manière de négocier avec les souverains*, Paris: Michel Brunet. [*On the Manner of Negotiating with Princes: Classic Principles of Diplomacy and the Art of Negotiation*, translated and published by Houghton Mifflin Harcourt]

CROCKER, Chester (1992), *High Noon in Southern Africa: Making Peace in a Rough Neighborhood*, New York: W.W. Norton and Company.

GEORGE, Alexander L. (ed). (1993), *Bridging the Gap: Theory and Practice in Foreign Policy*, Washington DC: United States Institute of Peace.

GEORGE, Alexander L. and BENNET, Andrew (2005), *Case Studies and Theory Development in the Social Sciences*, MIT Press. [Note: this is a re-edit of a 1982 edition]

GEORGE, Alexander L. and HOLL, Jane E. (1997), *The Warning Response Problem and Missed Opportunities in Preventive Diplomacy*, Washington, DC: Report to the Carnegie Commission on Preventing Deadly Conflict.

GEORGE, Alexander L. and McKEOWN, Timothy J. (1985), Case Studies and Theories of Organizational Decision Making, *Advances in Information Processing in Organizations* 2:21–58.

GIBBON, Edward (1776–1789), *The History of the Decline and Fall of the Roman Empire*, London: Strahan & Cadell; London: Penguin Classics (2001).

JENTLESON, Bruce W. (2000), *Perspectives on American Foreign Policy: Readings and Cases*, New York: W.W. Norton and Company.

MEERTS, Paul W. (2010), Egotiation: Ego as a Factor in International Negotiation Processes, *Pinpoints*, Laxenburg: IIASA, 35:28–29.

MILL, John Stuart (1861/2010), *Considerations on Representative Government*, London: Cambridge University Press.

MOORE, Barrington (1966), *Social Origins of Dictatorship and Democracy: Lord and Peasant in the Making of the Modern World*, Boston, MA: Beacon Press.

PARKER, Richard B. (1993), *The Politics of Miscalculation in the Middle East*, Bloomington: Indiana University Press.

RAGIN, Charles C. (1997), Turning the Tables: How Case-oriented Methods Challenge Variable-Oriented Methods, *Comparative Social Research* 16:27–42.

SHIELS, Frederick L. (1991), *Preventable Disasters: Why Government Fail*, Savage, MD: Rowman & Littlefield.

SKOCPOL, Theda (1979), *States and Social Revolutions: A Comparative Analysis of France, Russia, and China*, Canto Classics, Cambridge: Cambridge University Press.

SKOCPOL, Theda and SOMERS, Margaret (1980), The Uses of Comparative History in Macrosocial Inquiry, *Comparative Studies in Society and History* 22(2):174–197.

SAMBANIS, Nicholas (2004), Using Case Studies to Expand Economic Models of Civil War, *Perspectives on Politics* 2(2):259–279.

TETLOCK, Philip E. and BELKIN, Aaron B. (eds.) (1996), *Counterfactual Thought Experiments in World Politics: Logical, Methodological, and Psychological Perspectives*, Princeton, NJ: Princeton University Press.

THUCYDIDES [ed. and trans. Richard LIVINGSTONE] (1960), *The History of the Peloponnesian War*, New York: Oxford University Press.

TUCHMAN, Barbara W. (1984), *The March of Folly: From Troy to Vietnam*, New York: Knopf.

YIN, Robert K. (2003), *Case Study Research: Design and Methods*, Thousand Oaks, CA: SAGE Publications.

ZARTMAN, I., William (2005a), Comparative Case Studies, *International Negotiation* 10(1):3–15.

ZARTMAN, I., William (2005b), *Cowardly Lions: Missed Opportunities to Prevent Deadly Conflict and State Collapse*, Boulder, CO: Lynn Rienner.

ZARTMAN, I., William and RUBIN, J.Z. (2002), *Power and Negotiation*, Ann Arbor, MI: University of Michigan Press.

PART I

TO NEGOTIATE,
OR NOT TO NEGOTIATE

ROMAN DIPLOMACY DURING THE REPUBLIC

Do the Mighty Negotiate?

Ghislaine Stouder[*]

The Romans had a republican system from 509 to 30 BCE, during which time they extended the borders of their small Latin city until they reached the English Channel and the Rhine. Their empire thus encompassed the Mediterranean Basin and, since the time of Julius Caesar, even the Gaul territories. But even by 168 BCE the Romans had acquired a position of international hegemony that was without precedent in the ancient world, and which enabled them to impose their foreign policy militarily or, more and more frequently, simply by threatening to do so. In fact, at that time, the Romans had just won a decisive victory over Macedonia at Pydna that once and for all put an end to that realm – a legacy of Alexander the Great – and gave the Romans a *de facto* monopoly over a geopolitical world that had until then been multipolar and even anarchical.

This new position is illustrated by the embassy sent in late 168 BCE by Rome to the Seleucide king of Syria, Antiochus IV, another heir of a

---

[*] Poitiers University, France.

piece of Alexander the Great's empire.[1] Shortly before, Antiochus had tried to extend his reach to Egypt, which was under Rome's protection. To quell these expansionist desires, the envoy, C. Popillius Laenas, had been commissioned by the Senate to suggest that the king withdraw from Egypt or agree to war with Rome. Antiochus wisely preferred to withdraw. If the stories that have been handed down are to be believed, Popillius did something on this occasion that says a great deal about Rome's approach to diplomacy – which the Romans boasted of and which Popillius's interlocutors acknowledged. Having asked Antiochus to withdraw from Egypt, then repeating the request because the king refused to answer frankly, Popillius drew a line in the sand around Antiochus and his advisers and ordered them not to cross it until the king had spoken clearly with regard to the Senate's request. This shows that Rome's negotiating skills were limited, to say the least. During this period the ancient city was able to impose its decisions and gained little from diplomacy, which had become irrelevant. It must be admitted, however, that negotiation techniques were not much more developed in the earlier, and even much earlier period. Even when Rome was still in a modest position on the Italian peninsula's diplomatic checkerboard, the sources contain only a few more scenes of negotiation, which seems to have been foreign to Roman practices.

1. NEGOTIATING IN ROME: A PRACTICE NOT SEEN IN THE SOURCES

As a historian of antiquity, I must note here that I have no archives that enable me to assess, and possibly correct, the view of the ancient authors. Such authors probably tended to present Rome in a positive light, able to impose its will rather than having to negotiate its options. In addition, there is practically no trace remaining of a historiography hostile to Rome which would not hesitate to present diplomatic negotiations as they actually took place. Moreover, even when there is no ideological issue, the literary sources are not always interested in reporting negotiations, though they can be assumed to have occurred. As transcribed by Polybius, the three treaties between Rome and

---

[1]   For a full account of the event, see LIVY, *History of Rome*, book 44, chapter 19 (in LIVY, *The History of Rome, Volume XIII: Books 43–45*, (translation by A.C. SCHLESINGER, Loeb Classical Library 396, Cambridge, MA: Harvard University Press, 1951)).

Carthage (dating from 509, 348, and 279 BCE) include multiple, detailed clauses that were probably subject to negotiations between the Roman and Carthaginian agents. Polybius makes no mention of them, however:[2] like ancient Greek historians in general, he was more interested in the results of the negotiations than in the negotiations themselves.

Under such circumstances, Roman negotiations are hard to study for two reasons: Rome's position as a hegemon meant it did not have to negotiate; and the reports of such practices in the sources available to historians cannot be taken literally, but must be read critically.

2. THE ULTIMATUM ISSUED TO CARTHAGE IN 218 BCE, OR THE REFUSAL TO NEGOTIATE

The "space" for the negotiations mentioned in the sources generally arises in connection with a conflict: either before the conflict starts, or to resolve it. In such situations, more than in any other, it was important for the Romans to show they were in a position of strength, and there was little to no room for negotiation. As for pre-war diplomatic exchanges more specifically, they almost all ended in war. Were the Romans really such bad negotiators, or was declaring war their real goal? What criteria should we use to determine whether an embassy succeeded or "went wrong"?[3]

The Roman embassy sent to Carthage in 218 BCE on the eve of the Roman-Punic war provides an example. The Romans had sent a first delegation to the Carthaginian commander, Hannibal, to complain of the pressure he was putting on the city of Saguntum (now Zaragoza, Spain), which was then a Roman ally. After Saguntum was taken, the Romans sent a second embassy, this time to the Senate in Carthage, to ask for clarification about that Punic city's position on Hannibal's actions and to demand that Hannibal be handed over to them to right the wrongs suffered by a city allied with Rome. When the Carthaginians refused, the

---

[2]   POLYBIUS, *The Histories*, book 3, chapters 22–26 (in POLYBIUS, *The Histories, Volume II: Books 3–4* (translation by W.R. PATON. Revised by F.W. WALBANK, C. HABICHT, Loeb Classical Library 137, Cambridge MA: Harvard University Press, 2010)).

[3]   To paraphrase T.C. BRENNAN, "Embassies Gone Wrong: Roman Diplomacy in the Constantinian *Excerpta de Legationibus*" in C. EILERS (ed.), *Diplomats and Diplomacy in the Roman World*, Mnemosyne Suppl. 304, Leiden and Boston: Brill, 2009, pp. 171–191.

Romans decided on war: Quintus Fabius, the head of the delegation, got up, gathered his toga into a fold, and said that the fold contained both war and peace and it was up to the Carthaginians to choose between them. The Carthaginians refused to decide, and Fabius said he had brought them war.[4]

Sending two embassies shows that the Romans definitely knew how to create space for negotiation, but that space was often empty. The mission of Fabius and his colleagues was reduced to an exchange offering only two ways out of the diplomatic conflict: war or peace, and peace could only be obtained by Carthage submitting to Rome's will. In other words, the exchange was reduced to an ultimatum. This episode from 218 BCE is hardly the only example of how the Romans operated. According to the commentary of Livy, the Romans were aware and even proud of this way of doing things:

> This straightforward demand and declaration of war seemed more in keeping with the dignity of the Roman People than to bandy words regarding the rights involved in treaties, especially at that moment, when Saguntum had been destroyed.[5]

He indicates a pragmatic approach to international relations that implies that the Romans had made the decision to go to war before this exchange, and that they had weighed the risks of war and the chances of winning it.

In fact, since completing its conquest of Italy in 264 BCE, Rome had access to such vast human resources that there was no reason to fear armed conflict. Unlike almost every other ancient State, Rome had a policy of granting citizenship to the conquered population. This policy and the alliances formed with freshly subjugated populations meant not only that there was a much larger pool of soldiers available, but also that those soldiers cared more about defending Rome than mercenaries did. With such imposing military capabilities, the Romans were able to do without negotiation. To cite a contemporary concept, the Romans' "best alternative to a negotiated agreement" (BATNA)[6] was military and sufficiently well

---

4   The full account is in LIVY, *History of Rome*, book 21, chapters 18–19 (translation by B.O. FOSTER, *Livy. Books XXI–XXII*, Cambridge, MA: Harvard University Press; London, William Heinemann, Ltd., 1929).

5   LIVY, *The History of Rome*, book 21, chapter 19 (see above n. 4).

6   Roger FISHER and William URY coined this phrase in 1981 to refer to the best solution available to each party other than the negotiated solution under consideration: R. FISHER and W. URY, *Getting to Yes*, Boston: Houghton Mifflin Company, 1981.

maintained that no negotiations were necessary. At most, the negotiations Rome conducted were a "contest between alternatives, with the shape of the outcome being dependent on the strength of the non-negotiatory options of the parties".[7] If Rome negotiated, it was to better highlight its alternative options and to threaten to use them.

3. WAS NEGOTIATING FOREIGN TO ROMAN CULTURE?

Although the word "negotiation" derives from the Latin *negotium* (business, employment, occupation, affair), in antiquity the latter had nothing to do with diplomacy. The word was used as such only from the 15th century with the development of modern diplomacy.[8] In Greek, the concept of negotiation is expressed by the word's lexical scope, the *logos*: to negotiate means, above all, to establish dialogue and have a conversation with a foreign State. In Latin however, the Romans mainly used a vocabulary derived from the verb *disceptare*, which means to judge, decide, or resolve. The idea of justice can clearly be seen in certain diplomatic techniques that are almost identical to those used in a civil trial.

One of the particularities of Roman diplomacy is the use of "fetials", or "priest-ambassadors" as they are usually called, who in Rome were responsible for declaring war, entering into treaties, and managing hostile relations with foreign populations. One of Cicero's texts defines these priests as the "judges (*iudices*) of treaties, peace, war, and wrongs committed against ambassadors".[9] When war was being declared, their job was to state the Romans' claims, take the gods as witnesses, and if the claims were not satisfied, to declare war, properly speaking, and throw a lance into enemy territory as evidence of the state of war. Also called fetial law, the procedure probably dates from the archaic period and seems to have been abandoned at the end of the 4th century or the beginning of

---

[7]   I.W. ZARTMAN, "Negotiation: Post-Modern or Eternal?" in *Entrer en négociation*, Brussels: Larcier, 2011, p. 96.

[8]   G. STOUDER, "Négocier au nom de Rome" in B. GRASS and G. STOUDER (eds.), *La Diplomatie romaine sous la République: réflexions sur une pratique. Actes des rencontres de Paris (21–22 juin 2013) et de Genève (31 octobre–1er novembre 2013)*, ISTA, 2015, pp. 43–44.

[9]   CICERO, *On the Laws*, book 2, chapter 9 (in CICERO, *On the Republic. On the Laws.* (translation by C.W. KEYES, Loeb Classical Library 213, Cambridge, MA: Harvard University Press, 1928)).

the 3rd century. The activity of envoys, who were secular and inspired by the politics of the Roman Senate, is imbued with the same spirit because, to go back to the example from 218 BCE, Fabius does not do much more than a fetial would have done: he stated the Romans' claims to the Carthaginians and declared war when those claims were not met. To the Roman way of thinking, this fetial procedure, or any procedure like it, guaranteed that a war undertaken by the Romans would be a just war (*bellum iustum*). The discussions that preceded wars therefore never concerned responsibility for the wrongs, because for a Roman, it went without saying that the wrongs were committed by the enemy. The only question was whether or not the guilty parties would admit that they were at fault and agree to make reparations. The Romans were not negotiating, but seeking justice.

The fetial procedure was, more broadly, part of a legal conception of war in Rome: war was the means to right a wrong committed by an enemy. Victory was therefore not only obvious proof that the Romans were within their rights, it was also a practical way to impose on the losers the terms of an agreement that provided for compensating the original harm. Negotiation – which would be a compromise inconsistent with the search for justice inherent in inter-State relations – therefore played no role either before or after war was declared.

A comparison with contemporaneous practices, especially those of the Greeks, further underscores the uniqueness of the Roman concepts. The Greeks were not unaware of the legal aspect of international dispute resolution, but at the time, they followed an arbitration procedure that required a third State to resolve the dispute. The Romans also practiced arbitration in Greece for the Greeks, but they systematically refused it for themselves because they did not recognize any judges other than themselves, even if that meant being both judge and party.

The hypocrisy of such a position has been highlighted many times. Contemporary historians, in particular Anglo-American historians influenced by the criticism of 1970s U.S. imperialism, have stressed that the role of the fetial was limited to putting up a façade to hide the Romans' thirst for conquest: the refusal to negotiate was merely the result of a desire to conquer,[10] and the fetial procedure they so boasted of in fact amounted

---

[10]   Among the representatives of this critical school, see, in particular, W.V. Harris and his book *War and Imperialism in Republican Rome (327–70 B.C.)*, Oxford: Clarendon Press, 1979, pp. 163–254.

to issuing a non-negotiable ultimatum.[11] In addition to any reservations I may have about using a cultural reading to justify, rather than explain, a method for managing international relations dictated primarily by the imperatives of geopolitical contexts,[12] it cannot be denied that the fetial procedure dates to a time (the archaic era) when the Romans could not yet purport to have hegemonic ambitions. Rome's failure to negotiate therefore cannot be merely a result of their imperialist position – even if it was part and parcel of it – and the search for international justice cannot be deemed to be simply a cover for their hegemonic intentions.

4. ROMAN CRITIQUES OF THE PRINCIPLE OF NEGOTIATION ITSELF

In fact, negotiation was not so much foreign to the Romans as criticized by them, because they associated it with a ruse. To clarify this conception, I would cite the meeting that took place in 172/171 BCE on the banks of the Pineios between Roman ambassadors (one of whom was Quintus Marcius Rex) and Perseus, the young king of Macedonia. The Romans were preparing for war against Macedonia, believing that Perseus had violated the treaty of alliance that had just been concluded with Rome. The envoys had been sent east to tour Rome's allies to make sure of their support and assemble the armed forces. Perseus took advantage of their visit to ask for an interview with them to try to avoid war. Livy's long description undoubtedly refers to a scene of negotiation: the parties were on opposite banks of the river; discussion ensued to determine who – the Romans or the king – should cross the river, and the Romans persuaded Perseus to come to them; they then discussed the number of men that should be authorized to accompany the king, and the Romans got the king to come with only three companions. Having won two formal victories, the Romans finally obtained a truce so that Perseus could send ambassadors to Rome to defend his cause before the Senate. While sending an ambassador was decided at the king's request, it was to the Roman envoys' advantage to

---

[11]   J.-L. FERRARY, "*Ius fetiale* et diplomatie" in E. FRÉZOULS and A. JACQUEMIN (eds.), *Les Relations internationales. Actes du Colloque de Strasbourg, 15–17 juin 1993*, Paris: De Boccard, 1995, pp. 411–432.

[12]   See, e.g., Y. SCHEMEIL, "Des négociations interculturelles? Cultures, calculs, cognitions" in F. PETITEVILLE and D. PLACIDI-FROT (eds.), *Négociations internationales*, Paris: Presses de la fondation nationale des sciences politiques, 2013, pp. 141–168.

gain time so military preparations could be completed, even though they were further advanced than the Macedonians' preparations. Whatever the result, it is clear that the Romans, or at least some of them, had mastered the art of negotiation.

This diplomatic victory was not rewarded at the Senate, however. When he reported on his mission, Marcius was criticized by the old senators, who told him that:

> Not by ambushes and battles by night, nor by pretended flight and unexpected return to an enemy off his guard, nor in such a way as to boast of cunning rather than real bravery, did our ancestors wage war; they were accustomed to declare war before they waged it, and even at times to announce a battle and specify the place in which they were going to fight. [...] these are the acts of Roman scrupulousness, not of Carthaginian artfulness nor of Greek slyness, since among these peoples it has been more praiseworthy to deceive an enemy than to conquer by force. Occasionally a greater advantage is gained for the time being by trickery than by courage, but final and lasting conquest of the spirit overtakes one from whom the admission has been extorted that he has been conquered, not by craft or accident, but by the hand-to-hand clash of force in a proper and righteous war.[13]

This excerpt clearly reflects Roman beliefs. The old senators not only criticize Marcius for having used a ruse during the negotiations, they fail to praise the use of diplomatic techniques that demonstrate the Roman ambassador's negotiating talent. For them, the only alternative is war. The very fact of negotiating was thus likened to subterfuge, and thus to a practice inconsistent with the Roman way of thinking. More importantly, however, this senatorial discussion reveals how the Romans themselves were divided over the path to take. While the more traditional senators criticized it, others were clearly ready to use negotiation.

In fact, the sources recount scenes that may definitely be considered instances of negotiation. Two of the best known and most fully developed examples are the embassy of 212 BCE intended to convince the Aetolians to join Rome in a war against Macedonia, and the meeting in 198 BCE between the great general Flamininus and King Philip V of Macedonia

---

13   LIVY, book 42, chapter 47 (translation by E.T. SAGE, PhD and A.C. SCHLESINGER, PhD, *Livy. Books XL–XLII*, Cambridge, MA: Harvard University Press; London, William Heinemann, Ltd., 1938).

held in Nicaea to begin peace negotiations. The other examples primarily look at conflict resolution, or at least attempted resolution, and show that the Romans' interlocutors are essentially Greeks, who negotiated more frequently. These examples thus illustrate that Rome sometimes had to comply with foreign customs – in the days before it could impose its own diplomatic methods.

Such scenes were nonetheless rare, and became scarcer as Rome's power grew. A characteristic example relates to the issue of prisoners: the Romans had developed the habit of negotiating their exchange with the enemy, even if they had to pay for the men's return to their home country. But starting in the 2nd century BCE, almost all treaties contained a clause according to which the Roman prisoners had to be returned unconditionally and without ransom to Rome.[14] Another telltale change that could also be seen starting in the second century BCE was the almost systematic use of *deditio in fidem*: surrender to the winner's good faith. This procedure amounted to the loser's abandoning its right to negotiation in exchange for assurances that it would be treated benevolently by Rome. Such a procedure obviously could not be accepted voluntarily unless the Romans had previously exerted military pressure that left no choice between unconditional surrender and destruction. Thus, although it was practiced in certain situations in the early days of the Republic, little by little, negotiation disappeared from the Romans' diplomatic repertoire.

5. ROMAN NEGOTIATORS: MILITARY LEADERS WITH LIMITED POWERS

In all the discussions related to conflict resolution, Roman practices differ widely from those employed today, especially as regards the diplomatic official. Unlike ambassadors of the modern and contemporary eras, considered by themselves as well as others to be expert negotiators, Rome's legates had very limited powers. Merely envoys or commissioners of the

---

[14]   M. COUDRY, "L'or des vaincus: travestissement et occultation des transactions financières dans la diplomatie de la Rome républicaine" in F. MARCO SIMÓN, F. PINA POLO and J. REMESAL RODRIGUEZ (eds.), *Vae victis! Perdedores en el mundo antiguo*, Barcelona: Instrumenta, 2012, pp. 113–131.

Senate, they had little room to maneuver: their role was primarily to explain the Senate's decisions and make sure they were understood and possibly accepted; they were not authorized to negotiate their terms.

It is therefore usually a Roman general, acting as magistrate or promagistrate, that is seen conducting negotiations after a war. There may be several reasons for this. Generals had the benefit of effectiveness, as they could play on the impact of their recent victory to impose conditions that were more favorable to Rome. This approach aimed to overcome the problems posed by distance and helped build an imperialist diplomacy that clearly distinguished the center from the periphery. Generals were also familiar with the terrain, institutions, and peoples they had just fought, which made them expert treaty makers, as Cicero reports.[15]

Even in such cases, however, magistrates certainly did not have complete discretion: their conduct had to be modeled on the conduct of their predecessors. The treaty clauses that have been preserved are in fact relatively similar to each other, and magistrates had to use this foundation, borne of tradition and habit, to which any instructions the Senate gave before the armies departed may have been added. In addition, as the accounts reveal, magistrates were supposed to reach an agreement that satisfied a moral code that the Romans adhered to in their relations with foreigners. For example, in 256 BCE, when the Romans began the First Punic War by winning battles against the Carthaginians, the Carthaginians sent an embassy to the consul Regulus, who negotiated terms that were too harsh and which the Carthaginians eventually rejected. The ancient historians unanimously criticize Regulus, not because he made a mistake by overestimating his negotiating position with the Carthaginians, who at the time were far from having been subjugated, but because the measures imposed were not in harmony with Roman custom or the gods. Expertise, custom, and moderation were thus the limits placed on negotiations conducted by magistrates.

---

15   CICERO, *For Cornelius Balbus*, chapter 45: "Who therefore do we deem to be the most clairvoyant interpreters of treaties, the most experienced in the law of war, the most adept at analyzing the conditions and demands of cities? Those, of course, who have already done their duty and conducted wars. [...] Concerning treaties and all of the law of peace and war, who will not prefer our generals to all the best legal experts?" (in CICERO, *Pro Caelio. De Prouinciis Consularibus. Pro Balbo* (translation by R. GARDNER, Loeb Classical Library 447, Cambridge MA: Harvard University Press, 1958)).

But above all, the terms negotiated and imposed by magistrates were never final, and the Roman Senate felt itself free on several occasions to disavow the generals when the terms of the agreements they had made were no longer suitable. This happened in 152 BCE, when the promagistrate had obtained recognition of the defeat by the Celtiberian troops on the Iberian Peninsula. The Senate believed that the conditions that had been imposed were not harsh enough. To maintain the empire and keep it from breaking up, it had become necessary for a single institutional agent to have control over diplomatic discussions. That agent was the Senate, which also had the enormous advantage of being at the center of the empire.

Such two-step decision making meant that Rome's interlocutors knew they might have to negotiate twice. In Rome, the Senate was responsible for receiving ambassadors and talking with them. But there was no question of negotiating during Senate sessions, when the delegations stated their claims and the senators replied. Discussions were limited to a simple exchange that cannot be compared to negotiations. If there were any negotiations – and the evidence in the literary sources is extremely rare – they took place before the Senate session during which Rome's decision was definitively approved. They may have been held in a basilica (attached to the curia where the Senators met), where a committee of specialists studied the details of a foreign embassy's claims and the related issues. We also know that in very rare cases, negotiations took place at the forum, in the city's center, or in the private home of a Roman aristocrat or an influential senator, i.e., in an unofficial place for diplomacy.

In conclusion, knowledge of Roman negotiating practices is thin, not only because of the state of the documentation, but especially because this practice seems to have been largely foreign to the Roman mindset. This is easily understood given Rome's position of strength at the time. The basis for such an attitude may, however, be more closely related to the very characteristics of the Roman mindset, which was unaware of negotiation. I might suggest, however, that it is precisely the refusal to consider the option of negotiation that led Rome to conduct so many wars, which almost always ended favorably once the Romans began to integrate the losing populations into their citizenry and therefore their armies. In fact, both interpretations are equally supported by contemporary historians, depending on whether they criticize or defend Roman imperialism while having the U.S. "hyperpower" in their line of sight, because it is so easy to confuse the two.

REFERENCES

BRENNAN, T.C., "Embassies Gone Wrong: Roman Diplomacy in the Constantinian *Excerpta de Legationibus*" in C. EILERS (ed.), *Diplomats and Diplomacy in the Roman World*, Mnemosyne Suppl. 304, Leiden and Boston: Brill, 2009, pp. 171–191.

CICERO, *Pro Caelio. De Prouinciis Consularibus. Pro Balbo* (translation by R. GARDNER, Loeb Classical Library 447, Cambridge MA: Harvard University Press, 1958).

CICERO, *On the Republic. On the Laws* (translation by C.W. KEYES, Loeb Classical Library 213, Cambridge, MA: Harvard University Press, 1928).

COUDRY, M., "L'or des vaincus : travestissement et occultation des transactions financières dans la diplomatie de la Rome républicaine" in F. MARCO SIMÓN, F. PINA POLO and J. REMESAL RODRIGUEZ (eds.), *Vae victis! Perdedores en el mundo antiguo*, Barcelona: Instrumenta, 2012, pp. 113–131.

FERRARY, J.-L., "*Ius fetiale* et diplomatie" in E. FRÉZOULS and A. JACQUEMIN (eds.), *Les Relations internationales. Actes du Colloque de Strasbourg, 15–17 juin 1993*. Paris: De Boccard, 1995, pp. 411–432.

FISHER, R. and URY, W. *Getting to Yes*, Boston: Houghton Mifflin Company, 1981.

HARRIS, W.V., *War and Imperialism in Republican Rome (327–70 B.C.)*, Oxford: Clarendon Press, 1979.

LIVY, *The History of Rome*, book 21, chapters 18, 19 (translation by B.O. FOSTER, *Livy. Books XXI–XXII*, Cambridge, MA: Harvard University Press; London, William Heinemann, Ltd., 1929).

LIVY, *The History of Rome*, book 42, chapter 47 (translation by Evan T. SAGE, PhD and A.C. SCHLESINGER, PhD, *Livy. Books XL–XLII*, Cambridge, MA: Harvard University Press; London, William Heinemann, Ltd., 1938).

LIVY, *The History of Rome, Volume XIII: Books 43–45* (translation by A.C. SCHLESINGER, Loeb Classical Library 396, Cambridge, MA: Harvard University Press, 1951).

POLYBIUS, *The Histories, Volume II: Books 3–4* (translation by W.R. PATON. Revised by F.W. WALBANK, C. HABICHT, Loeb Classical Library 137, Cambridge MA: Harvard University Press, 2010).

SCHEMEIL, Y., "Des négociations interculturelles? Cultures, calculs, cognitions" in F. PETITEVILLE and D. PLACIDI-FROT (eds.), *Négociations internationales*, Paris: Presses de la fondation nationale des sciences politiques, 2013, pp. 141–168.

STOUDER, G., "Négocier au nom de Rome" in B. GRASS and G. STOUDER (eds.), *La Diplomatie romaine sous la République: réflexions sur une pratique. Actes des rencontres de Paris (21–22 juin 2013) et de Genève (31 octobre–1er novembre 2013)*, ISTA, 2015, pp. 43–44.

ZARTMAN, I.W., "Negotiation: Post-Modern or Eternal?" in *Entrer en négociation*, Brussels: Larcier, 2011, pp. 83–100.

THE TREATY OF DIJON (1513)

Or, the Art of Negotiating without a Mandate

Laurent Vissière*

At the end of summer 1513, the kingdom of France was under attack from a broad European coalition formed by England, the Holy Roman Empire, and Switzerland. While the English and imperial armies attacked from the north, taking Thérouanne and Tournai, the Swiss army, its ranks swollen with imperial contingents, laid siege to Dijon. Defense proved hopeless, but contrary to all expectations the governor of Burgundy, Louis II de La Trémoille, succeeded in negotiating a peace treaty with the enemy. In exchange for a little money and a lot of promises, the invaders lifted the siege and went home – where they learned that King Louis XII had refused to ratify the treaty, claiming that Louis II did not have a mandate to sign it.[1]

---

*   Sorbonne Université, Paris – IUF. The author thanks Emmanuel Vivet for his contribution to the third part, which was written jointly.

[1]   On the siege of Dijon and its European context, see Laurent Vissière, Alain Marchandisse and Jonathan Dumont (eds.), *1513. L'année terrible. Le siège de Dijon*, Dijon: Faton, 2013. On Louis II de La Trémoille, see Laurent Vissière, *"Sans poinct sortir hors de l'orniere", Louis II de La Trémoille (1460–1525)*, Paris: Champion, 2008.

1. THE HOLY LEAGUE VERSUS FRANCE

Until 1512, France was the most powerful state in Western Europe: King Louis XII (1498–1515) was also the Duke of Milan and played the referee in Italy. Unsurprisingly, such immodest prosperity aroused jealousy and Pope Julius II (1503–1513), who had sworn to drive all the "Barbarians" from Italy, managed to unite the Swiss cantons, the English, the Spanish, and various Italian powers into a "Holy League" that forced the French to retreat from northern Italy in the summer of 1512 after a series of messy campaigns. The war could have ended there, but continued with even greater force because Louis XII did not want to give up the Duchy of Milan, and his opponents had started thinking about launching a vast offensive against the kingdom of France. Before they did so, their coalition changed shape: the Holy Roman Empire joined but Spain dropped out, Venice switched its allegiance back to France, and Julius II died, although his successor, Leo X, continued to pursue his Holy League policy.

Meanwhile, Louis XII, who intended to make the first move instead of merely holding defensive positions, delegated a large part of his politicking to Louis II de La Trémoille (1460–1525), who was one of his best captains and governor of Burgundy. Hoping to persuade them to join the French alliance, Louis II conducted an embassy to the Swiss cantons in January–February 1513, but was unsuccessful: the Swiss demanded that the king abandon all claims to Italy, which the king would not hear of. Louis II returned to France only to be sent almost immediately to conquer Lombardy. But on June 6 he suffered a humiliating defeat at Novara at the hands of the Swiss, who occupied the duchy at that time. For the king to have sent all of his available troops to the other side of the Alps when he was well aware that the English and imperial forces were preparing a big offense was clearly a strategic error.

The coalition's plan was relatively simple. While Henry VIII attacked France from Calais – which was still an English possession – Maximilian of Habsburg was to attack in the northeast, in Champagne for example, and the Swiss were to attack in the east, in Burgundy. They agreed to meet outside the walls of Paris, and were already discussing how they would divide up the kingdom: Henry VIII dreamed of repeating his ancestors' exploits in France, while Maximilian claimed to be an heir of the Duchy of Burgundy. As with all large coalitions, the main problem was to coordinate the allies' efforts. Henry VIII landed in Calais with 35,000 men and heavy artillery (July 1), but since he had no real military skills he advanced rather slowly. Then, instead of launching all his forces against the army that Louis XII had managed, with great difficulty, to gather on the Somme River, he attacked Thérouanne, an isolated French city in the imperial province of Artois. He was joined in August by Maximilian, who had also advanced very slowly. After putting up a determined resistance, the city finally surrendered (August 23) and the two sovereigns, unable to agree on who would keep the city, decided to destroy it. Maximilian then went home, leaving the rest of the operations to Henry VIII, who took Tournai (September 23), another isolated French city within the Empire's territory. By then it was too close to winter to continue a war, so the English set sail for home without having tried to put the original plan into action.

Meanwhile the Swiss, to whom Maximilian had promised large amounts of money, had agreed (on August 1) to join the invasion of France despite the fact that military campaigns were generally conducted from spring to fall. Toward the end of the month, troops left Zurich and reached Besançon, in imperial Franche-Comté, on August 27. There they met up with the imperial contingents led by Ulrich VI (1487–1550), Duke of Württemberg and Count of Montbéliard, and Guillaume de Vergy, Marshall of Comté. These two supplied cavalry and artillery (26 big guns), as the Swiss had almost none. The combined army now counted nearly 40,000 soldiers who, lacking logistics, marched toward Burgundy pillaging everything in their path.

2. THE BEST DEFENSE OF DIJON: FIGHT OR NEGOTIATE?

The people of Burgundy had been French since the death of Charles the Bold in 1477, but the province was considered unsafe because the Burgundians continued to favor the Habsburgs, the only legitimate heirs of the former dukes. This is one of the reasons Louis XII had appointed Louis II governor in 1506: he was not only a warrior in whom the king had complete faith, but also the descendent of a family connected to the former dukes and related to all of the local lineages. In short, he was someone in whom the Burgundians could see themselves. From the day he was appointed, Louis II wrote often to the king to complain of the Burgundians' "ill will" and the province's military weakness. Finding the fortifications obsolete and poorly maintained, he tried to modernize them in various places (especially Dijon), but he lacked funds and the locals objected to paying for costly work that they considered unnecessary because France was at peace. With the first threat of a Swiss attack in the summer of 1512, Louis II scrambled to stockpile provisions, weapons, and ammunition, and to restore Dijon's fortifications. A year later, however, when the invasion really began, nothing concrete had been done about the fortifications.

In early September when the Swiss began their march, panic and consternation reigned. Louis II had taken the drastic measure of burning the neighborhoods immediately adjoining Dijon, as they were indefensible and would have enabled the invaders to advance, under cover, to the city's moats and set up their batteries right near the walls. Unfortunately it was too late, and the measure proved futile. The first Swiss troops arrived within sight of Dijon on the evening of Thursday September 8, and the next morning their cannons pounded the eastern wall. On Friday September 9, a second battery started bombarding the city from a rise on the northwest side, and continued without letup until Sunday September 11. After a short cease-fire in the afternoon, the firing started up again and lasted throughout the night. After three days of such bombardment, the intent of which was to terrify the civilians and create a breach in the ramparts, part of the walls collapsed into the moat. The assault was planned for Monday September 12 at dawn, but at 7 o'clock that morning, another cease-fire was agreed. That cease-fire led to a peace treaty and on Tuesday September 13, the Swiss packed up and marched home, pillaging as they went. They were very badly received when they arrived – accused of letting Louis II circumvent them and of having betrayed the coalition's cause. Meanwhile in Dijon, there was a celebration of the city's miraculous deliverance, which was attributed to the intercession of an antique Virgin venerated in the Notre-Dame church.

3. ANALYSIS: A NEGOTIATION BUT NO MANDATE

3.1. CONTINUING THE DIALOGUE

During the siege, contact was never completely lost between the two sides. While this was not exceptional in the Middle Ages, when battle was given only as a last resort, Louis II knew the Swiss mercenaries very well. Many had fought under his orders in Brittany (1488–1491) and Italy (1494–1495, 1500, 1502–1503, and 1509), and they had recently handed him a crushing defeat in Lombardy. Although he was leading seasoned and unharmed troops, he did not trust the Burghers' patrol and knew that in the event of an assault, he would commit all of his forces in a double-or-nothing bid to save Dijon because if he lost, the Swiss would not face any other obstacles on their way to Paris. As for the Swiss, they were not lacking in esteem for their adversary, whose military abilities and tenacity were well-known to them. They knew he would mount a fierce defense and that, regardless of the outcome, an assault would lead to a blood bath. While this may have given them pause, the fact was they had no real logistics and winter was approaching, so they could not linger in front of the walls of Dijon. If they were going to launch an assault, it had to be as quickly as possible. Also weighing in the balance was the fact that in the preceding months Louis II had been very active diplomatically in Switzerland, widely distributing the king's money in order to rebuild a network of allies and people indebted to him. Many of the Swiss wondered if there was a valid dispute with the king of France, who had been their traditional and favorite employer since Louis XI, and they were ready and willing to go back to him provided they did not lose face.

According to Pierre Tabourot, a municipal official who kept a diary of the siege, a first embassy went to talk to the Swiss on September 10.[2] It included Jean de Baissey, the official in charge of Dijon's waterways and forests; Jean de Rochefort, bailiff of Dijon; and René d'Anjou, lord of Mézières (and Louis II's nephew). There was no immediate result, but the next afternoon, the two sides called to each other over the walls. The Swiss demanded "the Duchy of Burgundy and the adjacent lands, the strongholds of Milan, Cremona and Genoa, the county of Asti, and four hundred thousand *écus* for interest, and that the king take ten thousand Swiss men back into his service".[3] Louis II had to refuse such terms – and the bombardment started again shortly thereafter – but the idea of a peaceful solution took hold and came to fruition the next day. Oddly, Pierre Tabourot does not cite Louis II's action at any time, but Jean Bouchet, who wrote his eulogy in 1527, told the story completely differently. He wrote that very early on, the governor sent the Swiss one of his most loyal officers, Regnaud de Moussy, as a deputy with the job of evaluating the enemy forces and above all, meeting the people "who had contracted secret friendship" with his master.[4]

---

2   VISSIÈRE, *L'année terrible*, (above n. 1), pp. 223–224 (citing Pierre TABOUROT, *Journal*).
3   Ibid., p. 224.
4   Jean BOUCHET, *Le Panegyric du chevallier sans reproche*, Poitiers: Jacques Bouchet, 1527, fol. 141v [scholarly edition by François CORNILLIAT and Laurent VISSIÈRE, forthcoming, Éditions Honoré Champion].

Regnaud accomplished his mission superbly, obtaining the safe-conduct that would enable Louis II to negotiate in person with the Swiss leaders on September 12. This account is not inconsistent with Tabourot's: the governor had probably appointed his agent without telling the members of the official embassy, whom he did not trust very much.

3.2. NEGOTIATING AT ANY COST

The treaty of Dijon, which contains only eight articles, was signed on September 13, 1513. In the king's name, Louis II agreed that the French would abandon all their Italian possessions, including the papal territories and the Duchy of Milan, along with Cremona and Asti (arts. 1 and 3). He promised to pay the Swiss 400,000 *écus à la couronne*, and 10,000 to the Duke of Württemberg and the Free Countians[5] (arts. 5 and 6). The king would not engage in reprisals against any Countians who had assets in France (art. 2), and any future disputes between the French king and certain Swiss parties referred to in the treaty would be resolved by the courts (art. 7). In addition, the king would no longer be allowed to recruit mercenaries in Switzerland without the cantons' consent (art. 4). The treaty was concluded subject to ratification by the king, the pope, the emperor, and the cantons (art. 8).

These eight, fairly disorganized articles partially satisfied the Holy League's objectives, i.e., to definitively drive the French out of Italy. But at the time, the French possessed only the strongholds of Milan and Cremona. Since they held no papal territory, the first article had only the symbolic value of putting the pope in the place of honor. The Swiss took the lion's share by claiming an absolutely exorbitant ransom (close to 1.5 tons in gold) and prohibiting the clandestine recruitment of mercenaries, a practice that had clearly existed in previous years. They seem to take the interests of their Free Countian allies to heart, but the treaty is in fact humiliating for them: they receive only 10,000 *écus* (forty times less than the Swiss), and a provision is thought to be necessary to protect them from the king. In short, they are treated as if they are under Switzerland's protection rather than its allies, and the treaty in fact marks the end of the alliance between the Swiss and the Countians, who were unable to forgive such humiliation.

---

[5]   Translator's note: residents of Franche-Comté (literally, Free County).

As an advance, the people of Dijon paid the Swiss 25,000 francs (roughly 8,300 *écus*), and the rest was to be paid by the king in two installments, on September 27 and November 11. This was a very optimistic promise given the calamitous state of public finances in late 1513. Dubious as to the possibility of receiving the rest of their money, the Swiss took five hostages when they left, including René de Mézières. But the real problem, which would be posed a few days later, was the treaty's legality: did Louis II have the authority to negotiate?

The governor reported to the king immediately regarding the treaty, sending him trusted men – Pierre Tabourot's journal mentions Lancelot du Lac, the governor of Orleans, and Jean Bouchet's *Panegyric* refers to Regnaud de Moussy. The discussion was heated: Louis XII thought some of the clauses were unacceptable and shameful.[6] The problem was not the ransom, huge as it was, but the idea of abandoning the Duchy of Milan and the county of Asti. The king had three *in rem* rights over the former and the latter was part of his estate. What right did Louis II have to dispose of territory that belonged to the family of Orleans and the French crown? Feeling he was in the king's "disgrace", Louis II wrote a letter on September 23 in which he argued at length in support of his actions: he had not been in a position to negotiate with the Swiss and had had to agree to all of their demands. But, he added cynically: "To denounce the treaty, you may always claim that I did not have your authorization to conclude it."[7] In other words, there was a reason other than article 8 that the king was not required to ratify the treaty. And he never did. He did begin to pay the Swiss according to its terms, but ultimately left it to his successor, Francis I, to resolve this thorny issue. It was only after the difficult victory at Marignan (September 1515) and tough negotiations that Francis I managed to bring the Swiss into the French alliance, with the perpetual peace of Fribourg (November 1516). That treaty was dearly paid (one million *écus*), but it was complied with until 1792, making it one of history's most durable peace treaties in history.

---

[6] Tabourot (above n. 2), p. 224; Bouchet (above n. 4), ff. 145v–146v. Guillaume du Bellay confirms Louis XII's fit of anger, explaining that "the treaty had terms that were not honorable for such a prince as the king" (Martin and Guillaume du Bellay, *Mémoires de Martin et Guillaume Du Bellay*, Victor-Louis Bourrilly and Fleury Vindry (eds.), Paris, 1908–1919, 4 vol., t. I, p. 37).

[7] Vissière (above n. 2), pp. 236–237 (citing letter from Louis de la Trémoille to the king).

3.3. NEGOTIATING WITHOUT A MANDATE: HOW TO ENDANGER THE TREATY'S RATIFICATION AND ONE'S REPUTATION

History is full of unratified international treaties such as Louis II's treaty with the Swiss. As discussed in the first chapter of this book,[8] the Roman Senate could reject certain treaties negotiated by its legates when it found them unsatisfactory for the glory of Rome. Two thousand years later, the United States Senate refused to ratify the Treaty of Versailles. And the problem is still with us, as shown by the more recent non-ratification of the Kyoto Protocol by the United States in 1997, and the French and Dutch referenda votes against the 2005 Convention on the Future of Europe.

To the extent that no one, or hardly anyone, negotiates for themselves, managing the principal-agent relationship, which some say is above all a "tension", lies at the heart of any negotiation. The problem is that while overly narrow mandates leave almost no room for creativity or power to invent useful solutions, overly broad mandates create unpleasant uncertainty about the results to be achieved. Every agent must therefore conduct two negotiations: one with the opposing party; and another, less visible but just as important, negotiation with their principal, in order to clarify the objectives and limits of what may be discussed. Research has explored this area extensively, in particular with the concept of "intra-organizational negotiation," or "intra-negotiation."[9] It is precisely because intra-negotiation between principal and agent tends to be neglected that it generally lags behind inter-negotiation, is often more chaotic, and is occasionally tougher. The time difference between the two types of negotiation can be a source of "misunderstandings and conflicts between the agent and the organization's members, because the former and the latter do not experience the passage of time the same way".[10] As indicated above, Louis II was pressed for time given the Swiss march on Dijon and the general military danger France was in. He lived far

---

8   See Ghislaine STOUDER, "Roman Diplomacy During the Republic: Do the Mighty Negotiate", in this volume.

9   Richard WALTON and Robert McKERSIE, *A Behavioral Theory of Labor Negotiations*, New York: McGraw Hill, 1965, considering intra-negotiation to be an essential part of all negotiations.

10   Christian MOREL, "La négociation intra-organisationnelle" (2009/2) *Négociations* 185.

from the king and was unable to consult with his principal quickly, or more precisely, to discuss each stage of the negotiation with him, and he knew it was highly probable that what he was going to agree to would displease the king so much that it would be disavowed. A negotiation is ultimately the principal's responsibility. But, as he put it so well in his letter of September 23, 1513, whether the treaty was ratified or not mattered little to him in the end: his only objective was to see the invader leave as soon as possible.

Negotiating with such ulterior motives carries significant risks, however, in terms of falling out of favor with one's principal and harming one's honor or reputation. If Jean Bouchet is to be believed, the treaty concluded by Louis II angered the king, and the flames of that anger were fanned at the court by Louis II's enemies, starting with the queen, Anne of Brittany. He lost the king's esteem for a while, a situation he called "disgrace". Meanwhile the Swiss were indignant over his double-speak, such that even though he had been one of their favorite interlocutors, he stopped negotiating with them almost entirely over the next few years. The issue of the hostages further complicated his task, as the Swiss made them pay dearly for the betrayal. Louis II therefore also had to face the discontent of the municipal officials in Dijon who were trying to save their family members imprisoned in Switzerland, whereas he had promised them the king would do his utmost to free them as quickly as possible. In any case, breaking one's word was a stain on a gentleman's honor, which must not have pleased an aristocrat like Louis II very much: until then, he had such a reputation for integrity he had been nicknamed the "knight above reproach."

3.4. NEGOTIATING WITHOUT A MANDATE IS SOMETIMES REASONABLE

Louis II's strategy was nonetheless a winning one, for the most part. The Swiss lifted their siege, Dijon was saved, and above all, the general military threat facing France was neutralized. Louis XII's subsequent refusal to ratify the treaty naturally had consequences, but given all that was at stake at the time, it seems clear that the most important and immediate interests were protected while less important, less pressing matters were left for the future.

Given modern communication methods, it does not seem that the approach Louis II took in 1513 would be common practice today.

A negotiator can simply use her mobile phone and a variety of other means to quickly submit a written version of her treaty proposals to her principal to obtain instructions. However, while such devices make distances irrelevant and can thus hasten negotiations in some cases, they cannot eliminate the issue of the agent-principal relationship. Contemporary negotiators may well find themselves in the position of having to decide immediately on an alternative to be suggested, or a concession to make, during a crucial negotiation (e.g., UN Security Council diplomats in the midst of intense negotiations may be unable to consult their governments due to time zone differences). Even if agents must consult their principals in theory, in practice it is sometimes impossible to avoid negotiating without a mandate and improvising. Louis II, who enjoyed his prince's trust and correctly assessed the situation, showed us in 1513 that such an unorthodox method can occasionally produce good results.

REFERENCES

DU BELLAY, Martin and Guillaume, *Mémoires de Martin and Guillaume du Bellay*, Victor-Louis BOURRILLY and Fleury VINDRY (eds.), Paris, 1908–1919.

BOUCHET, Jean, *Le Panegyric du chevallier sans reproche*, Poitiers, 1527 [scholarly edition by François CORNILLIAT and Laurent VISSIÈRE, forthcoming, Éditions Honoré Champion].

TABOUROT, Pierre, *Journal* [scholarly edition by Laurent Vissière, in Laurent VISSIÈRE, Alain MARCHANDISSE and Jonathan DUMONT (eds.), *1513. L'année terrible. Le siège de Dijon*, Dijon, 2013].

VISSIÈRE, Laurent, "Sans poinct sortir hors de l'orniere", Louis II de La Trémoille (1460–1525), Paris: Champion, 2008.

VISSIÈRE, Laurent, MARCHANDISSE, Alain and DUMONT, Jonathan (eds.), *1513. L'année terrible. Le siège de Dijon*, Dijon: Faton, 2013.

WALTON, Richard and MCKERSIE, Robert, *A Behaviorial Theory of Labor Negotiations*, New York: McGraw Hill, 1965.

DIPLOMATIC CRISIS IN JULY 1914

Secrecy, Ultimatums, and Missed Opportunities

Kevin HOMRIGHAUSEN*

On June 28, 1914, a Yugoslav nationalist named Gavrilo Princip assassinated the heir presumptive to the Austro-Hungarian throne, Archduke Franz Ferdinand. Over the next 35 days, it fell upon Europe's crowned rulers, ambassadors, and diplomats to navigate a complex web of international alliances and competing domestic policies in order to negotiate an alternative to world war. The European leaders would ultimately fail, and through a series of misrepresentations, ill-advised strategies, and missed opportunities, place the world on a path toward a "Great War" that would claim nearly 20 million lives, redefine the meaning of warfare, and permanently reshape a centuries-old geopolitical landscape.

---

*   J.D. Candidate, University of California, Irvine School of Law.

1. AUSTRIA-HUNGARY PLAYS THE "TWO-LEVEL GAME" AND RECEIVES A "BLANK CHEQUE" FROM ITS GERMAN ALLY

News of the Archduke's death on June 28 spread quickly, and Princip's actions were just as soon condemned by Europe's leaders. In Vienna, members of the Austro-Hungarian government rushed to blame the assassination on factions of the Serbian government, and debates over how to address the empire's southern neighbor intensified. Those like Count Leopold Berchtold, and Baron Franz Conrad von Hötzendorf, sought to capitalize on Austria-Hungary's present international sympathy by launching an immediate military attack on Serbia. In contrast, many of those close to the Habsburg Emperor, like Hungarian Prime Minister, Count István Tisza, cautioned against "making the abominable deed of Sarajevo a pretext for settling scores with Serbia" for fear of the international diplomatic fallout, including the potential intervention of the Slavic State's historical protector, the Russian Empire (Otte, 2015). Complicating these debates was uncertainty over whether the German Empire, then the most powerful military force in Europe, would honor its Bismarckian "Zweibund" alliance with Austria-Hungary.

This internal debate over Austria-Hungary's best course of action and the uncertainty of Germany's support reflect an important facet of international diplomacy. In many cases, parties to international negotiations are forced to navigate a "two-level game" wherein internal political groups and politicians promote their own policy, while at the same time national governments seek to "maximize their own ability to satisfy domestic pressures, while minimizing the adverse consequences of foreign developments" (Putnam, 1993).[1] At no point was this "game" played more poorly (and at such high cost) during the July Crisis, than when Austria-Hungary – itself a Habsburgian union between the Austrian Empire and the Kingdom of Hungary – sought the support of its most loyal ally, Kaiser Wilhelm II's German Empire.

Before the "divided counsel at Vienna" (Otte, 2015) could agree to a Serbian strategy, two Austro-Hungarian diplomats, Count Alexander Hoyos and Count László Szőgyény-Marich, endeavored to meet with

---

[1]   Putman was one of the advocates, in the international field, of the idea developed by Walton and McKersie (1965), according to which any negotiation has two sides, internal and external.

Kaiser Wilhelm on 5 July. These men's actions highlight a common problem in the "two-level" political game – how to handle the "divergences of interests between national leader[s] and those on behalf [of who they are] negotiating ..." (Putnam, 1993). Hoyos and Szőgyény both personally favored a military course of action toward Serbia and were careful not to inform the Kaiser of the fierce debate that continued in the Austro-Hungarian government.

In response to Austria-Hungary's seemingly unified course of action and Szőgyény's strong appeal to monarchal solidarity, the Kaiser offered Germany's unconditional support – a "blank cheque" (Otte, 2015). What prompted Wilhelm's unqualified support? Was his reaction a matter of honor, or a lack of proper consideration for his own interests? Whatever the Kaiser's reasons for lending unequivocal support to Austria-Hungary may have been, the effect in Vienna was clear. By bluffing their way into the unconditional support of the strongest military force in Europe, Szőgyény and Hoyos allayed the concerns of many in Vienna who cautioned against armed conflict with Serbia and "reinforced the belligerent attitude of senior Habsburg officials", increasing the chances "that Austria-Hungary's final reckoning with Serbia would be a military one" (Otte, 2015). Indeed, the negotiations in Berlin dramatically increased Austria-Hungary's bargaining power with regard to Serbia and its Russian defender. For the duration of the July Crisis, the leaders in Vienna would be more confident in making burdensome demands on Serbia and more willing to enter conflict. Perhaps as importantly, by issuing a "blank cheque" to its Zweibund ally, "Germany had surrendered her ability to restrain Vienna" and would now be subject to the ramifications of her emboldened ally's decisions (Otte, 2015).

2. AUSTRIA-HUNGARY DELIVERS AN ULTIMATUM TO SERBIA

2.1. DELIBERATING IN SECRECY

Armed with the support of her German ally and a unified government, Austria-Hungary assumed the lead role in dictating the course of July's negotiations. However, Austria-Hungary and the other great powers of Europe would soon discover the vital role of information sharing (or lack thereof). As important as the "blank cheque" was for Austro-Hungarian posturing, the agreement reached between the Zweibund allies remained a secret to the rest of Europe. Indeed, much of the diplomatic negotiations in Europe carried on as usual, and many of the great powers remained blissfully (or perhaps purposely) ignorant of a potential conflagration in the Balkans. In some cases, this ignorance was perpetuated by the Zweibund's own representations. For example, on July 9, the Austro-Hungarian ambassador to Serbia assured his Russian counterpart, that "Serbia's sovereignty would not be touched, and that, with some good will on the part of the Serb government, a mutually satisfactory solution will be found" (Otte, 2015). Similarly, the German Chancellor explained to a Russian ambassador that "no demands on the Serbian government ... would be irreconcilable with the dignity of the neighbouring state" (Otte, 2015).

The decision to keep the "blank cheque" secret from the rest of Europe represents an important concept in negotiation and game theory: "information asymmetry" (Mnookin, 1993). Although many negotiations require that parties keep some information private, information asymmetry may deprive parties the opportunity to explore potential solutions (Mnookin, 1993). For Germany, the decision to keep private the extent of its commitment to Austria-Hungary would ultimately limit its ability to negotiate a diplomatic solution. Because their agreement remained secret, Germany's unexplained and continuous defense of Austria-Hungary would come to be viewed by many Europeans as irrational, if not openly hostile.

Additionally, because the agreement between Austria-Hungary and Germany remained a secret, many of the European powers were unaware of the potential consequences of an escalating conflict in the Balkans. In France, diplomatic energy was spent developing positive relationships with Great Britain and the Russian Empire, and even in mid-July the French ambassador to Vienna found no reason to expect an Austro-Hungarian attack on Serbia (Otte, 2015). In Great Britain, leaders were occupied with surging Irish nationalism and fostering a positive new Anglo-German relationship. As one British diplomat explained, "[Franz Ferdinand's Assassination] will have no serious consequences, in any case outside Austria-Hungary" (Mnookin, 1993, p. 172). However, some in Britain saw conflict on the horizon. British foreign secretary, Sir Edward Grey, explained in a candid conversation to a German ambassador that he "would use all the influence [he] could to mitigate difficulties ... and if the clouds arose prevent the storm from breaking" (Mnookin, 1993). Indeed, Grey would ultimately offer to leverage Great Britain's relatively friendly relationships with Germany and Russia to facilitate a more open dialogue, though it would later prove to no avail.

2.2.   CAPITULATION OR WAR?

While the major continental powers remained largely oblivious to the impending conflict in Serbia, a mostly unified Austro-Hungarian Empire committed to issuing an ultimatum that would either force Serbia to make dramatic concessions or face a military response to the country's role in the Archduke's assassination. The ultimatum would, in theory, result in one of two responses – either Serbia would meet Austria-Hungary's demands, thereby severely weakening its diplomatic influence in the Balkans, or Serbia would reject the harsh terms and Austria-Hungary could commence military action against its southern neighbor while explaining to European leaders that it had afforded Serbia the opportunity to rectify its transgressions. As the Imperial Foreign Minister explained to the Kaiser:

> The text of the note to be addressed to Belgrade, agreed today, is such that we must reckon with the probability of a warlike confrontation. Should Serbia nevertheless yield and concede to our demands, then such a move by the kingdom [of Serbia] would not only mean its profound humiliation and pari passu a diminution of Russian prestige in the Balkans, but would also imply certain guarantees for us in the direction of a restraining of pan-Serb infiltration on our soil. (Otte, 2015)

However disingenuous this approach may have been, many in Austria-Hungary argued that framing the ultimatum in this manner would discourage other nations from involving themselves in a continental conflict.

At 6 pm on July 23, the Austro-Hungarian ambassador to Serbia delivered the 10-point ultimatum, setting out demands for the Royal Serbian Government "[t]o accept the collaboration in Serbia of representatives of the Austro-Hungarian Government for the suppression of the subversive movement directed against the territorial integrity of the Monarchy" and to allow "delegates of the Austro-Hungarian Government" to partake in "judicial proceedings against accessories to the plot of the 28th of June who are on Serbian territory". If Serbia did not accept these demands, Austria-Hungary would sever diplomatic ties with its Balkan neighbor and prepare for war. On July 25, Serbia surprised many by acquiescing to nearly all of the Austria-Hungary's demands, provided they complied "with the principle of international law, with criminal procedure, and with good neighbourly relations". However, Serbia flatly refused to permit Austro-Hungarian authorities to partake in judicial proceedings within its borders, citing a potential violation of Serbia's constitution. Austria-Hungary, which demanded nothing less that total capitulation, was unsatisfied with Serbia's response and declared war on July 28.

Austria-Hungary's July 23 demands and Serbia's conditional response provide a perfect example of the often ineffectiveness of ultimatums, or "take-it-or-leave-it" approaches to negotiation. First, when one party begins a negotiation with a "final offer" it is likely that the opposing party will find the terms "arrogant and demeaning", and thus less willing to engage in the negotiation (Adler, 2000). This was certainly the case in Serbia, where Austria-Hungary's ultimatum was viewed by many as a humiliating attack on Serbian sovereignty. As Prince Alexander of Serbia remarked, accepting the ultimatum unconditionally was "an absolute impossibility for any state which has the slightest regard for its own dignity".[2]

Second, the rigidity and uncompromising nature of ultimatums have a tendency to delegitimize the credibility of the negotiation process. When the terms of Austria-Hungary's ultimatum began to circulate through the foreign ministries across Europe, it became evident that the ultimatum was far from the "mutually satisfactory" proposal that would protect "Serbia's sovereignty", which Austria-Hungary had previously assured (Otte, 2015). In the eyes of many European leaders, Austria-Hungary's integrity was tarnished, as was the prospect of a reasonable diplomatic resolution.

Finally, when one party issues a hardline ultimatum, they may find themselves bound to proceed with their stated course of action, even if the opposing party offers a reasonable response. As Carrie Menkel-Meadow observes, "commitment to a particular offer may keep the adversarial negotiator from seeing variations of that offer that might be more advantageous for the parties" (Menkel-Meadow, 1984). This was certainly true on July 25 when Serbia was "prepared to hand over for trial any Serbian subject ... of whose complicity in the crime of Sarajevo proofs are forthcoming" and to "eliminate without delay from public instruction ... everything that serves or might serve to foment the propaganda against Austria-Hungary".[3]

Indeed, Serbia had capitulated more than many (including the Austro-Hungarians) could have expected. By all accounts, Serbia's response

---

2   Standmann to Sazanov, July 24, 1914, IBZL, series 3, vol. 5. doc. 35, p. 38, as quoted in Clark (2012, p. 464).

3   Duffy, Michael (August 22, 2009), "Primary Documents: Austrian Ultimatum to Serbia, 23 July 1914", <FirstWorldWar.com>, archived from the original on May 24, 2003, available at <https://web.archive.org/web/20041030212115/http://www.firstworldwar.com/source/austrianultimatum.htm>.

constituted a major diplomatic "win" for Austria-Hungary. Nevertheless, the Austro-Hungarian ambassador to Serbia was instructed to accept nothing short of an unconditional acquiescence to the ultimatum's demands, and finding the reply unsatisfactory, made the unilateral decision to withdraw from Serbia. Again, Austria-Hungary's seeming unwillingness to engage in diplomatic negotiations made the nation appear increasingly unreasonable in the eyes of many Europeans. Indeed, even those in Austria-Hungary who intended the ultimatum to act as an overly burdensome pretext for war had largely failed to consider its effect on the presently neutral nations of Europe. Austria-Hungary and Serbia would observe that "weakness can trump a stronger party's power if the powerful party faces public criticism for taking action against the weaker ..." (Adler and Silverstein, 2000). By accepting nearly all of Austria-Hungary's demanding terms, Serbia had essentially called their bluff, and Austria-Hungary's subsequent declaration of war would be viewed by the rest of Europe as irrationally hostile.

3. SIR GREY'S OFFER TO MEDIATE GOES UNHEEDED

One of the most tragic facets of the July Crisis was the futile efforts of the advisors, diplomats, and even monarchs who tried in earnest to prevent the dominos from falling, or at least limit the scope of a potential conflict. Since early July, Sir Edward Grey, the British Secretary of State for Foreign Affairs, had offered to capitalize on Great Britain's neutrality and offer his services to mediate between the Great Powers. As early as July 6, Grey proposed to "bring the two groups [of the Powers] closer together so as to prevent European complications and to facilitate an understanding about all emerging questions" (Otte, 2015). Given how these "European complications" would ultimately unfold, Grey's mediation proposal was more than apt. Though, as he would soon discover, mediations between sovereign States, whatever their form, are never easy to put in place.

Grey's initial offer to mediate between the powers was declined in early July, though Britain maintained its relatively neutral position and urged a policy of de-escalation to dignitaries on both sides of the Entente and Central Powers. If the conditions necessary to bring the major powers to the negotiation table were not yet ripe in early July, they certainly were by July 25. In the aftermath of Austria-Hungary's ultimatum, Grey again proposed a conference, wherein Italy, France, Britain, and

Germany could mediate the growing crisis between Austria-Hungary, Serbia, and Russia. Many diplomats across the continent began to accept Grey's recommendation of a "méiation á quarte", including German ambassador to London, Prince Lichnowsky, and Russian Foreign Minister, Sergei Sazonov. Yet when the State Secretary of the German Foreign Office spoke with the Austro-Hungarian ambassador, he assured his ally that he "was not in the slightest degree in favor of consideration being given to the English wish", despite his personal assurance to Grey that the German government shared Britain's hope. (Jannen, 1996).

Indeed, this seemingly duplicitous act was likely the result of Germany's refusal "to summon Austria before a European court of justice in her quarrel with Serbia" (Jannen, 1996). As recently as 1913 the Entente powers – Russia, England, and France – had agreed during an ambassador's conference to remove Serbians from Albanian territory, yet no action was ever taken. The ineffectiveness of this prior conference likely fueled a perception amongst the Central Powers that a diplomatic conference would be unlikely to result in a favorable outcome for Austria-Hungary.

Ultimately, Grey's proposal fell on deaf ears. No conference would ever take place, and a peaceful resolution seemed increasingly difficult to achieve. As Europe inched closer and closer to war, diplomacy in the form of secret assurances and false promises continued in closed-off rooms and coded telegrams. By the end of July 1914, not even the most powerful leaders in the world's most powerful nations could forestall the inevitable. On July 29, Tsar Nicholas II of Russia wrote to his cousin and life-long friend, Kaiser Wilhelm II of Germany;

> I foresee that very soon I shall be overwhelmed by the pressure forced upon me and be forced to take extreme measures which will lead to war. To try and avoid such a calamity as a European war I beg you in the name of our old friendship to do what you can to stop your allies from going too far. Nicky.[4]

The Tsar was correct, and by the end of July not even the two Emperors' appeals to familial bonds could prevent war. On July 30, Russia began a general mobilization of its military – the largest force in Europe. Germany answered in kind with a declaration of war on August 1, followed by a

---

4   World War I Document Archive, *The Willy-Nicky Telegrams*, available at <https://wwi.lib.byu.edu/index.php/The_Willy-Nicky_Telegrams>.

declaration of war against Russia's ally France on August 3. On August 4, Great Britain, who had to this point avoided involving itself, declared war on Germany, citing its violation of Belgian neutrality. "It has not been possible", Sir Edward Grey remarked, "to secure the peace of Europe" (Otte, 2015). One by one, countries from Europe, North America, South America, Africa, and Asia would find themselves consumed by a conflict that began so many miles away in the Serbian capital.

4. CONSEQUENCES OF FAILED DIPLOMACY

The 1914 July Crisis proceeded a global conflict that few could predict the consequences of. By the war's end, more than 30,000,000 men would be killed or wounded in action on battlefields stretching from the French country side to the Sinai Peninsula. Another 7,000,000 civilians would lose their lives as cities and villages the world over were introduced to a new, industrialized warfare. In addition to the devastating loss of life, the Great War, as it would soon be called, set in motion a chain of events, the ramifications of which are still felt today – from the post-war reparations that crippled the German economy and left a resentful population receptive to Hitler's rhetoric, to the Russian revolution, and the collapse of the Ottoman Empire.

The eruption of World War I is traditionally attributed to a combination of causes, but the cost of July 1914's failed diplomacy can be measured in human lives. While at the time the Austrian-Hungarian diplomats likely believed themselves to be making the best out of their alliance with Germany, bluffing their way into superior bargaining power, they were actually facilitating a narrative that would later allow observers to view the Central Powers as the primary aggressors. More seriously even, their short-sightedness made them lose sight of their true national interests, as World War I would ultimately see the end of the Austrian-Hungarian Empire they had been serving.

REFERENCES

ADLER, Robert S. and SILVERSTEIN, Elliot M., *When David Meets Goliath: Dealing with Power Differentials in Negotiations*, 5 Harv. Negot. L. Rev. 1, 92–103 (2000).

CLARK, Christopher, *The Sleepwalkers: How Europe Went to War in 1914*, New York: Harper Collins (2012).

DUFFY, Michael (August 22, 2009). "Primary Documents: Austrian Ultimatum to Serbia, 23 July 1914" <FirstWorldWar.com> archived from the original on May 24, 2003. Available at <https://web.archive.org/web/20041030212115/http://www.firstworldwar.com/source/austrianultimatum.htm>.

JANNEN, Jr., W., *The Lions of July: Prelude to War, 1914*, Novato, CA: Presidio Press (1996).

MENKEL-MEADOW, C., *Toward Another View of Legal Negotiation: The Structure of Problem Solving*, UCLA L. Rev. 754, 775–781 (1984).

MNOOKIN, R., *Why Negotiations Fail: An Exploration of Barriers to Conflict Resolution*, 8 Ohio St. J. on Disp. Resol. 235, 240–242 (1993).

OTTE, T.G., *July Crisis: The World's Descent into War, Summer 1914*, Cambridge: Cambridge University Press (2015).

PUTNAM, R., *Diplomacy and Domestic Politics: The Logic of Two-Level Games*, Double-Edge Diplomacy: International Bargaining and Domestic Politics, 436 (1993).

WALTON, R. and MCKERSIE, R., *A Behavorial Theory of Labor Negotiations*, New York: McGraw Hill (1965).

WORLD WAR I DOCUMENT ARCHIVE, *The Willy-Nicky Telegrams*, available at <https://wwi.lib.byu.edu/index.php/The_Willy-Nicky_Telegrams>.

THE GERMAN "ALL OR NOTHING" APPROACH IN 1917

Unwilling to Negotiate

Emmanuel Vivet[*]

In one of the chapters of his book *Thoughts and Adventures*, Winston Churchill examines Germany's attitude at the end of 1917, wondering why the Reich did not seek to negotiate peace even though for several months it had been in a good negotiating position – even a strong one – such that it could have avoided further losses and come out of the war with its head held high, instead of having to contend with the US army a few months later.

---

[*] Institute for Research and Education on Negotiation (ESSEC IRENE).

1. INCREASING THE MILITARY EFFORT RATHER THAN NEGOTIATING

1.1. A FAVORABLE NEGOTIATING POSITION FOR FIVE MONTHS

The former British Prime Minister (who in 1917 was the Minister of Munitions) presents the situation of Autumn 1917 as follows: after the October Revolution, Russia suddenly gave up the fight. Freed from this pressure on its eastern flank, Germany could release a million soldiers from that front and assign them to the Western Front. For the first time since the great battles of 1914, it again had the advantage in numbers. In the west, France had been going through a difficult period since the failure of its offensive at Chemin des Dames (in April) and because of repeated mutinies. The British army's offensives from June to November 1917 in northern France and Flanders failed one after another. Despite the fact that the fronts were at a standstill, generally speaking, Germany found itself in a favorable position.

At the same time, the Reich knew that the United States, which entered the war in April 1917, was preparing, slowly but surely, to go onto the battlefield. They still had to recruit, train and equip their army. It was thought – which proved to be true – that the American Expeditionary Corps would be operational in Europe in the spring of 1918. A nation of 100 million inhabitants with almost inexhaustible resources faced the Central European empires, which knew they would not be able to withstand such pressure in the long run. The favorable German position was therefore limited in time, a fact not overlooked by its commanding officers.

In theory, it was logical for the German authorities to seek to negotiate an honorable peace while there was still time, given the difficulty in breaching the lines and winning the war quickly (Verdun in 1916 convinced everyone of this point) and the certainty of eventually having to retreat when the US army was operational, especially as the Germans had security in the form of troop reinforcements from the former Russian front. This would have avoided hundreds of thousands of deaths, would have kept the German economy from getting progressively weaker because of the blockade and lack of coal, all while protecting the *Reichswehr* from the dishonor of defeat. The window of opportunity was between the beginning of November 1917 (the last British failure at Passchendaele[1]) and the spring of 1918 (the US push). For Churchill: "The German armies had saved their country in the field; now was the time for German statecraft to extricate the Empire from the hideous catastrophe into which it had blundered" (Churchill, 1932).

1.2. THE CHOICE OF WEAPONS

Despite these factors, the German Command took the decision to launch a major offensive in France. It was not a small "push" to enable it to negotiate from a better position, but a major offensive, allegedly of a new kind with shock troops: an offensive designed to win. Yet it would fail and mark the start of the German decline.

How was it decided? On November 11, 1917, Ludendorff, the quartermaster of the German General Staff, met his generals to consult them about where and when to attack. Ludendorff, focused on his military objectives and paying little attention to economic and political objectives, nor to his people's distress, wanted to fight to the bitter end. His approach was to use all the means at his disposal to try to win one last time. A very powerful German offensive was therefore launched four months later, which significantly weakened the British front (at Saint Quentin), threatened to break the Franco-British line, forced France to reorganize the front, and again cost hundreds of thousands of lives. But this offensive, like so many others, was eventually halted. The last German card had been played. The Allies were on the brink of a military disaster after this painful episode: "no one thought of peace or peace negotiations" (Churchill, 1932). The war would carry on to its end.

Churchill gives an initial explanation of the German attitude, seeing in this warlike relentlessness the result of the fact that the military in Germany had taken over the conduct of the war: not only the operations, but also the war's objectives, limits, and major decisions. The political authorities had gradually been removed from command, unlike in Great Britain and France – two countries where the political authorities maintained some control over the military sphere throughout the conflict. Surrounded by

---

[1] The British offensive at Passchendaele, near to Ypres, mainly failed due to the rain and mud. 262,000 British and 260,000 Germans were killed or wounded.

similar figures[2] and a soldier himself, the commanding general, Ludendorff, therefore did not have to pit his soldier's reasoning against different points of view that might have broadened or challenged his approach. This is a typical example of a *groupthink*, a cognitive bias described by Irving Janis (1972). Churchill speaks of Ludendorff as a leader who "loved his country, but [who] loved his task more. His task was to procure victory at all costs" (Churchill, 1932).

2. HOW CAN THE PARTIES' WILLINGNESS (NOT) TO NEGOTIATE BE EXPLAINED?

The sad story of the "missed opportunity" of autumn/winter 1917 raises a crucial negotiating issue, which is the parties' willingness to negotiate. Germany had an objective interest in opening discussions but did not do so. Conversely, there were opportunities – times when circumstances and personal inclinations made negotiation possible.

There were voices in Germany calling for an end to the fighting in 1917: industrialists were raising the alarm about the state of the German economy, and politicians were suggesting a peace of honorable compromise. The tragedy was that Ludendorff, as head of the Supreme Council of the Reich's General Staff, did not hear these warnings. He was not ready to negotiate and no one forced him to. But, had he been forced, he probably would not have been the most effective negotiator.

The parties must have a certain willingness to negotiate: they have to at least subscribe to the idea that at a given time, negotiation is a tool that may resolve your dispute or provide a solution that is preferable to the slippery slope you are heading towards. Otherwise, they will find themselves in that hopeless (yet common) situation where the parties go through the motions of "negotiating" in spite of themselves, or without believing it will lead to a solution. The parties must believe, deep down, that the discussions and their outcome serve a purpose.

To explain Germany's stance in 1917, this chapter applies three theories which are available to the contemporary researcher: *BATNA*, ripeness theory, and readiness theory.

---

2   The Mons Conference of March 21, 1917, during which the relaunch of the German offensive was decided, took place under Ludendorff's chairmanship in the presence of four generals. It did not include the emperor, the princes, the chancellor, the minister of Foreign Affairs, or any political party representatives.

2.1. GERMANY IN 1917 AND ITS *BATNA*

The concept of *BATNA*[3] is useful for reflecting on the value of negotiating. It reminds us that negotiation is not the only way to resolve crises, and that it is only justified if its result, or its expected result, is better than the best outcomes available through other means. It is pointless to continue a negotiation if it leads to a worse result than other methods. The negotiating table must therefore provide more favorable outcomes than those that can be reached "away from the table".

Let us look at the options Ludendorff had in 1917 other than peace talks, and what the best of them was. Surrender? Out of the question: the cost in terms of honor would be too high. A new major offensive? The gains would be high but uncertain, whereas heavy losses of human life were certain. The pursuit of a static battle? This solution was less costly in human lives in the short term, but had a high economic cost and offered little hope of victory while giving the Americans time to prepare. Mediation for peace, as proposed by Pope Benedict XV in August? This option was closer to negotiation and had the advantage of being at the initiative of a third party, therefore it saved honor; relieved the troops and the economy, while admittedly taking power from Ludendorff's military leadership. Unfortunately, it did not seem to be on Germany's agenda (the Reich gave the Pope an ambiguous response in September). Self-determination referenda in Belgium and Alsace-Lorraine? The risk of losing the territories was high, but the solution would be less costly.

As can be seen, in 1917 Germany was not lacking in comprehensive solutions "away from the battle" and was therefore not forced to increase its military effort. However, the major offensive planned by Ludendorff not only had a significantly higher cost-benefit ratio than many of these other alternatives, it was also a better option in this regard than negotiation was. The *BATNA* concept therefore cannot really explain Ludendorff's behavior in 1917.

2.2. GERMANY IN 1917 AND RIPENESS THEORY

The parties' willingness to negotiate may also be examined in light of the so-called "ripeness theory" developed by the American political scientist

---

[3]   *Best alternative to a negotiated agreement* – the best course of action if the negotiation fails.

I. William Zartman in 1988–1989, and updated in 2000. This theory is the result of studying and summarizing many 20th century cases from the Sudanese conflict to the Oslo Accords via the Tamil conflict and Colombia. Zartman is interested in the conditions necessary for rational actors to be receptive to the idea of a negotiated solution, and isolates two recurring factors:

- *a mutually hurting stalemate.*
- *a possible way out.*

In other words, the parties involved in a conflict first need to move toward negotiation. They must realize that pursuing their action will lead to long-term failure (a very bloody war and eventual defeat), an impression that is reinforced when, for example, a disaster has just occurred or is imminent. However, the parties must also be able to see that a solution is possible (for example, the Franco-British willingness sign an honorable agreement to cease fighting; Austria's desire to pull out of the war before it was too late; and Germany's good negotiating position). The solution need not be definite, it only has to be plausible.

A third, procedural factor is *the presence of a valid spokesman* (Zartman, 1988).

This additional condition reflects the fact that in a certain number of conflicts, for example ethnic conflicts, one of the "parties" is not really identified as such; they do not have representatives who would be able to make requests or complaints or demands and who would sit at the table. In such situations, the first task to bring about the possibility of a negotiated solution is simply to identify a representative – a spokesperson – capable of expressing diverse viewpoints.

If the situation in Europe in 1917 is considered from the point of view of ripeness theory, it is clear that the combatants were in a mutually hurting stalemate. The governments are clearly identified. The perception of a possible way out was also real, since diplomacy continued to play its part and discussions had already taken place in the previous months: in the first half of 1917, two serious peace proposals had been made.[4] First, a separate peace plan between France and Austria was initiated in April by the Emperor Karl and the princes of Bourbon-Parma

---

4   François-Georges DREYFUS, 1917, *L'année des occasions perdues*. These initiatives are summarized on pp. 374–375.

(and finally rightly rejected by Paris). Second, in August, the Pope made a very serious offer to mediate, but it was forcefully rejected by Woodrow Wilson, an anti-Papist, who was emulated by anti-clerical France and Italy, and hence a hesitant Germany. These lost opportunities involved an attempt to combine a few ideas that were always the same: the restitution of Alsace-Moselle to France; the re-establishment of Belgium (very important for London); and a plan for German territorial expansion towards Russia. Of course, there were doubts each time as to whether a referendum should be held in Alsace; whether Germany would retain its colonies; whether France would occupy the right bank of the Rhine; whether Italy would occupy Trieste; and what role Serbia would play in relation to Austria. In each case however, the alternatives to war were credible. Did Ludendorff disregard all this? In hindsight, it seems clear there was a way out, provided sincere negotiators made a genuine attempt to find it.

Why then did the war continue? The answer may lie in the third element of ripeness theory: it may be that Ludendorff was not a *valid spokesman* for Germany, that is to say his own personality kept him from being a negotiator who properly represented German interests. Still, he would have had to try. Did Germany even have any representatives to speak for it? While the political life of the Reich was fairly democratic in the beginning,[5] it had been permitted to evolve into a military directorate that controlled how the war was conducted, which determined the country's fate. But Ludendorff was not *politically representative*. That is ultimately the explanation given by Churchill, who takes care to note that the entire German political system had contributed to the emergence of a military directorate in Germany. Ludendorff's power should have remained that of a soldier and not become that of a *de facto* head of state. The issue was ultimately the lack of a satisfactory balance of powers in Germany in 1917, which is beyond the scope of this chapter.

In the context of ripeness theory, the willingness of the other parties would also need to be examined. Had Germany wished to negotiate peace in late 1917 or early 1918, would France have responded with favorable terms? And what about Great Britain? Even if Paris might have been enticed by the prospect of negotiations in late 1917, this is merely a hypothesis.

---

[5]   DREYFUS, ibid., p. 107.

2.3. GERMANY IN 1917 AND READINESS THEORY

In order to study the deadlock of 1917 further, we can also use readiness theory, which its author, Dean Pruitt, describes as "an adaptation of ripeness theory" (Pruitt, 1997). Readiness theory extends ripeness theory, but differs from it insofar as it studies not only the convergence of the parties' intentions (ripeness), but also each party's willingness to negotiate, emphasizing the analysis of psychological factors: "motives and perceptions – that make up ripeness on each individual side separately rather than focusing on joint states of mind such as a mutually hurting stalemate" (Pruitt, 1997).

Readiness theory thus lists many more psychological motivations, which are possibly not shared, that change the parties to the negotiation. It makes it possible to account for the fact that the parties are not ready to negotiate at the same time. Readiness, which is "the degree to which an opponent is willing to enter into negotiations or mediation" (Pruitt, 2005), breaks down the ripeness factors.

For Pruitt, the mutually hurting stalemate would depend on:

- the perception that the conflict is not going to be won;
- the cost of the conflict over time; and
- the perceived risk of continuing the conflict.

A dormant conflict, which people think they can eventually win and does not herald any immediate disaster, therefore encourages negotiation less powerfully than does a high-risk, active conflict in which victory is far off, or a low-intensity but long and risky conflict. A conflict that is "winnable", but only at a high and lasting cost, makes people think.

The perception of a possible solution (that is, ripeness) can be broken down into:

- working trust, that is to say the belief in the other party's willingness to negotiate; such trust can also be strengthened, especially with the help of a third party;
- the rank of the discussion partners: a high-level counterpart inspires trust in their ability to make decisions and meet commitments;
- the apparent closeness between the parties' positions, insofar as close positions make the negotiators optimistic about the outcome of a negotiated solution.

Pruitt also notes that third-party pressure contributes to a party's readiness to negotiate. He cites the example of Robert Mugabe, who took part in the negotiations that founded Zimbabwe despite being convinced that his army was winning the war. However, he was persuaded to enter into negotiations because the pressure exercised on him by third parties was very strong.

Ludendorff's behavior in 1917 is better explained by readiness theory. He was probably unaware that the parties' positions were close and did not know the details of the related diplomatic discussions (in 1917 the freedom of Belgium and the surrender of Alsace had become possible for Germany). This undoubtedly would have encouraged him to continue the fight at any cost. His perception of the risk in continuing the conflict seems to have been skewed, as he did not seem to have realized the gamble he was making by betting everything on a final offensive which, if it failed, would put Germany in an irremediably difficult position. His perception of the possibility of winning the conflict was surely too positive: the likelihood that his plan of attack could fail despite having been prepared much earlier, was not clear enough to him. He was: "Willful [...] very hard-working, but narrow-minded [...] a remarkable strategist and an excellent organizer, [...] convinced that '[t]he entire Reich's policy must be subordinate to the war"[6] who failed to see the benefits he would have achieved from timely negotiation. Finally, perhaps he underestimated the willingness of the other party to negotiate, accustomed as he may have been to considering the enemy as a force to be destroyed.

3. THE COST OF LOST OPPORTUNITIES

From late 1917 until its end, the Great War would account for 500,000 to 600,000 deaths. France had more deaths in 1918 (235,000) than in 1917 (164,000). Ludendorff was not the only cause of this, since other attempts at peace in other circles also failed.

However, his decision to increase a costly military effort, when everything was in place for favorable negotiations, is an example of both a groupthink and of poor analysis of the circumstances. Ripeness and,

---

[6]   DREYFUS, ibid., p. 121.

even more so, readiness theories provide tools to understand where his reasoning failed.

This lost opportunity was, in 1917, a very serious matter, and such lost opportunities are still seen in other political contexts. We need only look at the painful and unresolved ethnic conflicts in the world, at the political leaders who tend to favor international confrontation more than the well-being of their people and at the many dictators clinging to power instead of negotiating a peaceful way out. These cases should continue to make us reflect upon these lost opportunities in a rational way, analyzing the necessary conditions for a negotiation to start, or not to start.

Another possible track to follow would be to study the negotiators' personal beliefs. The beginning of a negotiation also takes place in a context where personal inclinations, emotions and affects, be they positive or negative, play a role. One example is given in a later chapter of this book, where the start of the 1950 Korean War is analyzed.[7] The war was set off without any clear evaluation of the situation and without even the usual exchange of military signals or threats; instead, it was based on surprise, anger, and the feeling of being insulted. This caused the conflict to escalate – just as, in 1917, the opportunity to de-escalate the situation was missed.

REFERENCES

CHURCHILL, W., 1932, *Thoughts and Adventures*, London, Thornton Butterworth, pp.147–162.

DREYFUS, F.-G., 1917, *L'année des occasions perdues*, 2010, Paris, éditions de Fallois, pp. 155–175.

JANIS, I., 1972, *Victims of Groupthink: A Psychological Study of Foreign-Policy Decisions and Fiascoes*, Boston, Houghton Mifflin.

PRUITT, D.G., 1997, "Ripeness Theory and the Oslo Talks", *International Negotiation*, 2, 237–250.

PRUITT, D.G., 2005, *Whither Ripeness Theory?*, Institute for Conflict Analysis and Resolution, George Mason University, Fairfax, Virginia.

ZARTMAN, I.W., 1988, "Common Elements in the Analysis of the Negotiation Process", *Negotiation Journal*, vol. 4, issue 1, 31–43.

ZARTMAN, I.W., 2000, "Ripeness. The Hurting Stalemate and Beyond", in Stern, P.C. and Druckman, D. (eds.), *International Conflict Resolution After the Cold War*, Washington DC, National Academy Press.

---

[7] See Emmanuel PETIT, "What Set Off the Korean Conflict of 1950?", in this volume.

PART II
BILATERAL NEGOTIATIONS

THE PHOENICIANS (960 BCE)

Long Distances, Close Business Relationships

Habib Chamoun* and Randy D. Hazlett**

Upon the Erythrean Sea the people live
Who style themselves Phoenicians.
These are sprung from the true Erythrean stock,
From the sage race, who first essayed the deep,
And wafted merchandise to coasts unknown.
These too, digested first the starry choir,
Their motions marked, and called them by their name.
Dionysius – *Pliny*, v. 965.

The Phoenician cities – and civilization – developed around the Mediterranean Sea from circa 1200 BCE to 300 BCE. Bold navigators, the Phoenicians had mapped the sky indeed. They were also famous craftsmen and are known for creating an alphabet that inspired later ones. They had

---

* Visiting Scholar, University of St Thomas Cameron School of Business.
** Professor, School of Mining and Geosciences, Nazarbayev University.

developed long distance trade routes, as their network extended from Mesopotamia to the Eastern coasts of the Mediterranean Sea, to Gibraltar and beyond. Their commercial enterprises resulted in the founding of colonies in Greek islands, Sicilia, and the North African coasts, the most famous of which became the ancient Carthage.

As Phoenician documents are very rare, we benefit from external sources, notably the Bible and Flavius Josephus (37 – circa 100). In this chapter, several historical documents from ancient historians, Hebrew and Christian scriptures are analyzed in order to find out how the Phoenicians negotiated. Some of the stories will tell us who the Phoenicians were, how they were perceived as negotiators, and what their values as negotiators were.[1]

1. FIRST CONTACT SALES OR SILENT NEGOTIATION

Herodotus (IV. 196) describes a typical first contact sales approach practiced by the Phoenicians:

> The Carthaginians also relate the following: – There is a country in Libya, and a nation, beyond the Pillars of Heracles, which they are wont to visit, where they no sooner arrive but forthwith they unlade their wares, and, having disposed them after an orderly fashion along the beach, leave them, and, returning aboard their ships, raise a great smoke. The natives, when they see the smoke, come down to the shore, and laying out to view so much gold as they think the worth of the wares, withdraw to a distance. The Carthaginians upon this come ashore and look. If they think the gold enough, they take it and go their way; but if it does not seem to them sufficient, they go aboard ship once more, and wait patiently. Then the others approach and add to their gold, till the Carthaginians are content. Neither party deals unfairly by the other: for they themselves never touch the gold till it comes up to the worth of their goods, nor do the natives ever carry off the goods till the gold is taken away (*The Histories*, pp. 381–382).

Here we see an example of a silent negotiation, which is also a cross-cultural negotiation, respectful and equitable. Herodotus hints that

---

[1] Some of the material in this chapter was originally presented in the book *Negotiate Like a Phoenician* (Chamoun and Hazlett, 2007).

the Phoenicians had developed extensive skill in communication without complete knowledge of their trading partner's native language.

As this account comes from the Carthaginian era, trades were no doubt brokered in gold as opposed to pure barter. The cited Pillars of Heracles is the ancient name for the Straits of Gibraltar. Herm (1975) adds: "In this way the first contacts were made. A counter-offer followed the first offering, and then the silent bargaining began, needing much tact, inventiveness and also honesty. The merchants did not want to spoil a possible new market before they had begun, a feeling apparently appreciated by their customers." Whether first contact or not, the Phoenician customer could feel he was dealt fairly.

2. NEGOTIATIONS OF KING HIRAM WITH THE HEBREW KINGS

2.1. BUILDING A PALACE FOR KING DAVID

We have gleaned the extensive product line and expansive trade latitude of the Phoenicians from Hebrew prophets. Likewise, we get good insight into the makings of a deal in the exchanges documented in the Bible concerning a big business proposition of ancient times – the most extravagant building project on record, the construction of the Hebrew temple to house the Ark of the Covenant, the place where God's presence dwelt – Solomon's Temple. The building of the temple was made possible through a business cooperation between the Phoenician and Hebrew kings. This deal led to a deep business alliance and probably ushered Tyre towards the pinnacle of its business empire. In this deal, the Phoenicians brought brilliant craftsmanship to Solomon. Let us examine the business dealings of the Phoenician King Hiram of Tyre in detail, which are well documented in various locations within the Hebrew Scriptures (notably in the *Samuel*, *Kings* and *Chronicles* books).

Once David, Solomon's father, had been installed on the throne, King Hiram sent an envoy bearing extensive gifts. 1 Chronicles 14:1 says: "Now Hiram king of Tyre sent messengers to David, along with cedar logs, stonemasons and carpenters to build a palace for him." This was neither part of a business deal nor a request of the region's newest monarch, but King Hiram took a proactive approach to lay the foundation for a long-term business alliance. In this sense, we can call these gifts *Tradeables*.[2] Hiram offered choice cedar and skilled laborers – a gift that was not refused and made a lasting impression. This was no doubt a costly gesture, but we can judge that Hiram had made a wise investment. His gift diffused any notion of political challenge and affirmed Hiram's belief that this kingdom was the new seat of regional power. A new king would, of course, require much more than a few pieces of wood, and Hiram wielded the trade network which could satisfy those needs.

In other words, Hiram brought to King David's doorstep the goods and precious know-how that the Hebrew king would otherwise have had to buy or seize by plundering conquered nations. Hiram thus started a long-lasting business relationship. As a matter of fact, when the time had come for Solomon to reign after his father David, the business relationship transcended his individual case and continued to the next generation.

2.2. BUILDING A TEMPLE FOR KING SOLOMON

King Solomon's wealth is described at length in the Bible, as well as his wisdom, as the greatest in mankind. King Hiram, for his part, was quick to continue the relationship with the son as he had with the father. 1 Kings 5:1 says: "When Hiram king of Tyre heard that Solomon had been anointed king to succeed his father David, he sent his envoys to Solomon, because he had always been on friendly terms with David." Solomon sent back this reply, asking for more.

1 Kings 5

3 "You know that because of the wars waged against my father David from all sides, he could not build a temple for the Name of the LORD his God until the LORD put his enemies under his feet.

4 But now the LORD my God has given me rest on every side, and there is no adversary or disaster.

---

2   Chamoun and Hazlett (2007) define *Tradeable* as: (1) A set of ideas or actions that help leverage a deal without being a part of the deal, or (2) Products and services that satisfy customer needs outside our own product line that are not in competition with our offerings. *Tradeables* create greater negotiation capacity for present or future deals. *Tradeables* literally means "able" to "trade" or bringing trading capacity. If we extract the word "deal" from *Tradeables* we are left with *Trabes*, which in Latin means the beam or the structure of the deal.

5 I intend, therefore, to build a temple for the Name of the LORD my God, as the LORD told my father David, when he said, 'Your son whom I will put on the throne in your place will build the temple for my Name.'

6 So give orders that cedars of Lebanon be cut for me. My men will work with yours, and I will pay you for your men whatever wages you set. You know that we have no one so skilled in felling timber as the Sidonians."

Speaking openly with Hiram of his divine mission, Solomon clearly implied the need for quality materials and workmanship. Saying that he has no one so skilled, he also pays the Phoenician people the highest of compliments. But, at the same time, we can see that no price was negotiated. This looks like a *carte blanche* offer. Would the wisest and richest man in the world not care about price?

1 Kings 5

8 "I have received the message you sent me and will do all you want in providing the cedar and pine logs.

9 My men will haul them down from Lebanon to the sea, and I will float them in rafts by sea to the place you specify. There I will separate them and you can take them away. And you are to grant my wish by providing food for my royal household."

10 In this way Hiram kept Solomon supplied with all the cedar and pine logs he wanted,

11 and Solomon gave Hiram twenty thousand cors of wheat as food for his household, in addition to twenty thousand baths, of pressed olive oil. Solomon continued to do this for Hiram year after year.

12 The LORD gave Solomon wisdom, just as he had promised him. There were peaceful relations between Hiram and Solomon, and the two of them made a treaty.

It is worth analyzing how King Hiram handled this blank check: he simply asked Solomon to provide food for his household. This looks like another open-ended deal. Later in the text, we are given the quantities that Solomon actually sent as annual payment. It must have been sufficient. This relates to the use of *tradeables* first introduced in this business relationship when there was no deal (or even the eventual dealer) on the scene. King Hiram must have supplied the royal family and household with enough goods in the intervening years. This led to an avenue of trust seen between these two parties in this deal.

The workers got to work on this massive construction project. In scale, it was not an impressive structure, but the materials and detail made it the top construction project of the time (cedar covered with gold for the interior, ornamental flowers, pure gold in the inner sanctuary, bronze pillars …). The artisanship had to be the best, so Solomon turned once again to King Hiram.

2.3. KING SOLOMON AND KING HIRAM: BUILDING A LEGACY

Further accounts, in the *Chronicles* book, mention a past business deal and a desire to continue this business relationship. There, we find references of the skill level required in the project, not just the simple felling of trees. Apparently no Israelite artisan was so skilled in working with metals and embroidered linen as found in the Phoenician society. This is why Solomon extended his requests, asking for the assignment of a Phoenician artisan to perform the most complicated and extravagant tasks in finishing out the temple.

> Send me, therefore, a man skilled to work in gold and silver, bronze and iron, and in purple, crimson and blue yarn, and experienced in the art of engraving, to work in Judah and Jerusalem with my skilled craftsmen (2 Chronicles 2:7)

In his reply, Hiram was to send Huram-Abi, a man of mixed Phoenician-Jewish heritage – a man of great skill. After an exchange of compliments preceding business, laying the groundwork for openness, we see that Hiram's response gives clues as to why a Hebrew king could have such a strong working relationship with a man of Canaanite descent.

2 Chronicles 2

11 Hiram king of Tyre replied by letter to Solomon: "Because the LORD loves his people, he has made you their king."

12 And Hiram added: "Praise be to the LORD, the God of Israel, who made heaven and earth! He has given King David a wise son, endowed with intelligence and discernment, who will build a temple for the LORD and a palace for himself.

13 I am sending you Huram-Abi, a man of great skill,

14 whose mother was from Dan and whose father was from Tyre. He is trained to work in gold and silver, bronze and iron, stone and wood, and with purple

and blue and crimson yarn and fine linen. He is experienced in all kinds of engraving and can execute any design given to him. He will work with your craftsmen and with those of my Lord, David your father.

15 Now let my Lord send his servants the wheat and barley and the olive oil and wine he promised,

16 and we will cut all the logs from Lebanon that you need and will float them in rafts by sea down to Joppa. You can then take them up to Jerusalem."

17 Solomon took a census of all the aliens who were in Israel, after the census his father David had taken; and they were found to be 153,600.

18 He assigned 70,000 of them to be carriers and 80,000 to be stonecutters in the hills, with 3,600 foremen over them to keep the people working.

Here we get the specifics – the when, where, and how. The cedar was to be floated to Joppa and hauled to Jerusalem. The manpower assigned to this task is large – 153,600 non-Hebrew residents conscripted into service.

Looking back at verse 12, we see that King Hiram uses for the second time the name for God, Lord, which the New International Version of the Bible transcribes in place of Yahweh. He said, *"Praise be to the LORD, the God of Israel, who made the heaven and earth!"* It seems as if the Phoenicians may not have allowed religion to be a stumbling block to business dealings, but to invoke the most holy name of God, giving him praise, and acknowledging him as the creator goes beyond business politeness. On this note, Johnston (1965) commented:

> The overtures of Hiram to Solomon could not fail, therefore, to have been viewed with grave suspicion by the priesthood, if the affection existing between the Tyrian and the Jewish monarchs had not had its root in a religious sympathy of a wholly different character from that which could have been possible at any later date, for between the pure and exalted worship of Jehovah and that of Baal there was a whole world of difference (p. 116).

Was King Hiram a worshipper of the God of the Israelites? Had he renounced the Baal worship prevalent in his culture? We may never know for sure, but it is doubtful that King Hiram would have put on a ruse just to swing a business deal. His sincerity appears genuine. His actions endorse his authenticity.

One can also wonder whether Huram-Abi was a *Tradeable* in the sense explained above. He was not part of the original deal. Was the deal in jeopardy if the added artisan was not supplied? Probably not, but it may have been in Hiram's best interest to send the best, not only to perform the task to satisfaction, but to oversee the quality of the project. Did Solomon request Huram-Abi? Maybe not, and perhaps the choice was left to King Hiram. Solomon asked for a skilled craftsman; Hiram chose to send the best – a most likely *Tradeable*.

Given that Huram-Abi's work proved to be very valuable, his inclusion most certainly strengthened the business relationship and gained leverage for future deals. The business relationship was quite mature at this stage and one may wonder whether there was need for further leverage. But if a business relationship continues, there is always need for increased leverage. Indeed, other building projects followed, all requiring materials to be supplied by King Hiram, including a second palace known as the Hall of the Forest of Lebanon and a separate palace for Solomon's Egyptian wife. Each project was more demanding from a materials perspective than the previous one.

Finally, following the 20-year building project collaboration on the temple and king's palace, King Solomon sent an unsolicited gift to King Hiram to show his pleasure – 20 cities in the region around Galilee. When Hiram went to inspect his gift, he was less than pleased. He questioned Solomon, "What kind of towns are these you have given me, my brother?" When delivering this negative report, King Hiram remains cautious and directs the focus of criticism onto the gift and away from the relationship. We are not given any follow-up on the disposition of these towns, but Solomon's use of *Tradeables* was not very effective in this instance. While their effective use involves meeting a client's need unrelated to the business deal, these towns apparently did not meet a need.

3. SOME NEGOTIATION PRINCIPLES FROM THE PHOENICIANS

3.1. BUILDING ON TRUST AND LONG-TERM RELATIONSHIPS

Analysis shows that the *Tradeables* concept (Chamoun and Hazlett, 2007) was actively used in the ancient culture of the Phoenicians. Are such dealings in 960 BCE applicable today? According to historian Sanford Holst (Holst, 2005), Phoenician negotiating style was characterized by being abundant and trustworthy. Customers' needs were satisfied by applying a set of principles where peacefulness, partnership and tolerance played a great role:

1. Create partnerships
2. Trade internationally
3. Resolve differences peacefully
4. Express religious tolerance
5. Respect women
6. Uphold equality
7. Retain privacy

As such, the Phoenician model seems to have put emphasis on mutual trust, reputation and long-term relationships. The Phoenician civilization could be one of the few that conquered commercially the ancient world without war but instead by negotiating (Chamoun and Hazlett, 2007). Respect was also part of the silent negotiation process as described in the story of Herodotus: the creation of smoke did open a communication process whose cooperative nature prevailed over competition. At some point, a process of distributive negotiation starts with the natives laying out as much gold as they thought the merchandise was worth, but this process remains within a process of mutual trust. If the sellers do not take the gold, a counter-offer was given with a gold supplement, and so on until the gold is taken away. In the same manner, the negotiation between King Hiram and King Solomon demonstrates full trust from King Solomon towards Phoenician King Hiram.

3.2. USING TRUST TO BUILD A COOPERATIVE STRATEGY

Gifting outside the deal (*Tradeables*), as a strategy executed by King Hiram with respect to the relationship with King Solomon and the neighboring growing empire under his control, can accelerate the approach to an agreement, or improve the negotiated equilibrium position. We assess that behavior aside from price that promotes mutual empathy acts as a catalyst to accelerate the relationship bonding process. Meeting the needs of a business partner fosters mutual empathy and creates significant leverage for the present and future deals.

In the same way as evolutionary game theory gives players opportunities to learn from repetitive interactions, repeated interaction has some semblance to a long-term relationship, such as the one between King Hiram and the Kings David and Solomon. Repeated interaction allows parties to assess collaborative tendencies. When the other party (King Hiram) consistently acts in a mutually beneficial manner, trust and mutual empathy is increased and risk decreased. Yet the risk of King Hiram not acting collaboratively was high, because Kings David and Solomon had extensive and often demonstrated military power and could easily become more competitive. If a competitive "price-focused strategy" had been used by both parties, most likely the negotiations would not have followed on to the next generation.

One might also point out that Phoenician strength was on the seas, while the Hebrews possessed an unmatched infantry. Thus, a physical confrontation was unlikely on the other party's domain of strength. Both King David and King Solomon had the capacity to be competitive in their respective fields. Conversely, on the cooperative side of their relationship, the fact that their interests and areas of expertise complemented each other help to understand the choices they made to collaborate; in a sense, Hiram and Solomon also introduce us to Ricardos theory of comparative advantage (Davis, 2005).

4. CONCLUSION: PUTTING TRUST AND RELATIONSHIP FIRST

At a time when international trade is not always a world of trust and balance, the Phoenicians, with some 3,000 years of distance, remind us of the importance of long-term partnerships. The Phoenicians were able to make themselves more valuable as business partners than as conquered foes. Using their natural resources, their skills, their business network and their business insight, they were able to land multiple construction projects with the regional power of the time. From the existing sources, King Hiram can be seen as introducing some basic yet crucial elements of international trade negotiations. All in all, the actual construction of Solomon's temple was secondary to the relationship that was fostered to the benefit of both parties. The texts emphasize very clearly the necessity of being proactive in building relationships based upon fairness and customer value, of keeping up these relationships, trusting partners as well as investing in their trust. The significant timespan of the Phoenician civilization argues in favor of such practices.

REFERENCES

CHAMOUN, Habib and HAZLETT, Randy D. (2013), *The Influence of Emotions in Negotiation: A Game Theory Framework*, in Christopher HONEYMAN, James COBEN and Andre WEI-MIN LEE (eds.), *Rethinking negotiation teaching series: Educating Negotiators for a Connected World. Vol 4* (pp. 569–586), St. Paul, MN: DRI Press.

DAVIS, Timothy (2005), *Ricardo's Macroeconomics: Money, Trade Cycles, and Growth*, Cambridge: Cambridge University Press.

CHAMOUN, Habib and HAZLETT, Randy D. (2007), *Negotiate like a Phoenician*, Houston: Key-Negotiations.

HERM, Gerhard (1975), *The Phoenicians*. Edited by Caroline HILLIER. New York, NY: William Morrow and Company.

HERODOTUS, (1997), *The Histories*. Translated by George RAWLINSON, New York, NY: Alfred A. Knopf.

HOLST, SANFORD (2005), *Phoenicians: Lebanon's Epic Heritage*, Los Angeles, CA: Cambridge & Boston Press.

Holy Bible, New International Version, Grand Rapids, MI: Zondervan, 1984.

JOHNSTON, Thomas C. (1965), *Did the Phoenicians Discover America?* Houston, TX: St. Thomas Press.

WHITE, Sherwin (1966), *The Letters of Pliny*, London: Oxford University Press.

CHRISTOPHER COLUMBUS AND THE CATHOLIC MONARCHS (1485–1492)

Negotiating Troubled Waters

Nancy CALDWELL*

While historians disagree about details concerning the negotiations between Columbus and the Catholic Monarchs, Queen Isabella I, and King Ferdinand II, there is a consensus as to the protracted and complex nature of the process, and to a series of events, which form the foundation of this analysis.

---

*   HEC Paris Business School.

1. REBOUNDING FROM A FAILED NEGOTIATION

In 1485, when King João II of Portugal rejected Columbus's proposed expedition to sail "West in order to reach the East and make discoveries along the way", the explorer left Lisbon to begin a new set of negotiations with Queen Isabella I of Castile and King Ferdinand II of Aragon.

One probable explanation for King João's refusal was that the king had already invested in an expedition to find a route around Africa to Asia. Although the results of that expedition were still unknown, if it proved successful, there would not be any perceived need to invest in a redundant exploration, which carried a great deal of risk, and no foreseeable advantages.

It is interesting to speculate why King João dismissed Columbus's "entrepresa". A strong possibility is that Columbus poorly managed a classic dilemma in negotiation. Whereas he was able to "sell his idea" by presenting somewhat plausible maps, he was unable to "sell himself." Only two years later, King João did agree to sponsor an expedition pitched by João Afonso do Estreito and Fernão Dulmo, which was in many ways similar to Columbus's earlier proposition. If the terms that Columbus later demanded from Spain are any indication, it is possible that Dulmo and do Estreito drove a softer bargain, which made their deal more attractive to the King. In 1487, do Estreito and Dulmo sailed westward under the Portuguese flag, but their expedition was unsuccessful, and both men died at sea.

Almost immediately upon João's rejection, Columbus left Portugal with his young son, Diego, to try his luck with "The Catholic Monarchs", Queen Isabella I of Castile I and King Ferdinand II of Aragon. There is some discussion as to whether Columbus's debts in Portugal expedited his departure.

2. FRAMING A NEW NEGOTIATION CONTEXT

2.1. FIRST CONTACTS

Upon arriving in the port of Palos in Andalusia, Columbus enrolled his son as a boarding student at the Franciscan monastery, La Rábida, before going on to plead his case with King Ferdinand II and Queen Isabella I. This monastery was not only located near Columbus's in-laws, but also proved to be strategic throughout his negotiations.

The prior of the monastery, Fray Antonio de Marchena, was known as the "astronomer priest", because of his interests in astronomy, maritime exploration, and geography, and was able to introduce Columbus to influential and wealthy nobles such as the Duke of Medinaceli. This introduction quickly led to the Duke's decision to equip Columbus's expedition himself, since he possessed his own merchant fleet.

Unfortunately, there was a huge structural obstacle. Explorations were "the exclusive prerogative of the Crown". Medinaceli, therefore, deferred to the King and Queen before making a commitment. This time, Columbus had been able "to sell both his idea *and* himself", but to a person who was not a decision-maker.

The response from the Queen was not the one Medinaceli was hoping for – a simple waiver giving him the authorization to finance an expedition on his own – but rather a summons for Columbus to appear before the court.

Fulfilling such a command was not simple: upon the marriage of Isabella and Ferdinand, their kingdoms, Castile and Aragon, were united and the court began moving nomadically from one city to another in the realm. Furthermore, the sovereigns were mainly focused on expelling the Moors from their last bastion on the peninsula, the mountain kingdom of Granada. Their active involvement in the military efforts to conquer this territory increased the cadence and unpredictability of their travels.

Making his way through the war's devastation, Columbus arrived at the city of Cordoba, on January 20, 1486, but missed the King and Queen by several weeks, because they had left for Madrid at the end of 1485. He stayed in Cordoba to await their return, but it was delayed by the birth of the monarchs' fifth and last child (Catherine of Aragon, who would eventually become the first wife of Henry VIII of England). The interval between Columbus's arrival, and his actual meeting with the monarchs, which is believed to have taken place in May 1486, proved to be crucial for Columbus both professionally and personally. From a professional point of view, it gave him an opportunity to gain favor with several dignitaries. From a personal one, he also met and fell in love with Beatriz Enriquez de Arana, with whom he had a son, Ferdinand, in 1488. Ferdinand would grow up to be become a scholar and his father's most important biographer.

2.2. PRESENTING A PROPOSAL TO THE "POWERS THAT BE"

When Columbus finally did meet the monarchs, he was careful to present his project in terms that reflected their interests: He would establish a route to Asia, which would bypass the Ottoman blockade of the spice trade. This would have the additional advantage of discovering new territories, enhancing the Crown's glory and wealth while opening opportunities for converting their inhabitants to Christianity. The last point was especially compelling to Queen Isabella, who was extremely devout.

Unfortunately, the context and timing of Columbus's pitch were working against him. Isabella and Ferdinand were feeling increasing pressures from their exhausting war against the Moors. Isabella's response to Columbus was to form a royal study committee of theologians, astronomers, and cosmographers. The commission was to be headed by Hernando de Talavera, a prominent political and religious figure, as well as the Queen's confessor, and was to begin its work the next fall. Since there was no deadline established for the committee to reach a conclusion, her action can be considered a stalling tactic.

Time passed. The court continued its peregrinations from place to place, and Columbus continued to establish and work his network among influential people. Although Columbus did meet with the Talavera committee to document and promote his ideas, he faced the predicament later described by his son, Ferdinand, who wrote that his father did not "wish to reveal all the details of his plan, fearing lest it be stolen from him in Castile as it had been in Portugal".[1]

While the Talavera Commission never formally rejected Columbus's proposal, the explorer learned through his network that the Commission was hostile.

At this point, the Queen may have revived Columbus's hope, without committing herself in any way to the expedition, by putting him on a retainer of about 12,000 maravedís a year to cover his travel and living expenses. One may wonder: was the Queen trying to buy time, keep him from going abroad to speak with competing monarchs, or even establish a sense of indebtedness toward her?

At some time between the fall of 1487 and summer of 1488, the royal stipends ceased and Columbus reacted by re-contacting King João II of Portugal, who invited him back to Lisbon, where Columbus's brother, Bartholomew, was living. The timing and context of this new attempt by Columbus to win King João's approval were even worse than they had been in 1485, when Columbus had failed previously. He arrived in Lisbon just in

---

[1]   COLUMBUS, Ferdinand, 1959, *The Life of Christopher Columbus by His Son Ferdinand*, trans. and edited by Benjamin Keen, Rutgers University Press, New Brunswick, NJ, p. 38.

time to witness Bartholomew Dias's triumphal arrival in December 1488. Dias had succeeded in sailing around the southern tip of Africa – thereby finding Portugal's long-sought route to Asia and causing King João II to lose all interest in Columbus's proposal.

With Portugal out of the picture and the years passing, Columbus and his brother decided to negotiate on two tracks at once: Bartholomew would try his luck with King Henry VII of England while Christopher returned to Castile, where he thought the war against the Moors was winding to a close, and the King and Queen would finally be able to focus on his "empresa".

While staying a second time at La Rábida, in May 1489, Columbus received a summons from the Queen to appear at the court at Cordoba to renew their discussions. The summons was accompanied by a grant of 10,000 maravedís and a royal warrant for provisions and lodging during the journey. Columbus left La Rábida feeling encouraged.

3. THE POWER OF PERSEVERANCE

3.1. NEW UNCONVINCING ATTEMPTS

At this point in the war, King Ferdinand's strategy against the Moors was to lay siege to an important frontier post, Baza, which was one of the three most important cities in the Kingdom of Granada. That spring the weather was severe and the roads were washed out by rains and flooding, causing such unsanitary conditions that six times as many Spanish soldiers died from disease as in combat. By the time Columbus arrived in Cordoba, the Queen was so consumed by the task of providing supplies for her husband's army that she had lost interest again in Columbus's project.

Another year passed before Queen Isabella's interest in Columbus's plans rekindled in the spring of 1490, when she convened another jury of experts to examine Columbus's proposal. Once again, though, they were unconvinced.

Despite the myth that Columbus had to persuade the Spanish court that the world was round, the actual blocking point was more a question of calculation. The Queen's advisors actually accepted that the world was spherical, but considered that the distance to be traveled by going west to reach India or the East Indies would be too great for contemporary ships to travel, let alone make the return voyage, if the western seas were navigable at all. (The fact is that they were right, or at least much closer to reality: it was too far to the East Indies. But, not, as it turned out, to the

West Indies, which neither Columbus nor the experts had factored into their calculations.) Although the jury rejected Columbus's proposal, for some reason the Queen let Columbus understand that this rejection should not be considered definitive and asked him to wait until the war with the Moors was over.

In the meantime, Columbus's brother, Bartholomew, had been captured by pirates while en route to England. And in Spain, the war with the Moors was dragging on. Finally, after laying siege to Baza for six months, King Ferdinand's forces broke through and went on to attack the last Moorish stronghold, the city of Granada.

In the spring of 1491, Columbus returned to the La Rábida monastery, where he learned that his brother, who had somehow gained his freedom and arrived destitute in England, had been turned away by Henry VII. Bartholomew had then traveled to the French court, where he was not meeting any more success with France's king, Charles VIII.

3.2. SENDING INDIRECT BATNA[2] SIGNALS

At La Rábida, Columbus spoke openly of plans to travel to France and personally present his proposal to the King. Fray Juan Pérez, a former confessor to the Queen and one of her most trusted advisers, was also staying at the monastery. Whether through luck, or strategic maneuvering, Columbus managed to let Pérez, and therefore Isabella, know, that she was on the verge of potentially losing her investment and the opportunities that Columbus represented.

Upon hearing of Columbus's plan to exercise his BATNA, Pérez rode off to meet with the monarchs, who were still in the process of trying to conquer Grenada.

As soon as Perez had laid out Columbus's supposed plans to take his proposal to the French king, a royal envoy was sent from Granada to La Rábida, not only with an order for Columbus to appear before the king and queen at their camp, Santa Fé, just outside of Grenada, but with 20,000 maravedís for the purchase of appropriate clothes and a warrant permitting Columbus the use of a horse.

By the time the Moors finally capitulated on January 6, 1492, Columbus had reached the royal headquarters and entered Grenada with the rest

---

2   Best Alternative To a Negotiated Agreement – his best course of action if his
     negotiation failed.

of the victors. It looked like the stage was finally set for him to succeed in persuading the Catholic monarchs: the war was over, the Queen had not only summoned him, but had invested in improving his stature. Everything seemed favorable for a positive outcome to Columbus's long and painful wait.

3.3. CALLING ONE'S BLUFF: TERMS AND CONDITIONS ARE NOT MERE DETAILS

The negotiation quickly bogged down, though, as soon as it came to negotiating the terms and conditions of the agreement. It is not clear whether these terms were the same that Columbus had demanded of King João or possibly mentioned in previous discussions with King Ferdinand and Queen Isabella, but history has preserved Columbus's requirements in Grenada in 1492, which included that he:

1. would have, for himself, his heirs, and successors in perpetuity, the office of admiral in all the islands and continents which he might discover or acquire in the ocean, with similar honours and prerogatives to those enjoyed by the high admiral of Castile.
2. would be viceroy and governor-general over all said lands and continents; with the privilege of nominating three candidates for the government of each island or province, one of whom would be selected by the sovereigns.
3. would be entitled to reserve for himself one tenth of all pearls, precious stones, gold, silver, spices, and all other articles and merchandise, in whatever manner found, bought, bartered, or gained within his admiralty, the costs being first deducted.
4. That he, or his lieutenant, would be the sole judge in all cases and disputes arising out of traffic between these countries and Spain, provided the high admiral of Castile had similar jurisdiction in his district.
5. That he might contribute an eighth part of the expenses in fitting out vessels to sail on this enterprise and receive an eighth part of the profits in perpetuity (Fiske, 1942, p. 417).

The Court summarily refused Columbus's terms and Isabella definitively rejected the Enterprise. But was that the end of the story?

Many historians have questioned why Columbus was so adamant – so stubborn even – about his terms that he risked losing a long-desired agreement? There has been considerable speculation that he was aware that there was something more in the Atlantic than he admitted knowing. If he believed this, and had reason to believe that the monarchs thought so as well, then he might have thought that his position was strong enough to risk a bluff. Finally, it is even possible that he was simply swayed by emotion and felt that he had to extract more from the King and Queen because they had played for so long on his patience and nerves.

Regardless of his motives for being so inflexible, upon being dismissed, Columbus left Santa Fé by taking the northern gate, which is known today as the Columbus Gate, toward France. "Then in the hamlet of Pinos just four miles to the north, where the trail crossed a gorge by way of an ancient three-arched bridge, Christopher Columbus heard the hoof beats of the queen's messenger pounding in hot pursuit".[3] The Queen had given in to Columbus's conditions.

4. GENERATING OPTIONS FOR MUTUAL GAIN

4.1. CALCULATING THE INTERESTS OF THE CATHOLIC MONARCHS

What happened during the interval? A wealthy and influential lawyer, with whom Columbus had (wisely) cultivated a relationship during this long and drawn out wait, had intervened. The lawyer, Luis de Santangel, handled the Court's finances and was able to present the queen with a global analysis of the situation, which is outlined in the following chart.

Based on the concept of Currently Perceived Choice,[4] Isabella's situation could be seen as follows.

As of: 1492

Currently Perceived Choice of Queen Isabella I of Castile

Question faced: "Should I authorize the Columbus expedition and thereby give in to his demands concerning title, role and wealth connected to his possible discoveries?"

---

3   DYSON, John, 1991, *Columbus For Gold, God, and Glory*, Simon and Schuster, New York, p. 93.
4   FISHER, Roger and URY, William, 1991, *Getting to Yes*, Houghton, Mifflin Company, Boston and New York, p. 45.

"If I say 'Yes' to Columbus"

And he is successful

+ I gain wealth, power and access to Asia
+ I gain the opportunity to spread Christianity
+ I make a small investment for huge potential gain
+ Columbus will only gain authority in territories not under my rule

And if he is unsuccessful

+ My sponsorship could be a useful extension of my policy to explore the Atlantic and exert authority beyond the Canary Islands
– I will be involved in a potentially embarrassing scheme
– I will waste (some) resources at a time when the royal coffers are empty

"If I say 'No' to Columbus"

And he is successful

– He may achieve success sailing under another flag, gaining glory and wealth for another crown
– I will appear foolish before the other courts of Europe
– I will lose an occasion to "catch up" with Portuguese maritime achievements

And if he is unsuccessful

+ I will not have invested uselessly

Santangel's main conclusion was that the potential gain far out-weighed any potential loss, and that there were ways to finance the expedition without costing the kingdom money it did not have. The war against the Moors had emptied the royal coffers.[5]

Using what we would now call a "creative financial engineering option", Santangel put together the following package to meet both the needs of the Crown to limit expenditure and Columbus's requirement of three fully supplied and manned caravels for his expedition:

1. Santangel suggested that a royal fine that had been imposed on the seaport of Palos in Andalucia for smuggling operations be paid in kind, by obliging the merchants of Palos to put two caravels at Columbus's disposal.

---

[5] The story of Isabella pawning her jewels to finance Columbus is probably a romantic myth. Her jewels had probably been put up as collateral to finance the purchase of supplies for the previously mentioned siege of Baza. That being said, it is interesting to note that putting royal jewels into hock was apparently not rare at that time in history.

2. Columbus would be able to raise 250,000 maravedís from a Genoese/Florentine merchant group in Seville toward financing the third ship.

3. The remaining 1,140,000 maravedís required for the third ship would come from the Holy Brotherhood,[6] of which Santangel was the treasurer, in the form of a loan to the Crown at 14 per cent over two years.

4.2. CONTRACTUAL AGREEMENT vs. ACTUAL IMPLEMENTATION

Upon reaching this agreement on April 17, 1492, Columbus finally seemed ready to begin preparing his voyage in earnest, but the context and timing still were not in his favor. While the agreement appeared feasible on paper, neither party had really considered the practical impediments to implementing it.

The month before, Ferdinand and Isabella had issued the Alhambra Decree, stating that all Jews who had not converted to Catholicism were obliged to leave the Kingdoms of Castile and Aragon and their territories by July 31. When Columbus arrived in Palos in May and handed the town's officials and merchants the royal order obliging them to supply him with two caravels, equipped with materials and crew, within 10 days, they neither acted nor opposed the order.

Ten days passed and nothing happened. It seems that most ship owners were focusing their resources on the brisk and secure business of transporting Jewish refugees to destinations around the Mediterranean. Another factor was that Columbus had acquired a kind of "crackpot" reputation with his strange ideas, and sailors preferred to set sail under safer commanders.

It is interesting to note that neither Columbus nor the King and Queen could negotiate for the ship-holders' and sailors' cooperation, but for opposite reasons. Whereas Columbus lacked the clout and stature to even coax agreements from them, the King and Queen were too highly placed to stoop to such transactions. From their regal heights, they supplied Columbus with decrees, but not necessarily the means for implementing them.

It was a highly respected local sea captain and third party in the negotiation named Martin Alonso Pinzón who finally saved the day by

---

6   A constabulary created in the late 15th century by the Ferdinand and Isabella to maintain law and order throughout the realm.

vouching for the "empresa" and leveraging his reputation to obtain the ships and recruit the sailors that made the voyage possible. In fact, some versions of the account claim that Pinzón had already made a voyage to the New World in 1488 under the French navigator, Jean Cousin.

The monarchs had also equipped Columbus with a decree granting amnesty for criminal activity for any sailor signing on for the expedition. But, in fact, of the 80 men who served on the three ships, only one was a convict–a man, who had killed another man in a fight, while three others were his friends, who were about to be tried for freeing him from prison.

In the end, two small caravels were committed to the expedition. The Pinta was commanded by Martin Alonso Pinzón, who obviously had a keen interest in facilitating a solution for Columbus, while the Nina was commanded by his brother, Vicente Yanez Pinzón. Given the caravels' modest size, Columbus was obliged to find a freighter to carry supplies for the expedition.

In Puerto de Santa Maria, Columbus was able to negotiate with the captain of a 70-ton three-master which was probably in port to load wool destined for Flanders. They contracted for a voyage of 2,400 miles from the Canary Islands on a course to be "advised".

The ambiguity of this agreement makes one wonder how carefully the captain of the ship protected his own interests. All three ships set sail on August 3, 1492, and the rest is history.

REFERENCES

COLUMBUS, Ferdinand, 1959, *The Life of Christopher Columbus by His Son Ferdinand*, trans. and edited by Benjamin KEEN, Rutgers University Press, New Brunswick, NJ.

DOR-NER, Zvi, 1991, *Columbus and the Age of Discovery*, William Morrow and Company, New York.

DYSON, John, 1991, *Columbus For Gold, God, and Glory*, Simon and Schuster, New York.

FISHER, Roger and URY, William, 1991, *Getting to Yes*, Houghton, Mifflin Company, Boston and New York.

FISKE, John, 1895, *The Discovery of America*, Vol. I, Houghton, Mifflin Company, Boston and New York.

MORRISON, Samuel Eliot, 1942, *Admiral of the Ocean Sea*, Little, Brown and Company, Boston, Toronto and London.

STUART, Nancy Rubin, 1991, *Isabella of Castile: The First Renaissance Queen*, St. Martins Press, New York.

THE 1998 ST MALO DECLARATION ON EUROPEAN DEFENSE

High Ambitions, Modest Results

Lord Peter Ricketts[*]

At their annual Summit in 1998 held in St Malo, the UK and France unexpectedly struck a deal which opened the way to the EU developing its own defense capability, breaking a taboo which had existed since the collapse of the European Defence Community project in 1954.[1] The structures and missions of the EU's Common Security and Defence Policy (CSDP) as they exist today would not have been possible without the breakthrough at St Malo. Yet the high hopes of that time were never fully realized. St Malo provides a case study in how political circumstances can align to enable two nations to reconcile longstanding differences. This was a necessary step for creating a strong and autonomous European defense capability. As subsequent history has shown, however, it was not in itself sufficient to make this happen.

---

[*] Former British diplomat, Visiting Professor at King's College London and Senior Associate Fellow, Royal United Services Institute London. This chapter is based on an article which appeared in the *RUSI Journal* vol. 162 no. 3 June/July 2017.

[1] The text of the St Malo Declaration is available at: <https://publications.parliament.uk/pa/cm199900/cmselect/cmdfence/264/26419.htm>. The story of the rise and fall of the European Defence Community is told in FURSDON (1980).

1. AFTER THE COLD WAR: NEW STIRRINGS IN EUROPEAN SECURITY

The fall of the Berlin Wall in late 1989 was an earthquake which transformed the European Security landscape. The 1990 NATO Summit held out the hand of friendship to former Warsaw Pact countries. The European Community decided that the end of East/West confrontation was the opportunity for Europe to step up its security role. This resulted in Article J.4.1 of the 1991 Maastricht Treaty, which set as a goal "the implementation of a common foreign and security policy, including the eventual framing of a common defence policy, which might in time lead to a common defence".

As so often, the formula was only agreed because it could be read in different ways. There were two distinct camps among Member States at that time. One group, led by the French, favored a European defense capability independent of NATO (reflecting long-held French reservations about the US dominance of NATO). For this camp, J.4.1 represented the first crucial step towards an autonomous European defense capability.

The other (smaller) camp was led by the UK. For John Major's government, there was no question of allowing the EU to develop a separate defense capability. Successive British governments had seen this as the task for NATO, an organization in which Britain had invested heavily and felt comfortable.

So, in the drafting of the Maastricht text, the UK blocked for months any reference to common defense. But in the end Prime Minister John Major, a shade more pragmatic than his predecessor Margaret Thatcher, accepted the need to include the words "common defence". They are tucked away at the very end of the phrase in J.4.1 quoted above.

The UK tried to buttress its position further, by resurrecting the Western European Union (WEU, a defense organization dating back to 1948, largely redundant after the creation of NATO) as the vehicle for European defense ambitions. So London proposed a declaration on the role of the WEU and its relations with the EU and the Atlantic Alliance. This declaration, signed the day after the Maastricht Treaty, echoed the ambitions of J.4.1 by stating that WEU members would "develop a genuine European security and defence identity and a greater European responsibility on defence matters". The declaration went on to define the role of the WEU as "the defence component of the European Union and as a means to strengthen the European pillar of the Atlantic Alliance". In other words, London's aim was to outsource European defense to the WEU.

2. THE APPROACH MARCH TO ST MALO

Maastricht put the concept of common defense into the EU Treaties. Using the WEU as a middleman between NATO and the EU was at best a temporary expedient. The reality was that the WEU was on the decline, while the EU was growing in number of Member States and in competences.

This is one part of the context which made St Malo possible. Two other building blocks were necessary. They fell into place with the election victories of a French President in 1995 – Jacques Chirac – willing to reconcile France with the military structures of NATO, and a British Prime Minister in 1997 – Tony Blair – ready to lift the taboo on an EU defense role, as part of putting the UK at the heart of Europe.

President Chirac had a respect for US military power. From late 1995, France took a series of steps to draw closer to the NATO military structure. The high-point of this process came at the Berlin NATO Foreign Ministers' meeting in June 1996, where it was agreed to build up a European Security and Defence Identity within NATO as part of the post-Cold War modernization of the Alliance. At the Berlin meeting, the US agreed for the first time that parts of the NATO command structure could be "lent" to the WEU to plan and command European operations where the US did not wish to be involved. Since much of the NATO planning and command machinery was made up of European military officers, this was not such a huge concession in practice. But this "Berlin process" was important in opening the door to European military operations using the command and control apparatus built up at great expense over the decades in NATO.

Tony Blair arrived in May 1997 determined to find areas where the UK could lead in Europe. The new government signed up to the EU's Amsterdam Treaty in October 1997, including its provision (Article J.7) that the WEU should over time be fully integrated into the EU, which would thereby inherit the WEU's planning capacity and some earmarked armed forces to give effect to the ambition of a "common defence". This was the next step in the institutional development set in hand at Maastricht.

Blair and his government also wanted the EU to play a more active role in the world. Memories were still fresh of the long and difficult period in 1993–95 fashioning a coherent Western response to Bosnia, with deep divisions between the US and the European countries about how to stop the ethnic cleansing and provide humanitarian support. In early 1998, the whole cycle of conflict in the Balkans seemed to be starting again, in Kosovo. Violent incidents between Serbian forces and the Kosovo Liberation Army led to a Serb crackdown in Kosovo, massacres of civilians, an international outcry, and, once again, the US pressing for NATO airstrikes. In the months leading up to the St Malo agreement in December 1998, Blair was increasingly frustrated at not being able to muster a credible threat of a ground force intervention in any form in Kosovo. In particular, as he makes clear in his Memoir A Journey, he found that President Clinton was very reserved, reflecting Congressional views.

3. ANATOMY OF THE ST MALO DEAL

All these factors put the British and French governments on converging paths. A small group of senior officials set to work to test whether common ground could be found. Despite several months of effort, and the exchange of several drafts, the two sides arrived at the annual UK-French Summit, held in December 1998 at St Malo, with nothing agreed. They started afresh from a blank sheet of paper, and after seven hours of negotiation produced a text at 2.30am. This was issued almost unchanged later the same morning.

The easiest way to show the careful balance of concessions which made this agreement possible is to consider the St Malo text paragraph-by-paragraph.

> The European Union needs to be in a position to play its full role on the international stage. This means making a reality of the Treaty of Amsterdam, which will provide the essential basis for action by the Union. It will be important to achieve full and rapid implementation of the Amsterdam provisions on CFSP. This includes the responsibility of the European Council to decide on the progressive framing of a common defence policy in the framework of CFSP. The Council must be able to take decisions on an intergovernmental basis, covering the whole range of activity set out in Title V of the Treaty of European Union. (St Malo Declaration para. 1)

The determination of the two leaders to develop a capacity for the EU to take military action is clear at the outset. The French also naturally exploited Tony Blair's acceptance, in the Amsterdam Treaty, of the principle that "common defence policy" was a legitimate area for EU action. This EU-friendly opening is balanced by the careful qualification that "the Council must be able to take decisions on an intergovernmental basis" and that defense issues sit clearly in Title V of the Treaty, that is to say the intergovernmental part. Neither the UK nor France wanted to see a role for the European Commission or the European Parliament in defense and security affairs.

To this end, the Union must have the capacity for autonomous action, backed up by credible military forces, the means to decide to use them, and a readiness to do so, in order to respond to international crises. (St Malo Declaration para. 2)

Agreeing to translate the Amsterdam Treaty opening into a "capacity for autonomous action" by the EU was a big move by the UK, away from its traditional position on NATO. However, the UK accompanied this with an important rider, that EU autonomous capacity was only "to respond to international crises". The significance of this becomes clear in the following paragraph:

In pursuing our objective, the collective defence commitments to which member states subscribe (set out in Article 5 of the Washington Treaty, Article V of the Brussels Treaty) must be maintained. In strengthening the solidarity between the member states of the European Union, in order that Europe can make its voice heard in world affairs, while acting in conformity with our respective obligations in NATO, we are contributing to the vitality of a modernised Atlantic Alliance which is the foundation of the collective defence of its members. (St Malo Declaration para. 2)

This intricate and carefully balanced paragraph makes explicit the condition that the EU would have no role in the territorial defense of Member States. This was a vital point for the UK: the collective defense of NATO territory was an exclusive role for NATO. There is a signal to non-EU NATO members in the commitment that a greater role for the European Union in defense would contribute to the vitality of a modernized Atlantic Alliance.

Europeans will operate within the institutional framework of the European Union (European Council, General Affairs Council, and meetings of Defence Ministers). The reinforcement of European solidarity must take into account the various positions of European states. The different situations of countries in relation to NATO must be respected. (St Malo Declaration para. 2)

This is a more procedural paragraph, which provides a further bulwark against any Commission attempt to assert competence over areas covered by the declaration. It also reflects the fact that four EU Member States (Sweden, Ireland, Austria, Finland) were neutral and not members of NATO.

In order for the European Union to take decisions and approve military action where the Alliance as a whole is not engaged, the Union must be given appropriate structures and a capacity for analysis of situations, sources of intelligence, and a capability for relevant strategic planning, without unnecessary duplication, taking account of the existing assets of the WEU and the evolution of its relations with the EU. In this regard, the European Union will also need to have recourse to suitable military means (European capabilities pre-designated within NATO's European pillar or national or multinational European means outside the NATO framework). (St Malo Declaration para. 3)

This is a crucial paragraph which moves the declaration on from statements of principle into the first outline of UK-French thinking about how the agreement would translate into practical military measures.

The opening half-sentence makes an essential point: the European Union will exercise its new capability to "take decisions and approve military action" where "the Alliance as a whole is not engaged". Behind this lies an argument between London and Paris, never fully resolved, as to whether NATO should have a right of first refusal over any military operation. Many on the British side favored this. The French side resisted it, because it undermined the principle of autonomous EU decision-making. The sentence merely states that the EU would only act when NATO had chosen not to do so, without saying whether NATO had any prescriptive right of first refusal or not. It covered the point adequately for the British, while leaving the door open to further evolution as the French required.

The sentence then moves on to spell out a vital point for the French, that the Union "must be given appropriate structures and a capacity for analysis of situations, sources of intelligence and a capability for relevant strategic planning". This opened the way to an EU Military Committee, Staff, Intelligence Cell and a strategic planning capability. The text also builds on the NATO agreement at the 1996 Berlin Ministerial that parts of the NATO military structures could be "lent" to the EU. The language is technical but the concept is clear. EU Member States would put in place arrangements to use their own planners working at SHAPE, and their own officers in the NATO Command Chain, to plan and command EU military operations.

Europe needs strengthened armed forces that can react rapidly to the new risks, and which are supported by a strong and competitive European defence industry and technology. (St Malo Declaration para. 4)

The sentence reflects a hope that a European defense initiative would be an incentive for EU Member States to keep up their levels of defense spending. The reference to the defense industry and technology was framed in general terms as this was the area on which least work had been done, and because London and Paris were wary of Commission initiatives in the defense equipment area.

4. AFTERMATH OF ST MALO: HIGH EUROPEAN AMBITIONS

So this was the St Malo Declaration, published on December 4, 1998. It was a genuine breakthrough, with each side moving beyond the positions they had occupied for decades. The British accepted that the EU should develop a real, useable military capability, and the means to plan for, and command, military operations. The French agreed that this would be done complementing, not competing with, NATO. Unlike the work done in 1967 on Resolution 242 about Palestine (see the chapter by Sami Faltas, "UN Security Council Resolution 242 of 1967", in this volume), on this occasion the diplomats managed to reach common ground on a sensitive issue without resorting to flagrant ambiguity in their drafting.

The announcement of such a substantive agreement had a huge impact. The shock was all the greater because no-one had been expecting it. The response in EU capitals was enthusiastic. The Vienna European Council a few days later welcomed the new impetus given by St Malo, adding: "in order for the EU to be in a position to play its full role on the international stage, the CFSP must be backed by credible operational capabilities".

The remarkable speed with which St Malo was translated into concrete EU structures and commitments owed much to the determination of President Chirac and Prime Minister Blair to see their initiative bear fruit, and to the sense of mutual trust which had developed among the small group of officials who had negotiated the deal. The UK and French defense ministries developed a "toolbox" of military capabilities that would be required. This led on to the adoption at the Helsinki European summit in December 1999 of the "headline goal": an objective that the EU should be able by 2003 to deploy within 60 days a force of up to 60,000 military personnel sustainable for at least one year (that is to say, at least 120,000 military personnel to allow for two six-month periods of deployment). In setting these goals, European leaders had in mind the two most recent Western military operations: the NATO-led interventions in Bosnia and Kosovo. Western forces had suffered few casualties in these operations, which were generally seen by public opinion as successful in halting ethnic cleansing. This was the scale of intervention that

President Chirac and Prime Minister Blair had envisaged the EU being able to take on in the future without having to rely on US support.

The 1999 Helsinki Summit also agreed that the EU should have the software to plan and direct military operations. So it called for the setting up of a Political and Security Committee (PSC), a Military Committee and a Military Staff. All came into being at the Nice European Council the following year (all the complex steps involved are summarized in Julian Lindley-French's invaluable "A Chronology of European Security and Defence 1945–2007.).

5. WHY THE HOPES OF ST MALO WERE NEVER REALIZED

St Malo created an opportunity to build a genuine EU military capability contributing to a modernized NATO. It opened the way to the EU defense and security structures that exist today, and the ambitious promises of military capabilities in the Helsinki headline goal. These reflected the widely held ambition at the time for the EU to be able one day to take on significant peace-keeping tasks without the involvement of the Americans or NATO. But they were never fulfilled. In the view of this author, there were three main reasons.

First, disagreements between Greece and Turkey prevented EU/NATO cooperation developing to the extent envisaged at St Malo. Turkey made clear from an early stage that it wanted to have the right to participate in EU-led military operations. Ankara was also concerned that that the EU could mount a military operation in its region without Turkey having any veto power or even a say at the decision-shaping stage. Greece for its part was determined to preserve the decision-making autonomy of the EU, and to ensure that Turkey did not use its membership of NATO to gain influence over ESDP. An agreement was brokered which enabled the EU to take over the NATO stabilization mission in the Former Yugoslav Republic of Macedonia, and later the operation in Bosnia. But that was as far as it went. The interlocking controls which Turkey and Greece (and Cyprus when it joined the EU) held on wider EU/NATO cooperation were used to ensure that there were no further uses of such cooperation, and no useful exchanges of information or analysis on any issue other than Bosnia. As a result, one of the key concepts of St Malo, that the EU would be able to use NATO planning and command capacities to underpin its own operations, has proved unworkable in practice beyond the Bosnia mission.

Second, the political context changed. All international agreements reflect a particular set of circumstances. In the case of St Malo, the international agenda moved on before the new arrangements could be tested in practice. With the Al Qaida attacks on the US in September 2001, the overriding priority became countering terrorism, and the focus quickly shifted to the military operation in Afghanistan. By the time of the Iraq war in 2003, the EU was bitterly divided, and the high hopes of St Malo seemed a distant memory.

Third, the ambitions reflected in the Helsinki Headline Goal, for the EU to command large-scale and long-lasting military operations of the kind NATO had undertaken in the Balkans, were never realistic. At its heart, the EU is an economic organization, with careful checks and balances between the institutions, each with their treaty-based roles and responsibilities. Even though security and defense policy sits in an inter-governmental section of the Treaty, the institutional arrangements of the EU were never conceived for the command and control of high-intensity military operations. Practice over the 20 years since St Malo years has shown that European leaders have chosen not to use the EU for such a role.

Instead, the EU has developed a distinctive capacity to blend military and civilian expertise in smaller missions focused on the complex and sensitive task of post-conflict stabilization. These have included a wide variety of capacity-building and training missions covering the spectrum from military and police forces to civilian administrators. The EU is also leading small naval operations dealing with piracy off the coast of Somalia, and the smuggling of refugees across the Mediterranean.

These operations are a valuable instrument in the EU's international engagement, but they are a far cry from the high ambitions of St Malo. The experience of St Malo suggests a number of lessons on the place of bilateral initiatives in influencing the direction of wider EU policy.

First, such agreements are sometimes *necessary* for progress to be made. As the two largest military powers in the EU, with strong and opposed views about the EU's role in defense, no progress was possible unless France and Britain found a reconciliation. The current EU defense and security policy would not have been possible without the agreement reached at St Malo.

Second, bilateral agreements are often not *sufficient* in themselves to unlock a change in EU policy. They provide a basis for progress, but the bilateral vision has to be embraced by a majority of other Member States, and the impetus has to be maintained from the initial euphoria to practical implementation. In the case of St Malo, there was an enthusiastic initial welcome, but in practice Member States were not willing the make the investments in military capabilities that were necessary to turn the St Malo vision into reality. With hindsight, the level of ambition was far too high, and failed to recognize that the EU was not well-adapted to command large-scale combat operations. In practice, both Britain and France have accepted the natural limitations of the EU in the military field, and have developed their military partnership bilaterally through the process launched at another bilateral summit, at Lancaster House in London in 2010.

The third lesson is that bilateral initiatives tend to be the result of a combination of circumstances and personalities, which rapidly change. That was certainly the case with St Malo, as described above. When the circumstances moved on, the euphoria rapidly evaporated, and EU practice developed on more modest lines. Britain's departure from the EU will change the center of gravity on defense and security issues, and create a new set of circumstances. France and Germany have suggested a new direction for European defense cooperation, with a heavy emphasis on European strategic autonomy both in military operations and in research, development, and industrial cooperation. The experience of St Malo suggests that the test will be whether these ideas meet the real needs of a wide range of Member States, and so can be sustained beyond the political imperatives of the moment. It is the hope of this author that they will also be sufficiently flexible for Britain to continue to play an active role in European security, as it has done for many centuries.

REFERENCES

BLAIR, T., *A Journey*, Hutchinson 2010.

FURSDON, E., *The European Defence Community: A History*, Macmillan 1980.

LINDLEY-FRENCH, J., *A Chronology of European Security and Defence 1945–2007*, Oxford University Press 2007.

RICKETTS, P., "The EU and Defence: The Legacy of Saint-Malo", *RUSI Journal*, vol. 162, no. 3, June/July 2017.

US–CHILE FREE TRADE
NEGOTIATIONS (2000–2003)

Linkage Analysis

Larry CRUMP*

Negotiations embedded in political and economic networks are not easily understood based purely on the interactions that occur between the primary parties. Negotiations between the United States and Chile, around the turn of the century, include numerous external parties that shaped negotiation process through linkage dynamics. This chapter presents an overview to this bilateral negotiation and then tracks the linkages that helped shape the Chile–US negotiation process and outcome. Of significance are the strategies each side used in managing these linkages. When properly applied, linkage strategies minimize risk and maximize opportunity for that party able to analyze linkage dynamics.

* APEC Study Centre at Griffith University, Department of Business Strategy and Innovation, Griffith University, Brisbane, Qld. 4111. L.Crump@griffith.edu.au. I would like to thank the many trade negotiators, diplomats and ambassadors who kindly gave of their time and shared ideas to support this study. I am especially grateful to Griffith University for continually supporting my research agenda by providing time and funding. I appreciate the assistance of Emmanuel Vivet and an anonymous reviewer from the Academy of International Business (US-West Chapter) for valuable comments on an earlier draft. However, the author is responsible for any errors or omissions.

1. THE PROPOSAL FOR A US–CHILE FREE TRADE AGREEMENT

The United States of America and the Republic of Chile (Chile) announced their intention to negotiate a free trade agreement (FTA) in November 2000, as the Bill Clinton presidency was coming to a close. Talks began quickly, although the office of the United States Trade Representative (USTR) held no hope that these negotiations would conclude swiftly. George W. Bush assumed the US presidency in January 2001 and negotiations paused, as the new US administration began to review the Clinton projects and programs and decide which would be terminated, suspended, or modified, and the projects that would continue. Eventually, the public learned that President Bush did not appreciate multilateral negotiations and so Chile–US free trade agreement (CUSFTA) talks were re-established in mid-2001.

2. FTA NEGOTIATIONS

Regina Vargo was chief US negotiator and led a team of 40–50 staff, primarily from the USTR. Osvaldo Rosales was Chile's chief negotiator and led a team of 90–100 staff, mostly from the International Economic Relations Directorate of the Chilean Ministry of External Relations. An overview of the negotiation process is shown as a timeline in Figure 1.

Initially, in consultation with their superiors, the chief negotiators outlined a 24-chapter treaty, which resulted in each side organizing into around 24 working groups. National working groups met privately to prepare for negotiations with their counterparts.

Figure 1. Chile–United States Free Trade Agreement: Negotiation Process

1995	11/2000	3/2002	8/2002	9/2002	12/2002	1/2003	3/2003	6/2003
Chile invited to join NAFTA (4-Amigo Talks: 3 rounds held in Mexico)	US & Chile announce intention to negotiate FTA	Talks suspended after 10th round	US Congress passes TPA	Talks resume	Agree at 14th round	Chile joins UNSC	FTA legal-scrubbing begins	Ministers sign FTA

Source: Produced by the author.

The two sides met every six to eight weeks for what is called a "negotiation round". During the first 16 months, the two sides held ten rounds, generally alternating between Washington, DC and Santiago, Chile. A round normally continues for one week and provides an opportunity for many joint working group meetings between the two sides plus meetings between the chief negotiators. Each joint working group begins by negotiating a treaty chapter framework or outline, and once this is agreed upon – which can take many months – the two sides fill in the details suggested by the adopted outline. If a joint working-group hits a deadlock, the issue is passed up to the Deputy Chief Negotiators, to the Chief Negotiators, and even to the Trade Ministers once negotiations move toward agreement.

Negotiations were suspended in March 2002, however, as the US Congress, mandated to approve all international treaties (US Constitution, Article II, Section 2), was attempting to work out a national trade policy framework that would provide the USTR and others with guidance. This came in the form of the US Trade Promotion Authority Act (US Public Law 107–210), or TPA, in August 2002. The USTR had advanced CUSFTA negotiations as far as it could without this mandate, so negotiations ceased in March 2002 and resumed a month after the TPA passed into law.

Reducing tariffs has been a fundamental part of trade liberalization since 1947, when the General Agreement on Tariffs and Trade (GATT) was initially signed by 23 nations (the United States and Chile are both GATT founding members). CUSFTA negotiations continued down this path, as Chile's largest export is copper, while the United States had a copper tariff. On the other hand, Chile had a tax on imported vehicles. These two tariff issues, and others, appeared on the CUSFTA negotiation agenda. But a trade negotiation is not only about tariffs, as a contemporary free trade agreement includes goods and services such as financial services, telecommunication services, and the movement of people who deliver services. Other issue areas include intellectual property, competition policy, transparency, government procurement, labor, and even the environment. All these topics were discussed and agreed upon during the 14 CUSFTA rounds required to conclude the basic text.

Many of the most difficult issues are negotiated in the final rounds. For example, the United States proposed that US banks be allowed to operate in Chile without committing capital – a policy known as branching. The United States was not successful in achieving this financial objective, but it was able to establish policies to assure that US business could transfer capital out of Chile. These final issues were part of a large bundle or package of issues that included some advantages for small and medium-sized Chilean companies operating in the US market.

Negotiations were concluded by US and Chile chief negotiators, and the Chilean Finance Minister, as many of the final unresolved issues pertained to financial sector demands made by the US. An in-principle agreement was achieved in December 2002 and finalized in early 2003. Lawyers on each side began the process of "legal scrubbing" to convert the negotiation text into an international trade treaty, although delays in this process were reported. The 313 page CUSFTA treaty (not including annexes and side letters) was finalized and then signed in Miami Florida in June 2003. An overview of the treaty (negotiation outcome) can be found in Table 1.

The CUSFTA treaty came into force in January 2004 and continues to support US–Chile economic relations, while harmonizing these two economies.

Table 1. Chile–United States Free Trade Agreement: Negotiation Outcome

Preamble	
1) Initial provisions	13) Telecommunications
2) General definitions	14) Temporary entry for business persons
3) National treatment and market access	15) Electronic commerce
4) Rules of origin	16) Competition policy
5) Customs administration	17) Intellectual property rights
6) Sanitary and phytosanitary measures	18) Labor
7) Technical barriers to trade	19) Environment
8) Trade remedies	20) Transparency
9) Government procurement	21) Administration of the agreement
10) Investment	22) Dispute settlement
11) Cross-border trade in services	23) Exceptions
12) Financial services	24) Final provisions

Source: Compiled by the author.

3. LINKAGE ANALYSIS: THEORETICAL FRAMEWORK

The negotiations people conduct, and life in general, are not a series of isolated events. The past is linked to the present, and it is reasonable to assume that the present will be connected to the future. My present, for example, is connected to my perception of my future just as your present is connected to your perception of your future. Might I be in a better position to understand your needs and interests, your opportunities and constraints, if I gain some insight into how your perception of your future is shaping what you seek today? Might I also gain greater understanding of your circumstances if I know something about how your past has shaped what you seek today?

Here we are considering *context*, or how a negotiation is embedded or linked to its social environment (see Crump, 2011; Jensen, 1963; Sebenius, 1983), although linkage dynamics do not involve some vague milieu or atmosphere. Linkages involve specific events and the ways in which they are linked to our current negotiation. One would expect that our theoretical and practical understanding of linkage dynamics would be substantial, given the prevalence of external events that are linked to issues at the negotiation table. Consider, for example, the role of precedents in political, commercial, and organizational life, and our lack of understanding of the strategic use of precedents at the negotiation table (see Crump 2016; Crump and Moon 2017). Indeed, our lack of understanding of linkage dynamics is surprising, since almost all negotiations are linked to one or more other negotiations or negotiated decisions.

Negotiation linkage theory is concerned with the ways in which one negotiation influences or determines the process and/or outcome of another negotiation. One way to understand negotiation linkage dynamics is to recognize their temporal quality, which is to say that linkages occur in the past, the present and in our perception of the future. *Concurrent linkages* pertain to events that occur during the same time period (see Crump, 2010); *consecutive-past linkages* consider how the past influences the present; and *consecutive-future linkages* examine how negotiator perception of the future might influence the present (see Crump, 2007). *Role theory* is useful for understanding concurrent linkages (see Crump, 2010; Wager, 1972; Watkins and Passow 1996) and *temporal theory* is helpful for understanding consecutive linkages (Crump, 2007, 2016; Crump and Moon, 2017). The utility of these concepts will become apparent shortly.

A full understanding of CUSFTA negotiations requires us to recognize the many linked events that influence negotiation process and its outcomes. Such events create linkage dynamics that are difficult to comprehend unless we recognize that these linked events illustrate patterns that contain strategic value or choices when properly understood. The following discussion re-examines the case presented initially by identifying how specific linked events influenced the negotiation process and outcome; this can offer strategic opportunities and/or constraints for either or all parties.

4. CUSFTA AND LINKAGE DYNAMICS

The following analysis is based on field research conducted by the author; this was undertaken by interviewing trade officials, diplomats, and ambassadors involved in Chile–US negotiations (28 total interviews), Singapore–US negotiations (30 total interviews), and Chile–EU negotiations (29 total interviews) in Brussels, Santiago, Singapore, and

Washington, DC in 2004–06, shortly after these three negotiations concluded. Several references at the end of this article provide detailed information on this research and the analysis of results.

Chile had a population of a 15.3 million in 2000. Did this relatively small market motivate President Clinton to commence trade negotiations two months prior to retiring from the US presidency? Past event (consecutive-past linkages) and contemporary event (concurrent linkages) provide understanding about motives and why CUSFTA commenced.

Chile and the United States had actually begun trade negotiations five years earlier through the Four-Amigo Talks, as Chilean leaders linked their national trade aspirations to NAFTA (a trade agreement involving Canada, Mexico, and the United States). Complications between Clinton and the US Congress did not allow the Four-Amigo Talks to proceed beyond three rounds, but negotiations had begun and apparently served as a precedent (consecutive-past linkage) with sufficient potency to re-start negotiations through the advent of a concurrent linkage, discussion of which follows.

After a late-night game of golf at the 2000 APEC Leaders' Summit in Brunei, the United States and Singapore announced their joint intention to negotiate a bilateral trade agreement in November 2000. Chile immediately reminded the United States that it had been waiting at the front of that line for five years. Shortly thereafter, the United States was concurrently negotiating two separate bilateral free trade agreements (FTA): one with Chile and the other with Singapore.

Singapore's population was even smaller than that of Chile, at four million in 2000. Clearly market access was not the motivation that drove the Clinton administration to seek to open these two markets. We will never secure full confirmation of the US motives, but interviews report that Clinton might have thought he could use these trade treaties to gain some small justice (consecutive-future linkage) involving the Clinton–US Congress relationship. It is important to recall that President Clinton was impeached by the US House of Representatives in December 1998 – and to recognize the public humiliation created by such a spectacle.

Reports indicate that Clinton hoped to present a "Democratic party trade treaty" – including issues like labor and the environment – to a Republican-controlled Congress. Curiously, this moment represents a significant shift in US trade policy, from a multilateral approach to a mixed multilateral-bilateral approach, which has been embraced by every US presidential administration since Clinton (excluding the Trump administration).

For the next three years, Singapore and Chile were each engaged in separate negotiations over the very same issues with the same party. Such circumstance have the potential to create a linkage-rich environment – but only the potential. For example, how should the US behave? Should it make the same proposals at the same time to each? More importantly, if the United States makes compromises, who should it compromise with first – Chile or Singapore? And does it matter? Such questions do matter, but only if Chile and Singapore are communicating formally or discreetly about their separate negotiations with the United States (this is international diplomacy – with all its opportunity and intrigue).

As previously mentioned, we can apply role theory to concurrently linked negotiations and define Chile and Singapore as "linked-parties", with the United States as the "link-pin party" that links Chile and Singapore together. But role theory generally is only relevant if the linked-parties are communicating with each other about their negotiations. I could not confirm that Chile and Singapore ever talked about their separate trade negotiations based on interviews with many negotiators at the table, including chief negotiators, ambassadors, and diplomats. Perhaps power relations between linked-parties and the link-pin party offers one explanation (with the United States being much more powerful than the two linked-parties).

Now it must be pointed out that this negotiation environment was even more complex than initially suggested. While Chile negotiated with the United States, we find that Chile was concurrently negotiating with the European Union. In applying role theory, Chile is defined as the link-pin party that links the United States and Europe together as linked-parties. In this case, linked-parties were communicating, which further supports the argument that asymmetrical power relations, when comparing the link-pin party and the linked-parties, can influence the negotiation process if the latter role is more powerful relative to the former role.

For example, a lead negotiator for Chile reported that "negotiations over financial services and investment were discussed by the United States and European Union. Clearly, communication moved across the Atlantic, as the same explanation with significant detail was presented separately by the US and the EU." This official's EU counterpart confirmed the overall approach: "There was an exchange of views between the EU and the US on negotiations with Chile ... On agriculture issues, for example the EU and US held two or three conference calls." A review of all interview data suggested that EU–US communication occurred irregularly and at upper levels of government. Such communication likely provided the linked-parties with a strategic advantage. Communication between linked-parties was not the only form of linkage dynamics that influenced the negotiation process.

A lead EU negotiator advised his counterpart from Chile that EU financial service goals were more reasonable than US financial service goals, then argued that Chile should "cut a deal on our more moderate financial services goals now and then you can use this agreement as a precedent in negotiating with the US". A Chilean financial services negotiator confirmed this EU approach, then explained how Chile used this outcome in its negotiations with the United States: "Chile achieved financial services policies with Europe that were much closer to our goal, as compared to US demands. Without this precedent, Chile would have had no argument with the US." As previously mentioned, Chile was forced to accept many US financial services demands, but this same negotiator reported that Chile successfully rejected the US proposal to allow foreign banks to set up in Chile without committing capital because of the precedent set in the EU–Chile trade agreement.

The European Union gained a strategic advantage by monitoring CUSFTA negotiations, as this allowed EU negotiators to establish educated guesses of US positions and goals on many issues relevant to their own negotiation. The European Union achieved some financial service goals by employing what we could term a "benchmarking strategy" (the EU–Chile agreement served as a positive benchmark for Chile). A linked-party may be more likely to achieve its goals by assisting a link-pin party to build positive benchmarks that are relevant to a concurrently linked negotiation or a consecutive-future linked negotiation.

Benchmarking also carried negative consequences for Chile. Shortly after being signed in November 2002, the EU–Chile treaty was posted on the internet by the European Union; this was about a month before CUSFTA negotiations were substantially concluded in December 2002. This development gave the United States a clear strategic advantage in concluding CUSFTA negotiations. For example, after reviewing the services portion of the EU–Chile treaty, the United States demanded the same or more on an item-by-item basis, then attached the EU–Chile services list as an annex to the CUSFTA services list to add clarity to Chile's services obligations to the United States. Chile was not at the complete mercy of the United States, however, as one US trade negotiator reported that Chile refused US demands to provide the same tariff reductions for chemicals, petroleum, and fuels that had been established in the EU–Chile treaty. A benchmarking strategy involves the use of agreements, agendas, arguments, concessions, goals, issues, and positions as a point of reference that can be applied to concurrently linked and consecutive-future linked negotiations.

As the link-pin party, Chile gained some strategic advantage by engaging in what might be called "outcome bundling". For example, Chile established the same outcome for each linked-party for its luxury tax on automobiles. Essentially, Chile concluded that more could be gained by compromising with the United States rather than with the European Union on their 85 per cent tax on the custom value of imported autos (above a threshold of US$15,740). An EU trade negotiator reported that "Chile and the EU were deadlocked on the auto tax and finally Chile told us that they would offer the EU whatever arrangement that was later offered to the US. The EU did not like this but accepted Chile's offer." If Chile had compromised with the European Union on this issue and reached an agreement, Chile would not have been in such a strong position to gain something of value from the United States later, as observed in the negative benchmarking example presented above. For example, this tax on automobiles was part of the final CUSFTA package, which contained many items including US copper tariffs; copper is by far Chile's largest export, which means a lot of money is involved in this US tariff. A link-pin party can gain benefits and/or minimize loss by protecting critical information through an outcome-bundling strategy in concurrently linked and consecutive-future linked negotiations.

A link-pin party engages in outcome bundling to protect valuable information that would normally disclose a compromise or a resistant point (bottom line). When a linked-party conducts this same strategy, it can be called "free-riding". The European Union gained substantial benefits by free-riding on US–Chile negotiations. For example, a senior Chilean official reported that "the EU understood that the US would establish a strong intellectual property regime in Chile. The EU strategy was: why make compromises with Chile to achieve something that the US will achieve for them?" Here the European Union simply secured Chilean agreement that the most favored nation (MFN) clause found in the WTO TRIPS (intellectual property (IP)) agreement would apply so that any IP regime negotiated by the United States would also apply to the European Union.

The European Union also gained a free ride on CUSFTA financial services arrangements, as Chile agreed that it would give the European Union whatever Chile offered the United States. A Chilean negotiation team member explained that:

> The EU was clever in how it managed policies related to the movement of capital out of Chile, as the EU probably concluded that the US would get a better deal

from Chile than the EU could achieve. Chile eventually accepted the condition that Chile would not discriminate against the EU in relation to any third-country regarding the movement of capital.

In this case, the United States is defined as a third country, so any agreement that the United States secured on movement of capital within Chile would automatically be transferred to the EU–Chile treaty. Months later, in Washington, DC, I spoke with a US trade negotiator who helped to conclude the CUSFTA finance chapter. He had no idea that during CUSFTA negotiations, in 2002, he was not only representing 288 million Americans but also 490 million Europeans. He said it would probably be the largest deal he would ever conclude.

In both examples, it is a linked-party that is gaining something of value from the link-pin party via a free ride that is based on work conducted primarily by the other linked-party. Furthermore, the linked-party conducting such work may be unaware that they are providing something of value to the other linked-party. Such a strategy offers one linked-party with a benefit at little or no cost. Understanding free-ride linkage dynamics thus has strategic utility.

One final linkage dynamic of significance can be identified in CUSFTA negotiations: the first linkage type identified in the international relations literature. "Issue linkage" involves the linking together of two discrete issues (see Jensen, 1963). For example, in CUSFTA we found that the United States sought to link international trade and international security – two discrete issues – to gain strategic advantage in pursuit of its international agenda.

Chile became a non-permanent member of the UN Security Council (UNSC), a two-year term that began in January 2003, near the conclusion of CUSFTA negotiations. The United States sought approval from all 15 UNSC members before initiating war against Iraq in early 2003 (claiming the existence of, although never finding, weapons of mass destruction). Chile was unwilling to link its trade agreement to this US initiative, but still had to manage US attempts to link these two issues together. Interviews with US and Chilean government lawyers confirm that legal scrubbing (to convert negotiated text into an international treaty, as already mentioned) was delayed. Intentionally or unintentionally, this delay put pressure on Chile to cooperate with the United States within the UNSC, although Chile did not bow to this pressure as it argued that diplomatic efforts should be pursued before military solutions. Interviews report that the Chile's UNSC position on this US proposal was established by Chilean President Ricardo Lagos.

The UNSC process only delayed the CUSFTA outcome, but there was clear potential that it could have derailed the outcome. Legal scrubbing concluded eventually, and then the treaty was signed by USTR Robert Zoellick and Chilean Foreign Affairs Minister Maria Soledad Alvear. Unlike the Singapore–US Free Trade Agreement, which was signed at the White House with substantial media fanfare in May 2003, CUSFTA was signed in a Miami hotel on the sidelines of an international trade ministerial the following month. Singapore's treaty closure provides a benchmark for evaluating Chile's experience. Apparently, the United States decided that having an ally in Latin America was more important than punishing a "recalcitrant" partner, so the United States proceeded to finalize CUSFTA.

All the linkage concepts and strategies introduced in this chapter are consolidated in Table 2, which identifies and describes each.

Table 2. Negotiation Linkage Concepts and Strategies

Linkage concept	Strategy
Negotiation linkage dynamics	The way in which a negotiation or negotiated decision influences or determines the process and/or outcome of another negotiation.
Linkage analysis	Establish or identify the patterns created by linkage dynamics that provides strategic opportunities and/or constraints for either or all parties.
Concurrent linkages	Pertains to two or more events occurring during the same time period that may influence one another, although typically one event influences the other (the direction of influence is useful to observe). Role theory can be applied to concurrent linkages.
Link-pin role	Creates the potential for negotiation linkage dynamics, as this role conducts two or more discrete negotiations that are linked together in a logical or practical manner. Each role (link-pin and linked-party) is presented with differing strategic choices related to position coordination, concession management, and opportunities for cooperative action.
Linked-party role	Two or more parties indirectly linked to each other through their separate interactions with a link-pin party. Linkage dynamics increase substantially when two or more linked-parties communicate directly or discretely with each other.
Consecutive linkages	Utilizes temporal theory to identity how past events and perceived future events influence contemporary events.

(continued)

Table 2 *continued*

Linkage concept	Strategy
Consecutive-future linkages	Examines how negotiator perceptions of the future influence present circumstances (often at the negotiation table).
Consecutive-past linkages	Examines how past events influence present circumstances (often at the negotiation table).
Precedents	A multifaceted tool created through a past event or decision (consecutive-past linkage) that evolves into a rule, standard, or guide. The effectiveness of a precedent is determined in part by its relevance to contemporary circumstances or the current situation.
Benchmarking strategy	The use of agreements, agendas, arguments, concessions, goals, issues, and positions as a point of reference that can be applied to concurrently linked and consecutive-future linked negotiations.
Outcome-bundling strategy	A link-pin party can gain benefits and/or minimize loss by protecting critical information (that would normally disclose a compromise or a resistant point to others) in a concurrently linked or consecutive-future linked negotiation.
Free-riding strategy	A linked-party gains something of value from the link-pin party based on work conducted primarily by the other linked-party in a concurrently linked negotiation.
Issue linkage strategy	The linking of two discrete issues such as security and trade. These two issues can exist in two separate contemporary venues or venues separated by time.

REFERENCES

CHILE–US FREE TRADE AGREEMENT, 2003, Foreign Trade Information System, Organization of American States, <http://www.sice.oas.org/Trade/chiusa_e/chiusaind_e.asp>.

CRUMP, L., 2007, A temporal model of negotiation linkage dynamics, *Negotiation Journal*, 23, 117–153.

CRUMP, L., 2010, Strategically managing negotiation linkage dynamics, *Negotiation and Conflict Management Research*, 3, 3–27.

CRUMP, L., 2011, Negotiation process and negotiation context, *International Negotiation*, 16, 197–227.

CRUMP, L., 2016, Toward a theory of negotiation precedent, *Negotiation Journal*, 32, 85–102.

CRUMP, L., and MOON, D., 2017, Precedents in negotiated decisions: Korea–Australia free trade agreement negotiations, *Negotiation Journal*, 33, 101–127.

JENSEN, L., 1963, The postwar disarmament negotiations: A study in American-Soviet bargaining behavior. PhD thesis, University of Michigan.

SEBENIUS, J.K., 1983, Negotiation arithmetic: Adding and subtracting issues and parties, *International Organization*, 37, 281–316.

WAGER, L.W., 1972, Organizational "linking pins": Hierarchical status and communicative roles in interlevel conferences, *Human Relations*, 25: 307–326.

WATKINS, M. and PASSOW, S., 1996, Analyzing linked systems of negotiations, *Negotiation Journal*, 12: 325–339.

NEGOTIATING PEACE WITH THE FARC (2010–2016)

Out of the Woods?

Frans SCHRAM*

After almost 60 years of suffering the most protracted conflict in the Western hemisphere, Colombia has been able to pass from a rare moment of negotiability toward the so-called "Havana talks" in 2012, and finally to the conclusion of a peace agreement in 2016. This turned a page in Colombia's history and its complex relationship with the continent's oldest and largest guerilla-movement, the *Fuerzas Armadas Revolucionarias de Colombia – Ejército del Pueblo* (FARC-EP).[1] The conflict has left deep wounds and significant distrust in Colombian society, together with a cultural acceptance of violence and a vast criminal infrastructure, spawning a multitude of illegal armed organizations and related problems. The rejection of the first

---

*   Dutch negotiation trainer and researcher, Berlin, Germany.
[1]   The Revolutionary Armed Forces of Colombia – People's Army (hereinafter: FARC).

agreement in a plebiscite in 2016 and the 2018 election of a new right-wing president who vowed to change the current agreement, are testimony to the large resistance against the FARC and its ambitions. However, considering that the Havana accord managed to achieve its principal goal – to convince the FARC to voluntarily set aside their weapons and start the transition to becoming a political party – the negotiation itself can indeed be regarded as successful (Segura and Mechoulan, 2017). How did this negotiation develop and result in the long-awaited agreement?

1. A HISTORY OF HALF-RIPE MOMENTS AND HALF-HEARTED ATTEMPTS

Colombia has been embroiled in internal conflict since the 1940s when the two main political parties, the Liberals and Conservatives, engaged in a civil war known as "La Violencia". As one of the offshoots of that war, the FARC-EP originated as a coalition of peasant self-defense forces with a marxist-leninist ideology and gradually morphed into the country's strongest guerrilla movement, ostensibly fighting to overthrow the oligarchic state and to achieve comprehensive socio-economic reforms. Since the government of President Belisario Betancur (1982–1986), almost every administration has engaged in peace negotiations with the FARC, despite the fact that none of the parties might actually have been earnestly ready for a negotiated solution. In 1984 the government and the FARC reached a ceasefire agreement that allowed the creation of a new leftist political organization, called the "Unión Patriótica" (UP), as a first step in the guerrilla's demobilization. The agreement however lacked the necessary support from key sectors of Congress, the country's chief economic groups and the military. As the peace process withered away, the members of UP were virtually exterminated by paramilitary organizations, often in collusion with (rogue) state security forces. The memory of the UP would linger as a powerful disincentive for the FARC to sincerely engage in peace processes, as it manifested the lack of security guarantees for those willing to disarm and transition into politics. A second try at peace negotiations was undertaken by President César Gaviria in 1991 and involved an alliance of several guerilla organizations including the FARC. Without a ceasefire in place, and with coordination problems on both sides, these negotiations also remained inconclusive.

In 1999 the government of Andrés Pastrana and the FARC engaged in a major series of negotiations after civil society had collected citizens' votes supporting re-engagement. The government agreed to demilitarize a territory the size of Switzerland in the "El Caguán" region, where the talks were to take place. Many issues however soured the process, rendering the Colombian public skeptical of further negotiations with the FARC for years to come. The level of trust in Caguán had been low, the agenda too comprehensive to be effective and the FARC's supreme leader did not show up at the talks, which was a looming symbol of the guerilla's weak commitment to engage in dialogue. The talks also happened at a time when the FARC was at the apex of its military strength and was accused of abusing the demilitarized zone to regroup and cultivate illicit crops. The FARC in turn accused the government of strengthening the paramilitaries and seeking too much military rapprochement with the United States. The talks collapsed in 2001 as it was evident that both sides lacked political will to fully commit. In 2002 a new president, the hard-liner Alvaro Uribe Velez, was voted into power on an election promise to solve the problem by military means and tighten the screws on the FARC.

What we see is that, in none of the above events had the parties apparently felt sufficient urge or pain to either inaugurate negotiations or to follow them through with sufficient motivation to reach closure. This invites the question of what factors are actually required for parties to first of all start negotiations and subsequently reach successful outcomes.

2. THE COSTS OF LINGERING ARMED CONFLICT INCREASE

Ten years after El Caguán collapsed, the conditions seemed to have improved, increasing the potential for the Colombian government to finally embark on successful negotiations with the FARC. It, however, required a new president, the former Minister of Defense Juan Manuel Santos, to appreciate and nurture these conditions. A series of events in the years 2002 to 2010 had dramatically raised the costs of the status quo. After his landslide election victory, the iron fist policy of the rightist Alvaro Uribe (2002–2010) significantly augmented the use of force against the FARC, leading the FARC to incur increasing losses and seriously affecting its perception of the functionality of the armed conflict. It had the effect of a "shock therapy" (Pruitt, 2005), ending the FARC's sense of invincibility (Rickmeyer, 2017). Opportunity costs for the FARC rose, as they became increasingly referred to as "terrorists" instead of a political subversive group. In March 2008 the military blows to FARC were compounded by the natural death of Manuel

Marulanda Vélez (a.k.a. "Tirofijo"), the founder and supreme leader of the organization. Yet the FARC was not defeated and even managed to increase its tactical military effectiveness under its new leader Alfonso Cano.[2] From a regional perspective, the arrival to power via the ballot – rather than through the bullet – of a number of leftist governments, weakened the FARC's case for armed revolution and warped its assessment of a feasible victory and unceasing ideological support. Venezuelan president Hugo Chávez and Cuba's Fidel Castro, both political backers of the FARC, had also started exerting pressure on the guerilla group to engage in peace negotiations and make a move towards political life.

A factor of considerable influence on each party's motivation to resort to negotiations were the political conditions in Colombia itself. The Government's military advantage gradually stalled and the scandal of extrajudicial killings by Colombian security forces, as well as the alleged links between politicians and drug trafficking right-wing paramilitary groups, harmed the political establishment's credibility. There was increasing pressure from foreign governments and the business sector to finally start a process that would create the stability outside of the urban centers needed for investors to work there with confidence.

Conversely, on the side of the FARC, support from their socio-political backbone – the agrarian rural population – had been dwindling due to its involvement in the drugs trade since the 1980s and increased (guerrilla) violence against civilians. Even though for a long time this does not seem to have significantly affected their military course of action, it probably did shape the thinking within the organization that a peace process would eventually present a more credible opportunity in the long term.

As both parties were enduring mounting costs and slowly understood that a definite solution would have to be found in the political realm, President Santos initiated, in September 2010, the informal and confidential talks with the FARC that would prompt a secret phase of negotiations in Havana, culminating in a framework agreement signed on August 26, 2012.

3. NEGOTIATIONS TAKE SHAPE

The ColGov-FARC negotiation process had two distinct phases: (1) initial clandestine talks between envoys of the government of President Santos

---

2   "¿Cuántos hombres y armas tienen las FARC?" Noticias RCN, available at <www.noticiasrcn.com/especialesrcn/conteo-hombres-farc/>.

and FARC representatives at the border with Venezuela in 2011; followed by secret negotiations in Havana, Cuba, starting in February 2012; and (2) four years of public talks, which officially started on October 18, 2012.

3.1. THE PRE-NEGOTIATION PHASE WITH GUARANTOR AND FACILITATING COUNTRIES

The first (secret) phase of the peace negotiations began with an exchange of paraphrased messages and letters between Henry Acosta, a Colombian economist who had facilitated contacts between Bogotá and the FARC before, and Pablo Catatumbo, a member of the FARC secretariat. A number of informal meetings took place throughout 2011, in which the parties decided not to have a mediated process but rather to invite a number of countries with other facilitating functions as a sort of "à la carte" approach (Acosta, 2016). The reluctance to involve external mediation probably had its roots in the much-criticized role of the UN during the El Caguan peace talks, as well as a desire to foster the sense of national ownership in finding a solution to an internal problem. Cuba and Norway would be called "guarantor countries", whose presence ensured that whatever was discussed would be verifiable by neutral agents and making the parties more inclined to find conciliatory language.

For reasons of a more political nature, the status of "accompanying countries" was assigned to Venezuela and Chile. It was also decided that the secret preparatory phase of the negotiations would take place in Havana and would serve to construct a "framework agreement" to guide the negotiations. The FARC initially wanted the dialogues to take place in Colombia, but the government was firmly opposed to demilitarizing a part of the country. The distance between Cuba and the rumble and tumble of Colombian internal conflict politics proved to be beneficial for the negotiations as it could keep those who might wish to derail the talks at bay, but, conversely, it did negatively impact Colombians' sense of ownership over the process (Segura and Mechoulan, 2017).

Just before the secret preparatory phase would start in February 2012, the FARC's top commander and political mind, Alfonso Cano, was killed in a military air raid by the Colombian army. Cano had actually been pushing for peace negotiations since 2010 and his assassination could have torpedoed the whole process. The FARC however sent a message to Santos two days after Cano's death asserting that everything that had been agreed upon in the preparatory talks would be upheld. This was interpreted by many in the Santos administration as an explicit sign that the guerillas were fully committed to the process (Acosta, 2016). Reassured, the government introduced a constitutional reform law which opened the door to a transitional justice system concerning the disarmament, demobilization, and reintegration (DDR) of illegal armed groups. This legislative act was symbolic because it acknowledged the existence of an armed conflict[3] in Colombia and, together with the insurances it offered, spurred confidence on the side of the FARC that a future agreement would be adhered to.

3.2. FORMAL PHASE: AN EFFECTIVE PROCESS STIMULATES OPTIMISM

On September 24, 2012 President Santos and the supreme leader of the FARC, Timoleón Jiménez (alias "Timochenko"), announced the formal start of negotiations. The FARC delegation was led by its second-in-command, Iván Márquez, and the Government delegation – composed of private and security sector members – was led by Humberto de la Calle and the peace commissioner, Sergio Jaramillo. At a press conference in Norway where the process was formally announced, the two sides still criticized each other in strong wording but, importantly, they stopped referring to each other as "terrorists".

The short, focused, and realistic agenda, covering both causes and effects of the conflict, proved to be very instrumental in smoothening the subsequent process. Previous negotiations had often become bogged down with agendas that were too comprehensive to be efficient. The agreement on the agenda presented a compromise of six issues: (1) a policy of comprehensive agrarian development; (2) political participation; (3) an end to the conflict; (4) a solution to the problem of illicit drugs; (5) victims' rights; and (6) implementation, verification, and endorsement of the agreement. The agenda was organized in a sequential format, with the exception of a few subcommissions where negotiations took place in parallel. The work that was done in these subcommissions turned out to be of particular relevance in breaking impasses at the negotiation table and enhancing mutual trust on both sides. Despite the parties' initial doubts about involving the UN, the organization had managed to gradually gain trust and a UN mission to Colombia was

---

3   Something which President Uribe had always refused to do, instead describing the violence as acts of illegal "narco-terrorist" groups attacking state forces.

established in 2016 with the mandate to monitor and verify the laying down of arms and the definitive bilateral ceasefire.

Importantly, the Havana process made it possible, for the first time, to invite the input of victims of the conflict at the negotiating table. This represented a watershed moment in the process, causing unexpectedly moving moments, which likely had an impact on the FARC's radical change of position on the issue of victims. Despite their initial reluctance, the government and the FARC increasingly acknowledged their responsibility for human rights violations and engaged in public acts of contrition, critically boosting mutual perception – and that of the public – of the feasibility of a final agreement.

On September 25, 2016, a peace deal was finally signed between Santos and Timochenko in Havana. However, not everyone in Colombia was happy with the outcome. As President Santos started to make moves towards peace talks with the FARC as of 2010, he had to break the coalition with his former ally and mentor, Alvaro Uribe, who positioned himself as the process' greatest nemesis and rallied much popular support against many provisions of the deal. The agreement was famously voted down in a plebiscite and had to be partially renegotiated. After intensive consultations between the parties a revised agreement was signed on November 24, 2016, and with ratification by the Colombian Congress an end to the conflict was finally marked.

4. RIPENING MINDS AND RISING READINESS

After such a long history of failed attempts, one of the main questions is what circumstances enabled the "Havana talks" to start in earnest in the first place and then sustain a fruitful process. Such circumstances are often described as constructing "a ripe moment" in a conflict, in which the effort for a negotiated solution finds fertile soil and time to prosper. Ripeness theory (Zartman, 1989, 2000) postulates that parties resort to negotiation in internal and international wars under two necessary, though not sufficient, conditions: (1) a Mutually Hurting Stalemate (MHS) and (2) a Mutually Perceived Way Out, in which both sides foresee that a negotiated solution is possible and that a formula can be found that is just and satisfactory to both parties. A third, procedural factor, is the presence of a valid spokesman (Zartman, 1989).

Dean Pruitt's "Readiness theory", an "adaptation of the ripeness theory" (Pruitt, 1997), can also help us in the analysis of the circumstances leading to the Havana negotiations. The theory argues that "all kinds of progress toward conflict resolution result from the existence, on both sides, of: motivational ripeness (motivation to achieve de-escalation) and optimism about finding a mutually acceptable agreement" (Pruitt, 1997). In that sense, it builds upon the same elements of MHS and a Way Out, but emphasizes the analysis of psychological factors – "motives and perceptions that make up ripeness on each individual side separately rather than focusing on joint states of mind such as a mutually hurting stalemate" (Pruitt, 2005, p. 6). These psychological states are variables, consisting of moving parts: "perception that the conflict is not being won, perceived costs, perceived risk of continuing the conflict, third-party pressure, working trust" that could compensate for each other in order to attain an end sum of "sufficient readiness" for negotiations, as also demonstrated by the Havana talks. In a sense, this allows for a greater reach in explaining phenomena such as the entry into informal prenegotiation discussions, followed by the likelihood of getting to an agreement. For negotiations to continue and succeed after the initial "ripe moment", the psychological state of "sufficient readiness" would then have to remain at least equal (although the different variables might shift) and preferably increase throughout the process.

4.1. SOURCES OF MOTIVATION TO END THE CONFLICT

The events in Colombia as described above indeed had a crucial influence on the FARC's perception that their military project was dysfunctional; third-party pressure from Cuba and Venezuela added further weight to the need for a political alternative. Conversely, the involvement of the UN, the guarantors and other international actors, instead played a significant role in increasing the optimism of both parties in the sense that an eventual agreement and its implementation would likely be supported politically, financially, and logistically.

On the side of the Colombian government, no impending catastrophe would tip the balance towards sufficient motivation, but mainly a calculus of opportunity costs. As both a former economic and defense Minister, Santos recognized that a trying to win the conflict would cost more lives, resources, and would reduce the potential for economic prosperity. Carrying on would not be worth drawing out these costs for an unforeseeable time to come. Moreover, trying to completely destroy FARC might also have perversely incentivized the guerilleros to continue their military struggle with an unprecedented vehemence. The successful targeting of high-ranking FARC leaders could have become counterproductive, because it risked leaving the FARC without the political capacity to engage in constructive peace negotiations.

4.2. SOURCES OF OPTIMISM FOR THE PARTIES

Just as important as the existence of certain "push" factors creating the psychological motivation to get parties to the table in good faith, is the perception that there is light at the end of the negotiation tunnel. "Optimism is a sense that it will be possible to locate a mutually acceptable agreement" and is thus initially "required for a party to enter negotiation" [...] and as negotiation goes along, this optimism must increase or the party will drop out" (Pruitt, 2005). Initial optimism often derives from what Kelman (1997) calls "working trust", which generates necessary concession-making. A key component of President Santos' peace policy was the adoption of the 2011 Land Restitution and Victims Law, which basically acknowledged the government's responsibility for the structural inequality of property rights and the disproportionate level of suffering it imposed on the rural population. The law aimed to redress human rights violations on all sides of the conflict, including violence by the Colombian security forces and paramilitaries, who had contributed to the almost four million displaced persons whose property had been confiscated or destroyed. As most of the victims came from formerly FARC-controlled areas, the law partially dismantled the conflict on the very issues of social justice, land reform, and reconciliation which were crucial in the political discourse of the FARC. The passing of this law might therefore have been a key tipping point for the FARC in establishing sufficient assurance that the two sides actually had compatible goals and thus creating an essential boost in optimism. Furthermore, as Colombia has a long history of guerilleros-turned-politicians being killed after demobilization and reintegration, the security guarantees which the Colombian government could offer would be key in scaling up the FARC's optimism. Consequently, the existence of ample peace infrastructures as well as a relatively developed participatory political system in Colombia probably helped to build some of the FARC's trust that its demobilization as well as the politicization of its project would be sufficiently facilitated.

"For optimism to be sustained once the process has commenced, the parties must eventually see the outlines of a possible agreement" (Pruitt, 2005). Indeed, the framework agreement reached in August 2012 (the "Global Agreement for the Termination of the Armed Conflict") functioned as a first codified proof of joint achievement, helping the parties to conceive "formulas" indicating the outlines of a possible final peace deal. It stipulated a number of process methods to smoothen further consensus-building, such as "nothing is agreed until everything is agreed", commitments to the confidentiality of the table's discussions, and agreements on strategic communication. The limited negotiation agenda expressed the guiding process methodology, which was a search for the middle ground between two opposite ways of understanding the conflict in Colombia: between the FARC's "positive peace" (reached through conflict *transformation*), a concept which relies on the argument that there cannot be peace until there is full and complete social justice; and the view of "negative peace" traditionally held by the state, which understands peace merely as the absence of violence.[4] For the Government, an important optimism-inducing breakthrough was accomplished here by convincing the FARC to focus on the topics that were strictly necessary to *end the conflict* and to perceive this as a starting point towards reaching "positive peace". The success in bridging these primary gaps was, together with the efficient process design, instrumental in cementing – or even augmenting – the levels of optimism in Havana, as each side perceived that it would now be feasible to reach agreement on the main issues within a reasonable amount of time.

4.3. REACHING AGREEMENT WITHOUT A CEASEFIRE

With the 1999–2001 El Caguán experience in mind, in which the FARC had used the opportunity to regain military strength, the government and the Colombian population did not deem a ceasefire to be the best idea to start negotiations with. The government probably believed that a continuation of military pressure would translate into positional strength at the negotiation table and would demonstrate determination to a variety of stakeholders. In terms of readiness, this would keep much needed motivational gravity on the FARC, as well as on some reticent members of the security forces and the internal political "spoilers". Santos insisted that a bilateral ceasefire would have to come at the very end of the process, although the FARC pushed for precisely the opposite. This led to a negotiation situation where "in Havana, negotiators talked as if war wasn't there; in Colombia, generals made decisions as if talks in Havana were not there.[5]

---

4   Concepts originally developed by Johan Galtung (1967).
5   D. MECHOULAN, <https://www.ipinst.org/2017/02/colombia-farc-agree-end-war#6>.

Although having a ceasefire in place generally brings a number of advantages in terms of stability and trust, it is not a conditional requirement for progress in talks and its absence can even be helpful as demonstrated in other cases.[6] No cease-fire was in place either in the Philippines' mediation case with the Moro belligerents (see Ariel Macaspac Hernandez's chapter, "Four Decades in the Southern Philippines (1971–2008)", in this volume). On their part, the FARC however initiated a number of sequential ceasefires throughout 2014 and 2015 and announced they had stopped all military training of its combatants while actively preparing them for demobilization and legal political activity. These unilateral steps probably helped to curry favor with an increasingly skeptical audience in Colombia and were met by the government's announcement that it would stop air-bombing FARC positions.

Nonetheless, the lack of a formal bilateral ceasefire and the inevitable ensuing acts of violence likely undermined public support for the Havana talks and affected the climate at the negotiating table to the detriment of mutual optimism. In the end, it remains hard to assess whether the positive effects of military pressure on "readiness", outweighed the lost opportunity of a ceasefire as confidence-building exercise.

5. PEACE FOR COLOMBIA

The levels of "readiness", brought about by the initial drivers of motivation and especially the momentum of optimism that had been fostered through the "magic of cooperation" in the formal negotiations, were sufficient to lead to signing a peace deal in Havana and probably also served as a sufficient buffer to weather the blow of the infamous "no" vote in the ensuing plebiscite. The final peace accord was ratified on November 24, 2016 between the Colombian government and the FARC after more than 50 years of conflict.

Despite the undeniable success of these negotiations, it is uncertain whether a bargaining strategy of similar motivation and optimism inducing factors – including a process design without ceasefire – could bear fruit in peace processes with other non-state armed actors

---

[6]   For example, in El Salvador the absence of a ceasefire had helped to foster an atmosphere of credible threats regarding the balance of power between the FMLN guerrillas and the government, which eventually brought the latter back to the negotiation table. *Private notes from a meeting with Alvaro de Soto at a Berghof Foundation event in Berlin, October 2017.*

in Colombia. Every conflict has its own logic; the country's last-standing guerrilla movement, the *Ejército de Liberación Nacional* (ELN) not only has a different agenda in current (stalled) negotiations, but is also skeptical towards a number of process design aspects of the Havana talks, including the timing and necessity of a ceasefire with the government.[7] This leaves another window of opportunity to be utilized, another process to be designed.

REFERENCES

ACOSTA, H., El hombre clave: El secreto mejor guardado del proceso de paz de Colombia, Penguin Random House Grupo Editorial Colombia, 2016.

"¿Cuántos hombres y armas tienen las FARC?" Noticias RCN, available at <www.noticiasrcn.com/especialesrcn/conteo-hombres-farc/>.

GALTUNG, J., *Theories of Peace: A Synthetic Approach to Peace Thinking*, International Peace Research Institute, Oslo, September, 1967.

KELMAN, H.C., *Some Determinants of the Oslo Breakthrough*, International Negotiation 2:183–194, 1997.

MECHOULAN, D. <https://www.ipinst.org/2017/02/colombia-farc-agree-end-war#6>.

PRUITT, D.G., *Ripeness Theory and the Oslo Talks*, International Negotiation, 2, 237–250, 1997.

PRUITT, D.G., *Whither Ripeness Theory?* Institute for Conflict Analysis and Resolution, George Mason University, Fairfax, Virginia, 2005.

RICKMEYER, P.F., *Establishing Ripe Moments for Negotiated Settlement in Counterinsurgency: An Example from Colombia*, School of Advanced Military Studies Kansas, 2017.

SEGURA, R. and MECHOULAN, D., *Made in Havana: How Colombia and the FARC Decided to End the War*, International Peace Institute, 2017.

ZARTMAN, I.W., *Common Elements in the Analysis of the Negotiation Process*, Negotiation Journal, 1988.

ZARTMAN, I.W., *Ripeness: The Hurting Stalemate and Beyond*. In Conflict resolution after the Cold War, ed. P.C. STERN and D. DRUCKMAN, 225–50, Washington, DC: National Academy Press, 2000.

---

[7] Private conversation with Pablo Beltrán, chief negotiator of the ELN, in January 2017 in Quito.

PART III
MULTILATERAL NEGOTIATIONS

CONSTANTINOPLE, THE ARMIES OF THE FIRST CRUSADE AND ALEXIUS I COMNENUS

How a Coalition was Built between Latins and Greeks in 1096

Jean-Claude CHEYNET*

In 1095 Alexius I Comnenus, the Byzantine emperor in Constantinople, was looking for help fighting the Turks. His empire was emerging from the most difficult period in its history, during which it suffered not only from political instability and a budget crisis, but also defeats at the hands of the Norman and Pecheneg invaders. The young emperor, who had taken the throne in 1081 (and would reign for 37 years), had progressively righted the situation.

---

*   Emeritus Professor, Sorbonne Université, France.

Now he wanted to solve the most difficult problem: to push back the Seljuq Turks who had just swept through the Near East and invaded Asia Minor. Thanks to effective negotiations and despite religious differences, in less than a year Alexius I Comnenus succeeded in forming a powerful Greek-Latin alliance that headed East, though it did not continue to Jerusalem.

1. THE LATINS ARRIVE AT THE GATES OF CONSTANTINOPLE

Led by the Seljuq sultans, the Turks had defeated the Byzantine imperial troops at Mantzikert in 1071, then swept across the Near East and invaded Asia Minor. In Nicaea, a dissident Seljuq branch had founded a Turkish state to challenge Constantinople. Having founded a new dynasty in 1081, Alexius I Comnenus was besieged on all sides, in particular by Pecheneg nomads in the Balkans, and was in danger of being defeated by the Normans of Italy led by Robert Guiscard and his son Bohemond. But 10 years later, the emperor had brought peace to the Balkans and was thinking of taking back Asia Minor, which was in the hands of the Seljuqs of Rum and various other emirs.

After 1092, Alexius sent emissaries to Western sovereigns, in particular the German emperor with whom he had a fairly warm relationship, because he wanted to bring together a large number of Latin soldiers. For more than half a century, the emperors had recruited heavy cavalry by the thousands. In particular, they recruited Normans, who became the Byzantine army's elite and attracted greater and greater numbers of warriors ready to make the pilgrimage to Jerusalem.

Despite the dogmatic split in 1054, the papacy supported this move. Alexius sent ambassadors to the council held in Plaisance with the new pope, Urban II, so that help could be brought to the East. In November 1095, at the regional council of Clermont, the pope appealed to Western chivalry to go to help the Christians of the East, and set the new goal of taking control of the Holy Sepulchre in Jerusalem (the pilgrimages had been disrupted by the actions of the Turkish emirs and the counter-offensives of the Fatimids of Egypt).

This appeal succeeded beyond all hope, resulting in the unprecedented event called the first crusade: important Western princes and crowds of pilgrims, often accompanied by their families, took the overland route, which necessarily went through Constantinople. The emperor was thus faced with an unheard of situation. He had asked for classic Western reinforcements, that is, mercenaries to back up his troops, but found himself with crowds that also included a large number of non-combatants who had undertaken a long pilgrimage – the precise nature of which was not immediately known, because the main leaders of this so-called crusade had no specific plans as to what they would do in the Holy Land other than reopen the route to the Holy Sepulchre to Christian pilgrims.

Alexius spoke with the expedition's leaders to try to gain the best advantage for the Empire. The Latin leaders, who headed separate armies, came from different backgrounds. They included Raymond, Count of Toulouse, a member of the proud Capetian royal line; Godfrey of Bouillon, Duke of Lower Lorraine, a descendent of Charlemagne; and Bohemond of Taranto, son of Guiscard, who had been Alexius's most formidable adversary during the Norman war of 1081 to 1085. He was perfectly familiar with the Byzantine institutions because many Normans from southern Italy had served the Empire.

2. NEGOTIATING TO BUILD A COALITION

The purpose of the negotiations between the emperor and the crusade leaders was to decide on the nature of the tie that would bind them in the future and determine what each side would bring the other. To help us understand these negotiations today, there is a remarkable Greek source, the *Alexiade* by Anne Comnenus, the emperor's daughter, who was about 12 at the time. She collected a number of accounts, and there are also accounts of the crusades written from the point of view of the Frank commanders, mainly Bohemond.

2.1. THE EMPEROR'S ADVANTAGES

– Alexius appealed to Christian solidarity, which was still quite strong given the Turkish invasion, despite the differences that the 1054 episode had highlighted. Byzantines and Latins shared the need to liberate Asia Minor from all Turkish presence. For the Byzantines, the issue was to regain provinces they had recently lost, and especially the city of Antioch, which the Turks had taken 10 years earlier and was pivotal to defending the Byzantine East. For the Latins, the goal was to make the Holy Sepulchre accessible by land again, as that was the only route that had been used extensively during the previous century. The sea route was still rarely used and in any case required control over the land because the ships still engaged in cabotage.

- He represented the only Byzantine position, even if advisors within the power circle took opposite sides in discussions on the concessions that should be made to the Latins.
- He had ways to put pressure on the crusaders. He guaranteed food supplies, which was a key issue for the armies because they had to cover several thousand kilometers. His recovered wealth enabled him to be generous with the pilgrims, who financed their long voyage themselves and were often short of resources. In addition, the objects he could offer them not only had intrinsic value, but also conferred prestige on the lucky recipients in the eyes of their followers. Moreover, the emperor provided guides who knew the roads of Asia Minor.
- The emperor was well informed and knew the crusade leaders' different interests. Some of them were thinking of staying in the East and carving out a principality there once they had completed their pilgrimage, so he knew what to offer to satisfy them.

2.2. THE CRUSADERS' ADVANTAGES

- Although the Latin armies arrived one by one and the pilgrims were far from their homelands, their numbers gave them an advantage: they could join forces and attempt an assault on Constantinople or one of the Empire's other large cities and, if they were not provided with adequate supplies, they could pillage the provinces they traveled through.
- The Western reinforcements were essential because they represented the only hope for Alexius to reconquer Asia Minor, where the Turks were now well entrenched.
- The crusaders had no direct ties with any of the Western sovereigns, though the papacy was represented by a legate. While their lack of unity gave the emperor an advantage because he could play on the rivalry between leaders, it complicated his task because he could not conclude a treaty in a single negotiation.

2.3. THE METHOD: DEAL WITH THE PILGRIMS SEQUENTIALLY

Alexius Comnenus therefore took advantage of the fact that the pilgrims arrived in sequential order, which logistics required in any case. He had time to prepare and engaged in separate bilateral negotiations with each of the armies. Once agreement was reached with one of the leaders, he made a point of boasting of it to the others.

The emperor was trying to send the Latins as quickly as possible to the Asian side of the Bosphorous or the Propontis, where he still had support. This saved him from the strong pressure he would have been under had all the armies of pilgrims arrived together. He applied this theory to Peter the Hermit, who was the first to arrive in 1096, leading disparate, undisciplined troops, as well as a large number of non-combatants. Alexius welcomed him with kindness and rushed to ship him across the Bosphorous, recommending that he wait for the others and not attack the Turks. This advice was not followed, which resulted in pilgrims being massacred and distrust of the emperor among some of the survivors who made it back to the capital.

Serious negotiations did not begin until 1096, when Godfrey of Bouillon, Raymond of Saint-Gilles, and Bohemond reached Constantinople. The emperor used the prestigious setting of the grand palace to impress his visitors. Issues of rank arose immediately, because the Latin and Greek conceptions were not the same. Alexius allowed the Latins to behave according to their custom, which scandalized his court: a Latin even dared to sit on the emperor's throne!

2.4. BINDING BOTH PARTIES ONCE AGREEMENTS WERE REACHED

Traditionally, when the emperor recruited Latins for his army, they became officers and temporary subjects of the emperor even if they came from illustrious families. Such subordination was unacceptable to the leaders of the crusade, and yet a way had to be found to confirm the agreements. Alexius agreed to adopt Latin methods. When the Latins were enlisted, they swore an oath of loyalty according to their customs, the idea being that they would feel more bound by the type of oaths they usually took in their homeland. Alexius thus accepted such an oath when he could get it.

2.5. THE DEALS

How did Alexius manage to take advantage of the arrival of this mass of warriors to clear Asia Minor? He played on the rivalries between the various contingents' leaders, especially between Bohemond and Raymond of

Toulouse, to win over the weaker ones. For example, Hugh of Vermandois, the king of France's brother, suffered a shipwreck off the Balkan coast and found himself utterly without resources. After being showered with gifts by Alexius, he had no trouble agreeing to swear the oath asked of him, and was then tasked with persuading Godfrey of Bouillon to follow his example. The emperor talked to each one separately as much as possible, then once a compromise had been reached, he brought all the partners together to swear the oath.

He was not unaware that Bohemond and his nephew, Tancred, came to seek their fortune in the East. Bohemond had shown great valor in combat against the Byzantines, but his contingent was smaller than those of the other leaders, which put him in a relatively weak position. Contrary to Anne Comnenus's intimations, Bohemond and Alexius reached an agreement fairly quickly, each probably thinking they would use the other later. The emperor relied on financial weapons, bestowing gifts on Bohemond and his followers. He also promised Bohemond territories to conquer at the expense of the emir of Aleppo and a large Byzantine military command in the East once Aleppo was liberated, as well as a substantial share of the spoils of the future victory.

Having won the first round, Alexius made Bohemond his agent vis-à-vis the other crusade leaders, who did not have the same motivation to reach a quick agreement with the emperor. In particular, Raymond of Saint-Gilles refused to do anything that might seem like an act of submission, citing his royal blood and relying on his army, which was the coalition's largest. The rivalry between Saint-Gilles and Bohemond permanently complicated the expedition and continued well beyond the crossing of the Bosphorous. Bohemond succeeded in pressuring his nephew Tancred to agree to the emperor's terms even though Tancred vehemently opposed making any concessions to Alexius. Alexius's gifts to the crusade's main representatives – gold, precious fabrics and objects, and imperial relics and dignities – helped persuade them to rally to the solutions he proposed. Some of them even went into imperial service completely and founded great Byzantine aristocratic lines.

3. WHAT DID ALEXIUS AND THE LATINS AGREE TO?

According to the treaties, the crusaders moved quickly into Asia Minor to take the old military road that connected the Empire's capital with Antioch.

Any territory or city they took back from the Turks and that had recently belonged to the Empire would be returned to the Byzantine authorities. The territories beyond Antioch and especially Jerusalem, which had not belonged to the Empire since the invasion in the 640s of the Arabs then-recently converted to Islam, would remain under the emperor's theoretical authority but tacitly would be left to the Latins. In all likelihood, the Latins did not have a clear idea of who would be in charge once they made their conquests.

Meanwhile, in addition to all the advantages he had granted, Alexius upheld his part of the bargain: he provided food supplies, loaned Greek guides, and sent a large contingent commanded by Tatikios, a general of Turkish descent who had grown up at the palace with the emperor and was very close to him. This contingent was the manifestation of the Byzantines' commitment to the pilgrims. The emperor also promised to come in person, with his entire army, to support the expedition for the time it took to bring all the contingents together, that is, one year. All the crusade leaders swore an oath of loyalty to the emperor except Raymond of Toulouse and Bohemond's nephew Tancred, who promised only not to harm the Empire's interests.

4. TREATY APPLICATION MADE DIFFICULT

The surrender of Nicaea in June 1097 revealed the first difference in how the parties interpreted the treaties. The Turks surrendered directly to the Byzantines, who treated the sultan's family with respect. This made the Latins, who had provided the main war effort, feel they were being denied their legitimate right to pillage, which would have made them rich at a time when their financial reserves for the long pilgrimage were dwindling.

The siege of Antioch brought things to a head. In the fall of 1097, the crusaders laid siege to this very strong fortress. Taking it meant maintaining a long siege while surrounded by the enemy, which limited the ability to obtain provisions. In February 1098, Tatikios (the leader of the Byzantine contingent) headed toward Cyprus to look for supplies, leaving the emperor without a direct, reliable witness to the Latins' fate. In June, the attackers' situation seemed so critical that the count of Blois (one of the main leaders) deserted the Latin camp and headed back to Constantinople. In the middle of Asia Minor he met Alexius, who was coming with all his troops to help the crusaders, as he had agreed. The count told him that the army at Antioch was lost and, on the advice of his advisors, the emperor turned around to avoid losing his army as well. Meanwhile Antioch had fallen and Bohemond, claiming that Alexius had betrayed them, refused to surrender this formidable fortress and former capital of the Byzantine East. Instead, he had it handed over to himself, starting decades of hostilities between Byantines and Norman princes of Antioch.

In his defense, Bohemond claimed Alexius had not come to the crusaders' aid when they were in great danger, while the emperor cited the treaties concluded in Constantinople and noted that he had gone far into Anatolia and had turned back only because of erroneous information. In fact, neither one had lost: the former had conquered a territory in the East, and the latter had recovered the rich plains of western Asia Minor.

5. THE ALLIANCE EVENTUALLY FELL APART

What was the end result for the partners of this alliance? What were the reasons for the final failure that eventually weakened the Greeks and Latins against the Turks? Negotiations had taken place in an atmosphere of distrust and, despite it being contrary to what many of the Latins wanted, they pushed for a compromise like the one the emperor had proposed because of the Byzantine military pressure and the threat of not being able to get supplies, which gave the emperor a formidable bargaining chip. Christian brotherhood no doubt played a role, as well as the desire to advance more quickly on the road to Jerusalem, but all the players had different objectives and concerns that varied as opportunities arose.

Bohemond provides the best example of this attitude. He had no chance of inheriting Guiscard's realm in southern Italy and had always been seeking his fortune in the East, initially at the expense of the Byzantines (until 1085). In 1096, he came to an agreement with the emperor fairly quickly because the emperor offered him the opportunity to become one of the most powerful, and therefore richest, officers of the Empire. Both partners were perhaps sincere at that time: such an arrangement would make up for Bohemond's disappointments in Italy, and the emperor would be recruiting one of the best soldiers of his time, who would also then cease to be a potential adversary. The siege of Antioch gave Bohemond the opportunity to cash in on what Alexius had promised him and to keep it for himself, without anyone above him. This change of position can be explained by the fact that the agreement was not based on long-term shared interests. It was also an opportunity for Bohemond to assert himself in relation to more powerful rivals, who had ceded Antioch to him after tough negotiations. Another event that was unforeseeable at the time of the negotiations occurred when the Armenians called Baldwin of Boulogne (a cousin of Godfrey of Bouillon) to Tarsus then Edessa, which he became the count of.

But the emperor was not without ulterior motives. The crusade's distant goal, Jerusalem, was not his priority: he was looking first of all for military strength to reconquer Asia Minor. From this perspective he succeeded, because he welcomed the Latin armies in disparate order and had them leave united to attack the Turks in Asia Minor. The full value of this exploit became clear in 1100–1101 when, faced with the successive arrival of yet more Latin contingents on their way to provide reinforcements to the new Latin states, the emperor did not manage to persuade the leaders of the various contingents to unite to cross the Turkish-held Anatolian plain, and the Turks destroyed the Latin troops as they arrived separately.

The emperor had succeeded in 1097, however, and after the Latins left, he made sure he took advantage of the expedition that had been so difficult to control. The advantage he gained was great, because the wealthiest portion of Asia Minor became Byzantine again.

But the role of chance and the unforeseeable must not be underestimated. Count Stephen of Blois, who persuaded Alexius that the Latins were in a hopeless situation at Antioch, left shortly before their great victory, on June 28, 1098, over Kerbogha, the emir of Mosul. Had Stephen stayed a month longer, it is highly likely that the crusade would have ended quite differently and the alliance between the Empire and the new Latin states would have lasted.

REFERENCES

MAIN SOURCES

SEWTER, E.R.A. and P. FRANKOPAN, trans. *The Alexiad*, revised, London, 2004.
Recueil des historiens des croisades. Historiens occidentaux, t. III, Paris, 1866 (Foucher de Chartres, Raoul de Caen, Raymond d'Aguilers, Robert le Moine).

SECONDARY LITERATURE

SETTON, K. (General Editor), *A History of The Crusades*, vol. I, Milwaukee, London, 1969.
SHEPARD, J., When Greek Meets Greek: Alexius Comnenus and Bohemond in 1097–1098, *BMGS* 12, 1988, pp. 185–277.

SHEPARD, J., "'Father' or 'Scorpion'? Style and substance in Alexius' diplomacy, Alexius I Komnenos" in *Alexius I Komnenos. Papers of the second Belfast Byzantine International Colloquium, 14–16 April 1989*, ed. by M. Mullett and D. Smythe (Belfast Byzantine Texts and Translations, 4/1), Belfast, 1996, pp. 68–132.

SHEPARD, J., "Cross-Purposes: Alexius Comnenus and the First Crusade" in *The First Crusade, Origins and Impact*, ed. J. Phillips, no. 6, Manchester, 1997, pp. 107–129.

THE CONSTANTINOPLE CONFERENCE (1876–1877)

Negotiating with Russia

Isabelle Dasque*

In the 19th century, international negotiations were generally conducted within the framework of the Concert of Europe, a dispute-resolution system based on informal multilateral cooperation, legal and diplomatic structures, and a feeling of shared values.[1] European diplomats were concerned with the Eastern Question, "together with the problems

---

* Sorbonne Université (Paris IV).
1 G.H. Soutou, *L'Europe de 1815 à nos jours*, Paris, Puf, 2nd ed., 2009, p. 26.

caused to the great powers since the end of the eighteenth century by the Ottoman Empire's withdrawal from territories in the Balkans and the eastern Mediterranean".[2] The 1856 Treaty of Paris had made them responsible for keeping the Ottoman Empire intact, and in exchange the Empire became subject to European public law:[3] to slow the Empire's decline, its leaders had launched a vast modernization program in 1839 called the *Tanzîmât* [reorganization], broadly based on the principles prevailing in Europe, but the interests of and rivalries between the foreign powers that had interfered in the Empire's domestic affairs on the pretext of protecting Christians limited the results of those reform efforts. Convened to put an end to the crisis that had been roiling the Balkans since 1875, the Constantinople Conference was conducted in two phases: (1) from December 11–22, 1876, nine preliminary meetings were held among the representatives of various European States, during which they negotiated to establish a program of reforms that was to constitute the conference's platform; (2) from December 23, 1876 to January 20, 1877, a plenary assembly was held with the Ottoman plenipotentiaries. The conference tested the ability of the Concert of Europe to serve as an appropriate framework for negotiations in the 19th century. Although the cooperative approach taken during the first phase allowed the powers to reach an understanding, the conference culminated in failure, partly due to competition among the participants.

1. TWO-STAGE NEGOTIATIONS

1.1. THE REASON FOR THE NEGOTIATIONS: INSECURITY IN THE BALKANS (1875–1876)

The Ottoman Empire had been dealing with a Christian peasant revolt in Bosnia and Herzegovina since July 1875, and since July 2, 1876 had been at war with Serbia and Montenegro which, helped by Russia, were supporting the rebels. In addition, the violent repression of uprisings in Bulgaria by irregular Turkish troops ("*bachi-bouzouks*") in June 1876 elicited very

---

2   F. GEORGEON, *Abdulhamid II, le sultan Calife*, Paris, Fayard, 2003, p. 20.

3   The Ottoman Empire's relations with European States had previously been governed by specific treaties called Capitulations. Now it was governed by the same rules of customary law as the Europeans were.

lively reactions from European diplomats and Europeans in general. Following Ottoman victories against the Serbs, in September 1876 Prince Milan I of Serbia appealed to the great powers to obtain an end to the hostilities. On October 31, 1876, General Ignatyev, the Czar's ambassador to Constantinople, issued an ultimatum to the Sublime Porte commanding it to accept a two-month armistice, subject to armed intervention. Completely isolated, the Ottoman government agreed.

On the suggestion of the Earl of Derby, Great Britain's Secretary of State for Foreign Affairs, the European powers decided to convene an international conference in Constantinople to resolve the issue of reforms in the Balkans. The Czar grudgingly agreed, threatening to act alone if the conference did not achieve anything. The Turkish government was highly averse to such a conference, which constituted interference in its domestic affairs, but agreed to attend it (and to the armistice) as a way to gain time in the face of Russian threats. Based on British and Russian memoranda written in 1875–1876, the purpose of the conference was to discuss peace based on the status quo with Serbia and Montenegro, and sign an agreement that would grant autonomy to Bosnia, Herzegovina, and Bulgaria and include guarantees to ensure effective enforcement.

1.2. SUCCESSFUL PRELIMINARY NEGOTIATIONS AMONG THE EUROPEAN POWERS

Against a backdrop of Anglo-Russian antagonism, the participants tried to agree in the pre-Conference meetings on options that were acceptable to the Ottomans but did not compromise their various interests.

Two, contradictory plans were proposed: one by the English and one by the Russians. According to a memorandum dated September 22, 1876, the English plan consisted of demanding a series of general guarantees from the Turks and a system of autonomy for the rebel provinces: in keeping with its policy of territorial integrity and intending to overcome Russian influence, Great Britain was counting on the Turks' good will and promises of reform. At the time, however, the Ottoman Empire was undergoing a governance crisis[4] compounded by economic difficulties, and English public opinion

---

[4]   In May 1876, Sultan Abdülazîz was deposed and replaced by Prince Mûrad V, who was deposed three months later and succeeded by his brother, Abdûl-Hamîd II, on August 31, 1876. R. MANTRAN, *Histoire d'Istanbul*, Paris, Fayard, 1996, p. 286.

was hostile to the Turks due to their treatment of Christians, in particular during the repression in Bulgaria. London was therefore becoming less and less inclined to believe that the Ottoman government was capable of reform.

Russia, meanwhile, was not put off by the idea of its troops intervening militarily and occupying Bulgaria, and in exchange it would consider having Austro-Hungarian troops stationed in Bosnia and Herzegovina: to achieve its ultimate goal of the Turkish Straits, Russia was pursuing a policy of entente with Austria-Hungary as a strong pan-Slavic movement, for which General Ignatyev was the spokesperson, was sweeping the country.

The outcome of the conference therefore depended on the relationship between General Ignatyev and Lord Salisbury, Secretary for India, whom the British government had appointed to attend the conference to temper the pro-Turkish positions of Sir Henry Elliot, its ambassador to Constantinople. The representatives of the other countries participating in the conference were trying to find a middle ground between the two plans on which the English and Russian representatives could agree after making mutual concessions, but were also defending their own interests. Italy was hostile to Russia's occupation of Bulgaria, which was likely to be followed by Austria's occupation of Bosnia. It therefore opposed Russia's claims. Austria-Hungary wanted, with Bismarck's benediction, to revise its policy regarding the Balkans to offset the territory and influence it had lost upon the unification of Italy then Germany. It also wanted to keep the Ottoman Empire intact, as it feared the crisis would benefit Serbia and enable it to take over Bosnia and Herzegovina. France, which had been excluded from the international scene since 1871, was favorable to looking for a negotiated solution to avoid an armed conflict that was likely to upset the European balance, to the advantage of States more involved in the region.

Despite these different approaches, and aware that the Turks counted heavily on divisions among the European States to gain time, the diplomats who were attending the conference agreed on a joint program that included correcting the borders between Turkey and its neighbors, Montenegro and Serbia; free navigation on the Boïana; and the idea of an autonomous structure for Bosnia, Herzegovina, and Bulgaria, under European control. While the administrative and judicial reforms planned for Bosnia and Herzegovina did not elicit opposition, Bulgaria's fate was the subject of more heated discussion. The Russians finally agreed to the principle of dividing Bulgaria into two administrative divisions (*vilayets*), each of which would have a provincial assembly and be governed by a prefect (*vali*) appointed by the Porte, with European approval, for a five-year term. Russia also agreed to abandon all ideas of occupying Bulgaria in exchange for setting up a European gendarmerie, composed of 6,000 men from neutral countries (Belgium, the Netherlands, and Switzerland), that would serve the international commission in charge of making sure the reforms were carried out. The plenipotentiaries also hoped to get the Ottomans to confine Turkish troops to fortresses and return the displaced Circassians who had set up colonies in the European portion of the Empire to Asia.

1.3. FAILURE OF THE PLENARY SESSION

With this agenda in hand, the delegation heads arrived for the conference's plenary session, which opened in the presence of the Ottomans on December 23 at the Palace of the Admiralty in the Kasimpasa quarter. As delegates were presenting their respective governments' points of view, rounds of artillery were being shot from the other side of the Bosphorus, from Seraskierart square in Stamboul, to announce that the new constitution had been promulgated. This announcement was the real answer to the representatives' speeches. Promulgating the constitution marked the end of the Tanzimât and served as a diplomatic weapon for the Ottoman delegates, who promised to improve the situation of the Christians, set new rules for the collection and distribution of taxes in the rebel provinces, and continue modernizing the Empire – but without supervision from the great powers.[5] The Sultan's representatives used the constitution as a basis for rejecting the draft agreements presented during the discussions, arguing in particular that this text enacted reforms applicable throughout the Empire, whereas the conference text would impose only partial measures. Despite the attempts of France and Austria-Hungary to obtain commitments from the grand vizier in exchange for concessions from them (i.e., the elimination of the international commission, as its tasks had been assigned to the European consuls), Lord Salisbury and General Ignatyev refused all attempts at conciliation. The Conference therefore ended on January 20, 1877 with no result.

---

[5] R. MANTRAN, *Histoire de l'Empire ottoman*, Fayard, 1989, p. 650.

2. BETWEEN A COOPERATIVE APPROACH AND A COMPETITIVE APPROACH: LESSONS FROM A FAILURE

2.1. WISELY CHOSEN NEGOTIATORS

While the conference was not attended by first rank diplomats,[6] the choice of negotiators had a significant influence on the discussions. Most important in this regard was the appointment of Lord Salisbury to direct the English delegation at a time when Great Britain was ready to change its policy concerning the Sublime Porte. When out of earshot of the Ottomans, he was likely to agree with the Czar's representative and more likely to listen actively than was Sir Elliott, who was close to reformist circles in Constantinople and toed the line of the territorial integrity of the Ottoman Empire set out in the Treaty of Paris. As Paul Desprez, secretary of the French delegation, noted: "The ambassador from England, with his British phlegm, could not please General Ignatyev, who on the contrary had a fiery, effusive nature. In addition, Sir Henry was the living personification of the old English politician in the East."[7]

Choosing negotiators who were able to understand the issue and each other made it easier to achieve success during the conference's first phase, by taking a predominantly cooperative approach to the negotiations between the European rivals, England and Russia. Convinced that the Ottoman Empire was in any event condemned, in particular in its European portions, Lord Salisbury preferred to reach an agreement with Russia in order to obtain guarantees from India, and opted for an integrative approach. The regional negotiation was part of a more global strategy. In any case, the informal and formal preliminary meetings gave the negotiators an opportunity to observe each other:

> Lord Salisbury's character added to his good chances. The vices of the social state and political customs of Turkey must have made a strong impression on

---

6   At the conference, France, England, and Austria-Hungary were each represented by two plenipotentiaries; the other powers by their accredited ambassador to the Ottoman government; and the Ottoman Empire by Safvet Pacha, the Minister of Foreign Affairs, and Edhem Pacha, the Porte's ambassador to Berlin.

7   P. DESPREZ, "La conférence de Constantinople, 1876–1877," in Archives of the French Ministry of Foreign Affairs (AMAE), Agents' Papers, Hippolyte Desprez, vol. 15. (Translator's note: P. Desprez, son of H. Desprez, kept a diary at the conference that is included with his father's papers in the archive.)

the rectitude of his conscience, the Christian and humanitarian, almost apostolic side of his nature. General Ignatyev did not neglect to take advantage of these tendencies in England's representative by constantly emphasizing to him the moral degradation of the Turkish regime and its oppression of the people. Lord Salisbury's language was the opposite of Sir Elliot's. There was therefore hope that the first task, to obtain agreement between England and Russia, was going to be accomplished.[8]

2.2. PRECONCEPTIONS INFLUENCED THE EUROPEAN APPROACH

The preconceptions the negotiators drew on to change their partners' positions may have made the second phase of the negotiations more difficult. In the eyes of the European diplomats, whose beliefs had been shaped by the Orientalist novels of the 18th century (Voltaire, Abbé Prévost, Fromaget) and the travel writings of the first half of the 19th century (Chateaubriand and Nerval), the Ottoman Empire was the embodiment of a despotic and fascinating East led by a sultan the Europeans referred to as an "Asian savage" or "semi-barbarian".[9] The European diplomats were also convinced that the Ottomans respected only strength, which explains the dominating behavior they exhibited, based on how they expected the Sultan's representatives to act. This type of "cognitive bias"[10] probably influenced the conference: the Europeans' shared preconceptions probably helped bring them together during pre-negotiations, but also led them to develop a negotiating position that was ultimately fairly harsh toward the Ottomans and led to failure in the plenary assembly.

2.3. CAN THE PLACE WHERE NEGOTIATIONS ARE HELD EXPLAIN THEIR OUTCOME?

The various places used throughout the Constantinople Conference influenced the negotiating process. Between the informal and formal

---

[8] Count Chaudordy letter to Duke Decazes, January 3, 1877, in AMAE, *Mémoires et documents, Turquie*, vol. 102.

[9] Melchior de Vogüé letter to his father, July 24, 1872, in French National Archives, 567 AP 39, Vogüe archives.

[10] D. KAHNEMAN and A. TVERSKY, "Subjective Probability: A judgment of Representativeness", Cognitive Psychology, 1972, 3, 430–454.

phases, which took place simultaneously or in succession, the conference was held on both official and improvised sites, in enclosed rooms or open areas, some of which were public while others were private.

The Russians took full advantage of the space during the first phase. The nine preliminary meetings between the European plenipotentiaries were held in the salons of General Ignatyev's hotel, and as Paul Deprez wrote in his memoirs:

> This was the best way for the general to advance his affairs: he was really himself only in the midst of his world, his colleagues, at work on his own territory, near his office. If one of his interlocutors seemed only half convinced by his arguments, it was easy for the general to lead him into the next room to speak to him more directly, if necessary read him a few documents methodically prepared for the occasion ... Not content with having the most serious of conversations with his colleagues, he overwhelms them with written communications, notes, and memoranda prepared in longhand by his secretaries: it is an arsenal of diplomatic documents, each of which must produce a given effect.[11]

The Russians led the negotiations, and used the places where they were held to put pressure on their interlocutors when presenting Russia's interests. Enclosed areas were the most effective, as they lent themselves to secrecy as well as to seeing shared interests in a "joint" program dictated largely by the Russians.

Conversely, while the European powers wanted to make a show of strength (peaceful, of course) by meeting on the banks of the Bosphorus, their choice of cities backfired: Constantinople was not a peaceful backdrop but a genuine participant in the negotiations. Holding the conference contributed to inflaming the Turks, in a city where rumors spread quickly and, as Count de Chaudordy, the head of the French delegation, wrote: "We took clever advantage of the secret necessarily kept by the plenipotentiaries regarding the discussions to thoroughly distort their significance. This silence left the field open for more than three weeks to the most erroneous revelations and inaccurate observations."[12] The preliminary negotiations elicited distrust from the Turkish negotiators, which from the outset endangered the minimum amount of cooperation required to negotiate. In addition, a Muslim community was emerging in Constantinople, its religious

---

[11]   P. DESPREZ, above n. 7.

[12]   Count de Chaudordy letter to Duke Decazes, January 9, 1877, in AMAE, above n. 8, fol. 363.

sentiments having been awakened on seeing the refugees from the Caucuses and the Balkans, and it intended to respond to foreign pressure and the reforms Turkish leaders had been carrying out up until then.

Similarly, the fact that the plenary session was held at the Hotel of the Admiralty on the Golden Horn was both the sign and the place of Ottoman resistance. This inlet in fact constituted a border between cosmopolitan neighborhoods such as Galata-Péra, where the embassies, commercial and insurance companies, and banks were located, and the predominantly Muslim neighborhoods of Stamboul where the ministries and administrative offices were located.[13] Colonized in the 19th century by prestigious constructions of the sultans and their dignitaries, the banks of the Bosphorus provided a genuine stage for the Empire around the water, while the neighborhoods that were distant from it were more or less synonymous with places of disgrace, exile, and confinement. The Turks' courteous indifference to the representatives who had come to impose an administrative reform program was reflected from the outset in the choice of the Admiralty. The Ottomans had retained one such official building (which represented the Tanzimat period during which the Empire had set up European-style administrative agencies, ministries and departments) in a Turkish quarter that was being completely renovated. But the European guarantors, and more specifically England, had made the modernization and reform process undertaken by the Porte the token of the Empire's integrity and independence, and the prerequisite for their support. The choice of the place was thus in itself a refusal to negotiate.

2.4. NEGOTIATING INTERESTS THEN POSITIONS: THE CONFERENCE STALEMATE

During the conference's first phase, informal negotiations were essential to clarify each party's motivations and make it possible to achieve an outcome. On the way to Constantinople, Lord Salisbury paid visits to Rome, Berlin, and Vienna, weighing the parties' interests and developing the strategy he would pursue in the name of Her Majesty's government. In Berlin and Vienna, he noted in particular that the embassies were opposed to the idea of an occupation, such that during preliminary discussions, he set aside all of General Ignatyev's proposed solutions: mixed occupation,

---

[13]   R. MANTRAN, *Histoire d'Istanbul*, above n. 4, p. 303.

Austro-Russian occupation, or Russian occupation of Bulgaria. He tried to persuade Russia to abandon its position (occupation of Bulgaria) and negotiate regarding one of its important objectives, i.e., guarantees for the Christian populations. The enterprise also owed its success to the secondary players who supported the opposing positions by suggesting other negotiable options. To avoid Russian occupation, France suggested that a Belgian gendarmerie supervise application of the reforms in Bulgaria. Other partners also obtained benefits because they managed to remove the Balkans from the exclusive influence of Russia, an influence henceforth contained in a collective system of guarantees and surveillance.

Despite backing down on its positions, Russia's negotiation with the Western countries was profitable: it won diplomatic neutrality[14] in its dispute with the Ottoman Empire, and kept its place in the Concert of Europe.

During the plenary assemblies, however, the negotiation concerned the positions of the parties rather than their interests. This is what led to the stalemate. Russia had already made concessions and did not want to make any more. Nor did the Ottomans, for the interference and reduced sovereignty imposed by the powers were even greater losses. Russia shifted from a cooperative approach to being competitive, which prevented the conference from achieving the desired result.

By supporting the idea of collective management of the Eastern Question, Russia gave the impression in Constantinople that it was negotiating its interests with the European powers and was being faithful to the spirit of the treaties and the Concert of Europe. But then its attitude changed:

> In the European assemblies, Russia listened wisely to arguments in favor of the balance of powers, but in practice it did not always comply with its maxims. Whereas the European nations had always supported that the fate of Turkey and the Balkans should be governed by the Concert of Europe, it invariably sought to resolve the issue unilaterally and by force.[15]

The failure of the negotiations with the Ottomans thus enabled it to return to the unilateral resolution it had aspired to and to which the Russo-Turkish war, declared on April 19, 1877, would lead.

---

14   In particular, it obtained Austria-Hungary's neutrality via the convention of January 15, 1877, in exchange for which Vienna would be able to occupy Bosnia-Herzegovina.
15   H. KISSINGER, *Diplomatie*, Paris, Fayard, 1996, pp. 155–156.

The Constantinople Conference was above all a theatrical illusion, with its individual and collective actors, meaningful backdrops, motives, and failure. Russia's outsized ambitions, which the European powers thought they had stifled in Constantinople, reappeared thanks to the Russo-Turkish war and the Treaty of San Stefano of March 15, 1878, and gave rise to new negotiations at the Congress of Berlin (June 13 to July 13, 1878).

REFERENCES

GEORGEON, François, *Abdulhamid II, le sultan Calife*, Paris, Fayard, 2003.

KAHNEMAN, Daniel and TVERSKY, Amos, "Subjective Probability: A Judgment of Representativeness", *Cognitive Psychology*, 1972, 3, 430–454.

KISSINGER, Henry, *Diplomatie*, Paris, Fayard, 1996.

MANTRAN, Robert, *Histoire d'Istanbul*, Paris, Fayard, 1996.

MANTRAN, Robert, *Histoire de l'Empire ottoman*, Paris, Fayard, 1989.

SOUTOU, Georges-Henri, *L'Europe de 1815 à nos jours*, Paris, Puf, 2nd ed., 2009.

YAVUZ, M. Hakan, *War and Diplomacy. The Russo-Turkish War of 1877–1878 and the Treaty of Berlin*, Salt Lake City, University of Utah Press, 2011.

YERASIMOS, Stefanos, *Visite privée. Istanbul*, Paris, Nouvelle édition du chêne, 1991, p. 94.

ZARTMAN, I. William (ed.), *International Multilateral Negotiations*, San Francisco CA, Jossey-Bass, 2010.

NO IMPUNITY FOR THE CRIMES IN DARFUR (2005)

Negotiations within the Security Council

Jean-Marc DE LA SABLIÈRE*

In the last decade of the 20th century our world, already scarred by the Holocaust and the tragedy of Cambodia, experienced two new monstrous tragedies: Rwanda and the "ethnic cleansing" in the former Yugoslavia. Fortunately, some States tried to respond. Efforts were made to get the United Nation's Security Council more closely involved in settling internal conflicts (which is in theory taboo) and in defending human rights.[1] In 2005 the international community even agreed that in the most egregious cases, it has a moral obligation to intervene, called "the responsibility to protect".[2] At the same time, progress was made on combating the impunity of the perpetrators of genocide, war crimes, and crimes against humanity. On July 1, 2002, the Rome Statute creating the International Criminal Court (ICC), ratified by 60 of its 120 signatories, entered into force.

---

*   Ambassador, former French permanent representative to the United Nations (New York).
[1]   Article 2(7) of the United Nations Charter prohibits the Security Council from intervening in matters that are within a State's national jurisdiction. This obstacle therefore had to be overcome.
[2]   See Articles 138 and 139 of the Final Document of the World Summit of September 2005.

All of this progress was erratic, however, with each step a hard-won battle against strong opposition.[3] For example, as soon as George W. Bush took office in 2001, his administration tried to sabotage the International Criminal Court. Through bilateral agreements, the United States prohibited numerous States Parties from ever transferring a US citizen to the court. In 2002 and 2003, it also obtained resolutions from the Security Council providing that for a one-year period, the ICC prosecutor could not investigate or launch a prosecution if, in the scope of an operation conducted or authorized by the UN, a case arose concerning the current or former officials or personnel of a contributing State that was not a party to the Rome Statute.[4]

It was in this context that the situation in Darfur arose. As the people of South Sudan were putting 20 years of war behind them through an agreement that provided for a referendum and the creation of a United Nations peacekeeping force, Darfuri movements in the western region of the country chose to press their claims by taking up arms. The reaction from Khartoum was horrific: sinister "Janjaweed" militias burned villages and engaged in mass killings and rape. Nearly 2 million people fled and ended up in displaced persons camps. Emotions ran high in Africa and even higher in the West. In September 2004 the Security Council, pressured by the Americans and Europeans to take action, asked Kofi Annan (the UN Secretary General at the time) to create an international commission of inquiry.[5]

The commission issued its report in January 2005. It not only characterized the violence committed in Darfur by the government and militias as crimes against humanity, and those committed by the rebels as war crimes, it also recommended that the Security Council refer the situation to the ICC – which the Security Council had the power to do even though Sudan was not (and still is not) a party to the Rome Statute. Thunder clap! What would the Security Council do? In other words, what would the position of the United States be, given that in September 2004, Secretary of State Colin Powell, following Congress, had spoken of genocide? A permanent member with a veto right, the United States could block everything. What would the Chinese do? China is also a permanent member, had opposed the Rome Statute, and enjoyed good relations with

---

3   On this issue, as well as on all of the negotiations concerning the Security Council decision to refer the Darfur situation to the International Criminal Court, see DE LA SABLIÈRE (2013, pp. 308–314).
4   See Resolutions 1422 (2002) and 1487 (2003).
5   See paragraph 12, Security Council Resolution 1564, adopted September 21, 2004.

the Sudanese government (dictated by oil). And what about the African States, which could influence other southern delegations and were careful about their positions because the conflict was taking place on their continent? The stakes were high for preventing new mass atrocities, and also for the future of the ICC. For nearly two years it had been restricted to secondary cases. Challenged by the High Commissioner for Human Rights Louise Arbour, who had come to New York to present the report, would the Council give the Court its chance by referring this major case to it, or would it show itself to be powerless, and thus toll the bell for the young Court? These questions provide some indication as to why the negotiations among the Council members were so important. France led the way, with help from the British.

1. CAREFULLY PREPARED, HIGH-PRESSURE NEGOTIATIONS

1.1. PREPARATIONS

French Mission to the United Nations meets in New York, draws up a road map, and gets the green light from the French government.

As soon as the report on Darfur was published, the French Mission in New York wondered whether it might actually be possible to have the situation referred to the ICC. To determine just how resistant to the idea the United States would be, the French ambassador questioned various Americans who were familiar with the issue and well-connected in Washington. The British were also approached, as the UK's active participation was essential. A permanent member of the Security Council and party to the Rome Statute, the UK is traditionally close to the Americans. Might it be ready for an adventure? The French and UK Missions came to the same conclusion: it was foreseeable that the United States would abstain if the resolution included a clause protecting US citizens from prosecution by the ICC for any acts committed in Sudan in the scope of a UN mission. While foreseeable, such abstention was not certain. The White House's opposition to the ICC was such as to create concern that Washington might wish not only to protect its citizens in the case of Sudan, where it was unlikely they ran the slightest risk, but also to weaken or even "kill" the ICC. All things considered, it was worth a try.

So the French Mission took a count. To be adopted by the 15-member Security Council, a resolution needs nine votes, with no opposition from a permanent member. While the relationship between the five permanent members is key, the composition of non-permanent members is also important. It changes every year according to elections,[6] and in early 2005 fate was with the pro-ICC camp: seven of the 10 non-permanent members (Argentina, Benin, Brazil, Denmark, Greece, Romania, and Tanzania) had ratified the treaty creating the ICC. That brought the number of Security Council members that were also parties to the Rome Statute to nine. Invited to a meeting by the French ambassador, all of these delegations ("the Nine") said that they were determined to support referral of the Darfur situation to the ICC. The Nine also indicated their willingness to stick together and talk frequently. The French Mission also had the support of the Philippines, which had already signed the Statute, and Japan, which intended to. It was betting that Algeria and China, which were sensitive to regional reactions, would remain neutral if the Africans held the line and that Russia, which had also signed the Rome Statute in 2000,[7] would be passive and in the end, depending on the circumstances, vacillate between abstention and a vote in favor. On this basis, the French government gave the ambassador the go-ahead.

1.2. A TWO-STAGE NEGOTIATION

After drawing the United States onto their turf, the States Parties to the Rome Statute obtain a hard-won agreement.

Before the ICC was created, the Security Council had established temporary international criminal tribunals and helped set up special courts on the basis of agreements with the United Nations.[8] In early 2005 the United States tried to return to this approach, but its attempts (as well as those by Algeria) to institute an alternative to the ICC were steadfastly resisted

---

6   Non-permanent members of the Security Council are elected by the General Assembly for a term of two years. They cannot be re-elected immediately. Every year, there is a partial renewal concerning the five seats occupied by the states whose terms have expired.

7   Russia signed the Rome Statute in 2000, but still had not ratified it in 2014.

8   The International Criminal Tribunals for the former Yugoslavia and Rwanda created by Security Council Resolutions 827 (1993) and 955 (1994) are subsidiary bodies of the Security Council, whereas the Special Tribunal for Sierra Leone is the result of an agreement between the United Nations and the government of Sierra Leone, promoted by Security Council Resolution 1315 (2000).

from the outset. In a show of unity, and with Louise Arbour's help, the Nine opposed the US alternative during a Council consultation session on February 16. The Department of State did not give up, however: it sent a mission to Africa to promote the idea of a mixed "UN-African Union" tribunal. But Benin and Tanzania, which were Security Council members, held firm. At the end of February things were going according to the French Mission's plan: the first battle (which would decide those to come) had been won, proving there was no alternative to the ICC.

The moment of truth had therefore arrived. Until then, the French and British had been distributing a preliminary draft resolution that was very informal, just a few paragraphs drafted in the form of a Council Decision, to refer the situation to the ICC prosecutor and obtain the cooperation of Sudan and other States. But nothing was circulated regarding the key paragraph on exempting nationals of countries that were not parties to the Rome Statute. The time had also come to decide on a schedule, i.e., the time when the text would be "officially" filed and submitted for a vote. The French Mission feared that the case would get bogged down in endless discussions, so the ambassador obtained agreement from Paris to try to connect this vote to the vote on sending forces to South Sudan, which was of major importance to Washington and was to take place in March. Since France had a majority, it hoped to control the procedure so that when the time came, it could speed up the final negotiations on the Darfur case.[9]

In early March, the French and British therefore proposed a paragraph to the Americans that was intended to neutralize them. As planned, the text referred only to the peacekeeping missions in Sudan, but the Americans rejected it out of hand. Realizing they were trapped, they intended to definitively resolve the issue of their relationship with the Court in the United Nations. They asked that their courts be given "exclusive jurisdiction" over their citizens for all current and future United Nations operations, regardless of the place of deployment. This was unacceptable, and the Americans were informed of that immediately. They refused to negotiate and wanted to force the issue. That's when the pressure started. Condoleezza Rice, who had recently been appointed US Secretary of State to replace Colin Powell, made phone calls to several foreign capitals. London started to vacillate. Paris held firm.

---

[9]   A permanent member's opposition cannot block adoption of a procedural decision that has obtained a majority of nine votes. The decision not to extend the veto right to procedural issues is the result of a compromise reached by the great powers before the San Francisco conference, at the meeting in Yalta among Roosevelt, Stalin, and Churchill in February 1945.

On Wednesday March 23, the US Mission tried to intimidate the other Council members in a consultation session by (i) announcing that it had filed a draft resolution creating the United Nations force in South Sudan in preparation for a vote the next day, and (ii) postponing the issue of the crimes committed in Darfur since there was no agreement. The French ambassador responded in the same session by announcing that he was officially filing the text on Darfur that was under discussion – which contained the Franco-British paragraph that the Americans had rejected – and stated that the vote on both texts should be held the same day.

The power struggle had begun. The French Mission did not believe the United States would veto the text, sensing the price would be too high for the Bush administration. How could it explain such extreme opposition when American citizens were protected? But France's inflexibility regarding procedure went too far for its partners. London insisted that it must be given time to negotiate with Washington. Others hesitated. Concerned with preserving the unity of the Nine and having received carte blanche from Paris regarding the procedure, the French ambassador agreed to separate votes on the two texts. However, he announced that the Security Council would decide on the draft related to Darfur within the next few days and set the date: Wednesday March 30.

On Monday March 28 the American steamroller started rolling. Washington asked for an extension: "the time needed to negotiate a counterproposal". Condoleezza Rice was insistent. The UK Foreign Secretary, Jack Straw, was willing to agree but his interlocutors in Paris (the minister of foreign affairs and the diplomatic advisor to President Chirac) referred the negotiations back to New York. On Tuesday Condoleezza Rice therefore asked the French ambassador, whom she knew well, to postpone the vote. He agreed, provided he received a "serious" counterproposal early the next morning. Wednesday March 30 was a tense day. The Americans started by announcing they would be a bit late; the French Mission agreed to postpone the vote for 24 hours, but given the American counterproposal, which had arrived in the late morning and was totally inadequate and even insulting to the ICC, it refused to negotiate, which Paris approved of. The French therefore decided to run the risk of voting the next day. Their determination worried their partners more and more, who feared that the Americans, pushed into a corner, would veto the text. Some wavered but continued to follow France, and firm resolve paid off in the end.

On March 31, the US Mission announced that Washington was giving up on its preferred goal, i.e. the general current and future exemption. In exchange, the text had to take note of (but not cite explicitly) the bilateral agreements concluded in the past by the United States and, in substance, provide for the "exclusive jurisdiction" of the US courts in any case concerning a US national involved in acts committed in connection with a peacekeeping operation in Sudan. While more presentable, this amendment still caused a problem because it encroached on the right of each State to prosecute the perpetrators of crimes committed against their citizens. But the Americans, who were engaging in a lot of diplomacy in foreign capitals, knew very well that most Security Council members would agree to a more limited request like this (which would become paragraph 6 of the resolution) because there is a precedent in a resolution related to Liberia.[10] They also knew that the French, who were less amenable than the English (who had abstained on the Liberian resolution), would no longer be able to carry their allies along with them. And that is exactly what happened. France's partners congratulated it, but declared themselves ready to agree to the compromise. For the French ambassador, the time had therefore come to wrap up the negotiations. He obtained the following instructions: he would vote in favor of the text but would make an explanation of the vote to specify that the immunity from jurisdiction that was provided for would, if applicable, be subject to interpretation by the French courts. The United Nations rules did not allow him to present a draft resolution on which his country would register a reservation, so he asked his English colleague to "carry" it to "get it across the finish line" without making any new concessions. This scenario played out and the two diplomats went together after the vote to present the results of these long negotiations to the press.

Adopted during the night on March 31 by 11 votes with four abstentions (EU, China, Algeria, and, oddly, Brazil[11]), Resolution 1593[12] was a great success for the Security Council, which is often accused of being passive.

---

[10] Security Council Resolution 1497 on the peacekeeping mission in Liberia, adopted August 1, 2003. France had abstained because of this paragraph and issued an explanation of vote.

[11] This surprising vote was motivated, in particular, by the concession made to the United States in paragraph 6, but many observers interpreted it as a sign of the Brazilian diplomats' very great caution: they were being careful not to displease the Arab countries while Brasilia was campaigning for a seat as a permanent Security Council member.

[12] "The Security Council ... 1. Decides to refer the situation in Darfur since 1 July 2002 to the Prosecutor of the International Criminal Court; 2. Decides that the Government of Sudan and all other parties to the conflict in Darfur, shall cooperate fully with and provide any necessary assistance to the Court and the Prosecutor ...; 6. Decides that nationals, current or former officials or personnel from a contributing State outside Sudan which is not a party to the Rome Statute of the International Criminal Court shall be subject to the exclusive jurisdiction of that contributing State for all alleged

At the time, it was considered to be a sign of major progress for the ICC. Alas, subsequent developments would not be equal to the hopes raised by Resolution 1593. The Security Council is a political body that acts on a case-by-case basis, without much concern for consistency. Divided and having to manage two difficult operations in the region with little support from Africa, which had become hostile to the ICC,[13] it did not continue to support the Court in the future. The arrest warrants issued for the parties responsible for crimes in Darfur, first among them President Omar al-Bashir, have therefore still not been executed.

2. HIGHLY DIVERSE FACTORS CONTRIBUTED TO THE NEGOTIATIONS' SUCCESS

In early 2005, the Bush administration's hostility to the ICC was such that many observers in New York doubted that the Security Council would follow the commission of inquiry's recommendations. They were therefore surprised by the results. Several factors explain this success:

- *The period was favorable to Security Council progress on human rights.*[14] The Americans did not find significant support, while China and Russia kept a low profile during negotiations.

---

acts or omissions arising out of or related to operations in Sudan established or authorized by the Council or the African Union, unless such exclusive jurisdiction has been expressly waived by that contributing State. See the text of the Resolution in the Annex to this chapter.

13 Little by little the African countries have distanced themselves from the ICC, and have been openly critical of it in recent years. Given the number of investigations the prosecutor has opened on the continent and the number of prosecutions of African heads of State, Africa believes it has been targeted by the court (see the conclusions of the African Union Summit of October 12, 2013).

14 During this period, the Security Council's progress in the area of human rights includes more than the creation of the international criminal tribunals for Rwanda and the former Yugoslavia and the referral of the situation in Darfur to the ICC. In 1991 it passed Resolution 688 concerning the Kurds, in which it found that mass repression could constitute a violation of international peace and security. Between 2005 and 2009 it made progress on protecting children and civilians in armed conflicts, including taking the "responsibility to protect" into account in its Resolution 1674 (2006) on the protection of civilians. A few years later, the period was much less favorable, marked in particular by three Russian and Chinese vetoes concerning the situation in Syria in 2011 and 2012. (On such progress and its limits, see DE LA SABLIÈRE (2013), at pp. 57–66, 299–307, and 318–322.)

- *The pre-negotiation analysis was accurate.* Not only did all of the French Mission's analyses prove to be absolutely correct, including with regard to the Chinese and Russian votes, but the Mission's assessment of the political situation was correct. It understood from the outset that the emotion created by the crimes in Darfur "changed things" in a way that made it possible to create a dilemma for the Bush administration: either "swallow" its hostility to the ICC but protect American interests, or assume the heavy burden of responsibility for blocking the Council's action to combat impunity – and open itself up to harsh criticism from its own people, since it had already characterized the crimes in Darfur as genocide.

- *A decision was made very early to base the negotiation strategy on the Mission's analysis.* The negotiators thus had a genuine roadmap and knew where they were headed, keeping the ball in their court and never losing control over the procedure.

- *The choice of a sequential approach, as is often the case in multilateral diplomacy, also proved to be a wise one.* It allowed for establishing a clear position for discussions from the very beginning: referral to the ICC was the only possible outcome. Once this obvious fact was pointed out, the Americans were trapped and had to negotiate on terrain that they had vainly tried to steer clear of.

- *The willingness of the nine delegations from States parties to the Rome Statute to remain unified behind a "lead" country was also a major condition of success.* Preserving unity was of constant concern and a daily task for the French ambassador and his staff. The nine countries met at the French Mission very frequently, and appropriated the operation for themselves. While the group's unity naturally broke down to some extent at the end, it was strong enough to isolate the Americans. Several of the Nine watched the British position, reassured by the thought that the English would not be able to openly oppose Washington. Other delegations, both among the Nine and not, kept their eyes on Benin and Tanzania, which had worked closely with the French Mission. These two delegations' efforts to defend the ICC prevented the alternative desired by the United States, i.e. an "African Union-UN" tribunal, from becoming a reality.

- *Determination in the face of the superpower's counterattack was especially effective because it stemmed from a desire to achieve a reasonable objective.* Concerned with improving relations between the ICC and the United States, the resolution's co-authors stressed to the media after the vote that there were no "winners" or "losers": it was an honorable compromise.

- *Another factor that warrants mention is the freedom the French negotiator was given with regard to tactics.* Authorized to officially file a text in the name of France alone if circumstances so required, the French representative was able to react immediately to the US attempt to separate the votes on South Sudan and Darfur. If France had not moved until after obtaining its partners' consent, it would have run the risk of a stalemate.

– *As is often the case, the relationship between the people involved played a role.* The good relationship between the permanent French and British representatives, who at the time were also engaged in a number of cases related to human rights, allowed them to find an elegant solution in the final stretch and wrap the case up by passing the "baton" to the UK when France was no longer able to "carry" the operation "across the finish line".

REFERENCES

La Sablière (de), Jean-Marc, *Dans les coulisses du monde*, Paris, Robert Laffont, 2013, pp. 308–314.

La Sablière (de), Jean-Marc, *Le Conseil de sécurité des Nations-Unis: ambitions et limites*, Brussels, Larcier, 2015, new print in 2018.

ANNEX

United Nations   S/RES/1593 (2005)

 Security Council   Distr.: General
                                                                 31 March 2005

Resolution 1593 (2005)

Adopted by the Security Council at its 5158th meeting, on 31 March 2005

The Security Council,

Taking note of the report of the International Commission of Inquiry on violations of international humanitarian law and human rights law in Darfur (S/2005/60),

Recalling article 16 of the Rome Statute under which no investigation or prosecution may be commenced or proceeded with by the International

Criminal Court for a period of 12 months after a Security Council request to that effect,

Also recalling articles 75 and 79 of the Rome Statute and encouraging States to contribute to the ICC Trust Fund for Victims,

Taking note of the existence of agreements referred to in Article 98-2 of the Rome Statute,

Determining that the situation in Sudan continues to constitute a threat to international peace and security,

Acting under Chapter VII of the Charter of the United Nations,

1.   *Decides* to refer the situation in Darfur since 1 July 2002 to the Prosecutor of the International Criminal Court;

2.   *Decides* that the Government of Sudan and all other parties to the conflict in Darfur, shall cooperate fully with and provide any necessary assistance to the Court and the Prosecutor pursuant to this resolution and, while recognizing that States not party to the Rome Statute have no obligation under the Statute, urges all States and concerned regional and other international organizations to cooperate fully;

3.   *Invites* the Court and the African Union to discuss practical arrangements that will facilitate the work of the Prosecutor and of the Court, including the possibility of conducting proceedings in the region, which would contribute to regional efforts in the fight against impunity;

4.   *Also encourages* the Court, as appropriate and in accordance with the Rome Statute, to support international cooperation with domestic efforts to promote the rule of law, protect human rights and combat impunity in Darfur;

5.   *Also emphasizes* the need to promote healing and reconciliation and encourages in this respect the creation of institutions, involving all sectors of Sudanese society, such as truth and/or reconciliation commissions, in order to complement judicial processes and thereby reinforce the efforts to restore long-lasting peace, with African Union and international support as necessary;

6.   *Decides* that nationals, current or former officials or personnel from a contributing State outside Sudan which is not a party to the Rome Statute of the International Criminal Court shall be subject to the exclusive jurisdiction of that contributing State for all alleged acts or omissions arising out of or related to operations in Sudan established or authorized by the Council or the African Union, unless such exclusive jurisdiction has been expressly waived by that contributing State;

7. *Recognizes* that none of the expenses incurred in connection with the referral including expenses related to investigations or prosecutions in connection with that referral, shall be borne by the United Nations and that such costs shall be borne by the parties to the Rome Statute and those States that wish to contribute voluntarily;

8. *Invites* the Prosecutor to address the Council within three months of the date of adoption of this resolution and every six months thereafter on actions taken pursuant to this resolution;

9. *Decides* to remain seized of the matter.

NEGOTIATING THE AMERICAN CONSTITUTION (1787–1789)

Coalitions, Process Rules, and Compromises

Carrie MENKEL-MEADOW[*]

No one really knows
How the game is played
The art of the trade
How the sausage is made

No one really knows
How the parties get to yess
The pieces that are sacrificed in
Every game of chessss

I want to be in that room
The room where it happens, in that big 'ol room ...
The art of compromise
Hold your nose and close your eyes.
We want our leaders to save the day –
But we don't get a say in what they trade away.

Lin-Manuel Miranda, *"The Room Where It Happens"*[1]

---

[*]   University of California, Irvine.
[1]   Lyrics of the Broadway show by Lin-Manuel Miranda and Jeremy McCarter, "The Room Where it Happens", *Hamilton: The Revolution: Being the Complete*

1. FRAMING A MORE PERFECT UNION: THE NEED FOR NEGOTIATION

In 1787, a mere four years after the close of the American Revolution, it looked as if the young nation, the American Confederation, might fail. Thirteen former colonies of England had fought one of the first successful wars to throw off a colonial power with claims of "no taxation without representation" and a mixture of economic and political grievances, famously outlined in Thomas Jefferson's *Declaration of Independence (1776)*. But 10 years after that Declaration, the substantial debt of the new nation (to its revolutionary soldiers, to France, to England for pre-revolutionary debts owed, and to others, including private citizens who helped fund the Continental army (Ellis, 2016), and regional differences about how to deal with new nationhood, threatened the very existence of colonies united weakly by the Articles of Confederation, a loose form of government granting most of the power to the 13 constituent states. Rumors circulated of possible reunification with England, secession of some of the new states pursuing different paths to economic development, and local violent protests and rebellions. When the Shays Rebellion (Massachusetts, 1786) erupted over taxation to pay the revolutionary debt, with violent attacks on government properties, it appeared that crisis was imminent (Klarman, 2016). After many negotiations to amend the Articles failed (a set of negotiations not covered in this chapter), since amendment required unanimity of all the states, proposals to re-negotiate the basic governmental structure prevailed, and a constitutional convention was called in 1787 in Philadelphia by the then existing Congress of the Confederation and with the approval of state legislatures, with delegates chosen by the 13 states in different ways.

The desire for a Constitutional Convention was actually the brainchild of a few brilliant and early "founding fathers": James Madison, Alexander Hamilton, John Jay, and eventually also George Washington, Thomas Jefferson (who was not present at the Convention because he was then ambassador to France, negotiating the revolutionary debt), and Benjamin Franklin, who sought a more "national" and less "federal" (states power) nation (Ellis, 2000, 2016). While admitting that the Articles of Confederation were not working, Washington recognized the important negotiation concept of "ripeness". In March of 1786 Washington wrote to his French friend and American patriot Lafayette and said, "matters are

---

Libretto of the Broadway Musical, with a True Account of Its Creation (New York: Grand Central Publishing and Melcher Media, 2016) at pp. 186–190.

not sufficiently ripe" for a complete governmental overhaul. He knew that there would likely have to be more generally felt "hurt" and harm to motivate the state delegates to come, as citizen apathy was so great that many of the early Confederation Congresses did not even reach a quorum of attendance.

The negotiations in Philadelphia in 1787 that forged the American Constitution, so far the most robust and long lasting constitutive written document of a nation state (Elster, 1995) almost failed many times, suffering from regional, economic, political, and moral (over slavery) differences. That the negotiations succeeded at all is a testament to the power of the process knowledge and political acuity (or manipulation) of Madison, Washington, and Franklin, as, in different ways, they managed a complex, interest-based multi-party, multi-issue negotiation (Lansky, 2000).

2. COMPETING INTERESTS IN PHILADELPHIA

Whatever united the colonies (distaste for taxation and despotic control from far away) enough to mount an army to defeat the English, that false unity soon collapsed in a series of conflicting economic, geographic, demographic, and political interests. Since many of the colonies were formed in reaction to developments in the home country (religious freedom for the Puritans and other religious groups, agricultural and farming policy, exportation of prisoners (the state of Georgia)), each one could be said to have developed its own political, social, and economic culture. Differences in the treatment of slavery, class interests (planter-owners of tobacco and cotton plantations in the south, shipping and merchant interests in the cities of the north), competition over ports and land and need to hold various tribes of Indians at bay outlined the diverging interests in Philadelphia.

There was, in addition, competition over who would control the new western land all the way to the Mississippi River. At the Treaty of Paris (1783) which ended the Revolutionary War, John Jay had skillfully separated the English, French, and Spanish; the Americans controlled a large domain of new territory west of many of the colonies, among which disputes were beginning.

The founding fathers of the United States were constituted by a well-educated class of lawyers (e.g. John Adams, Alexander Hamilton, Thomas Jefferson) or political theorists (James Madison), merchants and others, who hailed from either the more prosperous northern cities of New York (John Jay), Philadelphia (Robert Morris), and Boston, or the prosperous lands of Virginia (Washington, Jefferson, and Madison). Another set of prosperous planters from South Carolina (Charles Pinckney) and some agriculturalists and merchants from Pennsylvania (James Wilson) challenged the more elite framers on issues such as debt relief, import-export taxation, slavery, and the likely move from state to more federal/national power, such as in Hamilton's planned national central bank (Chernow, 2004).

While some reformers wanted piecemeal changes in the powers of the Confederation Congress, notably adding to them the power it lacked to levy tax and conduct foreign policy authority, the ultimately successful "framers" were much more interested in making a whole new compact with enhanced national unity and power. Unfortunately, the sectional interests and great differences among and between the states made negotiation over the content of the new Constitution a tug of multiple competing interests and issues.

The Constitutional Convention convened in Philadelphia in the hot summer months of May 25 to September 17, 1787 with uncertain legitimacy and authorization. Though the mandate from the Continental Congress and state selected delegates was to reform some elements of the Articles of Confederation, the leadership of the Convention eventually determined to make a total break with the Articles, wrote a new Constitution, and then created new rules for state ratification and approval. All of this was accomplished because of a skillful process management, marrying deep commitments to republican political theory to substantive compromises of cross-sectional and multiple interests. This included, unfortunately, as we see it now, the "compromise" of slavery, which 70 years later, necessitated a civil war to consolidate the achievements of the original framers.

This masterful (if very messy) negotiation is now labeled by at least one constitutional historian as the "framer's coup" – the negotiation of a new federal government with some strong central governmental powers, albeit limited by both separation of powers and federalism (Klarman, 2016). It is ironic that most of the citizens actually would have preferred to stick with the dysfunctional and weak government of the Confederation. The Constitution was finally ratified in 1789, though continued divisions about its meanings continue to the present day (Rakove, 1996).

3. ON THE IMPORTANCE OF PROCESS RULES: GROUND RULES AND DECISION RULES

With 55 different delegates, representing 13 different states, and ultimately factions that sometimes crossed state lines and made regional or economic coalitions, it was essential to structure what we would now call *process rules* – both rules for speaking (*ground rules*) and *rules for decision* (majority, super-majority or unanimity). Scholarly commentators on constitutional processes, mostly relying on the copious notes taken by James Madison (*Notes of the Debates in the Federal Convention of 1787*), have noted significant differences in what I call "*micro*" *process rules* (speaking rules, decision rules) and "*macro*" *process rules*.

The American Constitutional Convention owes its ultimate success in completing a document to the leadership of George Washington who presided over the meetings, James Madison who set the agenda and served as scribe and secretary, and Benjamin Franklin, who served as a sort of "*process facilitator*", commenting on process, and making suggestions in order to move the project of contentious discussion along.[2] There are many lessons provided by the processes used, which can now be contrasted to processes used in other constitutional negotiations (e.g. France, South Africa) as political theory intersects with the pragmatics of conflict resolution theory and practice.

Notably, those who first arrived in May 1787 (about 30 delegates) spent the first two and a half days negotiating their process and rules for speaking and deliberation. They began by making *role and committee assignments*, what we would now call *task groups* in complex negotiations, that eventually led to specialized committees working on particular topics for negotiation and later drafting. The delegates then explicitly discussed *procedural rules* (most were experienced politicians) and voted on those rules, all before they turned to the substantive debates and discussions that constituted the bulk of the four months of deliberations. Among the key process rules adopted were:

1. *Process leadership.* The first decision of the Constitutional Convention was to select George Washington (a reluctant attendee from his retirement as Commander in Chief) to preside (he was called President) over the deliberations. Washington's stature and ability to stay neutral and use his military sense of order (he spoke only once substantively at the Convention) produced a deliberative and calmer process than might have occurred without him. Though we know his actual preference for a strong national government to be developed,

---

[2]   Famously, at one contentious moment Franklin (probably an agnostic) suggested that each session begin with a prayer to God to invoke spiritual guidance in times of contest, see Ellis (2016, pp. 147–148).

he managed to exercise control primarily over process and left the "dealing" on substantive issues to his friends (Madison, Hamilton, and others). Comments at the Convention were to be addressed to him, he had authority to rule on procedural issues or conflicts between delegates, and sessions began and ended with his arrival and departure. In addition to those formal rules, of course, there was enormous respect and deference accorded to the man who had won the revolutionary war.

At a more informal level, Benjamin Franklin was an expert in diplomatic and human communications and served as a sort of *"process troubleshooter"* (Lansky, 2000), working to smooth out, both in sessions and out of session, conflicts and personal affronts between the delegates. As a seasoned diplomat by the time of the Constitutional Convention, Franklin knew how to manage and charm people. Even when people did not agree with him substantively, he was greatly respected as a scientist and learned man. As a scientist, Franklin tried to introduce a tone of study, curiosity, and inquiry – what we would now label a search for underlying interests and facts. He tried to move the delegates away from bombastic positional debate. Unlike Washington, he did offer substantive solutions, including offering ideas for totally new institutions.[3]

A third process function was performed by James Madison, *agenda manager, scribe, recorder and secretary.* Several participants at the Convention came with fully developed plans for the new Constitution (the "Virginia" plan, which was essentially Madison's plan; the "New Jersey" plan; and Alexander Hamilton's strong central authority plan).[4] The substantive negotiations mostly turned on which elements of these plans would make it into the final draft, eventually a compromise of many issues worked out by a Committee of Detail (see below). Having prepared well on the substantive issues *before* the Convention, Madison was able to keep his "eyes on his goals" and "control" the keeping of minutes and issues, and was eventually successful on some, though not all, of the ultimate treatment of issues he cared about.

---

[3]   Franklin tried to get slavery abolished at the Convention but saw it would not succeed. He put preservation of the United States as a nation above resolving this deeply troubling moral issue.

[4]   These competing plans were fully developed "packages" describing branches of government, voting, and representation rules. Ultimately, the design of the new government was assigned to special committees and then debated and discussed item by item in plenary session.

2. A rule of *confidentiality*. No public disclosure of the deliberations, thought to encourage honest and free debate, and prevent "erroneous and mischievous reports" (Letter from James Madison to James Monroe, see Lansky, 2000 and Klarman, 2016). This can be contrasted to the French constitutional process in 1789 (see Elster, 1995) where negotiations were held in public, in plenary/"committee of the whole" sessions, which encouraged daily and raucous public conflict. This is also in contradiction to current demands for transparency and publicity in many public negotiations.[5] *Secrecy* was considered an important aid to creative thinking, enabling the ability to trade and link issues, and departures from delegate committed-to positions, thus permitting the kind of flexibility, contingency, and trading that characterizes complex multi-party, multi-issue negotiation.

3. *Speaking rules* allowed a single speaker to speak no more than twice on a single issue and not for the second time until everyone else who wanted a say had had their chance.

4. *Attendance rules* required that for the full House to consider a matter only formally granted leaves would be tolerated. When the required attendance in a full session was not achieved, work continued in committee or task groups.

5. *Committees and task groups*. Unlike other constitutive processes which have been conducted totally in plenary session (which would have been possible with only 55 delegates) the American Constitutional Convention proceeded by committee on some issues, with representatives elected to committees to deal with difficult issues (such as representation) which allowed smaller groups to develop compromises which could then be presented to the Assembly of the Whole. This proved efficient, and allowed those who were committed and hard working to develop joint arguments across factional and regional interests to be presented to the whole group. In the end a Committee of Detail wrote most of the final text, which was then

---

[5] It should be noted that the Constitutional debates took place before the writing of the First Amendment guaranteeing freedom of speech and press, and so one might wonder if the Constitutional process would meet the process expectations of its own design for later legislative enactments and political deliberations. During the Convention, James Wilson of Pennsylvania argued against secrecy, saying the "people have the right to know what their Agents are doing". Benjamin Franklin was successful in persuading the delegates, at the end of the Convention, to keep all the deliberations confidential, as he feared public disclosure of the conflicts within would doom the ratification process.

corrected by the Committee on Style. Committees were formally agreed to and voted on.

Less formal were the "outside of the room where it happens" meetings that occurred over meals, drinks, and social occasions – some orchestrated by charming diplomats like Franklin, and others more contentious *caucuses* or *coalitions*. Outside meetings can be both helpful and dangerous as side deals are made and firm commitments are made to stay within the coalition. At the American Constitutional Convention both things happened, but outside meetings allowed someone like Alexander Hamilton, who was well prepared and articulate, to have more suasion in small groups than he was able to muster within his own New York delegation, which did not share his nationalist views.

6. *Votes were not attributable to particular delegates by name* (now called the "Chatham House rules"), so that personal affiliations or attributions would not be made public, thereby allowing some flexibility and the ability to change minds and votes.

7. *Vote revision* rules included that even if a matter passed by majority vote there could be a vote for reconsideration (after proper notice), allowing what we would now call both *contingent voting and agreement*, which in turn permits *linkage and trades* – altered votes on some issues after others are decided. Postponement of votes and issues was also permitted, also to permit some trading, linkage, and revision as the relation of one issue (e.g. representation in the House) to another (e.g. representation in the less democratic Senate) became evident. Madison explicitly saw that issues were likely to be linked and he rejected proposals that each issue that was addressed should be treated separately. He knew that ratification would depend on states getting *"packages"* or combinations of issues and terms they could live with, and so it was the "whole" (not the parts) that would matter in the end.

8. *Voting and decision rules.* Like so many multi-party negotiations, the Constitutional Convention more or less automatically assumed that *majority rule* would control most decisions. In the end 39 of the 55 (and 11 out of 13 states[6]) signed the final draft, which was then sent to the states for ratification. Art. VII required nine states for ratification, itself a change in the amendment rules of the Confederation, which had required unanimity. The ratification debates and negotiations (see Maier, 2010) were hotly contested and resulted in the drafting by the

---

6   The state of Rhode Island sent no delegates to the Convention.

first US Congress (James Madison, actually) of the Bill of Rights, the first 10 amendments to the Constitution, granting a series of individual rights (now called human or civil rights) and further limitations on national power with "reserved powers" for the states (Art. 10).

4. NEGOTIATING MULTI-PARTY AND MULTI-ISSUE COMPROMISES

Full discussion of all the substantive issues negotiated in Philadelphia are beyond the scope of this chapter, but a brief discussion of a few demonstrates how cross-cutting coalitions, trades, and compromises allowed a highly conflictual and diverse set of interests to be joined together to create a governmental structure, that although flawed, has operated for over 200 years.

4.1. THE MAIN ISSUES

The main issues which divided the delegates were:

1. The extent to which the new Constitution would create a *national, centralized government*, rather than a *loose Confederation*. This had to do with authority to tax, the conduct of foreign policy, commerce, boundaries and whatever other powers the nationalists could successfully claim (the "nationalists" vs. "the confederationists"). Despite many simplistic historical accounts that this was a North (nationalist) vs. South (confederationists, and pro-slavery) divide on issues, the fact is that several of the major architects of the nationalist plan were distinguished Southerners (and slave-holders), such as George Washington and James Madison (of Virginia). This allowed the strange "bedfellows" of later different political stripes (Hamilton, Jay, and Madison[7]) to join together in a coalition that was not based on sectional or even on economic interests.

---

[7]   These were the authors of the *Federalist Papers*, a series of essays appearing in the American press during the contests over the ratification process and now considered a classic of political theory and pragmatism. Madison would later in life join Thomas Jefferson in founding the Democratic-Republican political party, which challenged the Federalist Party, ironic as Madison had famously warned against the dangers of factionalism in *Federalist Paper # 10* (*The Federalist Papers*, Clinton Rossiter, ed., 1961).

2. Closely related to this issue was the question of *executive power*.
    Madison and Hamilton wanted a strong executive – however, most of
    the rest of the delegates and the people did not, remembering all too
    well their dissatisfaction with the monarchy of King George III. This
    topic occupied much of the plenary debate time at the Convention,
    with alternative proposals for a troika executive (representing the
    northern, middle, and southern states), a strong life-long executive,
    and an executive chosen by the Congress, not the people directly.[8]
    There were also debates about the length of term, bargained over
    with great energy, and resulting in a four-year term, which was
    not limited to two terms until the middle of the 20th century, by
    Constitutional amendment, after Franklin Roosevelt had been elected
    four consecutive times.

3. *The structure of the legislature.* During the Revolution the colonies
    (now states) had drafted their own Constitutions, and most had
    chosen bi-cameral legislatures allocating election and jurisdictional
    rules slightly differently. Though many of the founding fathers were
    actually afraid of totally direct democracy (and so voting rules included
    property requirements, etc. until much later), they were divided on
    whether there should be democracy by proportional representation
    (by number of inhabitants in a district) for both bodies or not. The
    "Connecticut compromise" (much opposed by James Madison)
    eventually had it that the House was to be elected proportionately
    (for two-year terms) and the Senate, with two senators from each
    State, no matter its size, elected indirectly (for six-year terms). This
    rule overrepresents the least populous states and underrepresents
    the most populous states, permitting "state" factions to continue to
    challenge the national government, a structure which has survived
    to this day. The US Constitution was totally silent (and still is) on the
    existence of and the role of political parties, despite clearly demarked
    interest groups at the Convention.

4. *The issue of slavery* clearly divided the delegates but was dealt with
    mostly obliquely under the rubric of the counting of "inhabitants" for
    representational purposes. The infamous "three-fifths" compromise
    allowed the southern states to count their slaves as three-fifths of
    a person for allocation of representatives, even though slaves, later

---

8   The compromise on the selection process of the executive has left the United States
    with the arcane and hard to explain Electoral College, which (as happened notably in
    2016) permits the selection of a President by state electors that may differ from the
    nationwide popular vote.

freed during the Civil War, could not vote until the 1860s. Ironically, as many commentators have noted, this compromise, which was seen as morally repugnant at the time (by some), but necessary to preserve the union, worked precisely because of what turned out to be false assumptions argued by Madison. The North was, at the time of the Convention, more populous and therefore delegates recognized they would have more "control" of the House in early years, but the South believed it had the future on its side, with greater population growth (later muted by the move west and creation of more states). Coalition negotiation depends on both accurate knowledge of present facts, and assessments (often hard to make) about the future consequences of "deals" made.

4.2. WAS THE WHOLE NEGOTIATING PROCESS LEGITIMATE?

The negotiating delegates to the Convention were charged to reform the Articles of Confederation, which required a unanimous vote of states to be amended. Perhaps the factor most responsible for the "miracle" in Philadelphia (Bowen, 1966) was that the particular people most opposed to the Constitutional process did not turn up as delegates. So historians for over 150 years have noted that a very well educated and elite group, who, for the most part,[9] supported a full revision and new constitutive order were able to do their work, in secret, but with free and open deliberations with each other. Thus, the highly robust (long-lasting, with one civil war and 27 duly enacted amendments) Constitution was not really representative of the people and certainly was not transparently enacted. In the end, legitimacy came from the highly contested state delegations which for the next two years (1787–1789) hotly debated the Constitution with and before "the people". After nine states ratified (not so obvious until it actually happened in 1789), the United States Constitution became the "law of the land". The first Congress' debates and enactment of the Bill of Rights continued those conflictual negotiations but ultimately legitimated the whole constitutional project.

---

9   Only three distinguished and heavily participatory delegates did not sign the Constitution: Edmund Randolph and George Mason of Virginia (later responsible for much of the Bill of Rights), and Elbridge Gerry of Massachusetts.

As the Broadway show *Hamilton!* and the more scholarly *Framers' Coup* have now demonstrated to many, the drafting of the US Constitution was successful because of many unsavory side and secret "deals" and "compromises" made "in the room where it happens", as skillful diplomats, lawyers, military officers, and patriots negotiated confidentially – trading interests[10] and making compromises.[11] This resulted in a constitutive document that both separates power into three branches of government horizontally and provides for a vertical source of governmental actions and contests (federalism), with these elements being thought to keep modern democracy always "negotiable".[12]

REFERENCES

ACKERMAN, Bruce, *We the People: Foundations* (Cambridge: Harvard Press, 1993).

BOWEN, Catherine Drinker, *Miracle in Philadelphia* (Boston: Back Bay Books, 1966).

CHERNOW, Ron, *Alexander Hamilton* (New York: Penguin Press, 2004).

ELLIS, Joseph J., *Founding Brothers: The Revolutionary Generation* (New York: Alfred Knopf, 2000).

ELLIS, Joseph J., *The Quartet: Orchestrating the Second American Revolution, 1783–1789* (New York: Vintage Books, 2016).

ELSTER, Jon, "Strategic Uses of Argument" in Kenneth J. Arrow, Robert H. Mnookin, Lee Ross, Amos Tversky, and Robert Wilson (eds.) *Barriers to Conflict Resolution* (New York: W.W. Norton, 1995).

---

10   The further importation of slaves was only prohibited in 1808 in the Constitution – so allowed to continue for 20 years after the Constitution was drafted. For many, the treatment of slavery in the Constitution has been a "fatal" flaw; for others the Constitution's ability to change in "constitutional moments" by amendment or judicial interpretation, given the doctrine of judicial review (Ackerman, 1993), and to incorporate compromises of diametrically opposed interest groups, is precisely what has made it so robust. Some Constitutional scholars urge that the "shame" of both this process and substance (slavery) should cause us to question the American "fidelity" to the Constitution, and to seek new revisions where appropriate. Thomas Jefferson himself argued that the Constitution should be revisited and perhaps revised in every new generation, as "new discoveries are made, new truths discovered, institutions must advance also and keep pace with the times", Letter to Samuel Kercheval, July 12, 1816, see *The Portable Thomas Jefferson* (Merrill Peterson, ed., 1975, pp. 558–559); Ellis, 2016, p. 203.

11   Elsewhere, I have argued that compromise is not without its own principled justifications (Menkel-Meadow, 2011).

12   Or, as historian Joseph Ellis has said, "The Constitution was intended less to resolve arguments than to make argument itself the solution" (Ellis, 2016, p. 172).

KLARMAN, Michael J., *The Framers' Coup: The Making of the United States Constitution* (Oxford University Press, 2016).

LANSKY, Dana, "Proceeding to a Constitution: A Multi-Party Negotiation Analysis of the Constitutional Convention of 1789", 5 *Harvard Negotiation Law Review* 279 (2000).

MADISON, James, *Notes of the Debates in the Federal Convention of 1787*.

MAIER, Pauline, *Ratification: The People Debate the Constitution, 1787–1788* (New York: Simon & Schuster, 2010).

MENKEL-MEADOW, Carrie, "The Variable Morality of Constitutional (and other) Compromises", 38 *Pepperdine L. Rev.* 903–914 (2011).

PETERSON, Merrill, ed., *The Portable Thomas Jefferson* (New York: Viking Press, 1975).

RAKOVE, Jack N., *Original Meanings: Politics and Ideas in the Making of the Constitution* (New York: Vintage Press, 1996).

ROSSITER, Clinton, ed., *The Federalist Papers* (New York: Penguin, 1961).

THE VIENNA CONGRESS (1814–1815)

A Security Council "Avant La Lettre"

Paul Willem MEERTS*

The 19th century witnessed a multitude of inter-state negotiation processes and this chapter will analyze one of the most outstanding: the Vienna Congress of 1814–1815. All of the concerned parties were invited to the congress, whether they were the former victims or the former allies of Napoleon. In that sense "Vienna" did better than "Paris" in 1991 when the Germans and the Russians were excluded from the negotiation process. There were two reasons for inviting all of the relevant countries – irrespective of size or importance – to participate: first, for a legitimate conference and therefore a legitimate Final Act, all stakeholders had to be present; and, second, if one country could be left out, why not another? Nevertheless, the negotiation process was run by only five out of about 200 stakeholders: Russia, Austria, Prussia, Britain, and France. This balance between exclusion and inclusion helped enormously to negotiate a quite effective charter that would be the framework for a relative peaceful 19th century. Such an equilibrium is mirrored in the construction of the

---

* Deputy General-Director (ret.) of the Netherlands Institute of International Relations "Clingendael". pmeerts@clingendael.org.

United Nations in our time. A Security Council of 15 members giving direction to a General Assembly of nearly 200 states, while within the Security Council five permanent members call the shots.

1. FROM WAR TO WORDS

How shall we structure post-Napoleonic Europe? This was the central question that gave rise to the Congress of Vienna in 1814–1815. An exhausted Europe needed a new order. Time was ripe for resolution (Zartman, 2001, p. 4). What should the new order be and what should it be about? Or better still, to what extent will we restore the pre-revolutionary Europe, and how are we going to do this? After the defeat of Napoleon at Leipzig, his opponents decided that the war was over and peace had to be secured through a process of diplomatic negotiation, involving all actors under the guidance of the most powerful ones.

On March 9, 1814 the allies signed the Treaty of Chaumont, which was published on March 31 when the allies entered and occupied Paris. In this treaty, the allies labelled themselves the "Grand Alliance" (also named the "Quadruple Alliance"); the nucleus of the "Holy Alliance" was proposed by Tsar Alexander one year later and signed by most continental powers, surviving for another 20 years. Chaumont was the first treaty in history that ruled that the parties had to act in the interest of peace in general. On May 30, 1814, the first Peace of Paris came into being. In June 1814, the allies decided that with regard to the unresolved territorial questions, no military action should be taken. It is interesting to note here that, with the sidelining of Napoleon, there was a growing risk of an inter-allied war. This risk only disappeared when Napoleon escaped from Elba in 1815, an event that finally pushed the allies to finalize their proceedings in view of a common enemy. Napoleon's return would then be the stalemate breaker, creating the ripeness that was needed to strike a deal.

From July until September 1814, the heads of state, ministers and ambassadors trickled into Vienna, and on November 1, 1814 the Congress of Vienna started, although the British had proposed August 15 and the Russian Tsar had opted for October 1. The Congress of Vienna was about to begin: "the last, and temporarily successful attempt at [the] preservation [of the Ancien Régime]" (Hroch, 1993, p. 43). Although the road to Vienna was long, most delegates were not prepared for it. Only one of the negotiators in the inner circle was a head of state: the Russian Tsar. He could act without any mandate and without taking into consideration the wishes of his populace. The other four were agents, representing their governments and – as far as the British were concerned – their parliament. They were diplomats/politicians who, de jure, had to take their constituency into account. Nevertheless, these constituencies did not go beyond their head of state and the circles around them. De facto, the Austrian, Prussian, British, and French representatives had a lot of room for maneuver.

2. THE BIG FIVE

The Russians were personified by Tsar Alexander I, an autocratic, imperious, generous, bullying, and spiritual ruler, who thought of himself as an enlightened man whose destiny it was to bring prosperity and stability to Europe. As years went by, Alexander I became more spiritual, influenced by Baroness Julie von Krüdener, and this made him even more inaccessible to his colleague negotiators than before. He saw himself as the liberator of the European continent, in parallel with idealist President Wilson of the United States a century later. In a way Alexander was precisely that, a kind of Messiah, although he had been Napoleon's ally for quite some time. He both admired and despised Napoleon.

Count von Metternich, who was Austria's Foreign Minister for 39 years, though being born in the Rhineland in Germany, was the nucleus of the Vienna Congress. As a counter-revolutionary, Metternich believed in the restoration of the old order. In that sense he was much more conservative, or actually reactionary, than Tsar Alexander I, who was Metternich's headache. Metternich managed to implement his plans, which were not to the liking of the British, who feared unrest among the European populations, and rightly so. The people had sniffed freedom and political influence, of which they were again deprived. Metternich's policy would spark civil unrest for at least half a century after the Vienna Congress came to a close.

The Prussian Chancellor, Baron (later Prince) August von Hardenberg, was the Prussian chief negotiator. Born in Hanover, he had previously been in the service of George III, King of England and Elector of Hanover. He had to leave England, however, when his wife started an affair with the Prince of Wales which became public. Hardenberg became Prussia's foreign minister and later its chancellor. He had to struggle with the Prussian military – which even mutinied against its political authorities and demanded a high price for Prussia's switch from France to Russia, a price for which the negotiations did not allow. Russia claimed Prussian territory in former Poland; Hardenberg had to compensate this in the Rhineland and Saxonia.

The British had been out of tune with continental Europe for a long time, and it took some trouble for them to become accustomed to the continental ways of life. British Foreign Secretary Lord Castlereagh headed the British delegation. Viscount Robert Stuart Castlereagh, later Second Marquess of Londonderry, was a figure with revolutionary ideas in his early years, and briefly an Irish patriot. He was seen as an honest man forced into dishonest proceedings. While Castlereagh saw Russia as a natural ally, Tsar Alexander I regarded Britain as his rival because of its maritime power and interests in the Mediterranean and Asia. Castlereagh tried to be a mediator, but he was fully drawn into the give-and-take of the Vienna conference.

France was only invited into the inner circle of negotiations after the discussion was well under way. Charles-Maurice de Talleyrand-Périgord, France's chief negotiator and minister of foreign affairs, had survived at least four regime changes in France and was still to survive another two. Talleyrand's aim was to save as much for France as he could, and he managed to maintain French territory after the Congress of Vienna as it had been before the Revolution, even a bit bigger. His farsightedness was combined with extreme pragmatism, his eloquence was merged with a creative mind, and his opportunism was coupled with a seemingly French legalistic approach, making him an example for diplomats even today.

The multitude of other negotiators were of very different levels and background. The Emperor of Austria and the Kings of Prussia and of France who were hardly involved and left the real negotiation process to their representatives. The monarchs of Bavaria, Saxony, Naples, Denmark and Sweden, having been allies of Napoleon, were deeply involved in the process as they had a lot to lose. Others were deeply ingrained as they had a lot to win, like Savoy, Spain, Portugal, and the Helvetian and Dutch Republics. They had a hard time in getting the ear of the negotiators in the inner circle, and were kept busy with social events. However, these corridors gave them the opportunity to lobby the representatives of the Big Five.

There were also representatives of minorities, such as Jewish leaders from Bremen, Frankfurt, Hamburg, Prague, and Lübeck, who pleaded for equality rights for the German Jews. As Metternich did not want to have the Jewish demands on the agenda, he ordered the police to expel them from Vienna. The Prussians and British supported the Jews, however, so they were allowed to stay – one reason (and perhaps the main reason) being the loans provided by the Jews to the rulers in their fight against Napoleon, for example from the British Rothschilds (Zamoyski, 2007, p. 379).

3. PROCEDURES AND PROCESSES

Communications in Vienna were facilitated by the use of French – the language of the "enemy" – as the lingua franca, but of course a common language did not lead to common ground. From a procedural point of view, the Vienna negotiations were quite messy. This had to do with the structure–content dilemma. The structure of the conference would, of course, have a large impact on the way in which the parties would deal with the content. A well-regulated Congress of Vienna, with clear procedures and an opportunity for all to participate and to vote on the Final Act, would give the small and middle powers a very strong finger in the pie.

However chaotic and ambiguous the rules of procedure were, and even if one could talk about official rules of procedure, they were a novelty to conference diplomacy in the sense that they established a structure consisting of circles and committees. The committees were meant to get all of the relevant countries involved, both for reasons of principle and practice. With the creation of the committees, those powers that could not participate in the core negotiations could be given some kind of legitimate place in the conference processes, which avoided further complaints about the hegemony of the inner circle.

The committees had specific tasks, dealing with specific issues. The following committees were installed: on Germany, Switzerland, Tuscany, Sardinia; Genoa, and Bouillon (on the border between France and the Austrian Netherlands, now Belgium); on international rivers, the slave trade, statistics, and diplomatic precedence; and, finally, on drafting the Final Act. The German Committee can be seen as the most important, most tricky and most emotional, as kings, princes, dukes, counts, barons, and other noblemen depended on this committee for their survival, and on the question of how they would survive. The German Committee was also responsible for tackling the Jewish issue – that is, the rights of the Jews in Germany – as the Jews tried to retain the rights bestowed upon them by Napoleon Bonaparte.

Other conferences in the 19th century profited from the procedural innovations that were made during the Congress of Vienna. They learned from its successes and from its failures. The Vienna Congress's construction tried to balance inclusion and exclusion in such a way that the number of decision-makers would be limited through exclusion, thereby avoiding too much complexity. The Great Powers were kept on board through inclusion, thereby avoiding the risk of deciding on a Final Act that would not survive the Congress for more than a few years. The procedures thus assured a European political constellation that would survive until deep into the 19th century. The procedures therefore helped to build a forward-looking state system. Yet the content was mainly reactionary and backward-looking, and this undercut the effectiveness of the forward-looking aspect.

The convergence of interests came to closure with the Final Act of the Vienna Congress, the drafting of which started just before Napoleon landed in southern France to start his march on Paris. The Final Act was signed on June 9, 1815, nine days before Napoleon was to be defeated at Waterloo. All of the countries participating in the Vienna Congress – apart from Spain, the Holy See, and Turkey – were signatories. Following Napoleon's abdication, the second Treaty of Paris was signed on November 20, 1815. It provided some changes to the Final Act of the Congress of Vienna, mainly to the detriment of France's northern border. France had to pay reparations and allow an allied occupation force of 150,000 men. The allies were in pains not to punish France too harshly for its recent behavior, as they did not want to undermine France's role as a future balancer in Europe, although severe punishment was demanded by public opinion.

4. THOSE NOT AT THE TABLE, ARE ON THE MENU

Inclusiveness and exclusiveness helped to get the work done. As mentioned earlier, the mass of the interested parties were included in the process through a series of festivities, but were excluded from the day-to-day decision-making process. This ongoing process took place between the five Great Powers. To include all of the major powers into this process was one of the Congress of Vienna's wise decisions, although it was not self-evident at the time. This inclusion had to do with the interests of most of the victorious powers, and with the negotiation skills of the French plenipotentiary, Talleyrand. At the very start, and at the very end after Napoleon's defeat at the Battle of Waterloo, the French were excluded. Later, as they took full responsibility for the Final Act of the Congress of Vienna and the negotiation process leading up to this agreement, the

Final Act was carried out by all five major European powers as its main stakeholders.

This Great Power inclusiveness gave the Congress of Vienna its forward-looking outlook and secured the survival of its accomplishments until the European revolutions of 1848. The Great Power inclusiveness in the inner circle of the Five, while excluding the smaller powers, gave the negotiators the opportunity to manage complexity, or even better to avoid complexity. It allowed for a rather smooth – be it ambiguous – bargaining process. The process involved playing chess with five parties and trying to forge majorities, although only a four-to-five stand-off could really be expected to wrench the isolated power into the agreement that the others wanted, and was achieved through political means or, on a few minor occasions, through the threat of war. This threat fostered the ripeness of the negotiation process, both to get it started and to finalize it.

An alternative process could have been to include more parties, but strict procedures plus strong presidents would then have been needed to facilitate this process. The world was not up to that at the start of the 19th century, as it was not a century later at the Paris Peace Conference in 1919. "Paris" and the Versailles Treaty excluded – with disastrous consequences – two of the major European powers: Germany and the Soviet Union. At a time when 17th and 18th century questions of precedence were still unresolved, the instalment of fixed chairs was not workable. The countries would not be able to allow their counterparts to take a formally higher position; everybody had to be equal, at least in theory.

Procedure was still too much of a political issue. It often is today as well, but we have overarching international structures and organizations that have a mandate to deal with those issues. Leaving it to the individual countries would even be a problem in today's world. Procedure also had to do with the perception of sovereignty and legitimacy, not only with power and equality. In an official sense, a breach of sovereignty was considered unacceptable, although it happened on a large scale when the Five thought that it was necessary. Having the kind of organization that would have a mandate of its own, with powers to do what states would normally be allowed to do, was not imaginable for the Great Five. It all had to come from their consensus-seeking proceedings, without any possibility of out-voting anybody in the inner circle. The lack of internal procedures created great flexibility and opportunities, but gave birth to technical problems at the same time.

The importance of the circles is mirrored by the number of times that these groups met. The Four/Five had 41 sessions, while the Eight, also signatories to the conference that gave Vienna its mandate and legitimacy, as well as the circle that had to ratify its Final Act, met only nine times. The Five then consulted – and negotiated with – members of the Eight during these nine sessions, but they had bilaterals with them as well, and they met them in the committees on specific subjects. Spain, Portugal, and Sweden were thus not completely neglected. One could say that they were partially excluded and partially included in the process. The fact that Spain refused to sign the Final Act, which strangely enough did not make the Act invalid, signals the danger of leaving some relatively important powers out of the process. However, if seven of the eight powers agree, what can the isolated party do?

One might conclude that in the end the decision-making procedure of the Congress of Vienna was consensus, but consensus minus one could still be regarded as a forum that could make a legitimate conclusion. This was a lesson learned by the Conference (later Organization) on Security and Cooperation in Europe (CSCE, later the OSCE) nearly 200 years later, when the issue of Yugoslavia had to be agreed. This issue of inclusion and exclusion is, of course, quite a dilemma, as the country that will resist until the end is likely to be a main stakeholder, and excluding a stakeholder raises problems in implementing the agreement.

Excluding the vast majority of the stakeholders could be seen as a bigger possible threat to the value creation of the Congress of Vienna and its sustainability over time. However, the Middle and Minor Powers of Europe were too dependent on the Great Alliance to be able to undermine the new old order. They had to cling to the Great Powers, as nearly all of these less-powerful countries were under increasing pressure from a growing middle class demanding more political influence or, at a later state, political independence if they were from a sizeable minority. Monarchs were pressured by their own populace and had to cling together as an overarching European ruling class, severely weakened by the ideas of the Enlightenment and the American and French Revolutions, not to forget the smaller spontaneous rebellions such as those in the Southern and Northern Netherlands, which had swiped away their rulers even before the French had staged their own regime change.

It should be noted, however, that the old order from before the French Revolution had been restored de jure, but the Congress of Vienna de facto sustained much of the status quo of 1813 and not the status quo ante of 1789. So did most of the countries. The vast majority of the civil servants in the new United Kingdom of the Netherlands were people who served the Batavian Republic and then Napoleon. King William of Orange preferred those who knew how to direct a centralized state over those who wanted to go back to the old particularism and regionalism: the "Orangists".

5. LESSONS FOR LATER

In his "Seven Lessons Learned from the Congress of Vienna", Guy Olivier Faure (Faure, 2004, pp. 12–13) concludes that the lessons from the Vienna negotiations are still highly relevant today. First, the effectiveness of a negotiation correlates strongly with the amount of advance preparation on formula and detail. This is certainly true. It is striking that the parties to the Congress of Vienna were ill-prepared, and the same is true for the other great congresses in European history, like the Conference of Westphalia (1648); the Peace of Utrecht (1713); and the Paris Peace Conference (1919). The effect of this in Vienna was a long search for common ground, which greatly undermined the effectiveness of the negotiation process and the durability of its Final Act – a Final Act that was basically a basket of different agreements, not the kind of Single Text that we know today (if any). Of course, today's preparedness for multilateral negotiations differs from country to country. In general, however, the meetings are well prepared and will often only materialize if the chances of success are more than 50 per cent at least. The pre-negotiation phase is often more important than the negotiation itself, especially in the European Union.

Faure's second point regarding enhancing effectiveness is about the importance of information-gathering, be it before the meeting starts, or during the meeting itself. As mentioned earlier, diplomats at the Congress of Vienna tried to gather as much information as possible, often in undiplomatic ways through secret police, festivities, and mistresses. They were aware of the importance of information and it helped them to oversee the process. They did not have the problem that information could leak to a strong public opinion at home and they could thus be more focused than diplomats in the new millennium.

The third point is about division of labor within the delegation, which should be adequate. In some delegations at the Congress of Vienna, there was indeed a division of labor, especially in the delegations of countries with a populace that was used to voicing its concerns, such as Great Britain and France. It seems that the British delegation under Castlereagh, and later Wellington, had the best division of labor. Diplomats were on the same wavelength, at a distance steered by the London cabinet. It was more difficult for the French, as Talleyrand had to manage ultra-royalists within his team who were influenced by their constituencies back home, while King Louis XVIII was not able to discipline them.

Faure's fourth point is to be soft on form and tough on which goals to achieve, which is in line with the ideas of Willem Mastenbroek (Mastenbroek, 2002), as well as with the profile of the average British negotiator (Meerts, 2012). In other words, be soft on the software of negotiations (for example, relationships and exploration), and tough on the hardware (interests and power). For the Congress of Vienna, this seems to have been true for all five main negotiators, except for the Russian Tsar, who could be unnecessarily rude, while giving away some of his goals too easily. For example, he gave in without any ado on the idea of putting Napoleon on Elba.

The fifth point is to prepare concessions carefully and to time them well. The impression of the Congress of Vienna is that concessions were often not prepared and not timed, leading to unnecessary mayhem. Diplomats nowadays will dig into the likeliness of their counterparts conceding on certain issues, while already asking themselves what they might give them in return. In long-lasting processes, like those in the European Union, the diplomats know perfectly well what the balance of concession is and when the time is ripe to strike the deals. The balance of interests in the EU changes slowly over time, but in general there are hardly any structural changes, unless there are "earthquakes", like the fall of the Berlin Wall and Brexit. On security, for example, the United Kingdom and the Netherlands are pro-Atlantic, joined by Portugal. France and Spain are pro-continental, joined by Germany. Countries such as Poland and Italy try to keep the balance between the two but rely heavily on the United States. However, the fall of Berlin Wall made Germany a Central European Power, instead of a border region. Brexit distorts the balance between those with an Atlantic orientation and others who focus on the continent.

The countries' positions are quite predictable, so concessions can be timed, and normally these are done at the very end of the process. Sometimes the concession kills that process, but as everybody knows that time is just a tactical device and not many want to derail the process, they normally succeed in solving the problem. Here we see a huge difference between "Vienna" and "Brussels". Its root cause is the difference of organization between the two: "Vienna" was under-organized; "Brussels" is over-organized.

The sixth point, Faure states, is that when involved in multilateral negotiations with coalitions, it is easiest to start by stating what one refuses to do. It is quite clear that this was very much the way in the

Congress of Vienna. Actually, states were hardly able to move from "no" to a "yes", something that can still be observed today in negotiations with representatives from countries south-east of the city of Vienna. Starting with a "no" might be easy indeed, but perhaps it is too easy. It often gives rise to "positional bargaining". It would therefore be better to start in a positive way by indicating options for convergence and stressing potential common ground. If stating demands, these should be linked to an indication of the trade-offs that one is willing to concede, provided that one's main priorities are met. As noted above, however, to bargain secondary priorities is often much easier than primary, implying that the negotiators will have to be very aware of their priorities.

Ambiguity is of the essence, as stated in point seven. Ambiguity helps the negotiator to manage complexity and to circumvent contradiction. This was true for Vienna and remains true today. Comparing the negotiations at the beginning of the 19th century and those in the 21st century, however, shows that there was more tolerance for ambiguity 200 years ago. The Congress of Vienna was as ambiguous as it could be, and not always in a constructive way, and this was broadly accepted by the negotiators. It served its purpose, which was one of the reasons why we had a Final Act at all. In today's world, ambiguity is much less tolerated, as it undermines control. Control is the password for conference diplomats in the new millennium.

6.   CONTINUITY AND CONTEXT CHANGE

The Congress of Vienna was chaotic, but because of its construction in several layers of influence, its relative power balance within the inner circle, and the relatively wide common ground among the Great Powers, it did reach a substantial outcome – an outcome that created stability, as well as laying the foundations for a lot of instability to come. The system of the Congress of Vienna did prevent another pan-European war in the 19th century. However, the international regime (Krasner, 1983) installed in Vienna could not prevent the world wars in the 20th century.

Serious attempts had already been made to guarantee a more stable Europe. Already before the Vienna Congress, Britain and Russia had agreed in 1805 on three principles to stabilize the continent: small states should be united in some kind of regional federation; an acceptable law of the nations should be established; and an international arbitration authority should be created in order to mediate disputes between states. In addition, the 1814 Treaty of Chaumont ruled that "the signatories were obliged, even after a treaty of peace, actively to promote an international peace" (Grüner, 1993, p. 24). "Vienna" had a positive effect on peace and stability in Europe, or at least on the balance of power among the powers.

Notwithstanding local uprisings and wars, the balance among the sovereigns was largely maintained for seven decades after Metternich lost control: "The European balance worked untrammelled in the seventy years between the fall of Metternich and its several repudiations by Lenin and Wilson" (Taylor, 1954, p. xxi). This did not mean, however, that "Vienna" could be seen as the beginning of a series of effective international conferences to secure the peace. Vienna did not yet provide the world with a "conference system", which came into being at the very end of the 19th century with, as a first step, the Convention for the Pacific Settlement of International Disputes (1899): the so-called "The Hague System".

Ripeness through deadlock and internal and external pressure, managing complexity by creating inner and outer circles, having professional negotiators to balance the fallacy – their inclination to "egotiate" – of political leaders, the importance of communication and empathy, the necessity of backchannel bargaining, all these factors helped to make Vienna a success. These elements are still of value today. However, in the modern world rigid structures are needed to make progress in the negotiation process. We owe it to international law and modern technology that we are now capable of developing complex institutions to keep the negotiation process on track and to protect the negotiators. At the same time these regimes can slow down these processes, or freeze them, as a consequence of gridlock. They also allow for politicians to bypass their negotiators, thereby breaking deadlocks or destroying the process of negotiation.

However, the main difference between "Vienna", and "New York" or "Brussels", is the role of the constituency. At the beginning of the 19th century there was hardly a home front to manage. Negotiators had an enormous freedom and could therefore use their creative minds to break deadlocks and find solutions for seemingly intractable problems. The "Two-Level Game" at the start of the 21st century forces the negotiators and their governments to take into account the wishes of their parliament, public opinion, trade unions, powerful private companies, the media, etc. And rightly so, as democratic states can conduct an international negotiation process in the interest of their populace. But it sometimes gives an advantage to authoritarian regimes who can decide quickly and without internal interference. Nevertheless, long-term stability of the state system relies on the readiness to take the public interest into account. Negotiation is its best instrument.

REFERENCES

FAURE, G.O. (2004), "Talleyrand: Prince of Negotiators", *PINpoints Network Newsletter*, Laxenburg: IIASA, 23, 12–13.

GRÜNER, W.D. (1993), "The Impact of the Reconstruction of Central Europe in 1814–1815 on the System of Peace in the Nineteenth Century", in: Goudoever, A.P. van (ed.), *Great Peace Conferences in History, 1648–1990*, Utrecht: Utrecht University Press.

HROCH, M. (1993), Comparing Early Modern Peace Treaties', in: Goudoever, A.P. van (ed.), *Great Peace Congresses in History, 1648–1990*, Utrecht: Utrecht University Press.

KRASNER, S.D. (1983), "Structural Causes and Regime Consequences: Regimes as Intervening Variables" and "Regimes and the limits of Realism", in: Krasner, S.D. (ed.), *International Regimes*, Ithaca and London: Cornell University Press.

MASTENBROEK, W.F.G. (2002), *Negotiation as Emotion Management*, Heemstede: Holland Business Publications.

MEERTS, P.W. Paul (2014), *Diplomatic Negotiation. Essence and Evolution*, The Hague: Clingendael Institute.

MEERTS, P.W. (2012), "Onderhandelen op zijn Hollands", *Internationale Spectator*, Clingendael Institute, 66: 12, 617.

TAYLOR, A.J.P. (1954), *The Struggle for the Mastery in Europe 1848–1918*, Oxford: Clarendon.

ZAMOYSKI, A. (2007), *Rites of Peace: The Fall of Napoleon and the Congress of Vienna*, London: Harper Perennial.

ZARTMAN, I.W. (2001), "Preventive Diplomacy: Setting the Stage", in: Zartman, I.W. (ed.), *Preventive Negotiation. Avoiding Conflict Escalation*, Lanham: Rowman and Littlefield Publishers, Inc.

THE 1856 CONGRESS OF PARIS

Putting Victory to Good Use

Yves BRULEY*

The Congress of Paris, although less well-known than the Congress of
Vienna described in the previous chapter, allowed Napoleon III to take
diplomatic revenge 40 years after Napoleon's defeat in 1814–1815. The
first major event to be held in the Quai d'Orsay (the French ministry of
foreign affairs), the Congress put an end to the Crimean War (1853–1855),
which Russia had lost to the Anglo-French coalition, and provided French
diplomacy the opportunity to move adroitly into the center of Europe's
diplomatic game. By taking advantage of France's victory, Napoleon III
acquired a position of moral leadership in Europe that lasted several years.
He also breathed new life into multilateral diplomacy and international
law – the most lasting result of the Congress of Paris.

---

*   Ecole pratique des Hautes Etudes (EPHE, PSL), Paris.

1. THE EUROPEAN BALANCE OF POWERS AFTER THE "PEOPLES' SPRING"

The Congress of Paris is all but forgotten today.[1] It is hardly known to anyone but the habitués of the Quai d'Orsay who frequent the Salon du Congrès on the ministry's ground floor, and historians of public international law who remember the 1856 Paris Declaration on Respecting Maritime Law, which instituted mediation rather than privateering in cases of conflict between signatory powers. In hindsight, the Congress of Paris does in fact seem to have been a key turning point in the development of international law, but the work it accomplished on a political level is no less interesting, if less permanent. The French saw the Treaty of Paris (concluded on March 30, 1856) as revenge for the Congress of Vienna, which had redrawn the map of Europe after Napoleon's defeat. This time, not only was France again led by a Napoleon, but it also played a key role in European diplomacy. England was undeniably still the world's greatest power in 1856, but France took over Russia's position as leader of continental Europe.

The history of the Congress of Paris is therefore the history of a victory. Not only for France, but also for Europe, which felt it had invented modern multilateral diplomacy, creating a new balance of powers and breathing new life into the Concert of Europe.

1.1. AFTER THE CRIMEAN WAR, EUROPE ATTENDED A CONGRESS IN PARIS

The Congress of Paris was designed to cement peace after the end of the Crimean War. That war was caused by Russia's desire to impose its influence over the Ottoman Empire, the "sick man of Europe", by taking advantage of the troubled situation in Europe following the "People's Spring." Contrary to expectations, France and England formed an alliance against Russia to defend the Ottoman Empire and, through it, the balance of powers. The Piedmont joined the alliance and Austria long threatened to join it, while Prussia remained neutral. The fighting began in 1853 and ended with the defeat of the Russians at Sebastopol on September 8, 1855.

---

[1]   In 2006, however, its 150th anniversary was celebrated by a colloquium at the Quai d'Orsay and an exhibit at the Invalides. See the colloquium proceedings, G. AMEIL, I. NATHAN, and G.-H. SOUTOU, *Le Congrès de Paris (1856), Un Evénement Fondateur*, Brussels, PIE-Peter Lang, 2009 and the exhibit catalogue, *Napoléon III et l'Europe, 1856: le Congrès de Paris*, Éditions Artlys, Paris, 2006.

Throughout that time, diplomatic efforts at the highest levels had also been unceasing. In 1854 and 1855, international conferences were held with Russia in Vienna to discuss conditions for a halt to the hostilities. Those conferences were unsuccessful, but on February 1, 1856 the armistice was signed in Vienna, where it was decided to hold a congress in Paris.

The congress was a symbolic victory for Napoleon III even before it began: by suggesting the negotiations be moved from Vienna to Paris, England and Russia recognized the merits of French diplomacy. An even stronger signal in this sense was the fact that the congress would be presided by the French minister of foreign affairs, who was none other than Count Walewski, the illegitimate son of Napoleon I and Maria Walewski.

Each power would be represented by two plenipotentiaries: their minister of foreign affairs and their ambassador to France. France's second plenipotentiary was Baron de Bourqueney, its ambassador to Austria, who thus provided continuity with the previous negotiations.

The congress did not have to discuss the main terms on which the war had been ended, as Russia had already accepted them: a neutral Black Sea; and the Ottoman Empire's independence and integrity, guaranteed by the major powers. In addition, before the congress started the Sultan promulgated a decree on the status of Christians in his Empire, and the issue of the holy places, which had been a trigger in 1853, was also set aside. That left the congress with responsibility for setting out all the details for applying the major principles and deciding the fates of Moldavia and Walachia – two Romanian principalities that were part of the Ottoman Empire but had to be given a new status. It resolved not only these issues, but also some that were beyond the scope of its initial program.

1.2. A CEREMONIAL OCCASION TEMPERED BY AN INFORMAL WORKING METHOD

At noon on February 25 a huge crowd gathered on the banks of the Seine in front of the Foreign Affairs Ministry, installed since September 1853 in what was then a brand new building that has since been called the "Quai d'Orsay". The plenipotentiaries arrived for the first session, which was held in the Salon des Ambassadeurs on the ground floor. A large table covered with a green velvet tablecloth made specifically for the occasion was set up in the middle of the room. The 12 plenipotentiaries took their seats around it in alphabetical order by country: Austria, France, Great Britain, Russia, Sardinia, and Turkey. A small square table was added for the congress's secretary, the French ministry's director of political affairs (Vincent Benedetti), who wrote the protocols. Noticeably absent was Prussia. It had been excluded because it had remained neutral during the war, but was "let in" by Napoleon III himself, who persuaded the powers to open the congress up to the Prussians. They took a seat at the table on March 18, after all the important decisions had been made.

The first order of business was to prolong the armistice until March 31, the congress thus giving itself more than a month to conclude a peace treaty. Over the first three weeks they held 11 sessions, one every two or three days, then picked up the pace on March 24, holding a conference every day to complete the treaty before the end of the month. The sessions, which lasted several hours, were described as follows:

> [T]hings went pretty much as they went at the council of ministers; no one gave any speeches. We freely exchanged ideas, and did not have the constraint of having to ask for the floor to respond to an argument or express our ideas. It was a conversation, often animated, sometimes a bit lively, but which was nothing like the regulated, methodical discussions of certain assemblies. Once the agenda was given, every member was free to talk when they thought the time was right. It goes without saying that this freedom from manners, governed by each person's conscience and the feeling of mutual consideration, never led the serious assembly into confusion. ... The sessions were usually broken up with a few minutes of distraction; I could almost say recreation. The plenipotentiaries adjourned to the salon de la Rotonde or went into the garden. We snacked, we took walks, we smoked.[2]

Let me add that the "Imperial Festival" was in full swing: every day, the plenipotentiaries were invited to the table of a dignitary of the regime, and their excellencies' stomachs were put to the test.

As in all large diplomatic meanings, there were two kinds of discussions: official and unofficial. In between official sessions, the plenipotentiaries shared their observations, discussed them, and negotiated, so that, in almost all cases, agreement had already been reached when they met in the plenary sessions. Therefore very few of those sessions disrupted the congress, and none of them endangered the peace in question:

> The plenipotentiaries often met in groups before the session began, either in the salon de la Rotonde or in the garden. These meetings always took place when the agenda indicated that serious difficulties would arise. It was the little meeting

---

2   E. GOURDON, *Histoire du Congrès de Paris*, Paris, Librairie nouvelle, 1957, p. 485.

before the big one, and sometimes the little meeting lasted (*sic*) much longer than the other one. In general, the plenipotentiaries who knew they were of the same opinion on a question that we were going to address formed a group, while their adversaries formed another. First we talked in low voices, then on a word, on a question, on a request for information, the men came together, the two groups blended and they exchanged ideas. ... The discussion quieted little by little, mutual concessions were made, and when the time seemed right to start work on the final version, the draft was set aside and the congress session began.[3]

1.3. A FLEXIBLE FORMAT: TAKING TURNS SPEAKING AND DRAFTING

A close reading of the minutes reveals that the congress did not follow an agreed format: the members felt their way, inventing negotiation and drafting methods as they went. They raised the major issues to be resolved one after the other at successive sessions, without waiting for agreement on one before raising another. The congress thus addressed several different topics at each session – the borders between Russia and the Ottoman Empire in Bessarabia and the caucuses, the problem of the arsenals on the banks of the now-neutral Black Sea, the terms for free navigation on the Danube, and of course the future status of the Romanian principalities – while also keeping track of progress on the negotiations. The plenipotentiaries often had to ask their government for agreement, but even with the telegraph it took four days to get an answer from St Petersburg or Constantinople. Fortunately, none of the governments ever overruled their representatives, which would have required them to renege on a negotiation and the terms of an agreement they had made subject to their government's approval.

In general, there was no unanimity with regard to issues introduced at the plenary sessions and the procedure was always the same: after an initial discussion, positions were explained and disputes noted, and the negotiation was adjourned. But it was not simply deferred to a future session: the habit developed of appointing special committees of plenipotentiaries from the countries most directly concerned so they could come up with a draft acceptable to everyone. The congress thus operated in an increasingly complex fashion over the month of March, as several committees met each day. In fact, the second plenipotentiaries had the heaviest workload, as they were generally responsible for preparing and negotiating new drafts

---

[3]   Ibid., pp. 486–487.

in between sessions. The increasing number of committees eventually led to the idea of creating a drafting committee composed of all the second plenipotentiaries and chaired by Mr. Bourqueney. In the end, he was assigned direct responsibility for drafting the articles, which were then proposed in the plenary session.

The congress thus made quick progress. On March 18, after only three weeks of work, Bourqueney was able to present the congress with an overview of the future treaty. But the hottest topic, the issue of the Romanian principalities, was set aside. The question was whether Moldavia and Walachia, whose peoples spoke the same language, followed the same religion, and had the same culture, should in the future be united in a single principality. Turkey and Austria were opposed to the idea, whereas France, England, and Russia were favorable to it, asserting that unification would make for a stronger "Romania". The argument in favor was based on the will of the people, who presumably wanted such a union. But the Turks and the Austrians claimed this was not true and that on the contrary, the people wanted to remain separate. A stalemate loomed. On March 10, the congress decided to form a committee of three of its members. In this context, the idea of consulting the people, under the supervision of a European committee, was put forward. The consultation would be followed by an international conference that would ratify the wishes of the Romanians, thus determining their status. Resolution of the issue was thus postponed, but it remained in the hands of the Concert of Europe. And, for the first time, the principle of consulting the people entered into diplomacy.

The last three sessions were devoted to a close reading of the entire treaty and the agreements attached to it. The treaty was initialed on March 29, and at noon on Sunday March 30, in the room where the discussions had typically been held, the plenipotentiaries signed and affixed the seals of their coats of arms. Clarendon then suggested they go to the Tuileries to inform the Emperor that the congress's work was finished and to thank him for his hospitality.

1.4. AFTER THE PEACE TREATY, THE SCOPE OF THE NEGOTIATION EXPANDED

In this atmosphere, which one could call not just irenic (which goes without saying when peace is concluded) but excessively optimistic, the congress entered its second phase. It had not been scheduled initially and was not directly related to the peace treaty, but the congress's organizers were not satisfied with simply bringing peace in the Near East and wanted to address issues weighing on the general situation in Europe. On April 8, at the 22nd session, Walewski took the floor and addressed three topics. He started with a long diatribe against the Belgian press, which he claimed was protected by very lax laws and had therefore allowed domestic policy attacks against the French Empire to increase. He then briefly addressed Greece's political and financial situation, which was a source of great concern, and finally, turning to Italy, expressed his desire to see the end of the double occupation of the Papal States (Austrian in the north, French in the South) and called on the king of Naples to show himself capable of leniency and moderation. A heated debate followed, primarily with respect to Italy.

The April 8 session continues to be famous. It was an undeniable victory for Cavour who, backed by the English, got Napoleon III to agree to have the congress talk about Italy one way or another. The discussion continued during the April 14 conference, but that session and the next, on April 16, which was supposed to be the last one, concerned essentially the rules of maritime law in time of war – yet another subject that was not on the original agenda. Here, the congress of Paris provides a particularly successful example of a "post-settlement settlement" (Raiffa, 1985): not satisfied with the initial agreement, negotiators continue to productively improve the result achieved during the first phase, going beyond the negotiation's original objective.

The plenipotentiaries began to leave Paris as soon as the April 16 session was over, but the seconds stayed for a few more days until ratifications were exchanged.

"It is beautiful, it is grand this peace that we have just signed", Bourqueney wrote. "Will it last forty years like the other?[4] We are not asking Providence to reveal its secrets; let's be content with its beneficence. As for the principal player (Napoleon III), he has never been so cool and calm: Europe is going to be thoroughly charmed with him."[5] In the small world of French diplomats, it was a time for enthusiasm. In a letter to one of his colleagues, an ambassador raves about how few years had passed

---

[4] I.e., the peace of 1815 after the Congress of Vienna.
[5] Private letter from Bourqueney to Edouard Thouvenel, ambassador to Constantinople, Paris, April 14, 1856. Archives of the French Ministry of Foreign Affairs (FMFA), Thouvenel Papers, vol. 5, f. 277.

since the commotions of 1848, and speaks "of an honorable peace that catapults France back to the head of civilized Europe".[6]

2. LESSONS FROM A MULTILATERAL SUCCESS

How did the congress realize its dream, which a columnist for the *Revue des deux mondes* defined as follows on February 14, 1856: "The congress must satisfy the winners without humiliating the losers" and offer "an elevated deal apt to preserve the peoples' dignity by becoming a new rule for European relations"?[7]

2.1. ISOLATE CERTAIN CONTENTIOUS SUBJECTS

Two weighty issues that could have caused the congress to fail were set aside: the Holy Places (the status quo resulting from the decrees of 1852 was maintained, thus implicitly deemed satisfactory); and the status of Christians in the Ottoman Empire, which was resolved before the congress opened, thus depriving Russia of the main pretext for its intervention in the Near East. As for the treaty's main subjects – the neutrality of the Black Sea and the integrity of the Ottoman Empire – they were deemed to be prerequisites and in theory would not be negotiated further. The issue of Romania was addressed at the congress but set aside for later. The idea of a preamble setting out general principles was also set aside to avoid needlessly destroying the agreement that was developing. The congress therefore essentially concerned fine-tuning the terms and did not discuss theoretical questions or the biggest issues. It defused the probable causes of failure or stalemate as much as possible.

2.2. MANAGE DISCUSSIONS FLEXIBLY

The congress gave itself five weeks, which is neither too short nor too long. It tabled issues one after another, without waiting to solve each

---

6   Private letter from General Aupick, former ambassador, to Edouard Thouvenel ambassador to Constantinople, Paris, March 31, 1856. FMFA, Thouvenel Papers, vol. 1, f. 352.

7   C. DE MAZADE, "Chronique de la quinzaine", *Revue des deux mondes*, February 14, 1856, 2nd period, Tome 1, 1856, p. 888.

problem before addressing the next. At the first sign of disagreement in the plenary session, issues to be negotiated were set aside and isolated. They were handled separately in small committees (even if those committees were generally composed of the same people), which allowed the negotiators to maintain an overall view. Once a compromise was found, a draft was proposed in the plenary session. The pace of the congress, an average of one session every two days, made it possible to go quickly. Diplomatic sociability, taken to its heights, fully played its role.

2.3. A MODEST, CALM APPROACH TO VICTORY

Russia did not come to Paris to be subjected to its victors' diktats: it participated in the discussions with the same dignity as the other powers. And even though Austria had not made war against Russia, it was not relegated to playing a minor role. Even Prussia was eventually invited. The winning coalition did not dictate its law: the cards were shuffled and new alliances could be formed. The game was open. The idea was therefore not so much to consecrate a victory and reap the dividends of a military investment as it was to show off a new Europe, one that was different from the Europe of 1815. Most importantly, France obtained great moral authority because it did not ask anything for itself: its war objectives blended with Europe's public interest (balance of powers through stability in the Near East, and a neutral Black Sea); and while it defended certain opinions (especially on Romania) that conformed to its interests or political outlook, it was never alone, but was joined by other powers (often even with Russia).

2.4. KEEP THE PUBLIC AT A REASONABLE DISTANCE

The Congress of Paris was a spectacular *huis clos*. It was held under the utmost secrecy – except that Cavour occasionally told journalists too much. Even the contents of the treaty of March 30, 1856 were not known to the public until after ratification. But if the public had to make do with rumors as to the treaty's substance, it witnessed a considerable historical event. The presence of men from foreign countries, the constant parties, and the announcement that the treaty had been signed all took place without any animosity toward the winners (this was before the days of nationalism). All eyes – not just those of imperial Paris but of all of Europe – were turned to the Quai d'Orsay, waiting for peace to be concluded. Without such public pressure, it would be difficult to understand why the major powers would have made so many concessions. The fact is, no one wanted to be held responsible for a fail or delayed peace.

The day after the congress, some observers pointed out – to complain – that on reading the treaty, one could not determine who had won and who had lost the war. The republican historiography then minimized the Congress of Paris, claiming that Napoleon III had made war for the benefit of strategic English interests rather than national French interests. This is a misunderstanding of the success of French diplomacy in 1856. After the Revolution and the Empire, France had been seen in Europe as a source of instability and war, and its diplomatic position was not on a level with its actual power. The Congress of Paris enabled it to present itself as a great but moderate victorious power playing the game of the Concert of Europe in the public interest, even when it recognized, for the first time ever, the principle of nationalities. In 1856, France was recognized as Europe's referee.

Victor Hugo was not wrong about it. Seeing his enemy win, he wrote an "Appeal to the Italians" that ends: "Italians! … Beware of what the congresses, cabinets, and diplomats seem to be preparing for you at this time. … Regardless of appearances, never lose sight of the facts. Diplomacy is darkness. What is being done for you conspires against you."[8]

"Diplomacy is darkness"! The congress was the height of diplomacy and therefore, in the eyes of Victor Hugo, the darkest hour of the night – that frightening moment when Napoleon the Small[9] became great.

REFERENCES

AMEIL, G., NATHAN, I., and SOUTOU, G.-H., *Le congrès de Paris (1856), un événement fondateur*, Bruxelles, PIE-Peter Lang, 2009.

ANCEAU, E., *Napoléon III*, Paris, Taillandier, 2008.

BRULEY, Y., *Le Quai d'Orsay impérial. Histoire du Ministère des Affaires étrangères sous Napoléon III*, Paris, Editions A. Pedone, 2012.

DE MAZADE, C. "Chronique de la quinzaine", *Revue des deux mondes*, February 14, 1856, 2nd period, Tome 1, 1856.

DUPUIS, C., *Le principe d'équilibre et le concert européen de la paix de Westphalie à l'Acte d'Algésiras*, Paris, Perrin, 1909.

ECHARD, W., *Napoleon III and the Concert of Europe*, Louisiana State University Press, 1983.

---

8   "Appel aux Italiens", *Actes et paroles*, Paris, Albin Michel, 1940, p. 135.
9   Title of a political pamphlet Hugo published in 1852.

Gourdon, *Histoire du Congrès de Paris*, Paris, Librairie nouvelle, 1957.

Napoléon III et l'Europe, 1856: le congrès de Paris, Artlys Ed., Paris, 2006 (exhibition catalogue).

Raiffa, H., Post-settlement settlements. *Negotiation Journal*, 1985, 1(1): 9–12.

Sédouy de, J.-A., *Le Concert européen. Aux origines de l'Europe, 1814–1914*, Paris, Fayard, 2009.

Soutou, G.-H., *L'Europe de 1815 à nos jours*, Paris, PUF, 2007.

Schroeder, P.W., *Austria, Great Britain and the Crimean War: the destruction of the European Concert*, Cornell University Press, 1972.

WOODROW WILSON IN VERSAILLES

A Transparent Diplomat's Frustrated Ambition

Aurélien COLSON*

When Woodrow Wilson (1856–1924) was elected president of the United States in 1912, several crises in Europe pointed up the growing risk of a continent-wide conflict. Against a backdrop of arms races and colonial rivalries, the main European powers had aligned themselves to create the Triple Alliance (Germany, Italy, and Austria) on the one hand, and on the other, the Cordial Entente between Great Britain and France, which entered into a Triple Entente with Russia. In keeping with the secrecy that had reigned in diplomatic negotiations since the Renaissance (Colson 2008, 2009), the precise clauses of these treaties were unknown to the citizenry concerned, despite the fact that they provided for going to war if the vital interests of an ally were threatened. A local *casus belli* could therefore drag the entire continent into war – which is precisely what happened when Archduke Franz Ferdinand of Austria was assassinated in Sarajevo on June 28, 1914.

---

*   ESSEC Business School, IRENE Paris, Singapore and Brussels.

Not wanting the United States to become embroiled in the European conflict, Wilson delayed the country's entry into the war until German aggression, among other things, made neutrality no longer possible. For example, in 1915 Germany increased its submarine activity in the Atlantic, including against civilian vessels: on May 7 it sank the *Lusitania*, sending 1,198 of the people on board, including 128 Americans, to the bottom of the ocean. In December Wilson began rearming the United States and started developing the political objectives the United States would pursue via this conflict, which he summarized in his famous "fourteen points" speech to Congress on January 8, 1918. The first was to institute a new system of international negotiations based on a transparent process and published results. This was the first time a head of state – the president of the United States no less – suggested putting an end to diplomatic secrecy. A few months later in Versailles, however, it was with the utmost secrecy that Wilson conducted negotiations in his hotel room. The purpose of this chapter is to shed some light on the contradiction between the desire for transparent diplomacy and the practice of international negotiations, which are still shrouded in secrecy today.

1. WILSON'S VISION FOR A NEW DIPLOMACY

1.1. CRITICISM OF TRADITIONAL DIPLOMACY

Criticism of the diplomatic conditions that may have facilitated or even provoked the war began immediately. Traditional diplomacy based on secret treaties that bound countries to each other in a system of alliances and counter-alliances was considered directly responsible for the start of this widespread conflict. In August 1914, well-known British university professors and members of Parliament, such as Ramsay MacDonald, E.D. Morel, and Bertrand Russell, therefore founded the *Union of Democratic Control* (UDC), which claimed that "[p]otentates, diplomatists and militarists made this war".[1] As MacDonald put it, "there must be an end of the secret diplomacy which has plunged us into this catastrophe".[2] In 1915 and 1916, several books were published in which the authors blamed old-fashioned diplomacy for the war. Morel wrote, for example: "We are

---

[1]   UDC, *The Morrow of the War*, London, 1914, p. 19.
[2]   D. MARQUAND, *Ramsay MacDonald*, London: Cohen Books, 1977, p. 209.

now in the presence of the utter failure of the old-fashioned methods of safeguarding peace by preparing for war."[3] On the cover of his book, a man blinded by the words "Secret Diplomacy" is on the verge of falling into an abyss opening up at his feet (Williams, 2006, p. 48). Secrecy in international negotiations therefore had to be done away with, which in particular meant that negotiations had to be supervised by representatives of the people.

In the United States, fear that the country would be dragged into the European conflict led to rapid growth in the pacifist movement. Groups such as the Woman's Peace Party, the Socialist Party of America (SPA), and the League to Enforce Peace (LEP) sprung up, and their platforms focused on eliminating secrecy and instituting popular control of diplomacy. The SPA proposed an "international parliament with legislative and administrative powers over international affairs and with permanent committees, in place of [the] present secret diplomacy" (Knock, 1992, pp. 53–54).

Wilson synthesized these ideological and programmatic movements into a political platform, with the intent of instituting a new international order based on nation-states and collective security.

1.2. THE WILSONIAN MOMENT: FROM IDEOLOGICAL SYNTHESIS TO POLITICAL ACTION

Formerly a professor of political science at Princeton, Wilson stayed abreast of such ideological movements, in which he saw himself. In 1908 he had joined the American Peace Society, and pacifism had nourished his thought and strengthened his desire to keep the United States out of the European conflict. He was convinced his country could foster a negotiated solution, but such a solution had to serve a lasting peace. To do so, he believed the international system of diplomatic negotiations had to be redesigned, which is the task he set for the United States on May 27, 1916 in a speech to the LEP: "We are participants, whether we would or not, in the life of the world. The interests of all nations are our own also. We are partners with the rest. ... The peace of the world must henceforth depend upon a new and more wholesome diplomacy" (Knock, 1992, pp. 76–77).

That speech sparked a wave of enthusiasm among pacifist movements in the United States and Europe. Wilson was reelected in 1916, but in

---

[3]   E.D. MOREL, *Ten Years of Secret Diplomacy: An Unheeded Warning*, London: National Labour Press, 1915, pp. xvii–xix.

January 1917, the disciples of excessive war won out in the German Navy: several ships were sunk and Wilson broke off diplomatic relations with Germany on February 3. The final straw came on February 26, when he learned of a telegram in which the German State Secretary of Foreign Affairs, Arthur Zimmerman, tried to persuade Mexico to declare war on the United States. On April 2, Wilson asked Congress to declare war on Germany, citing rigorous principles to justify the declaration and stating that the United States was not pursuing any of the typical objectives of war: "We desire no conquest, no dominion. We seek no indemnities for ourselves, no material compensation for the sacrifices we shall freely make."[4]

Wilson further clarified the objectives being pursued by the United States when he presented his 14-point program to Congress on January 8, 1918.[5] Rather than assign blame to one country or another for starting a world war, he talked about how the international system worked. For the first time ever, responsibility for a conflict was not attributed to a particular country (the loser, of course), but to the features of the international system itself (Williams, 2006, p. 49). In his speech, Wilson emphasized that he was opposed to the secrecy with which international negotiations were conducted, and claimed that transparency was a requirement for lasting peace:

> It will be our wish and purpose that the processes of peace, when they are begun, shall be *absolutely open* and that they shall involve and permit henceforth *no secret understandings* of any kind. *The day of conquest and aggrandizement is gone by; so is also the day of secret covenants* entered into in the interest of particular governments and likely at some unlooked-for moment to upset the peace of the world. (Williams, 2006, p. 49, emphasis added)

Wilson introduced his program for lasting peace as a logical extension of such openness: "The program of the world's peace, therefore, is our program; and that program, the only possible program, as we see it, is this: [the fourteen points]." Eight of them are specific to territorial disputes: points VI to XIII concern Russia, Belgium, France, Italy, Austria-Hungary, the Balkans, the Ottoman Empire, and Poland, respectively. With respect to colonial matters, the fifth point calls for taking into account the interests

---

4   "An Address of a Joint Session of Congress", April 2, 1917, in *Papers of Woodrow Wilson (PWW)*, A.S. LINK et al. (eds.), Princeton: Princeton University Press, 1984, XXXVIII, p. 348.

5   "An Address to a Joint Session of Congress", January 8, 1918, in *PWW*, 1984, XLV, pp. 534–539.

of the populations concerned. Three others refer to general principles: free navigation on the seas (II), free trade (III), and reduced national armaments. The two remaining points (I and XIV) frame the others, as if respect for them conditioned the whole:

> I. *Open covenants of peace, openly arrived at*, after which there shall be no private international understandings of any kind but diplomacy shall proceed always frankly and in the public view. ... (emphasis added)

> XIV. A general association of nations must be formed under specific covenants for the purpose of affording mutual guarantees of political independence and territorial integrity to great and small states alike.

"Open covenants of peace, openly arrived at" and an international organization – such were the two main pillars of the international negotiation system Wilson was proposing to replace the search for a balance of powers that had led to war. All he had to do was persuade his partners.

1.3. POPULAR SUPPORT FOR AN END TO SECRECY

Wilson's strategy was guided by his conviction that to institute a new international order based on open negotiations, the closed circuit of embassies had to be abandoned and citizens relied on directly: American public opinion is "as much a fact as a mountain and must be considered", he wrote.[6] The beneficiaries of Wilson's vision, the people, thus became the main source of his growing influence. Wilson had realized that obtaining popular support was his only option when saw how opposed European leaders were to the principles he was advocating to build a new international order, and wrote to a confidant: "Yes, I know that Europe is still governed by the same reactionary forces which controlled this country until a few years ago. But I am satisfied that if necessary I can reach the peoples of Europe over the heads of their Rulers."[7]

Reaching the people thus became his strategy. During the 1916 presidential campaign, creating a new international order based on a league of nations became a political subject of primary importance on Wilson's agenda.

---

6   *PWW*, LI, p. 416.
7   T.J. Knock, *To End All Wars. Woodrow Wilson and the Quest for a New World Order*, 1992, New York and Oxford: Oxford University Press, p. 162 (citing Wilson).

In speech after speech, Wilson explained the advantages of such a league and US participation in it to his fellow citizens. Reelected in 1916, Wilson gave his "peace without victory" speech on January 22, 1917.[8] This important speech had an enormous impact on American politics, but got a lukewarm reception from European governments. Wilson was targeting a different audience, however: "The real people I was speaking to was neither the Senate nor foreign governments, as you will realize, but the *people* of the countries now at war."[9]

The search for popular support was justified by the major disagreement between the Allies on the war's objectives, which illustrates the impact of secrecy in Europe. The Triple Entente's members had entered into secret treaties in which they set out, in advance, how they would divide up the territories they would gain control of if they won:[10] the Treaty of London (May 20, 1915) granted Italy part of Tyrol; the Sykes-Picot Agreement (June 16, 1916) split the Ottoman Empire between Great Britain and France, with Russia taking Constantinople. It was not until spring 1917 that the British foreign secretary, Arthur Balfour, told Wilson about these secret treaties. Wilson believed they violated the principle of self-determination and understood he was fighting a war alongside allies whose goals he did not share and who were far from espousing his.

Resolved to promote his ideas, Wilson found an unforeseen opportunity in the fall of the Czarist regime in 1917. One of the first acts of the new communist diplomacy was to criticize secrecy: on November 23, Lenin and Trotsky published the Allies' secret treaties to show that for the Czar, and by extension the European Allies, the war's real objective was territorial annexation.[11] These revelations struck a blow to the Allies in international public opinion (Mayer, 1959, pp. 245–266). In France, a so-called "committee to renew international relations" published a translation of a UDC pamphlet about the secret treaties.

The Fourteen Points speech of January 8, 1918 was therefore Wilson's reply to this new diplomatic context. Faced with the European Allies' procrastination following the publication of their secret treaties, Wilson wanted to remind the world that the United States had different objectives, and to tell its allies to abandon their objectives.

---

8   "Address to the Senate", January 22, 1917, *PWW*, XL, pp. 533–539.

9   "Letter to John Palmer Gavit", January 29, 1917, *PWW*, XLI, p. 55 (emphasis in original).

10   For example, Article 16 of the Treaty of London provides that the agreement must remain secret.

11   G.F. KENNAN, *Russia Leaves the War*, Princeton: Princeton University Press, 1956, pp. 71–84.

The increased American war effort helped degrade Germany's military position. On October 6, 1918, Germany made it known that it agreed to negotiations based on the Fourteen Points. Wilson sent his close advisor, Colonel House, to negotiate the general terms of the peace with France and Great Britain: he began the discussion on the Fourteen Points, but Clemenceau claimed he was not very familiar with them, and Lloyd George complained that Great Britain had not been consulted about them. However, whenever one of them blocked on one of the points (e.g., Lloyd George objected to free navigation), House reminded them that Wilson was going to have to give a public account of the Allies' conditions to Congress and the American people,[12] and they eventually agreed to a Pre-Armistice Agreement on November 5.

The armistice took effect on November 11, 1918. Wilson announced that he would lead the American delegation to the Versailles conference himself. But first he planned to visit the allied countries, where he intended to speak directly to the people so they could pressure their governments. The ground was especially fertile given the First World War's frightening human cost, which bolstered the trend toward pacifism. He was given a hero's welcome when he landed in Brest on December 4, and raved about everywhere on his European tour – Paris, London, Manchester, Rome, and Milan – as a "champion of human rights", "just", and "Moses from across the Atlantic". "Saint Woodrow" was so adored that several times Clemenceau stopped him from speaking at public meetings in France. Everywhere he went, Wilson called for an end to the old, bellicose diplomatic order based on a balance of powers and secrecy. He refused to sign a peace treaty that was only a ceasefire. He wanted to lay the foundations for perpetual peace guaranteed, in particular, by open diplomacy. But could a new balance be found given the institution of secrecy?

2. THE NEW BALANCE: SECRET PROCESS, PUBLIC RESULTS

The Wilsonian moment culminated in the Versailles peace conference, which began on January 18, 1919. Compared to his initial ambition – "open covenants, openly arrived at" – Wilson was only partially successful.

---

[12] A. WALWORTH, *America's Moment: 1918, American Diplomacy at the End of World War I*, New York: W.W. Norton, 1977, pp. 32–73.

While publication progressively became a legal as well as a practical requirement, treaties are still negotiated in secret, at the demand of diplomats.

2.1. PUBLICIZED RESULTS OF INTERNATIONAL NEGOTIATIONS

"Open covenants": the principle of public treaties became part of international law at the 1919 peace conference. The Preamble of the Covenant of the League of Nations provides: "The high contracting parties, [i]n order to promote international co-operation and to achieve international peace and security ... by the prescription of open, just and honorable relations between nations. ..."

To institutionalize "open" diplomacy, Article 18 of the Covenant provided for two new formalities: the registration and publication of all treaties. Mandatory registration was unprecedented: no previous treaty had mentioned secrecy with the intention of doing away with it. On the contrary, if the words "treaty" and "secret" were used together, it was sometimes to state the opposite, i.e., that the treaty would be kept wholly or partially confidential.[13]

In practice, Article 18 had very limited effect. Several League of Nations members felt that some matters that were in theory "technical or administrative" ought to be exempt from the new obligation (e.g., in 1920, France and Belgium did not register the military agreement appended to their alliance treaty).[14] But more importantly, the fact that certain countries had not joined the League, or had left it, reduced the provision's impact: neither Germany nor the USSR were League members in 1922 when they secretly concluded the Treaty of Rapallo, which allowed Germany to manufacture weapons in Soviet territory in exchange for technical assistance. In the early 1930s, the events that led to the Second World War (the affairs of Manchuria, Ethiopia, and the Anschluss, followed by the dismantling of Czechoslovakia, the invasions of Albania and Danzig, and the partition of Poland) were all signs of intense, secret diplomatic activity.

---

[13] M. DEHOUSSE, L'enregistrement des traités, Paris: Librairie du Recueil Sirey, 1929, p. 19; see also pp. 12–14.

[14] "When one analyzes precisely which types of agreements to which one wants to apply the exemption from registration, it seems clear that the words 'technical' and 'administrative' are merely euphemisms", ibid., p. 55.

After the Second World War, the San Francisco Conference heralded a return to open diplomacy. The successor to Article 18 of the 1919 Covenant, Article 102 of the United Nations Charter (adopted June 26, 1945, entry into force October 24, 1945) provides that:

1. Every treaty and every international agreement entered into by any Member of the United Nations after the present Charter comes into force shall as soon as possible be registered with the Secretariat and published by it.
2. No party to any such treaty or international agreement which has not been registered in accordance with the provisions of paragraph 1 of this Article may invoke that treaty or agreement before any organ of the United Nations.

Unlike Article 18, however, rather than provide that unregistered treaties are void, Article 102 simply prohibits parties to such treaties from invoking them. Article 80(1) of the 1969 Vienna Convention on the Law of Treaties strengthened this rule, and the International Court of Justice has enforced it. Like Article 18, however, Article 102 has had little effect, and it is estimated that only one-fourth of all treaties are registered.

Publicity nonetheless developed as democracy spread in Western societies and they attached increasing importance to having treaties ratified by elected representatives. Old-fashioned diplomacy placed little importance on ratification, as monarchs simply sent plenipotentiaries to negotiate in their name. But the new republican diplomacy conducted by the United States in the late 18th century changed this practice. The US Constitution (Article II, Section 2) provides that treaties must be ratified by the Senate, which means the results of negotiations must be discussed publicly and can be – and have been – rejected. In 1807 the Senate refused to ratify the Treaty of London; "a practice" the British statesman George Canning called "altogether unusual in the political transactions of States" (Nicolson, 1939, 45). Surprisingly, the Senate also refused twice (on November 20, 1919 and March 19, 1920) to ratify the treaty Wilson had negotiated in Versailles.

2.2. THE TRADITION OF SECRECY PERSISTS IN NEGOTIATIONS

"Openly arrived at": at the Peace Conference, Wilson contradicted himself and did not pursue his desire for public negotiations. In Versailles as in Vienna a century earlier, the "powers acting in the general interest", i.e., the large countries that had won, excluded the "powers with limited interests" (all the other countries). For Sir Harold Nicolson, a member of the British delegation:

> That treaty was certainly an open covenant since its terms were published before they were submitted to the approval of the sovereign authority in the several signatory States. Yet with equal certainty it was not "openly arrived at." In fact few negotiations in history have been so secret, or indeed so occult. (Nicolson, 1939, p. 43)

The Treaty of Versailles was in fact negotiated primarily by three statesmen, Wilson, Lloyd George, and Clemenceau, joined nominally by Italy's representative, Vittorio Emanuele Orlando. They negotiated the treaty behind closed doors, apart from even their own delegations, and thus wielded a kind of power their predecessors at Westphalia, Utrecht, and Vienna never had. And "the highest apostle of 'open diplomacy' found, when it came to practice, that open negotiation was totally unworkable" (Nicolson, 1939, p. 43).

Despite the increasing reach and entrenchment in international public law of the rule of open negotiations, diplomats from succeeding generations, as exemplified by Jules Cambon, Harold Nicolson, and Henry Kissinger, have all claimed that secrecy is vital to conduct international negotiations, as well to their results.

Cambon fits the stereotype of an inter-war negotiator who disagrees with Wilson. The French ambassador to Washington during the 1898 Spanish-American War and Berlin in 1914, he became the Secretary General of the Foreign Affairs Department during the Great War and published a summary of his experience in 1926. Noting that the era "does not like the bearers of secrets that ambassadors are" (Cambon, 1926, p. 11), he did not hesitate to refute the benefits of making the international negotiation process public:

> A negotiator must be discreet: it is a narrow obligation for him. ... I agree that today, discretion is not the fashion. ... Governments are no longer as free as they once were; they must take into account the public's impatience, but that is a far cry from negotiating in public. ... All it takes is for one to have been responsible for his country's interests abroad to realize that the day there is no more secrecy in negotiations, there will be no negotiations at all. ... It is elementary, in fact. Regardless of what revolutions the future brings, there will always be dunces, gossips, and muddle-heads, and as long as nations have interests to be discussed, the same rules of common sense will apply to those who are responsible for them. (Cambon, 1926, pp. 30–32)

Similarly, noting the impact of the telegraph, railroad, and public opinion, he wrote: "It is not to say for that that a new diplomacy is going to rise up that will throw the country back into the shadows of old diplomacy. New diplomacy, old diplomacy, are words that do not correspond to anything concrete" (Cambon, 1926, p. 119).

As for Nicolson, the assistant of Sir Eric Drummond (the first secretary general of the League of Nations), he left the Foreign Office in 1929 for a political career and to become a renowned essayist on diplomacy and its methods. He went even further than Cambon in his ironic denunciation of Wilson's ideal:

> All really good people speak of the "Old Diplomacy" – as also of her disreputable friend "Secret Diplomacy" – in a tone of moral censure. The implication is that, somewhere about the year 1918, diplomacy saw a great white light, was converted, found salvation, and thereafter and thenceforward became an entirely different woman. (Nicolson, 1939, p. 28)

Nicolson did not believe in the distinction between "old" and "new" diplomacies. Even if there were differences between the diplomacy of the 17th and 18th centuries and that of his era, there were not so marked as to be between "*their* darkness and *our* light". In 1939 he wrote that "[d]iplomacy during the last twenty years has become more personal, more secret, more occult even, than it was in the later nineteenth century". And he maintained this belief during the Cold War: "Any valid negotiation must be conducted continuously and confidentially."[15] Some diplomatic working formats were unfavorable to such discretion, which is one reason Nicolson criticized the diplomacy of multilateral conferences in particular as "perhaps the most unfortunate diplomatic method ever conceived".[16] For him, this format drew attention, increased expectations, and polarized personal relationships between the leaders who attended them. Conference diplomacy, insisted Nicolson, was similar to a "succession of propaganda speeches which took no account of the merits of the issues under discussion, which committed the several delegations to positions from which it would be difficult to retreat, which aroused resentment, and which filled the assembled delegates with weariness and despair".[17]

---

[15] H. NICOLSON, *L'évolution des méthodes en diplomatie*, Neuchâtel: La Baconnière, 1955 (translation of *The Evolution of Diplomatic Method*, 1954), p. 85.

[16] H. NICOLSON, *Curzon: The Last Phase 1919–1925. A Study in Post-War Diplomacy*, London: Constable, 1934, p. 397.

[17] H. NICOLSON, "Peacemaking at Paris: Success, Failure or Farce", *Foreign Affairs*, 1946, 2, pp. 197–198.

Throughout his essays, Nicolson claimed, targeting Wilson, that it was "ignorant to contend that [open covenants] should be openly arrived at. ... The endeavor to establish 'open diplomacy' has led delegates to make propaganda speeches in public and conduct serious negotiations in the privacy of hotel bedrooms – which leads to waste of time and farce."[18]

According to one of his contemporaries, "[o]pen diplomacy is a contradiction in terms; we may have publicity or we may have diplomacy, but we cannot have both".[19]

The third diplomat mentioned here to illustrate the persistency of secrecy is Henry Kissinger, whose approach to negotiation gave a major role to secrecy. Kissinger embodies the post-war realist paradigm, according to which states are the main players in the international system, they decide what to do based on a search for security, and the balance of powers is the key to peace. In the search for this balance, negotiations are unavoidable. For Kissinger they were a process of exchanges and contacts that were at least as important as the results one could obtain through them. He was a master who refined two techniques in particular. One is "linkage", i.e., linking various political issues so negotiations could be seen as a giant, holistic movement in which a series of intermediate agreements built on each other and where, as none of the partners could hope for unilateral victory, they agreed to play the game of mutual concessions. The other is "shuttle diplomacy", which saw Kissinger attending high-level meetings one after the other with the parties involved in regional conflicts, such as in 1973 when he met with leaders in the Middle East to bring an end to the Yom Kippur War. Shuttle diplomacy received a lot of media attention. Kissinger willingly sought contact with journalists and received exceptional personal media exposure, achieving a celebrity that was unprecedented in the history of American diplomats.

In a seeming paradox, this carefully orchestrated media coverage contrasts with Kissinger's determined use of secrecy: "Secret negotiations, indeed the clandestine meetings ... became a hallmark of Kissinger's diplomacy" (Berridge et al., 2001, pp. 198–199). Kissinger based his activities in back channels: secret, personal channels that short-circuited the usual procedures. In 1967, when he was a Harvard professor in contact with the White House but without an official position, Kissinger conducted secret negotiations between August and October to try to help end the

---

18 H. NICOLSON, "Perspective on Peace: A Discourse", in Carnegie Endowment for Peace (ed.), *Perspectives on Peace, 1910–1960*, London, 1960, p. 37.
19 I.L. CLAUDE, *The Impact of Public Opinion Upon Foreign Policy and Diplomacy. Open Diplomacy revisited*, The Hague: Mouton, 1965, p. 9.

Vietnam War. A classic example of a back channel is Kissinger's contact with the Russian ambassador, Anatoly Dobrynin, during negotiations that made US-Russian "détente" possible, in particular on the issue of nuclear arms. Describing back channels and how they were useful, Kissinger wrote: "We would, informally, clarify the basic purposes of our governments and when our talks gave hope of specific agreements, the subject was moved to conventional diplomatic channels. If formal negotiations there reached a deadlock, the Channel would open up again."[20]

But Kissinger also used secret back channels because he feared leaks from his own administration.[21] More broadly, because such channels are secret, this "twin track negotiating and decision-making process" (Berridge et al., 2001, p. 200) makes it possible to maintain contacts even with powers with which there are no official diplomatic relations. By making it possible to isolate oneself from outside turbulence and the pressure of public opinion, secrecy, or at least discretion, is an essential prerequisite for beginning certain key negotiations – such as the Oslo process between Palestinians and Israelis in 1993 (Colson, 2010).

Secrecy was increasingly criticized, however, as was Kissinger himself. In 1975, Congress started examining the CIA's activities over the previous quarter century (Church and Pike committees), and Kissinger was questioned about his activities with regard to Chile (the fall of Allende's administration in 1974) and Cyprus (1974 invasion of Turkey). In fall 1975, committee members criticized Kissinger for having used "secrecy for its own sake"[22] and during the 1976 presidential campaign, Jimmy Carter accused him of conducting secret negotiations unworthy of the United States. When Kissinger left the White House in January 1977, an editorialist wrote in the *New York Times* that "secrecy and deceit were levers of his power".

3. CONCLUSION: IS SECRECY ON SHAKY GROUND?

In the conflict between secrecy and transparency in diplomatic negotiations, there was clearly a "Wilsonian moment", which contributed to the

---

[20]   H. KISSINGER, *The White House Years*, Boston & London: Little, Brown, 1979, p. 138.
[21]   H. KISSINGER, *The White House Years*, Boston & London: Little, Brown, 1979, pp. 803–805.
[22]   R.D. SCHULZINGER, *Henry Kissinger. Doctor of Diplomacy*, New York: Columbia University Press, 1989, pp. 206–208.

establishment of secrecy as a norm in international negotiations. But the persistence of the realist paradigm and the effects of inertia specific to the diplomatic system support secrecy's predominance. A recent example dates from fall 2013, when then-US Secretary of State John Kerry conducted secret negotiations with Iranians at the same time as Catherine Ashton, the European Union's high representative for foreign policy, was facilitating official negotiations in Geneva. Over time, however, secrecy has become more limited. While negotiations themselves are still secret, little by little the pre- and post-negotiation phases have opened up: foreign policy objectives are no longer defined solely by the executive, and the treaties and agreements that result from negotiations must be ratified and published.

Seizing the *kairos* (moment favorable to action) presented to him in 1918–1919, Wilson did not succeed in imposing publicity on international negotiations, but a new balance was struck. Above all, Wilson followed his intuition and pursued a modern strategy, appealing directly to the people to promote a new system of international negotiations.

REFERENCES

BERRIDGE, G.R., KEENS-SOPER, M., and OTTE, T.G. (2001), *Diplomatic Theory from Machiavelli to Kissinger* (New York: Palgrave).

CAMBON, J. (1926), *Le Diplomate* (Paris: Hachette).

CLAUDE, I.L. (1965), *The Impact of Public Opinion Upon Foreign Policy and Diplomacy*. Open Diplomacy revisited (The Hague: Mouton).

COLSON, A. (2008), "The Ambassador Between Light and Shade: The Emergence of Secrecy as the Norm for International Negotiation", *Journal of International Negotiation*, 13, pp. 179–195.

COLSON, A. (2009), "La négociation diplomatique au risque de la transparence: rôles et figures du secret envers des tiers", *Négociations*, 1, pp. 31–41.

COLSON, A. (2010), "Le clair-obscur de la négociation: secret, transparence et asymétrie en négociation" in *Entrer en négociation. Mélanges en l'honneur de Christophe Dupont*, ed. A. Colson (Bruxelles: Larcier, 2011), pp. 287–304.

COLSON, A. (2013), "Machiavel, *Le Prince* et la négociation", *Négociations*, 2, pp. 147–157.

DEHOUSSE, M. (1929), *L'enregistrement des traités* (Paris: Librairie du Recueil Sirey).

KENNAN, G.F. (1956), *Russia Leaves the War* (Princeton, N.J.: Princeton University Press).

KISSINGER, H. (1979), *The White House Years* (Boston & London: Little, Brown).

KNOCK, T.J. (1992), *To End All Wars. Woodrow Wilson and the Quest for a New World Order* (New York and Oxford: Oxford University Press).

LINK, A.S. (ed.) (1984), *Papers of Woodrow Wilson* (Princeton: Princeton University Press).

MARQUAND, D. (1977), *Ramsay MacDonald* (London: Cohen Books).

MAYER, A.J. (1959), *The Political Origins of the New Diplomacy, 1917–1918* (New Haven: Yale University Press).

MOREL, E.D. (1915), *Ten Years of Secret Diplomacy: An Unheeded Warning* (London: National Labour Press)

NICOLSON, H. (1934), *Curzon: The Last Phase 1919–1925. A Study in Post-War Diplomacy* (London: Constable).

NICOLSON, H. (1939), *Diplomacy* (Washington, D.C.: Institute for the Study of Diplomacy, 1988).

NICOLSON, H. (1946), "Peacemaking at Paris: Success, Failure or Farce", *Foreign Affairs*.

NICOLSON, H. (1955), *L'évolution des méthodes en diplomatie* (Neuchâtel: La Baconnière) (translation of *The Evolution of Diplomatic Method*, 1954).

NICOLSON, H. (1960), "Perspective on Peace: A Discourse", in Carnegie Endowment for Peace (ed.), *Perspectives on Peace, 1910–1960* (London).

SCHULZINGER, R.D. (1989), *Henry Kissinger. Doctor of Diplomacy* (New York: Columbia University Press).

UDC (1914), *The Morrow of the War* (London).

WALWORTH, A. (1977), *America's Moment: 1918, American Diplomacy at the End of World War I* (New York: W.W. Norton).

WILLIAMS, A. (2006), *Liberalism and War. The Victors and the Vanquished* (London and New York: Routledge).

THE CONVENTION ON THE FUTURE OF EUROPE (2002–2003)

A Model Process for a Multi-Institutional Meeting

Francesco Marchi[*]

At its December 2001 meeting in the Brussels suburb of Laeken, the European Council decided to convene a convention on the future of the European Union to present the Member States with the reforms that would have to be made to meet the challenges of the 21st century, and in particular the EU's inclusion of 10 new Member States in 2004. Following that decision, the European countries agreed, for the first time ever, to share their power to revise the treaties with the supranational institutions that had hitherto been excluded from the process. The Convention,

---

[*]   Institute for Research and Education on Negotiation (ESSEC IRENE), France.

chaired by Valéry Giscard d'Estaing, was attended by just over 200 people representing European and Member State institutions, as well as candidate-country institutions. Despite the controversial subject matter and plethora of opinions, Giscard d'Estaing's chairmanship was a resounding success: after 18 months of intense effort, he obtained consensus on the text of the Treaty establishing a Constitution for Europe. His leadership and control over the process made success possible where several intergovernmental conferences, such as the 2001 Nice summit, had failed.

1. 1954–2001: A TRADITION OF INTERGOVERNMENTAL NEGOTIATIONS

Since it began, European integration has been based on negotiation, the cornerstone on which the Member States have built a supranational entity that has not only replaced intergovernmental agreements and evolved into a partly federal political system, but has constantly expanded geographically while acquiring more extensive political jurisdiction. Recurring cycles of treaty-revision negotiations have made it possible to make the changes such development has required while maintaining the delicate balance between sovereign-state equality and citizens' equality. However, the history of European construction is also full of treaty-revision negotiations that ended in a stalemate, which to a certain extent seems to support Jean Monnet's assertion that "Europe will be built through crises and will be the sum of their solutions"[1]

One of the central themes in the EU institutions' development has been the avoidance of the words "federal" and "constitution", which have always aroused distrust among the Member States. Despite their willingness to set up the European Steel and Coal Community (ESCC) in 1951, in 1954 the same governments called a halt to the creation of the European Defense Community and the European Political Community, which had strong federal connotations. In response to that crisis, Jean Monnet's functionalist method was used to create and consolidate the European Economic Community (EEC). While the plan for European integration had thus succeeded with respect to economic issues, resistance from Member States continued to make it difficult to develop a political dimension, notably in certain policy areas such as defense and foreign policy.

---

[1]   J. MONNET, *Mémoires*, Paris: Fayard, 2004.

The first election of the European Parliament by universal suffrage in 1979 laid the groundwork for Altiero Spinelli's[2] draft constitutional treaty, which the European Parliament approved on February 14, 1984. The Member State governments were not the least bit interested in this draft treaty, but the progressive ideas it contained played a key role in the discussions leading to passage of the Single European Act in 1987.

With the ratification of the Maastricht Treaty (1992), the inclusion of new areas of EU jurisdiction and the growing number of Member States came the question of whether or not the decision-making process was democratic and efficient. Beginning with the negotiations for the Amsterdam Treaty in 1996, changing the EU's institutional framework (the size of the European Commission, qualified-majority voting, and the scope of the co-decision procedure between the European Parliament and the Council of Ministers) became an important subject, but tensions between the Member States kept them from reaching a satisfactory agreement. Those tensions were greatest during the Treaty of Nice negotiations, which were supposed to prepare the European institutions to welcome 10 Eastern European countries as new members. Such institutional issues were labeled "leftovers", i.e., issues to be resolved later. The 1990s proved that the intergovernmental conference (IGC) method was no longer an effective way to overcome national self-interest when trying to redefine the delicate representational balance between sovereign states and European citizens.

2. THREE WORKING PHASES, FROM PERSONAL ASPIRATIONS TO PLENARY ASSEMBLY

Based on the positive experience of the first European Convention, which drafted the EU's Charter of Fundamental Rights, at its December 2001 meeting in Laeken the European Council decided to convene what it called a convention on the future of the European Union.[3] The purpose of this new convention would be to draft a document that would pave the way for the IGC to be held in 2004, before the EU enlarged to include the 10 new Member States. The European Council (heads of States and governments) established that the convention would be composed of 15 executive-branch

---

[2] Altiero Spinelli (1907–1986), an Italian MP and MEP, was the initiator of the European federalist movement.

[3] See Presidency Conclusions, European Council meeting in Laeken, December 14–15, 2001, Annex I: Laeken Declaration, p. 19.

representatives (one for each Member State), 30 members of the national parliaments (two per Member State), 16 European Parliament representatives, two European Commission representatives, and 13 observers from other European institutions. In preparation for the next enlargement, the 12 candidate countries and Turkey were invited to send two members of parliament and two executive-branch representatives. They were told, however, that their representatives could not block consensus.

The European Council appointed former French President Valéry Giscard d'Estaing (1974–1981) to chair the Convention, assisted by Vice Chairmen Guiliano Amato, from Italy, and Jean-Luc Dehaene, from Belgium. There were no official limits placed on the issues the Convention could address, but it was given only one year to complete its proceedings and produce a final document in which the Convention would indicate the various alternatives and degree of support each had received, or make recommendations if consensus had been reached. The Council also specified that the final document "[would] provide a starting point for discussions in the Intergovernmental Conference, which will take the ultimate decisions" In short, the European Convention would deliberate in the shadow of the IGC, where the Member States would have a veto.

The Convention's proceedings were broken up into three phases. During the first phase, which ran from February through July 2002, Convention members got to know each other and developed a shared feeling of belonging as they listened to each other express their aspirations for the Europe of the future. During the second phase, they broke into 11 working groups to examine the issues that had been raised during the first phase, analyze various alternatives, and make concrete proposals during the plenary session. The first six groups discussed economic governance, subsidiarity, the EU's legal personality, the status of the Charter of Fundamental Rights, additional areas of jurisdiction, and the role of national parliaments. On July 18, the Convention decided to set up a second wave of working groups, which tackled the issues of the EU's external activities, defense, simplifying legal framework, and the area of freedom, security and justice. Each working group had roughly 30 members, who chose which group to join based on their expertise.

When the working groups presented their reports to the plenary assembly, Giscard d'Estaing presented a draft treaty outline so a general structure could be decided on. This document signaled a sea change in the negotiation dynamics, as the Member State governments had begun to understand the European Convention's significance. The second phase ended in early February when the chairman decided to begin presenting and discussing the various parts of the treaty: the first part (Titles I, II and III) in late January; the second (Titles V, VII and IX) in late February; and the third (Titles IV, VI, VIII and X) in late March. The Convention then entered a phase of proposing amendments and refining the text in view of its final approval. The Praesidium[4] and Secretariat were in charge of summarizing the amendments proposed by the plenary assembly and incorporating them into a new version of the text, which was then submitted to the plenary assembly for discussion and final approval. Despite strong disagreements over the "leftovers", especially the institutional architecture, the heightened pace of plenary sessions enabled the Convention to reach broad consensus on Parts I and II before the European Council's June 2003 meeting in Thessalonica. An extension was nonetheless needed to discuss further refinements to Part III of the final text. The Convention's proceedings officially ended on July 18, 2003, with approval of the draft Treaty establishing a Constitution for Europe.

3. A TIGHTLY CONTROLLED NEGOTIATING PROCEDURE: TOWARD EXEMPLARY CONSENSUS?

The European Convention led to agreement on a text that contained innovative proposals on several aspects, and in particular on the "leftovers", which had been the subject of friction and reluctance from the Member State governments for more than a decade. The reasons for this success should therefore be analyzed, and a distinction made between the structural factors of the new negotiating context and those more closely related to Giscard d'Estaing's chairmanship and how he conducted the negotiation process.

3.1. THE SPIRIT OF THE CONVENTION: MEMBERSHIP AND BELONGING

Giscard d'Estaing opened the proceedings on February 28, 2002 with a speech that emphasized the Convention's inclusiveness and originality:[5] unlike

---

[4]   The Convention's executive body, composed of 12 members representing the Convention's various components.

[5]   CONV 4/02, Speech of Valery Giscard d'Estaing at the Convention's inaugural session, February 28, 2002, Brussels.

a classic ICG, the Convention was attended by representatives of both the European Union and the Member States, and the sessions and documents were public. In his speech, Giscard d'Estaing encouraged the participants to contribute to the Convention's work by distancing themselves from their partisan, institutional, or national affiliations and taking an individual approach instead. The fact that they were seated in alphabetical order favored this approach, by allowing Convention members to mingle more easily with members from other institutions or countries. His second point was to remind the participants of the enormous cost for the EU's future if an agreement was not reached. This reminder proved to be key in the multilateral negotiations, as the parties often had trouble making an initial estimate of the real costs of non-agreement.

Giscard d'Estaing also reminded the parties of the need for a new Europe, one that was ready to face the challenges of the 21st century, but did not suggest any solutions. The purpose of his approach was to convince the parties that these negotiations were truly necessary, without discussing preconceived outcomes. It also created a feeling of belonging to the process itself, including for those who were opposed to or had reservations about deeper European integration. He tried to give the proceedings a foreseeable time frame by describing the Convention's various phases; stressed the need to think openly about and listen actively to each participant's point of view as a point of departure for the discussions on Europe's future; reasserted the fundamental principle of active listening before active speaking, first as socialization tool but also to reduce the information gap among the Convention's participants; and clarified the importance of, and the need to gather enough, information before trying to develop any alternatives. By explicitly outlining this procedural sequence, he was able to protect the participants from one of negotiation's recurring pitfalls: value judgments about the alternatives before enough potential solutions have been proposed. He also explained how the Convention proceedings would be organized, because it is only when there enough options on the table and the consequences of each have been clearly defined that a decision can be considered. The organization and sequencing of the proceedings are key factors in successful multiparty negotiation[6] as research and practice have shown that an explanation of the proceedings' organization and schedule must be given as early as possible, while the stakes are still low and the parties have not yet become competitive.

---

6   I.W. ZARTMAN (ed.), *International Multilateral Negotiations*, San Francisco, CA: Jossey-Bass, 2010.

3.2. THE "AS IF" RULE, NON-DEFINITION OF CONSENSUS, AND "CRESCENDO" APPROACH

Giscard d'Estaing was aware, however, of the danger involved in producing a document that was merely the starting point for the IGC's work and might therefore be subject to endless haggling later. To increase the document's strategic weight, he therefore suggested that the Convention try to draft the text as if it were the final treaty text, with no open options. In this way, he correctly foresaw its anchoring effect, i.e., the ability of information known at the beginning of negotiations to influence the outcome. The anchoring effect was heightened by the fact that the text had garnered consensus. Although the IGC had the right to have the last word, it is harder to rehash an agreement when it has obtained consensus.

Another of Giscard d'Estaing's powerful tools was the decision not to hold formal votes, but to favor decision-making by iterative consensus. According to the Laeken Declaration, Giscard d'Estaing was in charge of declaring when consensus had been reached. This power was increased by the fact that consensus was never precisely defined during the Convention.[7] At each plenary session, the chairman summarized the previous discussions and the issues on which consensus had been reached. The lack of a precise definition of consensus was criticized numerous times – Giscard d'Estaing being reproached with declaring consensus based on his personal preferences.

He also displayed strategic skill in organizing the negotiations and setting the agenda to crescendo from the initial trust-building phase through the working groups' exploration of potential solutions in several EU policy areas, while taking care not to create a working group on redesigning the institutional architecture. The Convention proceedings began in February 2002, but Giscard d'Estaing postponed discussion of the highly controversial issue of revamping the EU's institutions until after the working groups had completed their analyses and the Convention had agreed to most of the other reforms. By not presenting the assembly with the text on reorganizing the institutional structure until late April 2003, when there was already broad consensus on most of the constitutional treaty's text and time was running short, he pressured the most conservative Convention members to abandon the status quo.

---

[7] F. DELOCHE-GAUDEZ, "La Convention sur l'Avenir de l'Europe: ruptures et continuités," in G. AMATO, H. BRIBOSIA, AND B. DE WITTE (eds.) *Genesis and Destiny of the European Constitution*, Brussels: Bruylant, 2007.

3.3. CENTRALIZED DRAFTING: STRATEGIC FILTERING OF AMENDMENTS, AND DRAFTING SUMMARIES

The Convention was finally working the same way a parliamentary assembly does. Another of Giscard d'Estaing's strategic calculations was to set up a procedure for amending the texts submitted to the plenary assembly. He encouraged Convention members to submit written amendments to the Praesidium, which summarized them. This enabled Giscard d'Estaing to discreetly set aside the most extreme amendments and isolate the spoilers and defenders of the status quo. He also gained a structural advantage with regard to processing and redistributing information, because he was the "author" of the new parts of text that would be submitted to the Convention's plenary assembly. By centralizing the amendment and summary-drafting procedure, Giscard d'Estaing strengthened the original text and confirmed the advantages of the technique known as "single negotiating text" or "one text procedure":[8] multilateral negotiations are more successful if only one text is discussed. This approach depersonalizes the amendments, as the chair is their only author and tries to reflect the outcome of the debate; the other parties are relegated to merely objecting, and must prove that each requested change is warranted.

3.4. CHANGING THE PROCESS AND THE BILATERAL CONTACTS

The Convention had almost finalized the treaty text by early 2003, but there was still strong disagreement over the institutional framework, and in particular the size of the European Commission, the new definition of what would constitute a qualified majority of the Council, and the replacement of the rotating EU presidency with a stable presidency. Giscard d'Estaing understood that the negotiation process had to be changed to allow for discussions by institutional components (national governments, European institutions, MEPs, national MPs, etc.) rather than in plenary sessions. Calling these bilateral component-based discussions "confessionals",

---

8   R. FISHER, *Beyond Machiavelli: Tools for Coping with Conflict*, Cambridge, MA: Harvard University Press, 1994, p. 148.

he set a prerequisite that for an amendment to be admissible, it had to obtain consensus within each component. This procedural change allowed Giscard d'Estaing to further isolate the most controversial elements of certain parts of the text related to the institutions and their organization. This "confessional" method, coupled with time pressure, made it possible to achieve consensus on almost the entire Treaty establishing a Constitution for Europe by June 12, 2003.

4. CONCLUSION: THE PROCESS OF NEGOTIATION SHAPES THE OUTCOME

From a methodological standpoint, this negotiation shows the fundamental importance of the role Valéry Giscard d'Estaing played as chairman, and therefore discussion organizer. While structural elements, such as the favorable context, time pressure before the 2004 accessions, a Convention not limited to executive-branch representatives, and transparent discussions and documents, contributed to the negotiation's success, it must be underscored that the control exercised over the procedure explains in large part the positive result obtained. The importance of the procedure is in fact a phenomenon observed in most major multilateral conferences.

History, however, has cruelly relegated this European Convention to failure, as the French and the Dutch rejected its final result in referendums held in 2005. The European Convention therefore cannot be compared to the American exploit of the Constitutional Convention of 1787 (as described by Carrie Menkel-Meadow in "Negotiating the American Constitution (1787–1789)" in this volume), where under the chairmanship of George Washington, 55 delegates representing 12 of the 13 states succeeded in drafting the Constitution of the United States in five months. One important difference is that the Constitutional Convention did not operate entirely by consensus, but held frequent votes instead. Another one is the relative absence of the media in the 1787 negotiation compared the 2003 one.

The results obtained in Europe in 2003 are nonetheless remarkable from a negotiation standpoint. Achieving consensus across 200 people on such sensitive European topics was a real challenge, and the results therefore largely exceeded expectations.

REFERENCES

CLOSA, Carlos and FOSSUM, Erik, "Deliberative Constitutional Politics in the EU", ARENA Report, Oslo: Arena, 2004.

CONV 4/02, Speech of Valery Giscard d'Estaing at the Convention's inaugural session, February 28, Brussels, 2002.

DELOCHE-GAUDEZ, Florence, "La Convention sur l'Avenir de l'Europe: ruptures et continuités" in G. Amato, H. Bribosia, and B. de Witte (eds.), *Genesis and Destiny of the European Constitution*, Brussels: Bruylant, 2007.

ELGSTROM, Ole and JONSSON, Christer, "Negotiation in the European Union: Bargaining or Problem Solving?", *Journal of European Public Policy*, Vol. 7(5), pp. 684–704, 2002.

FISHER, Roger, *Beyond Machiavelli: Tools for Coping with Conflict*, Cambridge, MA: Harvard University Press, 1994.

LAEKEN EUROPEAN COUNCIL PRESIDENCY CONCLUSIONS, December 14–15, 2001 (Laken Declaration).

MAGNETTE, Paul and NICOLAIDIS, Kalypso, "The European Convention: Bargaining in the Shadow of Rhetoric", *West European Politics*, Vol. 27, pp. 381–404, 2004.

MONNET, Jean, *Mémoires*, Paris: Fayard, 2004.

ZARTMAN, I. William (ed.), *International Multilateral Negotiations*, San Francisco CA: Jossey-Bass, 2010.

PART IV

BEYOND INTERESTS:
EMOTIONS, BELIEFS AND VALUES

AN INDUSTRIALIZATION DEAL IN 1868 JAPAN

Glover the Scotsman in Nagasaki

William W. Baber[*]

In mid-year 1868 Japan found itself in an uncertain space after the abdication of the Shogun, the restoration of the Meiji Emperor, and the standing down of the feudal clans. Though there were rumors of fighting, the country was in fact at peace and gathering itself for a shift from armed struggle to the greatest and fastest industrial leap forward that the world had yet seen. For the moment, however, the scores of clans in control of Japan did not know their futures and they struggled to shift from war readiness to a new footing that would replenish their funds and strengths. One clan, Hizen, had enjoyed control of the country's sole trading port from 1633 to 1859: Nagasaki. Hizen's ruler, the Daimyo Nabeshima, leapt for the opportunity to realize potentially immense cash incomes by exporting coal. Nabeshima was aware that his leading position on foreign

*   Associate Professor, Kyoto University, Graduate School of Management. The development of the concepts around negotiation schemas was supported by Japan Society of Promotion of Science grant number 17K03877.

contacts and ships was evaporating. His path to riches could however be opened with the cooperation of the rogue Scotsman who had managed volatile rebel samurai, Shanghai traders, and Shogunal officials, Thomas Glover. Success would cement Nagasaki's role in maritime industries. In the end, this particular deal turned out to be Japan's largest industrialization deal by 1868/9, preceded only by Glover's sale of a dry dock system in Nagasaki. Cognitive schemas help understand how the negotiation around the coalmine developed.

1. NEW BUSINESS OPPORTUNITIES UNDER THE MEIJI GOVERNMENT

When the negotiation on the Takashima coalmine started, in June 1868, steamships were arriving with greater frequency as the country opened new ports and granted greater freedoms to foreigners. The new government was in place with trade-friendly policies, especially with regards to importing foreign technology. Thomas Glover had been trading in Nagasaki since 1859. His dealings involving ships, weapons, and commodities were now on the wane, and some customers had trouble paying for their orders. Glover was hoping to shift from one-off deals on those goods and to return to long-term investments such as tea processing, production equipment, and speculating in land. Against this background of political and economic change, the possibilities around the Takashima mine piqued his interest.

The main subject of negotiation was the development of an existing coalmine on the island of Takashima, about 2 km off the coast of Kyushu and some 12 km from the city of Nagasaki. Japan at that time had few sources of coal and these were not well developed. There was almost no domestic market for coal as homes were not heated with that material, and existing industry, mainly small scale, relied primarily on charcoal. There was, however, an immediate market available in the servicing of visiting steamships. Glover proposed intensifying development of the Takashima mine knowing nearly nothing about mining, but confident of a growing market.

By 1868, the mine had been developed only to a very limited extent. Operations were conducted by traditional methods and manual equipment. Without pumps, flooded areas were simply abandoned. Despite lacking an engineering background, Glover felt at a glance that the mine could be made far more productive and profitable with modern European methods and equipment. Time would prove him right, but first he had to negotiate a profitable agreement with the Daimyo of Hizen.

2. TWO SIDES AND FIVE CHARACTERS SEEKING A DEAL

Glover, his counterparts, and the supporting figures knew one another and had interacted in the course of the 1860s. The actors include Glover, Matsubayashi Genzo, Kenneth Ross Mackenzie, Joseph Heco, and the Hizen clan Daimyo. None of these individuals were experts in mining or long-term finance. Yet they would have to negotiate one of the more important business deals of the early Meiji period; on one side was Glover and his supporters, Heco and Mackenzie; on the other side was the Hizen clan which had complete say over the land and the clan agent. The following paragraphs introduce each briefly.

Thomas Blake Glover arrived in Nagasaki in 1858, just as it was becoming a focus of resistance to the Shogunate. Glover became proficient in Japanese and took over from his predecessor, Mackenzie, before later establishing Glover and Co. Glover completed numerous deals in the decade before the negotiations around the Takashima mine. These deals ranged from mundane commodities such as tea and textiles, to guns fresh from the end of the American civil war and ships. Even more challenging were his dealings with revolutionaries who united the clans of Choshu and Satsuma. These interactions required political sensitivity and daring as they broke laws by smuggling individuals overseas and sometimes incurred the wrath of hot-headed reactionaries. Glover made profits for himself and his employer, but saw a decline of business and cash reserves in early 1868 as the Takashima negotiations began.

Kenneth Ross Mackenzie was a long lasting representative of Jardine, Matheson & Co., a trading company with a speckled history in the Chinese tea and opium trade. Mackenzie functioned as Glover's partner, advisor, and respected mentor. He was Glover's senior, by almost 40 years, with much experience in Nagasaki before Glover arrived.

Joseph Heco was an administrative assistant and interpreter for Glover. Although Glover spoke Japanese well enough to deal with revolutionaries and officials, he included Heco for his bilingual ability and experience. Heco was one of those rare castaways who had been rescued mid-ocean, transported abroad, educated, returned, yet avoided the summary execution most such returnees faced. His biography made him not only a useful employee to Glover but also a man of rare talents in Japan.

Matsubayashi Genzo was an experienced business agent of the Hizen clan. As the lead negotiator for the clan, he was the direct link between the negotiations and the final decision maker, the Hizen Daimyo.

Matsubayashi would have known both Mackenzie and Glover through previous dealings, such as acquisition of ships and the small scale sale of coal. Matsubayashi is described as a "hard headed man of business" and he was the head of the clan's commercial office (Checkland and Checkland, 1984). Like Heco, he had rich experience dealing with foreigners, exceeded in Japan perhaps only by individuals like the Tosa clan commercial representative, Y. Iwasaki, who would later found the Mitsubishi empire.

Nabeshima Naomasa was the Hizen Daimyo, a politically astute clan headman. He promoted western learning in his fiefdom, reformed its economy, advanced public health through smallpox vaccinations, managed decades of shifting alliances, and completed semi-legal purchases of foreign weapons during the last years of the Shogunate. He was inclined toward the modernization of the Takashima coal pits for income to pay off the debts of the arms race that led up to the restoration of the Meiji Emperor. One essential element of the Daimyo's relations with Glover was an outstanding debt for $43,000 for the purchase of the warship *Eugenie* from Glover some months prior to the Takashima negotiation.

3. A QUICK MOVING NEGOTIATION

From existing records and the work of historians we can roughly reconstruct a timeline of events.

It is not clear when Glover first discussed the Takashima mine, perhaps before his 1867 trip to Scotland, or even years before, since he had sold Takashima coal in small amounts since 1860. It seems that the initial formal contact was made by Mackenzie, at Glover's instigation, through Joseph Heco (Heco, 1895). Heco reports discussing the topic with Mackenzie and then delivering an anchoring offer to Matsubayashi who a few months later, on Sunday May 31, 1868, entered into talks with Glover and Heco (Sugiyama, 1993). Matsubayashi was well informed enough to reject the anchor proposal outright and to dive into much more serious talks armed with data and projections. The parties came to a rough agreement in a session on June 1. A first addendum was discussed the following day and agreed on June 3 as Matsubayashi attempted to get some support from Heco, his countryman, against Glover (Naito, 2001; Sugiyama, 1993). At this point, Glover left abruptly for Hyogo and Osaka to join land auctions in those ports, travelling on June 4–8. Matsubayashi agreed the second addendum on June 9, which the clan agent signed. After only three sessions in the midst of these other activities, the deal was agreed.

Hereafter, equipment was ordered and installed, technicians brought in, and sales consummated in short order. The mine was producing approximately 60–90 tons per day by January 1869 (Sugiyama, 1984).

4. A SUCCESSFUL DEAL AND THE SEEDS OF FAILURE

A first observation is that, for all actors in the deal, there was urgency to gain stable profits in a national atmosphere of relief, celebration, and concern.

Economically, there was a reckoning of debts in 1868 that had built up in the course of the revolt that restored the power to the emperor. The fiefs that had been spending and borrowing in previous years were taking stock of their situations and avoiding expenses (Sugiyama, 1984) and Nagasaki was in a downturn (Checkland and Checkland, 1984). The central government, undeveloped and unsure as it was in the earliest months of the Meiji period, was not yet making large investments. For Glover, this meant fewer transactions and earnest threat of defaults. For the Hizen clan leader, Nabeshima, this meant minimizing expenses, and a motivation to seek longer-term gains. One strategic change was however clear: trade was on and more ports were open, with more scheduled for opening. It would mean an increase in the number of foreign ship arrivals for Japan as a whole.

Nabeshima, the Hizen Daimyo, needed a stable income in order to manage clan debts. Foreign currency was a must, as the value of the Japanese *ryo* had decreased through most of his lifetime because the Shogun governments had successively debased the currency. In order to thrive in the unknown new order of the Meiji era, Nabeshima also needed to establish advantages over other clans that were likely to compete for resources and attention. With the port of Nagasaki apparently in decline, the clan's ancient advantage was eroding. A reliable sales channel for coal was an imperative if the coalmine was to bring any benefit at all. Beyond these immediate benefits, Nabeshima sought long-term control over the mine, low cash outlay, and strategic guidance regarding development and markets. What alternatives might a clan like Nabeshima's have had in 1868 Japan? The Daimyo could have searched for other partners with language, trade skills, and financing, perhaps in Yokohama; however, this would likely be time and cost intensive. Instead, the Takashima coalmine required resources he could realistically deploy: the island, its coal, manpower, permits, and useful local human networks, but only limited amounts of cash. His business agent, Matsubayashi, was skillful. Principal-agent conflict was minimal because Matsubayashi's position in a feudal society meant his success and satisfaction was synonymous with Nabeshima's. This ironbound connection may explain why Matsubayashi and Glover had apparently not developed a warm working relationship despite completing deals previously.

Glover's needs were relatively uncomplicated: income. Beyond this, he wished to diversify his business activities while ensuring low involvement in management of the mine, and a high share of profits. Glover appeared to have relatively strong business alternatives such as purchasing plots in Nagasaki, Osaka, and Hyogo ports as well as imports of marine and minting equipment, though we have noted these were in decline. He had, in addition, a vision that others seemed to lack, as well as access to finance, contacts to mining experts, sales skills, ability to buy equipment, and available customers (Checkland and Checkland, 1984; Gardiner, 2007; Sugiyama, 1984; Sugiyama, 1993).

In summary, Glover and Nabeshima, the two main actors of the deal, had complementary resources and skills; however they lacked experience in mining and resource development, a glaring gap. Glover had the better alternatives; nonetheless, his words and actions of the time indicate that he clearly felt the Takashima mine would be the most profitable among his choices. The sailing seemed clear for an agreement, but there were a few rocks in the Nagasaki waters.

4.1. BEWARE THE ROCKS!

The first rock to avoid was a clumsy effort by Glover to anchor the negotiation at a very low cost to himself. In exchange for the mineral rights of the island, he offered $6,000 to the Daimyo and another $6,000 for other leading families (karo) as a one-time transaction. Given his own expectations of $2 dollars profit per ton on 200–300 tons per day, this was an outrageously low anchoring offer. Matsubayashi's calculations laid this bare, but the Daimyo was not put off.

The next hazard was the small steamer *Eugenie* which had been purchased for $43,000 from Glover. Payment was not forthcoming, and default seemed likely. The first version of the agreement saw Hizen giving Glover $43,000 of credit in goods, and the final version saw the ship paid off through cash from mining profits. Thus the *Eugenie* was transformed from a problem to a solution that made the parties more dependent on their mutual success.

A final hazard to overcome was Glover's haste: after discussing and agreeing on June 1 with an addendum on June 3, he immediately took a week-long visit to Osaka and Hyogo to buy land. Directly upon his return, a second addendum was presented and agreed. In each addendum, Glover's positions improved by only minor concessions regarding monitoring and punitive clauses which neither side would have an interest in activating.

Thus the deal was completed. But why did this apparent triumph become a failure?

4.2. INSIGHTS THROUGH SCHEMAS

For Nagasaki and Japan, the development of the Takashima coalmine is considered a historical leap forward as one of Japan's first steps towards industrialization. Yet it is ironic that, despite the apparent success for Glover, the implementation of that negotiation quite rapidly went wrong for him. Despite his years of successes, deep knowledge of the environment, and substantial cultural skills, Glover the Scotsman went bankrupt within two years. How can we explain this?

One possible explanation for the mistakes made can be found in the field of cognitive psychology. We can analyze Glover and Matsubayahi's behaviors through *schemas*, a way of describing knowledge structures found in all people. As processes, specifically *procedure schemas* and *strategy schemas* (Nishida, 1999), schemas guide the thinking of people as they interact. They play a fundamental role in organizing routines and formal ways of behaving in many circumstances. But how do people envision negotiations? Beyond the broad definition of schemas as "mental representations of some aspect of experience that help interpret information" (Colman, 2009), negotiation schemas are guidelines, but not prescriptions, for processes and strategies that negotiators follow. The nature of schemas and their execution depend on one's experiences, culture, gender, age, and even rank in an organization (Baber and Ojala, 2015). Schemas guide the thinking and actions, but they do not determine interests and motivations. Schemas for negotiation include the processes negotiators execute to attain interests but they cannot prevent errors or guarantee best results; our schemas may lead us to success or doom.

Adjusting to, taking on or manipulating schemas of others is part of the cross-cultural experience of business people (Baber and Ojala, 2016). By 1868 Glover had a decade of experience with Japanese people, ranging from workers to a Satsuma Daimyo (Burke-Gaffney, 2009). He would have encountered and successfully used or adjusted a range of schemas as he negotiated in the fast-moving business and political environment of the times.

No one can conclusively determine the schemas in play among the actors in this long-past negotiation. Indeed, there may have been some schemas active that 21st century researchers might not recognize at all. Nonetheless, evidence from historical documents around the Takashima negotiation allow the investigator to infer a number of matches with procedure and strategy schemas around negotiation. Four of these are examined below, as they guided the negotiators to solutions and into eventual failure.

1. *Explore for cooperative solutions.* This widely used process schema, shared today amongst Western as well as Asian negotiators (Baber and Ojala, 2015) and apparently also with Glover and his counterparts in 1868, led the parties into restructuring the loan for the *Eugenie*. Linking the loan to mine development ensured that it would not go into default and took pressure off the cash strapped clan.

    However this negotiation schema was not used well. It can sometimes be dangerous to be over-creative. Paying the *Eugenie* debt from profits increased the likelihood that Glover would get payment, but eliminated any chance of getting cash or even trade goods in the near future. The risk became entirely Glover's, to whom slow payment seemed better than accepting payment in kind or non-payment. This short-term mutual win would turn out to be a serious mutual error later because their effort to resolve the point meant the critical loss of operating capital.

2. *Determine if there is suitable end to end business logic.* This of course very important strategy schema did not unfold properly for the parties to build a resilient agreement. Glover anticipated that, aside from large profits, there would be a long-term coal market accessible through his business network and a need for expert technicians. In addition, he expected the clan to take over day-to-day management of the mine, seeing to labor issues in particular.

    Glover did not, however, grasp the challenges of managing the mine including the high cost of maintenance and labor. Consequently he missed the need and opportunity to raise short-term capital by selling or mortgaging his land holdings. Poor execution of this strategy schema led him to bargain for only seven years, apparently not considering longer-term plans at all. As for the clan, Matsubayashi's report after the first communication with Mackenzie identified rough costs and break even projections, not merely profit hopes. His report also found that Glover held the keys to selling the coal, yet he misunderstood the capital needs of the mine. Both parties failed to follow through fully with this schema to accurately assess the lifecycle of the business.

3. *Get the deal and move on.* This strategy schema, which today seems more widespread in the West than in Japan (Baber and Ojala, 2015), perhaps caused Glover to rush into agreement in an attempt to gain the opportunity regardless of the details simply so he could hurry off to land auctions in Osaka. Upon returning, the second addendum amounted only to a few "band aids" and could not right the errors already built in.

4. *Secure an ally, develop the relationship.* This strategy schema seems to be widespread in today's Japanese negotiation behavior (Baber and Ojala, 2015). In 1868, it is likely to have applied to Glover and the clan; however, they did not develop it successfully. For the clan, alliance building was a main thread of their political maneuvering in those decades as the various clans plotted and squabbled (Jansen, 1994), but may not have applied to their business dealings. Regarding the coalmine, the parties needed skills and resources from each other for several years at least. Alliance building appears to have been part of Glover's thinking throughout his career as he had shown himself adept at building allies among the rebels seeking to overthrow the Shogun, as well as among Shogunal officials. Some of these alliances lasted decades and led Glover to new opportunities ranging from beer brewing to work for Mitsubishi Corporation. Although Glover attempted to build a deep alliance with the clan, this schema failed to bear fruits sufficient to weather the financial difficulties that soon arrived.

The schema framework offers an analytical lens to understand negotiators' actions and thinking and how they approach negotiations. Schema do not tell us precisely why negotiators succeed or fail. Rather, they help us understand what kind of thinking and guidelines the negotiators took into the deals they made.

5. TYING UP LOOSE ENDS

Takashima coal burned well – better than expected, as shown in a formal sea trial in the fall of 1868 (Gardiner, 2007). Captains quickly came to prefer it in East Asia (Sugiyama, 1984). Despite mechanized production from January 1869, the mine was slow to achieve the targeted +200 tons per day. Soon, labor became restive because of poor conditions. Even so, prospects looked good until a promissory note delivered by a visiting captain forced Glover into sudden bankruptcy. Glover could neither save the deal nor motivate his usual backers to do so and thus the Netherlands Trading Society took over Glover's share in the mine. His negotiation needs and wants were never fully met: he gained only little income and that too slowly; further, he could not avoid becoming the operations manager – the very task he had negotiated for the clan to handle. The clan lost some of the revenues it yearned for, and eventually also control of the mine.

The new owner required Glover to remain as operations manager and for the next several years he worked hard to manage the mine into success. Despite losing his ownership, he recovered his money in time as he earned the tangible gains of an employee and the intangible gains of becoming one of Japan's most seasoned industrial managers. Soon the mine would become a pillar of Japan's industrialization; a success for the nation although only a marginal win for the parties first involved. Decades later Glover would be recognized for this and other contributions with an award from the Meiji Emperor himself.

REFERENCES

BABER, W.W., and OJALA, A., "Cognitive Negotiation Schemata in the IT Industries of Japan and Finland", *Journal of International Technology and Information Management*, 2015, 24/3, 87–104.

BABER, W.W., and OJALA, A., Schemata, Acculturation, and Cognition: Expatriates in Japan's Software Industry. In Proceedings – Asia-Pacific Software Engineering Conference, Hamilton, NZ: APSEC, 2016.

BURKE-GAFFNEY, B., *Nagasaki: The British Experience, 1854–1945*. Folkestone: Brill, 2009.

CHECKLAND, S., and CHECKLAND, O., "British and Japanese Economic Interaction Under the Early Meiji: The Takashima Coal Mine 1868–88", *Business History*, 1984, 26/2, 139–155.

COLMAN, A., *A Dictionary of Psychology (Oxford Quick Reference)*, 3rd ed., Oxford: Oxford University Press, 2009.

GARDINER, M., *At the Edge of Empire: The Life of Thomas B. Glover*, Edinburgh: Birlinn, 2007.

HECO, J., *The Narrative of a Japanese: What He Has Seen and the People He Has Met in the Course of the Last Forty Years*, Vol. 2, (J. Murdoch, Ed.), San Francisco, CA: American-Japanese Publishing Association, 1895.

JANSEN, M.B., *Sakamoto Ryoma and the Meiji Restoration*, New York, NY: Columbia University Press, 1994.

NAITO, H., *Meiji kenkuo no youshou tomasu B. gurabaa shimatsu* [*Western Trade in the Meiji Period through the life of Thomas Glover*], Tokyo: Atene shobou, 2001.

NISHIDA, H., "A Cognitive Approach to Intercultural Communication Based on Schema Theory: What are Schemas?", *International Journal Intercultural Relations*, 1999, 23/5, 753–777.

SUGIYAMA, S., "Thomas B. Glover: A British Merchant in Japan, 1861–70", *Business History*, 1984, 26/2, 115–138.

SUGIYAMA, S., *Meishiisshin to igirisu shonin: tomasu gurabaa no shogai* [*The Meiji Restoration and English Businessmen: Thomas Glover's Lifetime*], Tokyo: Ishinami Shoten, 1993.

THE 1659 TREATY OF THE PYRENEES

France and Spain Negotiate Honor

Emmanuel Vivet*

In 1659, after their 150-year rivalry and 23 years of war, Europe's two main powers were ready for peace. Cardinal Mazarin, the French king's main minister, and his Spanish counterpart, Don Luis de Haro, undertook negotiations that would last two months. Combined with the 1648 Peace of Westphalia, the Treaty of the Pyrenees allowed stability and France's diplomatic advantage by means of a weakened Spanish Crown.

The modern diplomatic function was only just becoming an occupation during the classical period. The word "diplomat" did not exist yet, but the role of professional "negotiator", and in particular ambassador in residence, had been created three centuries earlier in Italy and was becoming more independent and clearly defined as practices became more efficient. Cardinal Richelieu had made a decisive intellectual contribution in this regard by transplanting Niccolò Machiavelli's concept of national interest

---

*   Institute for Research and Education on Negotiation (ESSEC IRENE).

into *raison d'Etat*, a moral and conceptual revolution that still permeates international relations. But this new approach came up against the old world, which based negotiations on ties of honor and blood. Between the national interests that Mazarin embodied and the Spanish world more attached to personal relationships, the gulf was wide.

1. TWO GREAT POWERS, FOUR NEGOTIATION TOPICS

1.1. SHIFT OF POWER IN EUROPE

In the mid-17th century, power was changing hands between the French and the Spanish. Thanks to its long-standing policy of territorial unification, France had been able to resist Habsburg encroachment and slowly but surely defeat the former empire of Charles V, wresting fortifications in Artois, Flanders, the Alps, the Roussillon, and even Catalonia from Spanish control. Meanwhile Spain, a great power weakened by insufficient economic and demographic growth, understood that it could no longer maintain its vast possessions outside Spain, which extended from the Kingdom of Naples to the Netherlands. In late summer 1659, the two countries' prime ministers, Cardinal Mazarin and Don Luis de Haro, headed toward the French–Spanish border to negotiate a peace treaty.

1.2. FROM NATIONAL INTERESTS TO LOGISTICAL DETAILS

Of the four main issues to be discussed, Mazarin began to resolve two while on the way to Saint-Jean-de-Luz.

The first was the marriage of King Louis XIV. During the classical period, a peace treaty between great powers was comprised of the resolution of a series of territorial issues, crowned by a marriage. To seal the peace of the Pyrenees, Louis XIV therefore had to marry the Infanta of Spain, Maria Theresa, even though he loved Mazarin's niece, Marie Mancini. The Cardinal was able to make the young king give up his passion and listen to reason. With this issue of principle resolved, the negotiations could focus on the precise content of the marriage contract with the Maria Theresa.

The second issue, which had much heavier strategic consequences, was the territory France would gain in exchange for peace. On June 4 Spain had agreed to a series of concessions, known as the Treaty of Paris, with Philippe IV's emissary, Pimentel. That agreement still had to be ratified. But when Mazarin arrived in Saint-Jean-de-Luz, he discovered he would have to do the work all over again because Pimentel had been disgraced in the interim, having been deemed overly complacent with regard to the French. This became Mazarin's main objective.

But there was also a highly sensitive issue of principle, a question of honor related to the fate of Louis II. An illustrious military leader known as the Grand Condé, Louis II was a *prince du sang*, cousin of the king of France and first in line after him. But the Condé had made the mistake of allying himself with Spain against France, which meant Mazarin had to make an example of him, punishing him by disarming him and taking away his property. The Spanish, however, wanted France to give Condé back his lands and the "responsibilities" that were in keeping with his rank. France wanted to punish him for treason, while Spain was intent on showing its loyalty to high nobility, not only for reasons of honor but also because it was in Madrid's interest to show Europe it was a reliable partner.

Lastly there were issues of logistics and protocol to be resolved before the negotiations could begin. In 1659, custom did not allow the king of France or the king of Spain to leave their realm except when in their armor leading their troops. How, then, could they negotiate and sign a document together? It took a little imagination to solve this. There was also a problem of protocol: etiquette required meetings before negotiations could begin, but who outranked whom? Who should make the first visit – a prince of the Church (Cardinal Mazarin) or a Spanish Grandee? This question remained unanswered.

The parties' meeting at the border was therefore based on an arranged marriage, preliminary negotiations that had been called into doubt by Spain, and a sensitive issue of principle.

2. CARDINAL MAZARIN: OR HOW TO HUMOR SOMEONE WHILE DEALING WITH SUBSTANTIVE ISSUES

The logistics and protocol issues were the easiest to resolve: when parties want to negotiate, they find a way around the procedural obstacles. These issues are worth discussing here, however, because the logistical solution is what fascinated people and has been best remembered.

2.1. SOLUTIONS TO THE ISSUES OF LOGISTICS AND PROTOCOL

Where to negotiate? To get around the fact that the kings could not leave their realms, Mazarin suggested meeting on Pheasant Island, which sits on the border in the middle of the Bidasoa River and was declared neutral for this purpose. A temporary building with a central ceremonial hall surrounded by perfectly symmetrical wooden apartments was built. A rug was carefully laid in the middle of the main room to mark the boundary between the two countries, and a table was set up across it so the negotiators and their kings could see and speak to each other while remaining in their respective kingdoms.

The only surprise was that Mazarin, an aesthete who was very concerned about appearances, had beautiful tapestries and paintings from his private collection brought from Paris to decorate the French side of the ceremonial hall. The French side was splendid and De Haro, who had been caught off guard, saved face by quickly hanging donkey blankets covered with his coat of arms on the walls on the Spanish side. Their skirmish over who could be more lavish reflected the impending battle for European domination.

This issue of rank was settled more expeditiously: they decided to dispense with preliminary visits and move straight to negotiating. The prime ministers and their deputies (Hugues de Lionne for Mazarin and Don Pedro Coloma for De Haro) therefore all arrived, ready to negotiate, on September 13, 1659.

2.2. THE TREATY OF THE PYRENEES: A BLEND OF INTERESTS AND VALUES

France and Spain sincerely wanted peace, but to achieve it, the negotiations between the two great military powers of the time had to resolve not only territorial issues, but also more symbolic issues of values.

A solution was quickly found for the territorial issues: Spain would abandon the fortifications the French had already conquered, in particular in the northern Artois, southern Roussillon, and Alsace. France's borders were thus consolidated, and in exchange Spain regained possession of northern Catalonia (Cerdanya) and various Flemish fortifications.

The fate of the prince of Condé led to a stalemate, however. Between keeping one's word (for the Spanish) and punishing an insubordinate rebel (for the French), they could not reach agreement. It was a question of principle for both sides. According to Simone Bertière, "it was a confrontation between two conceptions of the nobility's relationship to royalty, one clinging to the past, the other heralding the future" (Bertière, 2009, p. 754) De Haro said he would prefer that Spain grant territorial compensation to its ally rather than abandon the prince to his fate. But Mazarin's problem was not simply to punish the prince for treason: he also wanted to keep him from having lands that were too rich, and above all too close to Paris, which he might be able use as a staging ground to threaten the crown again.

When he raised the idea of Madrid compensating the French prince itself, De Haro said the compensation could take the form of a gift of the Franche-Comté region. This was out of the question for France, as the region's proximity to Paris would make it too threatening for the king, but Mazarin cleverly turned De Haro's suggestion to France's advantage: if Spain wanted to honor its ally, including by granting him lands, why not offer him lands along the border that he could then give to the king of France in exchange for his pardon? Spain would keep its word to Condé while at the same time giving in to French demands for restitution to the king, and the prince's honor would be saved.

It worked. The solution was accepted and after a few more delays, the stalemate could be broken. Even though Mazarin threatened to quit the talks at one point, the parties finally reached agreement on all issues. After further discussing territory, the French agreed to let Condé run the government in Burgundy and Spain agreed to dismantle the duchy's fortifications. The issue of Condé's honor had been resolved in principle, and agreement was reached on the details: he would lose his most important possessions, but would be pardoned by his cousin the king in exchange for the lands Spain would give him to be transferred immediately to the king.

That left the issue of the marriage contract between Louis XIV and the Maria Theresa. The marriage not only sealed the negotiations but was a subject of them, and there were heated discussions regarding the Infanta's waiver of her right to succeed to the Spanish throne, and with respect to the dowry, the amount (500,000 gold ecus), the currency in which it would be paid (French, as the Spanish real had lost its value), and the number of payment installments (three).

The final agreement had 180 official and eight secret sections. Louis XIV and Philippe IV signed it on Pheasant Island on November 7, 1659, swearing on their knees to faithfully uphold it, and Louis XIV married Maria Theresa in Saint-Jean-de-Luz on June 9, 1660.

3. HOW DOES ONE NEGOTIATE A QUESTION OF HONOR?

The negotiations on Pheasant Island were important for Europe as a whole because they brought an end to a war that had raged from the Netherlands to Germany, Flanders to Lorraine, and the Pyrenees to Piedmont; they capped the 1648 Treaty of Westphalia, which had ended the Thirty Years War and brought peace to the Germanic countries. Interest in the talks was so strong that diplomats from every country that was to have its fate decided by Mazarin and De Haro – including cardinal de Retz, the duke of Lorraine, and the king of England – rushed to Hondarribia in the hope of gaining some advantage from the negotiations. Even on their island, the negotiators therefore had to deal with a certain amount of external pressure during the discussions.

Beyond the territorial issues, the question of honor was key for both of them. Spanish honor had already kept Madrid from asking for peace for too many years, and during the negotiations it almost caused the delegations to get mired in the issue of the prince of Condé's status, which only Mazarin's flexibility and quick-wittedness allowed them to resolve. Two years earlier, De Haro had said with regard to other negotiations: "First we looked at the question of honor, and only thereafter at preserving the nations, because without honor, all nations lose themselves in the end, and it is only with honor that one can hope to re-enter those one has lost."[1]

Clearly there was a difference between the somewhat chivalrous Spanish conception and that of Mazarin, who for 20 years had been working to build a strong, centralized government where, if necessary, government authority trumped princely honor. The negotiation of values, which modern theory calls "value-based negotiation" (as opposed to interest-based negotiation), complicated the discussions considerably. Value-based negotiation goes beyond managing mere "passions", i.e., individual feelings that make it hard to stay on rational ground and thus hinder negotiations. How do negotiators deal not just with emotions, but with more deeply rooted beliefs, such as the parties' world view or faith? It is interesting that Mazarin, who was disturbed by the value-related discussion, did not try to deny there was an issue. On the contrary, he agreed that the Spanish had a problem and took it into account while trying to work around it. In doing so, he confirmed a well-known lesson in the art of negotiation: issues

---

[1] Remarks quoted in "Lionne," *Dictionnaire du Grand Siècle*, p. 883.

of honor, emotions, or other values (especially identity-related issues, which are very important in some modern conflicts) cannot and must not be ignored. They must be taken into account one way or another, even if doing so is difficult.

But if the discussions moved forward, it was also because Mazarin was imaginative and suggested new combinations. The transfer of borderlands to Condé, then from Condé to the king so the king could enlarge his realm, was a sophisticated as well as an elegant solution.

In short, to avoid getting trapped in value-based discussions, to keep a rift from becoming a stalemate, negotiators must not only acknowledge such issues, they must tie them to the interest-based concerns that modern theory recognizes as the key issues in a good negotiation. In the 17th century, the interests were territory, fortifications, "responsibilities", tax revenues, and the dismantling of military constructions. Seen from Pheasant Island in 1659, the issues of principle had no solution per se. To resolve them and move on to the substantive issues, Mazarin had to admit there was a problem of honor and combine it with the more concrete concerns – which he succeeded in doing.

Looking back today it is clear that national interests were never far behind: if the Spanish agreed to negotiate, it was because they could no longer hold out militarily. Negotiating became an option once France's repeated victories (the battle of Dunes in June 1658 and the taking of Dunkirk, Gravelines, etc.) reinforced Spain's losses, making them inescapably clear. To make sure these were on the parties' minds, Mazarin asked the Viscount of Turenne to stay posted with his army at the Dutch border during the negotiations, thus belying De Haro's claim that he was negotiating only with respect to values.

4.   A GOOD BUT SHORT-LIVED AGREEMENT

While the negotiations led to an agreement, one can't help noting a minor paradox: the Peace of the Pyrenees, which was negotiated professionally and voluntarily by two great powers in a normal climate, did not usher in a lasting peace. A few years later, Louis XIV renewed the war in Flanders, in particular over the question of Spanish succession.

Such instability may naturally cast doubt on the quality of the negotiations. Should the negotiators be accused of negligence? Were they responsible for the agreement's lack of permanence? Should they – could they? – have dealt with the issue of the Spanish succession in advance so it would not reignite war in Europe? These questions are beyond the scope of this chapter, but the Treaty of the Pyrenees contained some "constructive ambiguities" that may have weakened its ability to withstand the test of time. In addition, Mazarin died two years after the negotiations ended. Given his personality and understanding of the issues, this may have compromised the peace's stability.

I prefer to believe, however, that the attitude of the young Louis XIV in the years following 1659 played a significant role. After he took the throne, he took French foreign policy in a bellicose direction that eventually accentuated, rather than tempered, the tendency to make the formation of nation states a cause of war. In the 17th century, war seemed to be a childhood disease of newly formed states. The Sun King even accused himself of promoting it, if one believes the claim that his dying words were: "I loved war and buildings too much." Mazarin, his illustrious Italian mentor, preferred the arts and the art of negotiation.

REFERENCES

ALLAINVAL (D'), Abbé, 1745, *Lettres où l'on voit la négociation pour la paix des Pirénées*, Amsterdam: Z. Chastelain.

BERTIERE, Simone, 2009, *Mazarin, le maître du jeu*, Paris, Poche.

CALLIERES (DE), François, 1716, *De la manière de négocier avec les souverains*, Paris. New edition Geneva, Droz, 2002, Translated and published by Houghton Mifflin and by A.F. Withe, University of Notre Dame Press.

GOMBERT, Pierre, 2008, *Mazarin*, Paris, Fayard.

HOFSTEDE, Geert, 2001, *Culture's consequences: Comparing values, behaviors, institutions, and organizations across nations*, 2nd ed., Thousand Oaks, CA, Sage.

KUTY, Olgierd, 1998, *La négociation valorielle*, éd. de Boeck.

MÉNDEZ DE HARO, Luis, 2000, *Letters from the Pyrenees: Don Luis Méndez de Haro's Correspondence to Philip IV of Spain, July to November 1659*, edited by Lynn Williams, Exeter, UK.

PRUITT, Dean, 2001, "Negotiation Theory and the Development of Identity", *International Negotiation*, vol. 6, pp. 269–279.

ZARTMAN, I. William, 2001, "Negotiating Identity: From Metaphor to Process", *International Negotiation*, vol. 6, pp. 137–140.

THE MACARTNEY EMBASSY TO CHINA (1793)

Negotiating Face and Symbols

Guy Olivier FAURE*

Nothing could be more fallacious than to judge of China by any European standard.
Lord Macartney, 1794

At the end of the 18th century, the British Crown was vying to develop its trade with China. An embassy headed by an experienced diplomat, Lord Macartney, representing King George III, was sent to meet Qianlong, the emperor of the Celestial Empire. In practice, the mission had to negotiate the opening of new ports, the setting up of a permanent diplomatic representation in Peking, the cession of a convenient offshore island, and the lessening of restrictions on business in Canton. It was

---

* CEIBS, Shanghai; PIN, GIGA, Hamburg.

the first time a formal British embassy was sent to meet the emperor of China. Such a mission represented a turning point in East-West relations with major consequences for future relations. Despite its extremely careful preparation, this historical negotiation between maritime England and continental China did not turn as expected by London.

1. BRITISH TRADE WITH CHINA: THE CANTON SYSTEM (1757–1842)

At that time, the Chinese government would issue trading licenses exclusively to authorized merchants and in very limited numbers. Foreign trading was only allowed during five months in the year. The British were not allowed to communicate directly with Court officials, and trade was limited to the ports of Macao and Canton (now Guangzhou). Furthermore, the rules enacted by the Chinese were extremely erratic; restraints, abuses, exactions and corruption were extremely common. The merchants, often called "foreign devils", were sometimes in danger of their lives. For several decades this system had been accepted by the Europeans because they had no other choice. Then, the British demand for tea increased, and the Industrial Revolution required new markets for the manufactured goods. Great Britain had become China's largest trading partner, accounting for 61 out of 86 foreign ships landing in Canton in 1789. The British East India Company sought to increase its trade with China and establish more openness, transparency, stability, and safety for all activities. It became a political affair and the British government decided to get involved.

2. PREPARING FOR THE MISSION

The Crown decided to send to China an embassy headed by Lord Macartney on board of three ships sailing around the Cape of Good Hope. It was an extremely long trip, lasting one year each way. As one of the goals of the embassy was to demonstrate the utility of British science and technology, in hopes of encouraging Chinese purchases of British goods, the mission was to bring with it a number of gifts including clocks, telescopes, weapons, textiles, and other products of technology. Macartney intended the display of technical prowess to reflect Britain's remarkable characteristics, ingenuity, entrepreneurship, and curiosity about the world. He had also in mind to bring back new and deeper knowledge about the Middle Kingdom, as well as artifacts and strategic plants such as tea, which was only grown in China and was controlled by a monopoly exporting only the leaves of the tea.

2.1. THE LONG MARCH TO PEKING

The embassy sailed from Portsmouth on September 26, 1792 and arrived at the port of Tientsin (now Tianjin) on August 5, 1793. Representatives of the East India Company had previously met with the military governor of Guangdong ahead of Macartney's arrival, in order to request permission for the embassy to land at Tientsin instead of Canton. The governor at first refused, as it was considered improper for a foreign mission to select its own port of arrival. The British officials pointed out that the ships carried many fragile and precious items that might be damaged if taken overland. Furthermore, the embassy had travelled a great distance, and would be considerably delayed if sent back to Canton from Tientsin. The Court agreed to the request, and instructed officials to lead the embassy to Tientsin, then the Court of the "Son of Heaven", Emperor Qianlong (Macartney, 1908).

In accordance with the Chinese custom of considering all gifts to the emperor as tribute, and before the mission landed, the Chinese placed a flag on the admiral vessel, on which was written "Tribute-bearer from England". The viceroy of Chihli came to greet the embassy, which was supplied with transportation including – 600 cases of presents being carried to Peking. As a royal envoy, Macartney made a point never to appear as a mere commercial emissary. However, while displaying the utmost civility, the Chinese court wanted the foreigners to understand clearly that both parties were not to be considered as equals. Again, the boats and carts used for the transport bore flags with the inscription: "Ambassador bearing tribute from the country of England." Macartney, who knew about this, made no protest in order to not jeopardize the overall project (Cranberg-Bing, 1961).

En route, Macartney was informed that the meeting with the emperor was not to take place as expected in Peking but at Jehol (now Chengde), a mountain resort, a week's trip beyond the Great Wall. The mission reached Peking on August 21. It was escorted to a residence north of the city. The British delegation was not permitted to leave the premises during the whole duration of its stay. Only Macartney, on his demand, was allowed to move to a different residence in Peking. On September 2, 70 members of the mission left the capital for Jehol (Hevia, 1995).

2.2. MATTERS OF PROTOCOL: KOWTOW OR GENUFLECTION?

The Chinese Empire had always considered itself as the center of the world and all other states as tributaries. However, the Macartney embassy was given special treatment and a higher degree of tolerance for conforming to rituals because it was sent officially as such for the first time in history and to commemorate an exceptional event, the emperor's birthday. Another reason for special care was that the embassy had traveled an extremely long distance to come before the emperor's court.

Normally, the observation of the Court etiquette was an absolute obligation. All people approaching the "Son of Heaven" should follow the ritual of the kowtow, which required people to kneel three times with both knees on the ground and bow three times for each kneeling so as to touch their forehead to the ground. Even when receiving imperial edicts from the emperor's envoys, people, whoever they were, had to abide by this ritual of the kowtow (Hevia, 1995; Backhouse and Bland, 1914).

Macartney had been instructed to accept "all ceremonials of the Court which may not commit the honor of your Sovereign or lessen your own dignity". Portuguese and Dutch merchants had agreed to kowtow but Macartney regarded this ritual as clearly humiliating. For him, he was representing the most powerful nation on Earth and the best he could accept was that King George and Emperor Qianlong has an equal status.

Macartney was persistently urged by officials to perform the kowtow when he would meet the emperor. In return, Macartney issued a written proposal in line with the principle of equal status: whatever the ceremony, a Chinese official of equal rank would have to do the same before a portrait of King George III. The Court objected that this notion of reciprocal equality was totally unacceptable because the "Son of Heaven" could have no equal.

The Court compromised on the issue and stated that Macartney could perform a single kowtow. Even there, Macartney did not give in and stuck to his position. With no agreement in sight and the ceremony coming very soon, the Court even contemplated cancelling the meeting. Ultimately, it was agreed that Macartney would only "genuflect" before the emperor as he would do before his own sovereign, touching one knee to the ground, although without the usual hand kissing, as it was not customary for anyone to kiss the emperor's hand.

3. MEETING EMPEROR QIANLONG

The meeting with Qianlong took place on September 14, 1793. The British set off from their residence at 4 am in darkness, arriving at the imperial encampment at 5 am. The ceremony was to be held in the imperial tent, an immense yellow yurt in which the emperor's throne was standing at the center of a raised platform. Several thousand attendees were present, including other foreign visitors. Qianlong arrived at 7 am and sat on his throne. Lord Macartney entered the tent along with George and Thomas Staunton, secretary and page to Macartney, and their Chinese interpreter. The other members of the embassy waited outside.

Macartney stepped up to the platform first, went down once on one knee, exchanging gifts with Qianlong and presenting King George III's letter. He was followed by George and Thomas Staunton. As Thomas Staunton could speak Chinese, Qianlong exchanged a few words with him. The British were followed by other envoys, all tributaries of Asia, strictly following the traditional rituals and doing the kowtow. A banquet followed the whole ceremony. The British were seated at a table at the emperor's left, in the most prestigious position.

Qianlong sent to Macartney several dishes from his own table, together with a few liquors. Later on, he sent for Macartney and Staunton to come to his table and gave to each of them, with his own hands, a cup of warm wine. Macartney, in his personal report, described the manners of Qianlong as "dignified, but affable, and condescending, and his reception [...] very gracious and satisfactory" (Peyrefitte, 1993).

The form was there only to compensate the lack of positive substance and despite gestures of great courtesy, the embassy was ultimately a failure. Not a single point was settled, or even really discussed. Qianlong made it clear in his written answer presented in the form of a letter to King George III:

> ... all European nations, including your own country's barbarian merchants, have carried on their trade with our Celestial Empire at Canton. Such has been the procedure for many years, although our Celestial Empire possesses all things in prolific abundance and lacks no product within its own borders. There was therefore no need to import the manufactures of outside barbarians in exchange for our own produce. But as the tea, silk and porcelain which the Celestial Empire produces, are absolute necessities to European nations and to yourselves,

we have permitted, as a signal mark of favor, that foreign hongs [merchant firms] should be established at Canton, so that your wants might be supplied and your country thus participate in our beneficence. But your Ambassador has now put forward new requests which completely fail to recognize the Throne's principle to "treat strangers from afar with indulgence," and to exercise a pacifying control over barbarian tribes, the world over. Moreover, our dynasty, swaying the myriad races of the globe, extends the same benevolence towards all. Your England is not the only nation trading at Canton. If other nations, following your bad example, wrongfully importune my ear with further impossible requests, how will it be possible for me to treat them with easy indulgence? Nevertheless, I do not forget the lonely remoteness of your island, cut off from the world by intervening wastes of sea, nor do I overlook your excusable ignorance of the usages of our Celestial Empire. I have consequently commanded my Ministers to enlighten your Ambassador on the subject, and have ordered the departure of the mission (Backhouse and Bland, 1914).

Thus, the demands concerning the opening of new ports, the establishment of a permanent diplomatic representation in Peking, the cession of a small island along the coast, and the lessening of restrictions on business in Canton were simply turned down and, moreover, the mission was kicked out of the empire. However, there were some side benefits, because the mission gathered intelligence, brought back artifacts and detailed observations previously unknown. As mentioned by Macartney in his journal, "We are now masters of geography of the north-east coast of China, and have now acquired a knowledge of the Yellow Sea which was never before navigated by European ships".

4. MEETING CONFUCIANISM

4.1. THE CULTURAL DIVIDE

As underlined by Peyrefitte (1993), "The encounter of 1793 was truly a collision of two planets. [...] the mutual discovery of two refined yet incompatible cultures, one celestial and lunar; the other with its feet firmly on the ground – mercantile, scientific, and industrial". The gap between them was so huge that Qianlong could not avoid mentioning it in his official letter to King George: "If you assert that your reverence for Our Celestial dynasty fills you with a desire to acquire our civilization, our ceremonies and code of laws differ so completely from your own that, even if your Envoy were able to acquire the rudiments of our civilization, you could not possibly transplant our manners and customs to your alien soil." Further on, Qianlong insisted on the fact that "Our dynasty observes the severest restrictions respecting the admission of foreigners within its boundaries", making clear that in the future there would be no way for any foreigner to get in as "The distinction between Chinese and barbarian is most strict".

4.2. TWO COGNITIVE MAPPINGS CONFRONTING EACH OTHER

Is the failure of the primary objectives due to Macartney's refusal to kowtow before the emperor, as it is sometimes believed? It could, rather, be the result of the Chinese tradition in foreign policy, which was to a large extent incompatible with the British view.

Macartney saw his mission as the historical encounter between the world's two greatest and most powerful monarchs: George III of the maritime West and Qianlong of the continental East. He came to meet the emperor with the conviction of a European superiority based on modern ideas stemming from the French Enlightenment philosophers and from the new scientific knowledge of Galileo, Newton, and Watt, furthermore, strengthened by an economic vision inherited from Adam Smith.

On the Chinese side, the indications of sinocentrism are very clear, stemming from the document issued by the Court: "You, O King, from afar have yearned after the blessings of our civilization and in your eagerness to come into touch with our converting influence have sent an Embassy across the sea bearing a memorial. I have already taken note of your respectful spirit of submission."

Many such sentences strongly confirm how Qianlong sees the king of England: "your humble desire to partake of the benefits of our civilization [...] To show your devotion, you have also sent offerings [...] I have perused your memorial: the earnest terms in which it is couched reveal a respectful humility on your part, which is highly praiseworthy [...]. It behooves you, O King, to respect my sentiments and to display even greater devotion and loyalty in future, so that, by perpetual submission to our Throne, you may secure peace and prosperity for your country".

Then, comes the conclusion: "You [...] who have shown your submissive loyalty by sending this tribute mission [...] Tremblingly obey and show no negligence!" (Backhouse and Bland, 1914) Thus, King George, the most powerful monarch of Europe and probably of the world, is treated not so much better than a Chinese subject.

Both sides had a radically different framing of the overall situation and Macartney, in all probability, could not have been accepted as a diplomatic bridge by the imperial court, as it had been cleverly managed by Matteo Ricci in the 16th century, because he was identified as a representative of a remote foreign power whose fate was to be and to remain a vassal of the "Son of Heaven" – an absolutely unacceptable status for the representative of King George.

In Chinese eyes, Great Britain could receive some benefits from trading with the Empire provided that it would be understood as a contribution to the glory of Chinese civilization. The letter of Qianlong offers a vision of the world that tends to show that the Empire is not an oriental version of a nation-state but a civilization-state extending its good deeds to the whole world.

Macartney also made an attempt to get some facilities in the religious domain for foreign missionaries. Again, the Throne made absolutely no concession and even caught this opportunity to promote the Chinese moral system, "which from time immemorial has been religiously observed by the myriads of my subjects". Ultimately, Qianlong rejected the idea that a foreign religion be spread in the empire as "The distinction between Chinese and barbarian is most strict, and your Ambassador's request that barbarians shall be given full liberty to disseminate their religion is utterly unreasonable". This message did not leave any room for negotiation.

4.3. THE STRATEGIC ISSUE: RELATIONSHIP vs INTERESTS

One of the fascinating aspects of this 1793 British mission to China is that, despite the cultural divide, an extremely high level of respect and courtesy was always maintained. This pomp compensated, as is often the case in diplomacy, for the differences in terms of interests. It normally creates some ground for negotiation. However here, courtesy was in complete contrast with the strong divergence of interests, and did not bring any positive outcome for Macartney.

For some time during the presence of the embassy in the Middle Kingdom, negotiations were kept going on with compromises and concessions made on both sides. An encounter became possible and finally happened. Most of the time, the embassy was treated with great pomp and ostentatious respect. The real obstacles were still to come, and were so much deeper that they led to a dialogue of the deaf. What has been commonly concluded as a failure of the mission was in fact more of a standstill. The situation could not be characterized as a mutually hurting stalemate and both parties had an acceptable BATNA. The status quo was still the best option for the Chinese Court, which wanted to keep the British as far away as possible from the Empire. The peremptory refusal of any of the British requests reflected the apprehension of the Chinese to engage in trade and diplomatic relations with the Western world.

Even though the trade balance was negative for Great Britain, the existing situation was still acceptable because London had other options for increasing its trade: manufactured products, technology, and, as history has shown, warships and opium with gunboat diplomacy.

The most important concern for Qianlong was the control of his vast empire. Any change coming from outside the Empire would be viewed as a risk rather than as an opportunity. Thus, he had to ensure that China be kept at the center of the world and any other state would not become anything more than a tributary, even if scientifically and technically speaking much more advanced. This was the condition for not having to reconsider the balance of the world. The strategic objective of Qianlong was not the development of the economy of the Empire but its status and stability. The benefits to China of European enlightenment probably did not make any sense to him. This is why the imperial court ended up spending so much time and energy just to try to work out how to get Macartney and his mission out of China.

In the Chinese culture, doing business and negotiating require, first, establishing a friendly relationship. Such a relationship was a necessary though insufficient condition for reaching any agreement, given the high stakes at play (Faure, 1998). It was somewhat achieved at the imperial banquet. Nevertheless, if states have no friends but only interests, extreme formal courtesy would only compensate for negative answers on the substance, as in any good diplomacy. Clearly courtesy, pomp, and even friendship do not make a negotiation effective, if interests do not meet.

Ultimately, the power balance was greatly asymmetric as the Court had a full control over the context and conditions of the embassy. The only limit to the exercise of blunt power was the concern to avoid a clash for which there would have been no additional gain for the Court and that would have elicited strong resentment on the British side, with possible consequences in the long term.

4.4. THE FINAL WORD GOES TO CONFUCIUS

The Macartney embassy is often considered as a turning point in Chinese-Western relations. This embassy dramatically shaped the way in which

China would be perceived. The Chinese had frequently been portrayed as unreceptive to foreign ideas and arrogant in their behavior towards foreigners. The lack of receptiveness that the embassy had to endure did not find its source in Chinese cultural arrogance, but rather in strict adherence to the principles of Confucianism. Confucianism has to be understood as a political, social, and cultural construct which has governed China since the Han Dynasty, and has penetrated every sphere of Chinese life. The kowtow, for instance, was not so much an expression of a Chinese arrogance but rather a ritual symbol of the Qing Court; a ritual used to enact a hierarchical relationship between the emperor and the person performing the gesture (Backhouse and Bland, 1914). The fulfillment of the kowtow was seen as a means of maintaining the social and moral order of the Chinese society, which was an essential requirement of Confucianism. However, the refusal of the traditional kowtow was not the explanatory factor of the failure of the British mission. The next year, a Dutch ambassador, Isaac Titsingh, agreed to do it but was, in the end, not better treated than Macartney.

The major reason behind the failed mission was much deeper than a divergence on abiding by a formal procedure. The failure was rather a consequence of the Confucian legacy, anchored in the mindset of the Chinese court, bringing about a rigidity that left no room for negotiation. In this mindset, hierarchy and subordination are fundamental principles for both Chinese society and for China's external relations with other states. The tributary-state system has been embedded in the Chinese psyche since the Han dynasty (202 BCE–220 AD), with Chinese emperors asking neighboring kingdoms to accept submission in return for China recognizing their legitimacy (Chen, 2016). Only after 1860 was a "Ministry of Foreign Affairs and Representations" in foreign countries established. Until that time the only institution dealing with foreign issues was the "Court of the Tribute from Vassals", which was the recipient of the tokens of allegiance. Confucianism claims that authority is necessary to properly manage a complex system of relations leaving very little free space for negotiation. In the traditional Chinese culture, the necessary flexibility comes from Taoism, with its unique way of managing a yin-yang balance.

Saving face, though, was one of the few things left to do. Qianlong personally was extremely interested in Western technology, and the common view of him having no interest in modern artifacts is baseless. The Jesuits had had a number of contacts with the imperial family throughout the reign of the Qing Dynasty and had already brought some of the "strange or ingenious things" to Qianlong before Macartney's visit.

(Qianlong collected clocks, scientific instruments and telescopes in their most sophisticated versions, and even welcomed Italian painters at his court.)

So, when Qianlong states in his letter "As your Ambassador can see for himself, we possess all things. I set no value on objects strange or ingenious, and have no use for your country's manufactures", the real issue may not really be technology but rather keeping British influence as minimal and as distant as possible. Furthermore, saving face is much more important from a Chinese standpoint than losing on the substance of the deal. In spite of the real interest he had for western technology, Qianlong had to appear to look down on what had been brought to him.

This 1793 British mission shows that modernizing and opening up China to the world was a most complicated challenge, due to the need to adhere to Confucian values and political requirements of that time. Half a century later, further rejections of equal trading opportunities within China led Britain to launch the Opium Wars under the justification that its "trading requests" were constantly denied.

Irrespective of the period in history, every Chinese negotiator is at the same time a Confucian gentleman and a Sunzi style warrior (Faure, 1998, 2017). If he benefits from a strong power position, once he is recognized as the legitimate authority, he may act as a Confucian showing benevolence and doing good deeds. If he is not sure about his position and his ability to influence the counterpart, he may then resort to hard bargaining tactics, even tricks, to reach his goals. However, the warrior has to be realistic and at some point may have to compromise. It was not so with the Macartney embassy, because it was Confucius who, ultimately, had the last word.

To negotiate in a Chinese context was and still is to engage in issues of maintaining face during trading, in producing reputation, in building up and validating a self-image. In Chinese culture, face concerns are never paltry. They are the *sine qua non* condition for entering the real substance of the negotiation (Faure, 1999).

Especially in diplomatic relations, resorting to rituals may be understood as a facilitator for negotiations. The rituals shape, strengthen and validate expressions. Thus, they tend to enhance the status of the relation, to pacify this relation through the avoidance of personal involvement with its attached consequences. Rituals properly performed show respect for tradition and for the counterpart. This is either a way to open a concession-making phase or to move into a stonewalling attitude still acceptable for the other.

At the same time, the manipulation of symbols tends to increase power, i.e., to increase one's own weight in the negotiation process. Using symbols is playing with a transcendent reality to strengthen communication and position.

Resorting abundantly to symbols feeds the communication system of the negotiation, enriching it and strengthening its substance. But what can be seen from the 1793 case is that the Confucian verticality can also leave little room for negotiating. Confucianism calls for a unique decision-maker. Thus, the negotiation is turned into a decision-making process with a main actor confronting not a counterpart but a given situation, which is not quite what an effective negotiation, where the power imbalance should not be too great, normally requires.

REFERENCES

BACKHOUSE, Edmund and BLAND, John Otway Percy, 1914, *Annals and Memoirs of the Court of Peking*, Houghton Mifflin.

CHEN, Zhimin, 2016, "China's diplomacy", in CONSTANTINOU, C., KERR, P. and SHARP, P., *The Sage Handbook of Diplomacy*, Sage Publications.

CRANMER-BYNG, John Launcelot, 1961, *Lord Macartney's Embassy to Peking in 1793 from Official Chinese Documents*, University of Hong Kong.

FAURE, Guy Olivier, 1998, "Negotiation: The Chinese Concept", *Negotiation Journal*, vol. 14, no. 2, 13–148.

FAURE, Guy Olivier, 1999, "The Cultural Dimension of Negotiation: The Chinese Case", *Group Decision and Negotiation*, Kluwer Academic Publishers, vol. 9, no. 3.

FAURE, Guy Olivier, 2017, "China in Central Asia: Negotiating Cooperation for Mutual Benefits", in HAMPSON, F. and TROITSKIY, M.: *Tug of War: Negotiating Security in Eurasia*, CIGI/McGill University Press.

HEVIA, James Louis, 1995, *Cherishing Men from Afar: Qing Guest Ritual and the Macartney Embassy of 1793*, Duke University Press.

PEYREFITTE, Alain, 1993, *The Collision of Civilizations*, HarperCollins Publishers.

ROBBINS, Helen Henrietta, 1908, *Our First Ambassador to China: An Account of the Life of George, Earl of Macartney*, E.P. Dutton and Company.

WHAT SET OFF THE KOREAN CONFLICT OF 1950?

Interests, Reputation, and Emotions

Emmanuel PETIT*

In April 2018, a historic meeting took place between the North Korean leader, Kim Jong-Un, and the president of South Korean Moon Jae-In, starting with a highly symbolic handshake in the demilitarized zone separating their two countries. This came as a cooperative move that helped greatly to pave the way to the ground-breaking US-North Korea summit in June 2018 (as studied by Mark Young in his chapter "The Run up to the Trump/Kim Singapore Summit" in this volume) and later in February 2019. As the whole world still watches two countries that are theoretically still at war and wonders if the two Koreas will be able to sign a peace treaty (only an armistice was signed on July 27, 1953, at the end of the conflict that began in 1950), I will review, following Jonathan Mercer's analysis (2013), the unexplored affective reasons why military conflict took place between these countries.

* GREThA, University of Bordeaux. Emmanuel.petit@u-bordeaux.fr.

1. UNEXPECTED HOSTILITIES

To everyone but those who knew it was going to take place, the attack launched by North Korea against South Korea at 4 am on June 25, 1950 was a genuine surprise.

For the three years preceding the war, and contrary to the policy actively conducted at the same time in Western Europe, American leaders had not thought it necessary, or wise, to supply the South Korean government with the means to defend itself. The CIA had of course thought an invasion by North Korea was "probable" (Mercer, 2013, p. 231[1]) – once the US troops withdrew from the peninsula in 1949 – but it was far from suspecting that an attack was imminent. The possibility there would be an attack was known and often discussed, but its launch so soon after the troop withdrawal caught the US president and his staff by surprise.

According to the historian Allan Millet, President Harry Truman felt offended, even insulted, by the attack. On the day of the attack, he told his Secretary of State, Dean Acheson, "Dean, we've got to stop the sons of bitches no matter what" (Mercer, 2013, p. 232). The next day he wrote to his wife: "Haven't been so badly upset since Greece and Turkey fell into our lap" (Mercer, 2013, p. 232). The surprise intensified the emotional reactions of the American leaders and contributed to their viewing the North Korean invasion as completely immoral. But the surprise elicited by North Korea's offensive was followed by even greater astonishment when, contrary to all expectations, the US leaders decided to actively engage in combat on the side of South Korea. It was now the turn of the belligerents and their supporters – the Soviet and Chinese governments – to be deeply surprised. Joseph Stalin, in particular, had not thought the United States would respond militarily to defend a small territory where US interests were not obviously at stake.

The decision to start the Korean War was made by North Korea's leader, Kim-il Sung, but he could not have done so without the support of the Soviet Union and communist China. Stalin's position was in fact key. At first he opposed Kim-il Sung's plan to invade, especially because he thought the United States would feel obliged to intervene militarily as long as US troops were still present in Korea. But by starting to withdraw its troops in June 1949, the United States seemed to be opening the door to North Korean intervention.

---

[1]   Citing US Central Intelligence Agency, Consequences of U.S. Troop Withdrawal from Korea in Spring, 1949, February 28, 1949.

In the United States as well, a large number of commentators and government or military personnel were caught short by the government's sudden response, which seemed to be a complete reversal of its prior strategy: from withdrawing troops to supporting South Korea through totally unexpected military intervention. The Truman administration's decision to send combat troops to South Korea stunned General MacArthur, who told a colleague, "I don't believe it ... I don't understand!" (Mercer, 2013, p. 231). Historians also report that on the day of the invasion, General Omar Bradly, an Army Chief of Staff and first Chairman of the Joint Chiefs of Staff, "evidently had little or no thought that the United States might reverse its earlier decision and fight to save South Korea" (Mercer, 2013, p. 232). Most American politicians were extremely surprised by the armed intervention. Hadn't Secretary of State Dean Acheson, in his speech at the National Press Club on January 12, 1950, clearly limited the defensive perimeter of the United States to a line running from the Aleutian Islands to Japan and from Japan to the Philippines, thus excluding Korea and Taiwan? Shortly before North Korea attacked, the CIA knew that North Korea had greater military capability than South Korea did, and that it could take Seoul. Even so, a US response was deemed highly improbable.

The parties thus found themselves in a situation where neither had anticipated the other's move: the North Korean attack or the US response. Surprise was a crucial factor in starting the conflict, which was long, costly, and still has serious consequences. To avoid it, could both the Soviet and American decisions have been foreseen? Could anyone have more accurately predicted, and perhaps prevented, the escalation? And, if the parties did not have rational expectations of each other, could a correctly worded threat have been an effective deterrent?

2. THE FAILURE OF RATIONALITY, OR THE EFFECTS OF SURPRISE AND FEAR

2.1. THE LIMITS OF RATIONAL ANALYSIS BASED ON INTERESTS AND REPUTATION

One way to interpret the situation is to use the theory of rational choice (von Neumann and Morgenstern, 1947), which posits that decision makers seek to maximize their interests by taking into account the costs associated with their decisions. They take into account all the information available to them, and are able to reexamine their beliefs on a probabilistic basis by assimilating any new information they obtain. According to the "common knowledge" hypothesis of rationality, they also believe that the other parties involved are rational and know that they are. If one focuses on questions of strategic conflict from the perspective of the American game theorist Thomas Schelling (1960), the parties' signals and reputations are two key decision-making factors. Decision makers can signal their intentions to prevent the action of one of their partners or adversaries. However, signals can only be effective, i.e, credible, to the extent the action they underlie involves a cost for the party for whom the signal is intended. For example, a verbal threat of reprisal (in the case of a military invasion) may be made credible if armed forces are amassed at the border, or if mutual defense agreements between partner countries are affirmed and renewed. However, a threat's credibility crucially depends on the belligerents' reputation, past behavior, and especially their ability to meet their commitments. In this sense, reputation represents a substantial (and costly) investment for a decision maker, and it must be preserved in the long term.

In the case of the Korean War, the stakeholders' interests in this "blitzkrieg" were clear and simple: to unite a territory that had suffered under the yoke of the Japanese for 35 years and been split in two after World War II, and to take the enemy's lands. Since North Korea was militarily superior to South Korea, the temptation to go to war was naturally stronger there. Its significant military superiority led the North Koreans to believe that even if the United States intervened, the conflict would be so short (a few weeks) that the US would not have time to oppose the invasion. For North Korea's supporters, China and the Soviet Union, the stakes of an invasion were more limited given the low costs they each anticipated (delivery of materiel, and logistics), but significant enough to persuade them to agree to this request from a friendly communist country. In addition, as the US Joint Chiefs of Staff had underscored in 1947, and as many were thinking when the war started, the South Korean peninsula was of practically no interest to the United States from the standpoint of defending its interests. Geostrategically speaking, the United States was mainly concerned at the time with Western Europe, and its defense of its interests in Asia focused on Japan, rather than Korea.

The rational actors in a conflict are, in theory, able to discern the other parties' interests. That is why the Soviets doubted that the Americans would fight for South Korea: they knew that the United States had only minor interests there and that the cost of a military response would be high. Mao Zedong also supported initiating hostilities because he thought the United States would not get involved in the defense of such a small country. Stalin took the withdrawal of American troops in June 1949 as a signal that the United States would not get involved and that, on the contrary, South Korea might attack. Mao and Stalin therefore rationally believed that the American "resolutions" (the withdrawal followed by Dean Acheson's speech in January 1950) were the logical result of the defense of US interests and of American capability. For example, the US will intervene in various regions of the world only when its interests are truly endangered and when the costs of an intervention will be offset by the expected benefits.

On the basis of these factors, the North Korean invasion was logical, rational, and could have been foreseen. What was less so was what seemed to be a sudden "about-face" by the US government. Reputational considerations must therefore be taken into account. It was in fact possible that the United States feared that unless it gave a firm military response to an invasion by an ally of communist regimes, its international reputation would be damaged and weakened. The American government saw the attack by North Korea as a challenge from the Soviet Union, which required a preventive response to avoid the erosion of the United States' prestige and credibility in the world. Dean Acheson feared that failure to engage would encourage the enemies of the United States and leave its allies perplexed. President Truman, who was afraid of a "domino" effect, warned Congress in this sense, saying "If we were to let Asia go, the Near East would collapse and no telling what would happen to Europe" (Elsey Papers, 1950). In particular, he thought Stalin had defied the US government in the past and would continue do so in the future (in Yugoslavia, Turkey, or Iran). Truman believed Stalin had interpreted the American decisions of the eight months preceding the attack as signs of weakness and had given the go-ahead to the North Korean invasion on that basis. And he was determined not to repeat the mistakes of Neville Chamberlain, the British leader who had been unable to halt Hitler's progress with the 1938 Munich Agreement.

There could therefore be some rationality to the American response. But the reputational argument does not explain why the fear of being seen as indecisive, or weakened, caused the United States to change position so radically. Did the Korean "affair" really endanger the unequaled prestige the United States enjoyed after World War II? And why did North Korea's (rational) supporters not foresee this change?

To understand the strategic decisions of the main actors in the Korean conflict (Kim-il Sung, Stalin, Mao, and Truman), one must also remember that emotions have a significant effect on a person's beliefs and how people interpret the signals they are sent. Credibility and the search for prestige are among the beliefs that can be called "emotional" (Mercer, 2010). If, in particular, the Americans reacted very quickly to North Korea's intervention, even though the costs inherent in taking such a position were very high, it is probably because they *believed* there was something crucial at stake that would lead to undermining their international reputation. However, nothing indicates that such a belief was shared at the time by the belligerents, or even by the United States' allies. Was it the fear (unjustified) of losing its reputation that pushed the US to intervene in Korea? Does an actor's credibility therefore depend on what it thinks?

2.2. BEYOND RATIONAL ANALYSIS: THE WEIGHT OF EMOTIONS

Stalin would probably have been very surprised to learn that the American leaders believed he thought they might be weak or indecisive. Had he suspected this belief, or been better informed, he probably would have more accurately anticipated the risks North Korea was running by going ahead with the invasion, and opposed it. In fact, Stalin incorrectly assessed the developments in American policy and the new foreign policy direction taken in spring 1950. The main reason for this is that Stalin was unaware of the emotional climate that went along with the turnaround in the American position.

In early 1950, communism's progress across the globe – the crisis in Berlin in 1948–1949; the fall of nationalist China in spring 1949 and the proclamation of the Republic of China the following fall; the Soviet Union's successful test of an atomic bomb on August 29, 1949 – had planted the seeds for a climate of fear, worry, and even paranoia to develop, and led the US government to rethink its foreign policy (Cadeau, 2013). In January 1950, President Truman demanded that a working group be set up to review the country's peace and war objectives. The working group advised a harsher US policy against communism coupled with significantly increased military potential, as the containment policy instituted after World War II was turning out to be weak, ineffective, and overly narrow. Not everyone agreed with the working group's report, however; Truman himself was very reticent and asked for an assessment of the costs of such a policy change. In this climate, the North Korean offensive caused surprise and tipped the scales in favor of following the working group's recommendations.

Because a military decision had to be made quickly and the Americans had not foreseen that the North Korean attack was imminent, the choice to support South Korea was made precipitously, without cool reflection. Relying on the work of historians, Mercer (2013) in particular reports that the State Department and the CIA never conducted any investigations to determine whether not intervening in a conflict in Korea would harm the international reputation or prestige of the United States. Even Dean Acheson's position seems largely introspective: "During the afternoon [of the 25th] I had everyone and all messages kept out of my room for an hour or two while I ruminated about the situation" (Mercer, 2013, p. 238). The next day, he isolated himself for several hours to write the speech in response to the attack that Truman would give the following day to Congress and the public.

In that speech, two explanations were given to defend a firm attitude and take military action in support of South Korea. Firstly, the North Korean command was weak and indecisive, and defeat was foreseeable. Secondly, the reputation of the United States was at stake: the governments of several European countries were wondering, "in a state of near-panic", what the American position would be. For Acheson, whether the outcome of the military intervention was favorable or not, "it was important for us to do something" (Mercer, 2013, p. 234).

While American leaders feared their credibility was in danger, it is highly probable that neither Stalin nor Mao thought so. But what about the governments of the United States' allies? Contrary to what the American leaders believed or expected, reactions abroad were far from unanimous. For example, the British Cabinet did not meet until June 27, 1950, and the situation in Korea was relegated to fourth position on the meeting's agenda. While the invasion was of course denounced, prudence was suggested and priority given to the continued presence of the United States in Europe. Its reputation did not seem to be in doubt at any time. In France, the start of the conflict elicited greater concern and misgivings; there was fear of American involvement, the extension of the conflict, and even use of the atomic bomb. The newspaper *Le Monde* underscored the inconsistency and uncertainty of US policy, recalling that the troop withdrawal in 1949 had been driven by the fact that Korea was of little strategic interest. In Canada, the

US response elicited surprise. Like the British, the Canadians wanted the US intervention to be conducted under the supervision of the United Nations.

The paradox of this escalation is that it was based on mistaken beliefs about reputation. The United States was not likely, in the eyes of its allies and probably even more so of its enemies, to lose credibility, prestige, or even its ability to contain communism, by failing to engage in South Korea. Or at least, such a scenario was doubtful. And yet the Truman administration entered the conflict primarily to defend the country's reputation: "[I]f we just stand by," said Truman, "they'll move into Iran and they'll take over the Middle East. There's no telling what they'll do, if we don't put up a fight now" (Mercer, 2013, p. 234). The Americans were above all afraid of being seen as weak, uncertain, indecisive, or weak-willed. These feelings, the prevailing climate of fear, and the astonishment caused by the attack dictated how US leaders interpreted the events of June 25, 1950. Surprise shaped their judgment and led them to believe their credibility was in real danger. American decision makers used their feelings and intuition as unseen proof that others, both allies and adversaries, suspected that they had little determination or desire to be involved in international affairs. To correctly anticipate events, Stalin would have had to accomplish two difficult tasks (Mercer, 2013). On the one hand, he would have had to foresee that the United States would take a (new) strategic direction that it had not yet adopted and that would be surprising. On the other, he would have had to be able to imagine what the Americans were thinking about him with regard to the alleged weakness of their foreign policy. To foresee and prevent the American response, he would therefore have had to imagine what emotions the Americans would feel (worry) and above all, foresee what they would feel after the North Korean attack (panic). The emotional climate at the time explains the turnabout in the American strategy, their mistaken belief that their reputation was in danger, and their costly and "disinterested" armed involvement in the Korean civil war.

3. CONCLUSION: EMOTIONS IN INTERNATIONAL RELATIONS

The analysis presented in this chapter highlights the advantage of using emotional tools (fear and surprise) in the field of international relations.

Other historical cases have illustrated this, such as the role of fear after the September 11, 2001 attacks (Hall and Ross, 2015), anger in managing the Taiwanese crisis (Hall, 2011) or very differently, affective relations in resolving conflicts between Allies during the Suez crisis in 1956 (Eznack, 2011). The history of the Korean War and its sudden start show a specific moment when negotiations that could have been undertaken were not. Before negotiations or a conflict, rational actors generally form expectations on the basis of their interests and those of their adversaries, evaluate the various parties' reputations, and send various signals or threats to clarify their intentions. In the case of the Korean War, this type of rationality failed completely, such that not even a first phase of negotiations could be initiated. Against a background of concern that turned into panic, surprise caused the armed conflict to escalate.

REFERENCES

CADEAU, Ivan, *La guerre de Corée: 1950–1953*, Perrin, 2013.

ELSEY PAPERS, 1950, *Notes Regarding Meeting with Congressional Leaders*, June 27, 1950. Available at <https://www.trumanlibrary.org/whistlestop/study_collections/koreanwar/>.

EZNACK, Lucile, Crises as Signals of Strength: The Significance of Affect in Close Allies' Relationships, *Security Studies*, 2011, vol. 20, no. 2, pp. 238–265.

HALL, Todd H., We Will Not Swallow This Bitter Fruit: Theorizing a Diplomacy of Anger, *Security Studies*, 2011, vol. 20, no. 4, pp. 521–555.

HALL, Todd H., ROSS, Andrew AG., Affective Politics after 9/11, *International Organization*, 2015, vol. 69, no. 4, pp. 847–879.

MERCER, Jonathan, Emotional Beliefs, *International Organization*, 2010, vol. 64, no. 1, pp. 1–31.

MERCER, Jonathan, Emotion and Strategy in the Korean War, *International Organization*, 2013, vol. 67, no. 2, pp. 221–252.

SCHELLING, Thomas C., *The Strategy of Conflict*, Cambridge, Harvard University Press, 1960.

US CENTRAL INTELLIGENCE AGENCY, Consequences of U.S. Troop Withdrawal from Korea in Spring, 1949, February 28, 1949, Available at <https://www.cia.gov/library/readingroom/docs/DOC_0000258388.pdf>.

VON NEUMANN, John, MORGENSTERN, Oskar, *Theory of Games and Economic Behavior*, Princeton University Press, 1947.

THE CUBAN MISSILE CRISIS, 1962

Overt Confrontation, Covert Diplomacy and Downright Luck

R. Gerald Hughes*

I never thought I would live to see the day when I wanted to go to war.

General Earle Wheeler, Chief of Staff of the United States Army,
October 20, 1962[1]

If they carry out an attack on Cuba, a barbaric, illegal, and immoral act, then that would be the time to think about liquidating such a danger forever through a legal right of self-defense. However harsh and terrible such a decision would be, there is no other way out in my opinion.

Fidel Castro to Nikita Khrushchev, October 27, 1962, "Black Saturday"[2]

The Cuban Missile Crisis, known as the October Crisis to the Cubans; and the Caribbean Crisis to the Soviets/Russians, was a 13-day standoff

---

* The author would like to thank Len Scott for his invaluable assistance in the preparation of this chapter.

[1] Ernest R. MAY and Philip D. ZELIKOW (eds.), *The Kennedy Tapes: Inside the White House during the Cuban Missile Crisis* (Cambridge, MA: The Belknap Press of Harvard University Press 1997) p. 203.

[2] Michael DOBBS, *One Minute to Midnight: Kennedy, Khrushchev, and Castro on the Brink of Nuclear War* (New York: Alfred A. Knopf 2008) pp. 204–205.

between the United States and the Soviet Union in the autumn of 1962. For the US, the crisis was initiated by the deployment of Soviet ballistic missiles in Cuba. In the end it was resolved by negotiation, although the clandestine nature of much of this meant that the details remained a closely-guarded secret for many years after the crisis. The reasons for Soviet leader Nikita Khrushchev's decision to deploy the missiles have been hotly disputed ever since although, as James Hershberg argues, Khrushchev's decision "defies mono-causal explanation".[3] The confrontation is widely considered to be the closest that the Superpowers came to a nuclear war during the entirety of the Cold War and was later described by one Kennedy aide, Arthur Schlesinger, Jr., as "the most dangerous moment in human history".[4] Against this, Assistant Secretary of Defense Paul Nitze argued that US local superiority in the Caribbean, allied to global strategic nuclear superiority, meant the risk of nuclear war over Cuba was minimal.[5] The Cuban Missile Crisis represented the culmination of a period of tension that began with the Cuban Revolution of 1959. In April 1961, a US-sponsored invasion of Cuban exiles failed miserably (at the Bay of Pigs) and relations deteriorated further as the US launched Operation Mongoose (which included a program of sabotage and an intention to assassinate the Cuban leader, Fidel Castro). It seemed only a matter of time before the United States would invade Cuba and end the Cuban Revolution permanently.[6]

1. A NUCLEAR CRISIS IN THE CARIBBEAN

1.1. FROM ESCALATION TO SECRET AGREEMENT

By June 1962 Castro had acceded to Khrushchev's request to install ballistic nuclear missiles on Cuba. The installation of these missiles began later that summer in strict secrecy. By this time President John F. Kennedy

---

3   James HERSHBERG, "The Cuban Missile Crisis" in Melvyn LEFFLER and Odd Arne WESTAD (eds.), *The Cambridge History of the Cold War Volume 2* (Cambridge: Cambridge University Press 2010) p. 68.

4   Arthur SCHLESINGER, Jr., *A Thousand Days: John F. Kennedy in the White House* (New York: First Mariner 2002) p. xiv.

5   Paul H. NITZE, with Ann M. SMITH, and Steven L. REARDEN, *From Hiroshima to Glasnost: At the Center of Decision* (New York: Grove Weidenfeld 1989) p. 205.

6   Hugo ABEDUL and R. Gerald HUGHES, "The Comandante in his Labyrinth: Fidel Castro and his Legacy", *Intelligence and National Security*, 26/4 (2011) pp. 548–555.

was under no small amount of domestic political pressure over Cuba. Republican politicians such as Senator Homer Capehart (R-IN) and Senator Barry Goldwater (R-AZ) gleefully denounced Kennedy for his weakness in the face of the communist threat posed by Cuba. On August 31, 1962, Senator Kenneth Keating (R-NY) stated on the floor of the Senate that the USSR had sent 1,200 servicemen to Cuba (and these were not harmless "technicians", but combat troops). In the Senate on October 10, 1962, Keating warned that the Soviets were actually installing nuclear missiles in Cuba. These charges were strenuously denied by the Kennedy administration, which was acutely aware that the impending mid-term elections would result in disastrous losses for the Democratic Party if there was shown to be any substance to Keating's charges. In order that the Soviets should be under no illusions as to his resolve, and in order to counter his domestic critics, Kennedy had stated publicly, on September 4, 1962, that "the presence of offensive ground-to-ground missiles ... [in Cuba would create] the gravest issues". On September 19, the CIA asserted that it was unlikely that the Soviets would deploy missiles in Cuba.[7] In this assessment, the agency was erroneous.

On October 14, 1962, a US U2 spy plane photographed Soviet R-12 (SS-4) medium-range ballistic missiles in Cuba. The president was briefed on this two days later. In *Essence of Decision*, Graham T. Allison and Philip D. Zelikow identified six basic policy options that were now open to Kennedy:[8]

- Do nothing: US vulnerability to Soviet missiles was hardly new.
- Overt diplomacy: pressurize the USSR to remove the missiles.
- Covert diplomacy: make an approach to Castro to try and split him from the Soviets.
- An invasion of Cuba.
- Air strikes against Cuba.
- A blockade of Cuba.

These options were summarily reduced to three by the Chairman of the Joint Chief of Staff, General Maxwell Taylor: one, "take them out";

---

[7]   SNIE 85-3-62, "The Military Buildup in Cuba", September 19, 1962. CIA Freedom of Information Act Electronic Reading Room, <https://www.cia.gov/library/readingroom/docs/CIA-RDP80B01676R001800050003-7.pdf>.

[8]   Graham T. ALLISON and Philip D. ZELIKOW, *Essence of Decision: Explaining the Cuban Missile Crisis*, 2nd edition (New York: Longman 1999) pp. 111–116.

two, "squeeze them out"; and, three, "buy them out".[9] Thomas Powers noted that Kennedy made only two crucial decisions in the first week of the crisis. First, the Soviet missiles in Cuba had to go. Second, he would state this publicly before taking any action.[10] On October 16, the main actors in the National Security Council (NSC) began to meet as the so-called Executive Committee (ExComm), although this body was only officially established on October 22. By the afternoon of October 19, 1962, senior figures in the Kennedy administration were leaning towards the blockade option, but a significant – and skeptical – minority advocated air strikes to neutralize the threat from Cuba.[11] In particular, Kennedy's military advisers remained unconvinced,[12] and it was clear that more moderate responses were strictly limited in the time they had to effect a change in Soviet policy. On October 22 Kennedy addressed the nation and made it clear that he would not permit offensive weapons to remain in Cuba. The US was thus imposing a naval blockade on Cuba (this was termed a "Quarantine" as, under international law, a "Blockade" was an act of war).

After several days of tension, on October 26 Khrushchev sent a conciliatory proposal that, whilst still under consideration in Washington, was followed by a letter setting out a hard-line position. The world seemed to be on the brink when, on October 27 ("Black Saturday"), a U2 was shot down over Cuba by a surface-to-air missile (killing the pilot, Major Rudolf Anderson). Crucially, Kennedy decided not to retaliate. At this juncture Attorney General Robert F. Kennedy, the president's brother, suggested replying only to Khrushchev's first letter, and accepting its terms. This proved acceptable to Moscow. The deal that ended the crisis entailed the Soviet Union dismantling and removing its offensive weapons from Cuba. In return, the US agreed to issue a "no-invasion" pledge. (If one accepts that Khrushchev's motive was to defend Cuba and not to restore nuclear parity, then the guarantee not to invade Cuba casts the Soviet leader in a more favorable light.) The deal also involved a secret assurance whereby the US agreed that it would dismantle

---

9   Raymond GARTOFF, *Reflections on the Cuban Missile Crisis*, revised edn. (Washington DC: The Brookings Institution 1989) pp. 44–45.

10   Thomas POWERS, "And after we've struck Cuba?" (1997) in *Intelligence Wars: American Secret History from Hitler to Al-Qaeda* (New York: New York Review Books 2004) pp. 183–184.

11   David R. GIBSON, *Talk at the Brink: Deliberation and Decision during the Cuban Missile Crisis* (Princeton, NJ: Princeton University Press 2012) pp. 99–101.

12   ALLISON and ZELIKOW, *Essence of Decision*, pp. 189–203.

all its Jupiter MRBMs in Turkey. The first letter on the fateful weekend of the crisis had requested only the "no-invasion" pledge from the US; the second additionally demanded the removal of the Jupiters from Turkey. To accede to this latter demand in public would have been political suicide for Kennedy. A secret agreement effectively robbed Khrushchev of any significant political capital he could derive from the resolution of the crisis.

1.2. HESITATING AT THE BRINK OF NUCLEAR WAR

For many years, the members of the group that had conducted US policy during the crisis (the ExComm) acted to preserve the myth that Kennedy had stood firm and refused to withdraw the Jupiters. Kennedy's National Security Adviser, McGeorge Bundy, eventually conceded that "we misled our colleagues, our countrymen, our successors, and our allies".[13] For his part, Kennedy aide Ted Sorensen admitted that he had deliberately falsified Robert Kennedy's posthumous memoir[14] of the Cuban Missile Crisis.[15] The president's willingness to remove the Jupiters was made clear by his brother to Soviet ambassador Anatoly Dobrynin on October 27, 1962 (Dobrynin's report to Moscow corroborated this).[16] Thus whilst Khrushchev may have "blinked", so too did Kennedy. The archival record thus demonstrates the lack of appetite for nuclear war on both sides that fateful weekend; at the meeting of the Soviet Presidium on October 28 it is clear that Khrushchev had already told his comrades it was necessary to retreat *before* he learned of Robert Kennedy's meeting with Dobrynin.[17]

The "Quarantine" of Cuba ended on November 21, 1962, following the departure of the Soviet missiles. Influential insider accounts cast Kennedy in heroic mold, an individual who had mastered the structures

---

[13]   McGeorge BUNDY, *Danger and Survival: Choices about the Bomb in the First Fifty Years* (New York: Random House 1988) p. 434.

[14]   Robert F. KENNEDY, *Thirteen Days: A Memoir of the Cuban Missile Crisis* (New York: W.W. Norton 1969).

[15]   Bruce J. ALLYN, James G. BLIGHT, and David A. WELCH, *Back to the Brink: Proceedings of the Moscow Conference on the Cuban Missile Conference, January 27–28, 1989* (Lanham, MD: University of America Press 1992) pp. 92–93.

[16]   Richard Ned LEBOW and Janice Gross STEIN, *We All Lost the Cold War* (Princeton, NJ: Princeton University Press 1994) pp. 523–526.

[17]   ALLISON and ZELIKOW, *Essence of Decision*, pp. 283–287.

of international politics.[18] And, in fairness, the taped consultations demonstrate that Kennedy had successfully managed the crisis to a remarkable extent, although he had been assisted by Khrushchev and enjoyed some real strokes of fortune.[19] Secretary of Defense Robert McNamara opined that the Cuban missile crisis was "the 'best managed' crisis of the last half of the century, but we were very lucky as well".[20] Former US Secretary of State Dean Acheson ascribed the avoidance of nuclear war to "plain, dumb luck".[21] Sheldon Stern, former historian at the John F. Kennedy Presidential Library, asserted that "Nobody really 'managed' the Cuban missile crisis. That's the greatest myth of all."[22] Traditional crisis management was plainly inadequate for a nuclear age. The nuclear age demanded better lines of direct communication and, in June 1963, the Moscow-Washington Hot Line was established. The pursuit of détente, so Kennedy's admirers insisted, would have been a central policy of a Kennedy second term.[23] The Cuban Missile Crisis stands as Kennedy's monument in history, a reminder to the world that, in the international politics of the nuclear age, what doesn't kill you makes you stronger.

2. AVOIDING WAR THROUGH LUCK RATHER THAN CRISIS MANAGEMENT?

Between 1987 and 1992, the historiography of the crisis was driven forward by critical oral history conferences. Certain of the participants were able to reinforce the narratives established by the first wave of informed assessments of the crisis (often comprising their own writings).

---

18   R. Gerald HUGHES, "'The Best and the Brightest': The Cuban Missile Crisis, the Kennedy administration, and the lessons of history" in SCOTT and HUGHES (eds.), *The Cuban Missile Crisis*, pp. 124–128.

19   Sheldon M. STERN, *The Cuban Missile Crisis in American Memory: Myths versus Reality* (Stanford, CA: Stanford University Press 2012) p. 158.

20   Robert S. McNAMARA, James BLIGHT, Robert K. BRIGHAM with Thomas J. BIERSTEKER, Col. Herbert SCHANDLER, *Argument Without End: In Search of Answers to the Vietnam Tragedy* (New York: Public Affairs 1999) p. 151.

21   Dean ACHESON, "Homage to Plain Dumb Luck" in Robert A. DEVINE (ed.), *The Cuban Missile Crisis* (Chicago, IL: Quadrangle 1971) pp. 197–198.

22   Sheldon M. STERN: E-mail to the author, September 17, 2014.

23   SCHLESINGER, Jr., journal entry for January 15, 1963. Arthur SCHLESINGER, Jr., *Journals: 1952–2000*, edited by Andrew SCHLESINGER and Stephen SCHLESINGER (New York: Penguin 2007) p. 334.

After the first conference in Florida in 1987, Schlesinger recorded that he was "struck ... with special force [by] JFK's absolute determination to avoid a military confrontation".[24] McNamara's public insistence that there was not going to be war in 1962 was challenged by historians who deployed McNamara's own words against him.[25] During the 1989 Moscow conference, McNamara continued to downplay the risk of war in October 1962 and found support for his position from Sorensen and Bundy. This caused Pierre Salinger, Kennedy's press secretary, to write of his "disappointment [that] ... some of the participants seemed to judge the events of 1962 from the perspective of the cooled political climate of 1989 détente".[26] When, at the Havana conference in 1992, it was revealed that the Soviets had a large number of operational nuclear weapons in Cuba, McNamara was alarmed when Castro confirmed that the Soviets would have used tactical nuclear weapons against a US invasion. McNamara concluded: "The indefinite combination of human fallibility and nuclear weapons carries a very high risk of potential nuclear catastrophe."[27] For Salinger: "Neither side "won" the Cuban missile crisis. Rather, two leaders reached an understanding that nuclear war was unthinkable."[28] That neither the crisis in Cuba, nor the (intimately related) confrontation in Berlin,[29] led to war was more down to good fortune rather than crisis management or skilled negotiation. Indeed, the underestimation of Soviet forces in Cuba in 1962, allied to the pressures for a military solution, meant that the US was far closer to war with the USSR than anyone realized at the time.

In negotiation terms, the absence of trust, the information asymmetry between the two sides and the lack of direct communication between the military headquarters make the event look very vulnerable to an escalation. Precisely those very elements led to a general confrontation in relation to Austria-Hungary in 1914, as discussed by Kevin Homrighausen in "Diplomatic Crisis in July 1914" in this volume. That the crisis in Cuba avoided this trap – mainly due to luck – should encourage political leaders

---

24 SCHLESINGER, Jr., journal entry for March 24, 1987. Schlesinger, Jr., *Journals*, p. 631.

25 Deborah SHAPLEY, *Promise and Power: The Life and Times of Robert McNamara* (Boston: MA: Little, Brown and Company 1993) pp. 183–185.

26 Pierre SALINGER, "Gaps in the Cuban Missile Crisis Story", *New York Times*, February 5, 1989.

27 McNAMARA *et al.*, *Argument Without End*, pp. 9–11. Quote at p. 11.

28 SALINGER, "Gaps in the Cuban Missile Crisis Story".

29 Christof MÜNGER, *Kennedy, die Berliner Mauer und die Kubakrise: Die westliche Allianz in der Zerreißprobe 1961–1963* (Paderborn: Ferdinand Schöningh 2003).

to continue to think about how to handle such extreme cases. Not surprisingly, the main practical lesson derived from the 1962 crisis was that communication between the protagonists was paramount. This led directly to the establishment of the Moscow-Washington hotline. This demonstrated that, beyond whatever strategies can be put in place in order to handle such gamed theoretical cases (one could think of the Thomas Schelling's "chicken game"),[30] crisis management and détente require constant interaction and negotiation. That the Cuban Missile Crisis so nearly ended in nuclear holocaust is hardly surprising. In "chicken", *war* is the mutual worst option, whilst *defeat* is the second-worst option.[31]

2.1. THE MUNICH SYNDROME

The disastrous policy of Appeasement in the 1930s had forever handicapped policymakers in their pursuit of peaceful solutions to diplomatic crises.[32] USAF Chief of Staff, the hawkish General Curtis LeMay, had been well aware of this when, on October 19, 1962, he raged at Kennedy: "This blockade and political action, I see leading into war. I don't see any other solution. It will lead right into war. This is almost as bad as the appeasement at Munich."[33] And, even after Khrushchev had accepted Kennedy's proposals on October 28, LeMay opined: "The Soviets may make a charade of withdrawal and keep some weapons in Cuba."[34] When the crisis was over LeMay, told a stunned Kennedy to his face: "We have been had. It's the greatest defeat in our history. We should invade today."[35] LeMay's opinion echoed Churchill's verdict on Appeasement: "We seem to be very near the bleak choice between War

---

[30] Thomas SCHELLING, *Arms and Influence* (New Haven, CT: Yale University Press 1966) pp. 116–125.

[31] Frank C. ZAGARE, *Game Theory, Diplomatic History and Security Studies* (Oxford: Oxford University Press 2019) p. 155.

[32] R. Gerald HUGHES, *The Postwar Legacy of Appeasement: British Foreign Policy since 1945* (London: Bloomsbury 2014).

[33] Kennedy meeting with the Joint Chiefs of Staff, 9.45 am, October 19, 1962. MAY and ZELIKOW (eds.), *The Kennedy Tapes*, p. 178.

[34] Aleksandr FURSENKO and Timothy NAFTALI, *"One Hell of a Gamble": Khrushchev, Castro Kennedy, and the Cuban Missile Crisis, 1958-1964* (New York: W.W. Norton 1999) p. 287.

[35] Michael R. BESCHLOSS, *The Crisis Years: Kennedy and Khrushchev, 1960–1963* (New York: HarperCollins 1991) pp. 543–544.

and Shame. My feeling is that we shall choose Shame, and then have War thrown in a little later on even more adverse terms than at present."[36] For his part, after the missile crisis a shaken President Kennedy confided to an aide that his military was "mad".[37]

2.2. DOMESTIC POLITICS AND INTERNATIONAL POLICY

It was the combination of high-risk nuclear gamble and volatile domestic political considerations that made the Cuban missile crisis so dangerous. Although Kennedy was wont to observe that "[d]omestic policy can only defeat us; foreign policy can kill us",[38] John Kenneth Galbraith was correct when he recalled that the "political needs of the Kennedy administration [caused] it to take almost any risk to get [the missiles] out".[39] That said, the nuclear near-miss of October 1962 underlined the fact that the fear of being labelled an "appeaser" was increasingly being offset by a fear of nuclear war. In the nuclear age the delicate art of balancing the maintenance of vital national interests against the danger of nuclear war has strained the sinews of statesmen for over 70 years now. In 2018, James Blight and Janet Lang declared that their book, *Dark beyond Darkness*, had been "written as an act of resistance [...] to the widely-accepted idea that we can live forever with nuclear weapons without another Cuban missile crisis-like event, but this time, one in which our luck runs out and we destroy ourselves irreversibly".[40] In the aftermath of the First World War Georges Santayana memorably observed that "only the dead have seen the end of war".[41] That being so, we would be well advised to remember that the *"warning in the Cuban missile crisis is this: it nearly happened once; it can happen again."*[42]

---

36   Churchill to Lord Moyne, September 11, 1938. Martin GILBERT (ed.), *Winston S. Churchill: The Official Biography: Companion, Volume V, Part 3: The Coming of War 1936–1939* (London: Heinemann 1982) p. 1154.

37   Len SCOTT, *The Cuban Missile Crisis and the Threat of Nuclear War: Lessons from History* (London: Continuum 2007) p. 127.

38   SCHLESINGER, Jr., *A Thousand Days*, p. 380.

39   Russell D. BUHITE, "From Kennedy to Nixon: the end of consensus" in Gordon MARTEL (ed.), *American Foreign Relations Reconsidered: 1890–1993* (London: Routledge 2002) p. 131.

40   James G. BLIGHT and Janet M. LANG, *Dark Beyond Darkness: The Cuban Missile Crisis as History, Warning, and Catalyst* (Lanham, MD: Rowman and Littlefield 2018) p. xiii.

41   Georges SANTAYANA, *Soliloquies in England and Later Soliloquies* (New York: Charles Scribner's Sons 1922) p. 102.

42   BLIGHT and LANG, *Dark Beyond Darkness*, p. 93.

REFERENCES

ABEDUL, Hugo and HUGHES, R. Gerald, "The Comandante in his Labyrinth: Fidel Castro and his Legacy", *Intelligence and National Security*, 26/4 (2011).

ACHESON, Dean, "Homage to Plain Dumb Luck" in Robert A. Devine (ed.), *The Cuban Missile Crisis* (Chicago, IL: Quadrangle 1971).

ALLISON, Graham T. and ZELIKOW, Philip D., *Essence of Decision: Explaining the Cuban Missile Crisis*, 2nd edition (New York: Longman 1999).

ALLYN, Bruce J., BLIGHT, James G. and WELCH, David A., *Back to the Brink: Proceedings of the Moscow Conference on the Cuban Missile Conference, January 27–28, 1989* (Lanham, MD: University of America Press 1992).

BESCHLOSS, Michael R. *The Crisis Years: Kennedy and Khrushchev, 1960–1963* (New York: HarperCollins 1991).

BLIGHT, James G. and LANG, Janet M., *Dark Beyond Darkness: The Cuban Missile Crisis as History, Warning, and Catalyst* (Lanham, MD: Rowman and Littlefield 2018).

BUHITE, Russell D., "From Kennedy to Nixon: the end of consensus" in Gordon MARTEL (ed.), *American Foreign Relations Reconsidered: 1890–1993* (London: Routledge 2002).

BUNDY, McGeorge, *Danger and Survival: Choices about the Bomb in the First Fifty Years* (New York: Random House 1988).

DOBBS, Michael, *One Minute to Midnight: Kennedy, Khrushchev and Castro on the Brink of Nuclear War* (New York: A.A. Knopf 2008).

FURSENKO, Aleksandr and NAFTALI, Timothy, *"One Hell of a Gamble": Khrushchev, Castro Kennedy and the Cuban Missile Crisis 1958–1964* (London: John Murray 1997).

GARTOFF, Raymond, *Reflections on the Cuban Missile Crisis*, revised edn. (Washington DC: The Brookings Institution 1989).

GIBSON, David R., *Talk at the Brink: Deliberation and Decision during the Cuban Missile Crisis* (Princeton, NJ: Princeton University Press 2012).

GILBERT, Martin (ed.), *Winston S. Churchill: The Official Biography: Companion, Volume V, Part 3: The Coming of War 1936–1939* (London: Heinemann 1982).

HERSHBERG, James, "The Cuban Missile Crisis" in Melvyn LEFFLER and Odd Arne WESTAD (eds.), *The Cambridge History of the Cold War Volume 2* (Cambridge: Cambridge University Press 2010).

HUGHES, R. Gerald, *The Postwar Legacy of Appeasement: British Foreign Policy since 1945* (London: Bloomsbury 2014).

HUGHES, R. Gerald, "'The Best and the Brightest': The Cuban Missile Crisis, the Kennedy administration, and the lessons of history" in Len SCOTT and R. Gerald HUGHES (eds.), *The Cuban Missile Crisis: A Critical Reappraisal* (Abingdon: Routledge 2016).

KENNEDY, Robert F., *Thirteen Days: A Memoir of the Cuban Missile Crisis* (New York: W.W. Norton 1969).

LEBOW, Richard Ned and STEIN, Janice Gross, *We All Lost the Cold War* (Princeton, NJ: Princeton University Press 1994).

MAY, Ernest R. and ZELIKOW, Philip D. (eds.), *The Kennedy Tapes: Inside the White House during the Cuban Missile Crisis* (Cambridge, MA: The Belknap Press of Harvard University Press 1997).

MCNAMARA, Robert S., BLIGHT, James, BRIGHAM, Robert K. with BIERSTEKER, Thomas J., SCHANDLER, Col. Herbert, *Argument Without End: In Search of Answers to the Vietnam Tragedy* (New York: Public Affairs 1999).

MÜNGER, Christof, *Kennedy, die Berliner Mauer und die Kubakrise: Die westliche Allianz in der Zerreißprobe 1961–1963* (Paderborn: Ferdinand Schöningh 2003).

NITZE, Paul H., with SMITH, Ann M. and REARDEN, Steven L., *From Hiroshima to Glasnost: At the Center of Decision* (New York: Grove Weidenfeld 1989).

POWERS, Thomas, "And after we've struck Cuba?" (1997) in *Intelligence Wars: American Secret History from Hitler to Al-Qaeda* (New York: New York Review Books 2004).

SALINGER, Pierre, "Gaps in the Cuban Missile Crisis Story", *New York Times*, February 5, 1989.

SANTAYANA, Georges, *Soliloquies in England and Later Soliloquies* (New York: Charles Scribner's Sons 1922).

SCHELLING, Thomas, *Arms and Influence* (New Haven, CT: Yale University Press 1966).

SCHLESINGER, Jr., Arthur, *A Thousand Days: John F. Kennedy in the White House* (New York: First Mariner 2002).

SCHLESINGER, Jr., Arthur, *Journals: 1952–2000*, edited by Andrew SCHLESINGER and Stephen SCHLESINGER (New York: Penguin 2007).

SCOTT, Len, *The Cuban Missile Crisis and the Threat of Nuclear War: Lessons from History* (London: Continuum 2007).

SHAPLEY, Deborah, *Promise and Power: The Life and Times of Robert McNamara* (Boston: MA: Little, Brown and Company 1993).

SNIE 85-3-62, "The Military Buildup in Cuba", September 19, 1962. CIA Freedom of Information Act Electronic Reading Room, <https://www.cia.gov/library/readingroom/docs/CIA-RDP80B01676R001800050003-7.pdf>.

STERN, Sheldon M., *The Cuban Missile Crisis in American Memory: Myths versus Reality* (Stanford, CA: Stanford University Press 2012).

STERN, Sheldon M., E-mail to the author, September 17, 2014.

ZAGARE, Frank C., *Game Theory, Diplomatic History and Security Studies* (Oxford: Oxford University Press 2019).

THE RUN UP TO THE TRUMP/KIM SINGAPORE SUMMIT

Playing Red and Playing Blue

Mark Young*

Donald Trump is almost certainly the most unlikely and disruptive President in US history. From the moment he descended the elevator in Trump Tower in June 2015 to announce his candidacy for the US Presidency, he has continued to confound and repel his critics and delight his loyal supporters. His stock in trade is to upend the establishment, joker style, which usually means demonstrative belligerence and politically incorrect messaging. But it can also, surprisingly, include unexpectedly and excessively cozying up to America's traditional enemies, with Russia the most obvious example.

---

* President of Rational Games, Inc. Markyoung@gmx.net.

North Korea, in the meantime, has continued doggedly on its quest for atomic weapons, first tested in 2006. Undeterred by the principled but ineffectual diplomatic moves of the Obama administration, President Kim Jong-Un has made steady progress in developing and testing short-range, intermediate, and even long-range missiles, along with the means to fire them. Ignoring the noise from Trumpian Washington, he has steadily advanced in this quest, while the whole world watched the growing escalation between the two countries with fear and trepidation.

Somehow, however, in early 2018, something changed. Sparked by remarkably deft and helpful diplomatic overtures by South Korean President Moon Jae-In, the two Koreas began a startling rapprochement, soon augmented by a new dialogue between Washington and Pyongyang as well. Out of the confusing mix of the incoherent bluster at the UN and what seem to have been more conciliatory private communications, the almost unthinkable became reality: Mr Trump and Mr Kim met for the first American/North Korean summit meeting ever in Singapore on June 12, 2018. This was not peace yet, but it surely was a possible step towards it.

What prompted this remarkable turnaround? How did this diplomatic miracle happen? How were these two decidedly power-conscious men, their countries for decades implacable enemies, able to decisively turn the tide, first interrupting the torrent of mutual vitriol and then both taking the risk of appearing together publicly to seek a more equitable solution? Who exactly made the decision to give peace a chance, and to take the risk of negotiation?

1. THE TRUMP/KIM NEGOTIATIONS: SEEKING COOPERATION IN A COMPETITIVE ENVIRONMENT

Telling the story of the Trump-Kim encounter is in effect to show just how cooperative moves can emerge from a highly competitive, if not conflictual, situation. As such, the vitriolic shouting and tweeting match between Mr Trump and Mr Kim in the second half of 2017 was the culmination of a classic competitive and aggressive cycle which had built up steam over three decades and looked very dangerous indeed – well capable of escalating into a bloodbath and destroying both Koreas. It is therefore quite remarkable that, barely a year later, the two men managed to meet amicably, even cordially and at least initiate a more productive dialogue. Thus, the competitive cycle was halted with some initial cooperative moves. The stage was set for a new kind of game.

A closer look not only at the larger political situation in both the United States and North and South Korea but also at the personal dynamics of the fast-changing relationship between Trump, Kim and also Moon Jae-In reveals an intricate series of cooperative and competitive moves on both sides. With the license of fairly selective historical analysis, three principal stages of the negotiation can be identified: a Competitive stage, a Cooperative stage and a still very uncertain Intermediate one. The combination of the three has been, so far, fortunate and successful and has made a win-win solution to the crisis possible.

In order to analyze the sequence of events leading to the first Trump/Kim meeting in June 2018 in a more illuminating way, this chapter will make use of a common negotiation game used in negotiation studies. Drawing on game theory, including the Prisoners' Dilemma (PD) (Tucker, 1950), it seeks to shed new light on the question of exactly what turns the tide in protracted situations of conflict. This most famous dilemma (Axelrod, 1984), now a household word in game theory and central to the work of several Nobel Prize recipients, is indeed about cooperation and competition. But it is also all about trust, an important factor in International Relations, especially when distrust has become deeply entrenched in the negotiators' minds.

2. THE RED/BLUE GAME

A particularly insightful and playful illustration of the PD can be found in the "Red/Blue" training exercise.[1] Framed in a more abstract way, this interactive simulation puts the players in a situation where they come to realize the value of good communication, trust, and precise goal-setting, as well as experiencing the rewards of a Win/Win outcome that makes the pie bigger.

In this game, two teams, sequestered in separate rooms, must, over 10 rounds, each (independently) reach a joint decision to play a color: Red or Blue. Points are awarded to both teams at the end of each

---

[1] Originally created by the US military during the Korean War, then further developed by various negotiation trainers, and finally copyrighted by Huthwaite International Ltd, with whose kind permission I include the description here.

round depending on what they have both chosen to play, as depicted in Figure 1.

Figure 1. The teams are mutually interdependent

	TEAM TWO:	
TEAM ONE:	RED	BLUE
RED	+ 3 / + 3	– 6 / + 6
BLUE	+ 6 / – 6	– 3 / – 3

Source: Huthwaite International.

The participants soon learn that, tempting as playing "Blue" may seem, it is virtually impossible to win the game (whatever that means) without the cooperation of the other side. They experience the importance of wise goal-setting with an understanding of trade-offs, the challenges of internal negotiation within teams, and the need to adroitly navigate the "Negotiation Triangle" between discussions with the other side and then with their mandate-giving home front. They learn to value good communication and trust, clear messaging that brooks no misunderstanding and respect for non-rational motivators such as pride and fear.

Perhaps most importantly, the Red/Blue game teaches its players the importance of integrative bargaining, *making the pie bigger* by working together creatively to increase the value of the pie, and searching for value that can be provided by third parties.

And perhaps most relevant for this discussion of Trump and Kim, the game lays bare the power of *"systems dynamics"* in which "Blue/Blue" or "Red/Red" cycles take on an energy of their own which accelerate and are increasingly difficult to break, as assumptions about the other side harden and creativity is stifled. The players come to realize that even smaller, short-term moves contribute to overall dynamics and can lead to powerful positive or negative cycles. They learn to think carefully about each move that is made, and to anticipate both immediate and long-term responses from the other side, both in the immediate round and over the longer course of the ten-round game. We see all of this clearly in the behaviors of the two protagonists. Trump and Kim, in the period between July 2017 and June 2018.

3.   PHASE ONE: BLUE FUTILITY

This first phase began with a bang with the election of the iconoclastic Donald Trump in the United States, who within hours of inauguration made his penchant for conflict all too clear and who daily used his Twitter weapon to surprise and intimidate friend and foe alike. What followed, at least for North Korea, was a fairly monotonous series of Blue (competitive) moves in both word and deed. Kim, for his part, returned the fire, with escalating tests of weapons and also with highly personal attacks on his new nemesis in Washington.

Viewed through the template of the Red/Blue exercise, the 65 years from the end of the Korean War in 1953 to early 2018 can fairly be viewed as an almost uninterrupted Blue/Blue game. In repetitive cycles of warmongering and weapons development, each side sought to win the game on its own terms, expressing and increasing its power by means of threats, intimidations and real damage inflicted on the other side, with hapless South Korea caught in the middle.

On the US side, the Obama Administration had decided on a three-pronged strategic attack: first increasing economic sanctions (as far as the Chinese would allow them), and then combining those with the installation of the THAAD nuclear defense system in South Korea. Finally, this was augmented by a fairly sophisticated cyberattack on the still clandestine North Korean nuclear development program. It is difficult to say how effective this rational strategy was, but the observable results did not offer much room for hope. The situation on the Korean peninsula, frozen since 1953, was getting more and more dangerous.

The Blue response from the North Koreans was predictable and not long in coming. First short-range and then longer-range missiles were tested, some of them falling harmlessly into the ocean, others landing closer to the mark, not far from Guam, which is officially US territory. It became increasingly clear that North Korea was ever closer to joining the nuclear club. And their realization that achieving this goal would represent a major shift in power only fueled the effort. Kim was on a mission and seemed likely to achieve it.

All of this was duly accompanied by an escalating war of words. At his UN speech in September 2017, Trump issued dire warnings of "fire and fury" to rain down on the Korean people. Like many of Trump's domestic political opponents, Kim was given a derogatory nickname: "Little Rocket Man". The verbal histrionics became ever more absurd, culminating in

Trump's schoolboy bully proclamation that "my Button is bigger than your button. And it works."

Not to be outdone, Kim responded in kind. Trump was "senile and a dotard" and "mentally deranged". He was "ignorant and impotent". While journalists had a field day translating these fairly sophisticated insults, the temperature rose. The Blue cycle was firmly in place, both in terms of weapons and words, already out of the control of both protagonists.

The allies on both sides looked on passively and rather helplessly. The Europeans made earnest entreaties to tone down the rhetoric, the Japanese tried to keep their heads down and the Chinese repeated the mantra of the need for a peaceful solution, while all the while enabling the North Koreans to violate the sanctions. There really was no sign of possible intervention, either between the two protagonists or from those outside. And there was no clear way out of the spiral: neither side could afford to shift to Red. (See Figure 2.)

Figure 2. July to December 2017: The Futility of Playing Blue

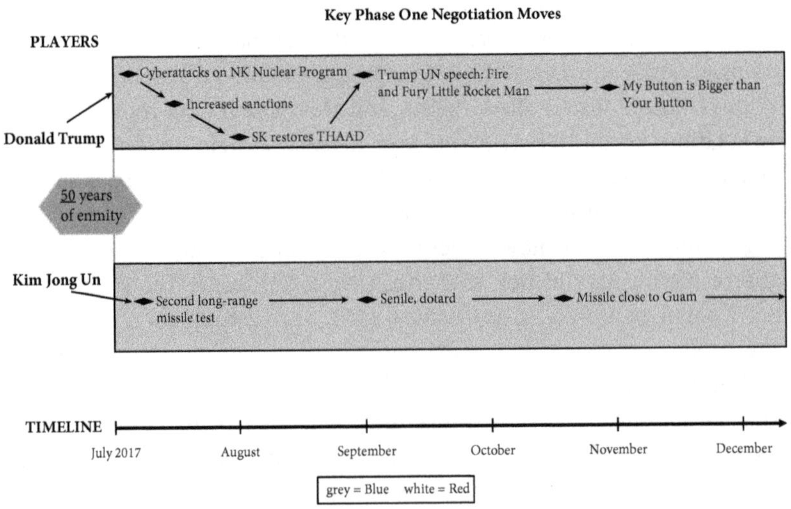

Source: Produced by the author.

But what about third parties? Who else might be able to help to change the rules of the game? The impetus came, quietly and skillfully, from South Korea. First hesitantly, and then with increasing confidence, South Korea's President Moon made discreet back-channel overtures which soon became more public. With great popular support including by his business community, he began a revival of the "Sunshine policy", even in the face of the brewing storm.

The welcome occasion, one which could bring an opportunity for change, was the Seoul Olympics.

4. PHASE TWO: RED CAN CHANGE THE GAME

A closer look at the events of early 2018 in both the United States and the two Koreas shows growing momentum towards a switch to a Red game, albeit with significant backsliding on both sides. Until literally hours before the morning of June 12, it was not entirely clear whether the summit would actually be held. But the Red dynamic held, and the two protagonists eventually limped into the arena in Singapore.

The first move came from President Moon in South Korea. Seizing on the upcoming event of the 2018 Winter Olympics in Seoul, he issued an invitation to President Kim to attend the opening ceremony. In a somewhat cautious second Red move, Kim responded with the offer to send his sister, one of the few Kim relatives who apparently enjoyed his ear and trust. Kim Yo-Jong was later dubbed "North Korea's secret weapon" as her charm and natural grace led Seoul to welcome her warmly, with giddy press accounts of all details of the brief visit. The cycle had been broken and the Enemy had a new and surprisingly attractive face.

But the Americans were not ready yet. In an astonishing act of disrespect, Vice President Pence, seated directly behind Kim Yo-Jong at the opening ceremony, chose to shun her, refusing to even acknowledge her presence. And no further word came from Washington despite the press storm there as well pushing the détente forward. It is to the great credit of the South Koreans that they decided to continue on their new path alone and undeterred, hoping the Americans would eventually catch up and join the train before it left the station.

To be very clear: this first mutual shift to Red was no act of goodwill. Both sides in this conflict remained deeply interest-driven, each seeking to take the upper hand. Slowly, however, each came to understand that Red moves could often accomplish this goal far more effectively than could Blue.

And a key realization for the South Koreans was that taking the lead, even with small steps, would eventually spark President Trump's narcissistic hunger to make history and compel the Americans to get on board while they could still plausibly claim credit for the shift in strategy. (See Figure 3.)

Figure 3. January to June 2018. Red can Change the Game

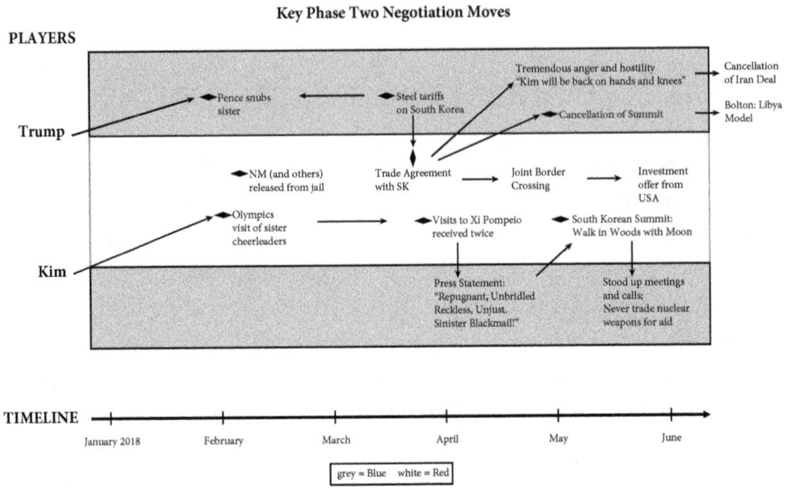

Key Phase Two Negotiation Moves

Source: Produced by the author.

In typical Trumpian style, the US Administration continued with yet another Blue move, slapping tariffs on the South Koreans in a highly unfortunate parallel effort to renegotiate the US/South Korean trade agreement, much as they would later try to do with many other trading partners. The South Koreans, out of either weakness or prescient grace, acceded to at least a few of the American trade demands and thus removed this potential barrier to the continuing rapprochement. In any case, the ice was broken, and the Blue cycle brought to a halt.

Kim, in the meantime, energetically and adroitly commenced two-pronged negotiations, first with the new American Secretary of State, receiving Mike Pompeo in Pyongyang twice, and, perhaps more significantly, with two longer and apparently fairly substantive visits to Beijing. The first of a series of discreet "back-channel" negotiations began in earnest, with the North Koreans making sure that their Chinese home front was in approval before beginning logistical discussions with the Americans to plan a possible ground-breaking first meeting between Trump and Kim.

And the pan-Korean spring lovefest blossomed. There was a highly photogenic and historic first summit between Moon and Kim at Panmunjom in April 2018, complete with a joint border crossing by the two Presidents, then a walk in the woods and an exchange of gifts, including a USB stick which was reputed to contain substantial first investment offers by the South once hostilities with the North formally ceased. Notably, Moon seems to have engaged in these discussions, so crucial for laying the groundwork for the later negotiations, at some risk to his own negotiating authority given, on the one hand, the still tepid American backing and, on the other hand, the fierce criticism by his domestic opposition for "playing the North's game" and opening up to the Enemy in this imprudent way.

With back-channel contacts thus established at least on the North Korean side, Kim was now ready to make his first tentative moves towards direct negotiations with the Americans. But Washington sent confusing signals. Pompeo and his staff pushed for fairly hastily arranged meetings, but these had more to do with logistics than with substance. A major topic was where the summit would be held, given the need for neutral territory, Kim's famous aversion to flying and the power games that go with hosting such a meeting.

No sooner had the Singapore venue been officially announced, things began to go sour, at least on the public relations front. Bold statements from the North Koreans that they would "never trade nuclear weapons for aid", repeated cancellations or no-show at planning meetings – all this sorely tried Trump's famously thin patience. Finally, in a fit of pique, he announced that the summit was off. This veering into Blue was fairly typical for Trumpian negotiation tactics, and many watchers did not take it seriously.

But the North Koreans certainly did. Fresh vitriol spewed from Pyongyang: this was "sinister blackmail", and the Americans (especially Trump) were "unbridled, reckless, repugnant and unjust". Trump responded by lamenting the "tremendous anger and hostility" on the North Korean side, predicting that Kim would soon be back "on his hands and knees". This schoolyard bickering would have been almost comical, were the stakes not so high.

Two further moves on the American side made matters far worse. Trump's triumphant retreat from the JPCPA nuclear deal, laboriously signed in 2015 after nearly a decade of negotiation between Iran and six Western powers, was a powerful confirmation to the North Koreans that the Americans were not to be trusted, even after signing a deal. And John Bolton, the new National Security Advisor, poured oil on the fire with impolitic (and inaccurate) comparisons of the emerging North Korean agreement with those reached a decade ago with Libya, leading directly to the violent demise of Mr Gaddafi. Unwise or simply belligerent, this talk was poison to the pan-Korean efforts to establish at least minimal communication and trust.

Despite all of this, the momentum towards a meeting had been established, so that there was already no alternative to continuing on with the highly public announcement of direct North Korean/American negotiations, whether in Singapore or elsewhere. There was nowhere to go but forward, even given the strong emotions and misgivings on both sides. The pull of history and the cost of failure were powerful forces indeed. Singapore was on again, and the world waited to see what happens next.

5. PHASE THREE: PURPLE UNCERTAINTY

On June 12, 2018, the summit went off without a hitch. Despite the hasty preparations, the logistics were flawless, the mood upbeat and the pageantry impressive. The final communiqué after the four-hour meeting, extolling the encounter as an "epochal event of great significance" (see the Annex to this chapter) was thin in the extreme. But observers chose to put their faith in the follow-up to come. Unfortunately, the relative inactivity and the re-emergence of Blue dynamics since Singapore must be cause for concern. The problem is by no means resolved.

As he did with Vladimir Putin in Helsinki a few months later, the truculent and aggressive Trump displayed an almost kittenish desire for harmony with Kim. Whether this was due to his firm conviction that he can do almost any deal as long as there is a personal relationship, he seemed sure that his sudden offer of bonhomie between leaders would heal all wounds. Kim, while far less demonstrative, played along. The closing ceremony was Red in the extreme.

Most puzzling was the four-minute video that the Americans had prepared and apparently showed to Kim in a private session. This gauzy Hollywood concoction put forward two alternative futures for North Korea: one a bright, colorful world of scientific progress and happiness, the other a desolate and monochrome landscape full of weaponry accompanied by ominous music. Only one person could choose between these two destinies, the film's narrator said. Kim's reaction was not publicly reported.

But the tangible results of the meeting left most questions open. Critics called it a "drive-by negotiation". Beyond the grand wording and mutually professed fealty to abstract principles in the one-page declaration, it was clear that none of the thorny problems had been addressed. There was no mention of North Korea's nuclear program. Just what does "nuclear disarmament" mean? Is there to be a formal peace treaty? What about the THAAD nuclear shield over South Korea? How and when will sanctions be lifted? In what sequence will the next moves be made, and how will they be verified? How to build trust at the working level after six decades of Cold War?

Astonishingly, there was one very Red unilateral concession made by the Americans: the immediate cancellation of the annual Freedom Guardian joint military exercises. Trump proudly framed this as "a way to save money" and did not seem to realize the value of this concession to the other side: the North Koreans had chafed under these exercises for decades and complained bitterly and publicly about them. But it was the one tangible result of the summit, so Kim could go home pleased and boasting of his success.

Communications after Singapore continued to be warm for several weeks. Trump announced that there would be "no more talk of maximum pressure" and proclaimed Kim to be "smart, gracious and very reasonable". Trump promised Kim that very soon he would be "happy, safe and prosperous". Kim, somewhat less effusively, offered to "talk anytime". A schedule of working-level meetings was agreed with the intention of perhaps meeting again for a second summit before the end of 2018. And several weeks after Singapore, an envoy arrived in Washington from North Korea with a theatrical "Giant Letter" proclaiming the release of three American prisoners. Now Trump had a tangible success to report as well.

Fairly soon, however, Blue tendencies reasserted themselves. This was not just due to recidivism, but also to the realization of both sides that some element of power remains key in negotiations, and that keeping Blue options alive is a necessary enrichment of any Red approach. In the end, it was to be a mix of both – Purple, if you will – that might make the breakthrough possible, with Red predominating but with Blue never quite out of sight. (See Figure 4)

The Chinese did their part as well in furthering the new détente. Somewhat surprisingly, North Korea was accepted into the massive Chinese "One Belt, One Road" initiative, signaling an end to its economic isolation. They also offered to fill in the detail left open in Singapore by fleshing out what a "phased approach" to disarmament might look like, a principle to which the Americans had still not officially agreed, despite Mr Trump's implied approval at the meeting.

Figure 4. June 2018. A Picture-Perfect Summit … But What Happens Next?

Key Phase Three Negotiation Moves

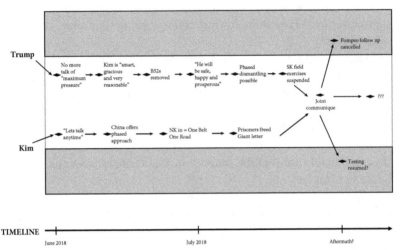

Source: Produced by the author.

In the ensuing months, things chilled again. The pattern of cancelled meetings and no shows on the North Korean side reappeared, accompanied by widespread rumors of resumed nuclear testing. Pompeo had to publicly cancel a much-vaunted visit to Pyongyang for no apparent reason. Jarringly, Trump told the press in that he had "fallen in love" with Kim, to which the North Korean leader responded with disdain for "conniving American psychological tactics". While the rhetoric between the two certainly did not match Phase One levels, the long weeks of passivity and the long list of unresolved issues did not bode well for the future.

At the time of writing (March 2019, just after the failed Hanoi summit), the author would certainly not be foolish enough to venture a guess as to what the final outcome will be. The opportunity offered by the Blue to Red turnaround in Singapore was unique and historic. But what will the two parties do with it?

6. TAKEAWAYS FOR THIS NEGOTIATION

So what are we to make of all this? Does the possibly emerging Trump/Kim negotiation breakthrough, especially when viewed as a Red/Blue game, offer lessons for other negotiations or conflict situations? It seems that the (admittedly anecdotal) analysis in this short chapter suggests at least three preliminary "takeaways".

In general, the best strategy for effective negotiation especially in an intractable situation of conflict is probably *a judicious mix of Red and Blue*, with the former predominating, but the latter also kicking in occasionally to give each partner bite and to keep the other honest.[2] Also, due to the power of the moral high ground, playing Red can be powerful in itself: far from being a sign of weakness or naïveté, playing Red can literally shame the opponent into reciprocity.

Beyond these thoughts, three lessons are perhaps unique to the Trump/ Kim situation. The first was the importance of a personal bond. Neither of these two protagonists were particularly empathetic, but the overwhelming cost of failure to not only both sides but potentially the whole world made walking away from the table for good not a realistic option. To this one could add the somewhat odd personal chemistry which still seems to exist between these two Alpha leaders, and the shared culture that between them they will work things out amicably. Just two guys solving a problem with a mutual pride in making history together.

Second, *back-channel efforts were particularly helpful here*. Tellingly, it was neither Trump nor Kim who started the dialogue here, but rather President Moon in South Korea, (the true candidate for the Nobel Peace Prize) whose discreet and deft outreach to the "other side" got the process started after decades of hardened inertia. In the difficult first few weeks of "Phase One", it was these back-channel negotiations that created the momentum that neither side could then stop.

The Chinese certainly also did their part, both in serving as a surprisingly constructive home front and sounding board for Kim, and for making substantive proposals after Singapore to help in implementation. These unofficial initiatives, deliberately unsanctioned by the official decision-makers, can yield breakthroughs on "dealbreakers" and point a way forward.

Finally, one should never underestimate *the role of externalities and luck*. The hosting of the Olympics, the surprise election of Trump which

---

[2]   This is likely to happen anyway, as in any situation with an established Blue/Blue dynamic, the temptation for "backsliding" will always be great, at least for some factions on each side. Thanks to Linda Marsh at Huthwaite for making this point to me.

allowed a "Nixon in China" effect, the rise of President Moon in South Korea: these were all contextual events that strongly mitigated the North's fear of invasion and change, while at the same time inspiring both leaders to live up to the ideals of non-violent political and social change. In 2018, the time seemed to be right for a dialogue to start, and the seeds of constructive negotiation, once thrown, fell on fertile soil. It is unlikely that the Singapore encounter would have transpired in this way had the ground been rockier.

7. CONCLUSIONS: NEGOTIATION DYNAMICS

The 2017–2018 emerging nuclear negotiations between the US and North Korea were breath-taking to watch, shaped by externalities and strongly influenced by personal relationships. Seen especially through the sobering lens of the failed follow-up summit in Hanoi in end February 2018, it seems impossible to venture any prediction as to how this conflict will end. But the analysis of the Red/Blue game does shed light on the importance of negotiation dynamics and how even small moves can change them. And that is cause for hope, not only in this particular negotiation.

REFERENCES

AXELROD, R., (1984), *The Evolution of Cooperation*, New York, Basic Books.

BINMORE, K., (1991), *Fun and Games: A Textbook on Game Theory*, London: D.C: Heath & Co.

McADAMS, D., (2014), *Game-Changer: Game Theory and the Art of Transforming Strategic Situations*, London: W.W. Norton and Company.

OSBORNE, M.J, with RUBINSTEIN, A., (1994), *A Course in Game Theory*, London: The MIT Press.

RAIFFA, H. with LUCE, R.D., (1957), *Games and Decisions*, New York: Dover Publications.

TUCKER, A. W. and KUHN, H. W., (1950), "Contributions to the Theory of Games" (eds), *Annals of Mathematical Studies*.

YOUNG, M., (2007), "Playing Red and Playing Blue: the 1990–94 Negotiation Miracle in South Africa", *International Negotiation*, volume 12, 2.

ANNEX

Joint Statement of President Donald J. Trump of the United States of America and Chairman Kim Jong Un of the Democratic People's Republic of Korea at the Singapore Summit

President Donald J. Trump of the United States of America and Chairman Kim Jong Un of the State Affairs Commission of the Democratic People's Republic of Korea (DPRK) held a first, historic summit in Singapore on June 12, 2018.

President Trump and Chairman Kim Jong Un conducted a comprehensive, in-depth, and sincere exchange of opinions on the issues related to the establishment of new U.S.-DPRK relations and the building of a lasting and robust peace regime on the Korean Peninsula. President Trump committed to provide security guarantees to the DPRK, and Chairman Kim Jong Un reaffirmed his firm and unwavering commitment to complete denuclearization of the Korean Peninsula.

Convinced that the establishment of new U.S.-DPRK relations will contribute to the peace and prosperity of the Korean Peninsula and of the world, and recognizing that mutual confidence building can promote the denuclearization of the Korean Peninsula, President Trump and Chairman Kim Jong Un state the following:

1. The United States and the DPRK commit to establish new U.S.-DPRK relations in accordance with the desire of the peoples of the two countries for peace and prosperity.
2. The United States and the DPRK will join their efforts to build a lasting and stable peace regime on the Korean Peninsula.
3. Reaffirming the April 27, 2018 Panmunjom Declaration, the DPRK commits to work toward complete denuclearization of the Korean Peninsula.
4. The United States and the DPRK commit to recovering POW/MIA remains, including the immediate repatriation of those already identified.

Having acknowledged that the U.S.-DPRK summit – the first in history – was an epochal event of great significance in overcoming decades of tensions and hostilities between the two countries and for the opening up of a new future, President Trump and Chairman Kim Jong Un commit to implement the stipulations in this joint statement fully and expeditiously. The United States and the DPRK commit to hold follow-up negotiations, led by the U.S. Secretary of State, Mike Pompeo, and a relevant high-level DPRK official, at the earliest possible date, to implement the outcomes of the U.S.-DPRK summit.

President Donald J. Trump of the United States of America and Chairman Kim Jong Un of the State Affairs Commission of the Democratic People's Republic of Korea have committed to cooperate for the development of new U.S.-DPRK relations and for the promotion of peace, prosperity, and security of the Korean Peninsula and of the world.

DONALD J. TRUMP
President of the United States of America

KIM JONG UN
Chairman of the State Affairs Commission of the Democratic People's Republic of Korea
June 12, 2018, Sentosa Island, Singapore

PART V

MIDDLE EAST NEGOTIATIONS:
INTERESTS OR EMOTIONS?

NEGOTIATING IN SYRIA IN 1920

Gouraud and Faisal before
the Battle of Damascus

Julie D'ANDURAIN*

The Battle of Maysalun (July 24, 1920) between French and Sharifian forces is known for having brought an end to the Arab Kingdom of Syria, i.e., the political organization of Hashemite power that revolved around Faisal bin Hussein and the city of Damascus. The battle occurred despite the fact that earlier that year Georges Clemenceau, the chairman of the French Council of Ministers, had agreed in principle to an independent Syria under French mandate, and Faisal had many

---

*   Sorbonne Université, Paris – Roland Mousnier Center.

supporters in Damascus, as well as the support of two French officers (Sylvain Cousse and Maxime Toulat) who had rallied to his cause and provided a useful link with the French command. And while he no doubt cut the figure of a grand colonial leader, Henri Gouraud, the high commissioner and commander-in-chief of the French Army of the Levant who had just arrived in Syria, was not likely to disobey his superiors. What happened, then, between January and June 1920? Why did the Franco-Syrian negotiations, which had begun during the Paris Peace Conference, continued in Beirut and were consistent with Syria's agreements with the British, culminate in the "Battle of Damascus"[1]?

1. FRANCE IN SYRIA, OR THE FAISAL-GOURAUD NEGOTIATIONS

The negotiations that ended abruptly at Maysalun in July 1920 were between Faisal bin Hussein and General Gouraud.

1.1. FAISAL

Born into a prestigious Hashemite family in 1885, Faisal was the third son of Hussein bin Ali, the Grand Sharif of Mecca and governor of the Hejaz.[2] Since the rules of primogeniture meant he had no hope of succeeding his father, he gladly became his father's soldier when Hussein launched the "Arab revolt" against the Turks in Syria in May 1916. The issue for Hussein, who in October 1916 had crowned himself "king of the Arab countries", was to lay claim to an Arab kingdom larger than the Hejaz;[3] for his son it was simply to conquer a kingdom through armed struggle. The revolt was not led exclusively by the English because the

---

[1] The name the French initially gave to this battle, which opened up Damascus to them (*La Syrie*, July 31, 1920). Faisal supporters preferred to call it the battle of Maysalun (or Maysalun Pass), in reference to its location.

[2] His elders were Ali (1879–1935), who became king of the Hejaz in 1931, and Abdallah (1882–1951), who became king of Transjordan. His younger brother was named Zeid or Zaid (1898–1970). For an Arab, and more particularly Jordanian, view, see Suleyman Musa (1989).

[3] It was important for future events that Hussein was not recognized by his allies as "king of the Arab countries", but only as the "king of the Hejaz", with transmission of the title by primogeniture.

French, through the French military mission in the Hejaz brought over by Colonel Edouard Bremond,[4] very quickly joined the Anglo-Arab forces. In this way Faisal got to know the English (in this case, the famous Colonel Edward T. Lawrence) as well as the French, especially Captain Rosario Pisani, who was in charge of creating the embryonic Arabian regular army. As a result of his military and political victories, Faisal established credibility with the English and French – taking his brother Abdallah's place – and his father sent him to represent the Hejaz at the Paris Peace Conference in 1919. He was well liked by the French, who saw him as an ally,[5] and in particular by General Gouraud, who awarded him the Legion of Honor in Strasbourg in December 1918.

In January 1920 after meetings with Clemenceau, Faisal obtained a temporary agreement in which France "asserts its recognition of the right of the Arabic-speaking peoples of all religions living in Syrian territory to unite to govern themselves as an independent nation". In exchange, Faisal

> recognized that due to the disorganization resulting from Turkish oppression and the damage suffered during the war, it is in the Syrian peoples' interest to ask for counsel and assistance from a great power, to realize their union and organize the operations of the nation, counsel and assistance that shall be registered with the League of Nations, when it materializes.[6]

1.2. GOURAUD

General Gouraud arrived in Syria in November 1919 with both a military and a political title: commander-in-chief of the French Army of the Levant, and France's High Commissioner in Syria. He had reached the pinnacle of his professional glory: after having stopped Samory, the last black emperor, when he was a young captain in 1894, he was involved in all the major conquests in West Africa (e.g., Mauritania and Chad),

---

[4]   The group was comprised of (generally Muslim) French officers (squadron chief Cadi and captains Regui Saad, Raho, Pisani, and Cousse), important North African leaders (Si Kaddour Ben Ghabrit), and interpreters (Bercher, Cuny, and Streiberg). Regarding the military mission in Hedjaz, see the books by Pascal LE PAUTREMAT (2003), Jean-Yves BERTRAND CADI (2005) and Rémy PORTE (2008).

[5]   Maurice BESSON (1918).

[6]   Gérard D. KHOURY (1993).

thus making his reputation as a "colonial party" strongman. Just before the war in Morocco, he became a brigade general (1912) and continued to win promotions for his courage in World War I. He was seriously wounded in the Dardanelles and had an arm amputated (1915); in spring 1918, he stopped Erich von Ludendorff's offensive in the Champagne region and thus actively took part in retaking that territory between spring and fall.[7] Although a colonial, at the end of the war he wanted to stay in France in the position of governor of Strasbourg. Clemenceau decided instead to send him to Syria, initially to relieve the British troops along the Syrian coast, then to Cilicia in accordance with the agreement signed in Deauville on September 15, 1919.

The four cities occupied by Arab troops – Damascus, Hama, Homs, and Aleppo – were to serve as the base of the future Arab State or confederation of Arab States, in accordance with discussions held in 1916 between the British and French diplomats Mark Sykes and François Georges-Picot. But these cities were in "Zone A" of the Asia Minor Agreement (generally referred to as the Sykes-Picot Agreement), and so were indirectly under France's administrative mandate. The Arab government therefore had to ask for assistance and support from the French rather than the British. On the date of the Deauville agreement, Syria (including Lebanon) was divided into two separate areas: a coastal area under French control (called the Western zone), and the interior (Eastern zone) under Arab control. While Gouraud and his team were trying to determine how a "mandate" differed from the protectorate system applied to Morocco, he discovered that he and Faisal agreed on one thing: the concept of a "Great Syria", i.e., the creation of a Syria as large as possible. They disagreed, however, as to the precise contours of this "Great Syria" and the operational terms of the French mandate.

2. POOR NEGOTIATING CONDITIONS

2.1. UNCERTAINTY SURROUNDING AN IMPORTANT ISSUE: THE RAYAK RAIL HUB

In keeping with his reputation for being an obedient soldier, Henri Gouraud did not challenge Clemenceau's decision or try to prevent a Faisal-led Arab nation from being created, even though he thought

---

[7]   Julie d'Andurain (2009).

Faisal would not have risen to prominence without the pro-Muslim policy of Gouraud's predecessors, Colonel Antoine Philpin de Piépape during the war and François Georges-Picot thereafter. As soon as he was appointed, he noted that Faisal "did not exist ten months earlier"[8] but assured his superiors of his goodwill toward him. It far exceeded that of his civilian deputy, Robert de Caix, who never changed his view of Hussein's son as the embodiment of the "Sharifianism introduced by the English" to destabilize the French in the East.[9]

Applying the fundamental principles of any military or political leader, Gouraud first asserted that order had to be reestablished, as the country was still suffering from the war's side effects (famine in the area around Beirut, revolts against Mustapha Kemal in northern Cilicia, and a poorly organized Sharifian army). His remarks pertained especially to the central corridor formed by the Bekaa Valley (the fertile area between Lebanon and the Anti-Lebanon Mountains), which separated the two Syrian zones at the time. Strategic for many reasons, the area is claimed by both Lebanese and Syrian nationalists.

While waiting for a vote and a decision by the Peace Conference, the Clemenceau-Lloyd-George agreement signed on November 26, 1919 provided a temporary solution: the Bekaa and its three main cities, Rayak, Baalbeck, and Rebaya, would remain under Sharifian administration but the Arab gendarmerie would be supervised by French military inspectors. In Faisal's absence, his younger brother Zeid was appointed to implement the decisions with help from General Nouri Saïd, who was well appreciated by the French at the time.

At first the negotiators displayed obvious goodwill. In January 1919 the French withdrew from Baalbeck as agreed, but stayed in Rayak[10] to secure their troop transports because pressure from Mustapha Kemal was mounting in the north and they had to be able to reach Aleppo quickly. Faisal insisted on taking back all authority over Rayak, the Syrian territory's central hub. In new negotiations in February, Gouraud acceded to the Faisal's demand, agreeing to withdraw his troops from

---

[8]   Draft by General Gouraud, December 1919, Gouraud Archives, PA AP 399, C63-D2 (hereinafter PA AP 399 and the box number).

[9]   Handwritten letter dated January 22, 1920 from Robert de Caix to Gouraud, PA AP 399, C55-D1.

[10] Rayak is a very important rail hub linking Damascus and Beirut, as well as Syria's north and south (on the Aleppo, Homs, Damascus, Daraa line). The border between the East and West zones is near Baalbeck. See the maps at the end of the chapter (Figures 1 and 2).

Rayak and Moallaka except for small detachments left in the Rayak workshops, in exchange for assurances that train traffic would be protected.[11] But Faisal was unable to keep his word: he was immediately threatened with insurrection by his troops, who were the Damascus administration's most extreme nationalists. On February 9 the French High Commission's intelligence services told General Gouraud that Faisal had reneged on his promises regarding Rayak.[12]

2.2. DOUBT ABOUT THE PARTNER

The French leaders quickly began to wonder about Faisal and his behavior. They had been well informed since the beginning by two Arab-speaking French officers, Lieutenant-Colonel Cousse, a liaison officer in Damascus, and Colonel Toulat, Faisal's personal attaché. Robert de Caix criticized them, considering them to be "completely under the Sharifian spell"[13] while Gouraud, aware of how difficult their mission was, behaved in a fatherly way and continued to have faith in them. Cousse, who had been in Damascus since 1919, knew the city where Faisal had set up his government extremely well and quickly understood the magnitude of Syrian nationalism. Toulat deeply admired Faisal, whom he praised constantly, but he nonetheless recognized "that he will never be anything other than an Arab acting to further Arab interests, and to that end using the French, English, Americans, Italians and Turks all with the same indifference".[14] They had both helped Faisal establish himself in Damascus while favoring Zeid and especially Nouri Saïd, convinced that he would be able to disarm Damascus's lower classes and prevent the Bedouins from pillaging the Jews and the Christians, and would rally the political clubs in Damascus (the Arab Club, the National League, and the National Defense Committee) to his cause.

But what had worked between late 1919 and early 1920 started to prove less successful shortly after Faisal returned from Paris (January 16, 1920). Acclaimed by a crowd shouting "long live Arab independence", he was immediately assailed by Syria's staunchest nationalists, Dr. Abderrahman

---

11 Letter from Gouraud to Toulat dated February 4, 1920, PA AP 399, C62-D1.
12 Second office general staff, report dated February 9, 1920, PA AP 399, C74-D1.
13 Letter from Robert de Caix to Berthelot dated March 9, 1920, PA AP 399, C55-D1.
14 Letter from Colonel Toulat to General Gouraud dated March 10, 1920, PA AP 399, C62-D1.

Chabendar, Sheik Kamel Kassab, and Adel Arslan, who took advantage of the circumstances to shut out Nouri Saïd. While the Arab general the French listened to was being discredited, Faisal tried to institute mandatory military service to constitute an army without necessarily showing he could solve the problem of the gangs committing exactions in the country.[15] Gouraud wrote to Cousse that "it pain[ed him] to note that the Emir continues to beguile [them] with promises"[16] and, believing responsibility includes authority, told Faisal he had to make himself obeyed if he wanted to appear credible.[17] Faisal initially complied by setting up a new government, but its members seemed much too favorable to the French for the extremists. A few weeks later, he was forced to agree to a Syrian Congress of 60 members, who proclaimed him "King of Syria" on March 7, 1920.[18]

3. LESSONS: A NEGOTIATION DERAILED BY THE RISE OF EXTREMISM

3.1. "KING OF SYRIA": A SYMBOLIC CLAIM THAT ENDANGERED NEGOTIATIONS

By agreeing to become "king of Syria", Faisal indicated that he wanted to definitively cut ties with Turkey and continue to fight for the independence of the Arab nations. While the substance of his message had not changed, as a practical matter the French saw the decision of March 7, 1920 as an anti-French move that also put the new head of state in a "position of rebellion against the Conference" in Paris. At Lord Curzon's insistent invitation, Faisal therefore had to go to European to explain himself.

Millerand, the French foreign affairs minister, still thought it possible to "manoeuver diplomatically to try not to have to manoeuver

---

[15]   In late January 1920 a French officer was taken prisoner then assassinated in horrific conditions at the Hamman army post. On the gangs and how the high commission tried to deal with them, see Jean-David MIZRAHI (2003).

[16]   Letter from Gouraud to Cousse dated January 26, 1920, PA AP 399, C62-D1.

[17]   Gouraud became convinced of Faisal's weakness in February 1920. Toulat eventually admitted it in May, when he wrote to Gouraud that "I don't believe in the Emir's duplicity either, but alas, I have to believe he is weak". Letter dated May 20, 1920, no. 457, PA AP 399, C62-D1.

[18]   Declaration of the Syrian National Congress of Damascus, March 7, 1920.

militarily". And yet, while Cousse and Toulat continued to insist on the need to keep trusting Faisal, Gouraud considered the situation particularly serious, believing that Faisal could not be considering war with France and England.[19] Given Faisal's hesitations, he decided not to recognize him as king, symbolically refusing the authorization to fly the Syrian flag and refusing to allow the title of "king" to be added to Faisal's name in the prayers at the Damascus mosque. At the same time, the Syrians who did not support him tried in numerous ways to show that the election was not valid.

3.2. FAISAL OVERPOWERED BY HIS ADVISORS

More importantly, Faisal seemed to be a leader overpowered by his advisors. Cousse and Toulat both remarked that the nationalist movement had grown in the preceding months, especially due to the loss of Mosul and Palestine, which the nationalists (whom the high Commission called "the Extremists") considered an unwarranted amputation of land they laid a claim to. They were also worried about Lebanon's borders, which were being negotiated at the time. They had been very active for a long time and had set up special organizations, such as the Arab Club, the National League, and the National Defense Committee. The main representatives were men who held important positions, were very close to Faisal, and were therefore highly influential. They maintained constant pressure on all the political decision makers, including Faisal and the High Commission's representatives, and the National Defense Committee even proclaimed publicly that political assassination of traitors, like insurrection to obtain absolute independence, was a duty. Since they were the ones who controlled the Rayak rail hub, they were able – and did not hesitate – to stop trains from running between Aleppo and Rayak.

The unconditional support Cousse and Toulat had given Faisal began to falter in mid-April 1920: Toulat learned that the order prohibiting weapons from circulating by rail (and therefore through Rayak) came directly from Faisal and, despite his reminding Faisal that the French were fighting the Turks for Syria's northern border, the "king of Syria" refused to cede any ground. Use of the Aleppo railroad thus became yet again a major topic of negotiations, and a stumbling block. Tension then continued to

---

[19]   Letter from Gouraud to Toulat dated March 15, 1920, PA AP 399, C 62-D1.

increase. In May 1920, while Damascus government's new foreign affairs minister (Dr. Chabendar) reiterated his demands for total independence, Gouraud was insisting on a series of guarantees. He demanded the evacuation of Sharifian troops from the Bekaa Valley, including Rayak; abolishment of mandatory military service; punishment of those responsible for exactions; and agreement to the mandate that was to be discussed in San Remo. Nothing worked, and the situation worsened, to the great dismay of Cousse and Toulat. On May 19, 1920 Toulat wrote to Gourand that "we don't know whether he is motivated more by cynicism or madness ... I thought it my duty to warn the Emir, in a personal and private capacity, that in my opinion we were heading quickly toward war. ... The Emir told me I was demoralizing him ...".

3.3. MARCHING TOWARD WAR WHILE NEEDING TO MAINTAIN ORDER

Tensions increased even further when signature of the San Remo accords was announced (April 25, 1920), as they placed Syria under French mandate rather than granting it independence, and placed Mosul, which the Syrians claimed, in Mesopotamia and thus under British control. Faisal immediately protested, saying he had expected something else.[20] Meanwhile the Bekaa erupted, increasing civil unrest, and Christians in Beirut and Lebanon issued "threats, almost ultimatums"[21] to the French, causing them to intervene. Faced with being overwhelmed, Faisal tried to strengthen his army, which also served as his police force. Given their own inadequate numbers, the French agreed to this build-up of the Faisalian army under their supervision, while naturally fearing that nationalist hopes were being stirred up. Recruiting was difficult, however: some Arabs were extremely hostile to the idea of Hashemite military service, and Faisal was in dire financial straits and unable to pay his troops. Nationalists hostile to the French presence redoubled their efforts in Damascus while the milieus more favorable to the Hashemites had become weary, such that at the end of June, Gouraud was convinced that even the Muslim communities would start expressing a desire for "any situation, but quick".[22]

---

[20] Letter from Cousse to Gouraud dated May 27, 1920, PA AP 399, C62-D1.
[21] Six-month report from Lt. Col. Nieger to Gouraud, July 1, 1920, PA AP 399, C49-D1.
[22] Letter from Cousse to Gouraud dated June 20, 1920, PA AP 399, C62-D1.

When the idea of a French expedition to Damascus formed in Gouraud's mind on June 21, the situation had deteriorated to such an extent that he was "surprised by the Emir's surprise".[23] The break with Gouraud was approaching, and while the French were drafting a memo of their main complaints against the Arab government, Faisal was desperately – and vainly – seeking support, first from politicians in Paris, then from the English. In the context of the divvying up of the Middle East, a rapprochement with the English seemed practically a *casus belli*. The French, and especially Robert de Caix, were convinced that the English were secretly maneuvering the Hashemites to increase the centers of hostility. Gouraud therefore sent orders on July 13 to his two main generals, Clément de Lamothe and Mariano Goybet.

The Damascus expedition was seen as a way to "teach the hostile elements a hard and healthy lesson".[24] The next day, Gouraud sent Faisal an ultimatum and informed him of his intent to enter the city to restore order. Faisal replied late, on July 19, 1920, asking for two more days. Believing Faisal had not been able to take control of the situation to prevent war, Gouraud sent instructions to General Goybet at the Mezzeh encampment, asking him to start marching on Damascus and insisting heavily on the need to not harass the people regardless of class, and to use restraint when disarming them. On the morning of July 24 in the long Maysalun pass, the Faisalian positions were taken out by bayonet. The battle ended around 11 am with the defeat of the Sharifian army, which saw its commander-in-chief, General Yusuf al-'Azma, abandon 15 canons, 40 machine guns, and large quantities of ammunition on the battlefield. Faisal was forced to flee and join the British, who made him king of Iraq in August 1921.

4. CONCLUSION ON A NEGOTIATION WHICH DID NOT TAKE PLACE

During the first six months of 1920, Syria suffered from the very difficult application of the initial Faisal-Clemenceau agreements, which eventually turned into armed conflict. As important as it was, the international context does not seem to have been responsible for

---

[23] Letter from Gouraud to Toulat dated June 21, 1920, PA AP 399, C62-D1.

[24] Gouraud to Goybet and de Lamothe, Policy Directives dated July 13, 1920, PA AP 399, C57-D4.

derailing negotiations. Faisal was interfered with in his own camp – pushed by extremists he had to placate; Gouraud, on the contrary, was far from Paris and thus had fairly broad negotiating authority with respect to both weighing events and making decisions. Their uneven stature as legitimate representatives surely did not help the negotiations, any more than the symbolic but all-too-real quarrel in March over flying the flag and the title of "king of Syria". Most obviously, and as seen in other cases in this book (e.g., Emmanuel Vivet's chapter, "The German 'All or Nothing' Approach in 1917", in this volume), the situation was not ripe for negotiation.

REFERENCES

ALI-EL EDROOS, Syed, *The Hashemite Arab Army 1908–1979*, Amman, The Publishing Committee, 1980.

ALLAWI, Ali, *Faisal I of Iraq*, New Haven, Yale University Press, 2014.

BESSON, Maurice, "Notre allié, le roi du Hedjaz", *Revue Politique et Parlementaire*, August 1918, tome III, no. 285, pp. 182–187.

CADI, Jean-Yves Bertrand, *Le colonel Chérif Cadi*, Paris, Maisonneuve, 2005.

D'ANDURAIN, Julie, *Le général Gouraud, un colonial dans la Grande Guerre*, PhD. dissertation under the direction of Jacques Frémeaux, defended at the Sorbonne in October 2009.

D'ANDURAIN, Julie, *Henri Gouraud. Photographies d'Afrique et d'Orient. Trésors des archives du Quai d'Orsay*, Paris, Éditions Pierre de Taillac/Archives diplomatiques, 2016.

KHOURY, Gérard D., *La France et l'Orient arabe, Naissance du Liban moderne, 1914–1920*, Paris, A. Colin, 1993, p. 290.

LE PAUTREMAT, Pascal, *La politique musulmane de la France au XXe siècle. De l'hexagone aux terres d'islam, espoirs, réussites, échecs*, Maisonneuve et Larose, 2003.

MIZRAHI, Jean-David, *Genèse de l'Etat mandataire. Service des Renseignements et bandes armées en Syrie et au Liban dans les années 1920*, Paris, Publications de la Sorbonne, 2003.

MUSA, Suleyman, *La Grande révolte arabe, la guerre au Hedjaz (1916–1918)*, Amman, 1989.

PARRIS, Timothy, *Britain, the Hashemites and Arab Rule, 1920–1925*, The Sherifian Solution, London, Frank Cass, 2003.

PORTE, Rémy, *Du Caire à Damas, Français et Anglais au Proche-Orient, 1914–1919*, Saint-Cloud, Soteca, 2008.

The letters quoted in this chapter are from the Gouraud archives, which are kept at the French Ministry of Foreign Affairs.

MAPS

Figure 1. Rayak, rail hub between Beirut and Damascus

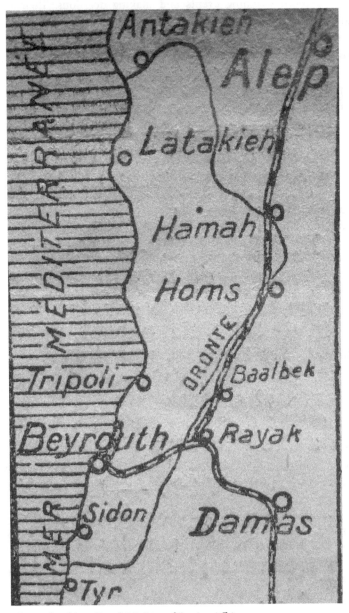

Source: Gouraud archives, French Ministry of Foreign Affairs.

Figure 2. Maysalun, at the gates of Damascus

Source: Gouraud archives, French Ministry of Foreign Affairs.

UN SECURITY COUNCIL RESOLUTION 242 OF 1967

Ambiguity in International Agreements

Sami FALTAS[*]

On November 22, 1967, the United Nations Security Council passed a resolution on "the grave situation in the Middle East" following the Six-Day War. This resolution, number 242, was adopted unanimously, which was highly unusual during the Cold War. The price for this achievement was a perceived ambiguity on the most urgent issue at hand: Israel's withdrawal from recently occupied land. Many observers consider this ambiguity a fundamental flaw, but this chapter will argue that it fulfilled a useful purpose. We will see that in general, ambiguity can facilitate peace negotiations in various ways. In the short term, it may be needed for any agreement at all to be reached. In the longer term, under more favorable conditions, it may provide a formula or framework for agreement on a wider range of issues.[1]

---

[*]   University of Groningen, the Netherlands.
[1]   The historical information in this chapter is mostly based on Bailey (1985).

1. ISRAEL BECOMES A REGIONAL SUPERPOWER

Israel won the war of June 1967 swiftly and overwhelmingly. Egypt lost the Sinai, an important part of its territory, and the Gaza Strip, a part of Palestine that it had previously administered. Jordan lost East Jerusalem and the West Bank – parts of Palestine that it had annexed – and Syria the Golan Heights. Once the Arab public realized the full extent of the military and political defeat, the shock was traumatic. Formerly considered the underdog, Israel was now recognized as the most powerful and successful state in the region. The Palestinians were now further than ever from regaining their homes and their land. The leaders of the defeated states, especially Egypt's charismatic president Gamal Abd el Nasser, were humiliated.

In the summer of 1967, relations between the US and the USSR were tense. After the Cuban missile crisis of 1963, the superpowers had installed a hotline between the Kremlin and the White House in order to prevent an unintended war between East and West. In the crisis caused by the June war of 1967 this hotline was used for the first time. The East-West divide had long prevented, and for over 20 years would continue to prevent, the UN Security Council from taking decisions on matters of great importance. But in November 1967, the East and the West were able to overcome their differences.

Israel was a new state mostly ruled by socialist Zionists of European descent, with a narrow and vulnerable territory, enjoying support from the United States and Western Europe. It was developing nuclear weapons and faced a hostile front of Arab states backed by communist-ruled and non-aligned states. The PLO had been founded three years earlier, but Palestinian nationalism was still in its infancy. The hijacking of international airliners and attacks on Jewish targets around the world would come later. Egyptian President Abd el Nasser was hugely popular in the Arab world, which believed he had restored its dignity by throwing the British troops out of Egypt and successfully nationalizing the Suez Canal.

Despite growing Soviet support for Egypt, the USSR did not encourage Arab aspirations, real or feigned, to destroy the Jewish state. In fact, Moscow had at first supported Israel. Nasser's crushing defeat of June 1967 meant the end of his international popularity, the demise of the Pan-Arabism he had championed and the rise of Israel to military superiority in the region. It also marked the beginning of a period in which terrorist violence would put Palestine on the international political agenda.

2.   THE ROAD TO 242

After the war of June 5–10, 1967, the members of UN Security Council recognized that the United Nations needed to act quickly and decisively. The Council had to address the consequences of the Six-Day War, but also to try to prevent further violent conflict and, if possible, foster a lasting peace between Israel and its Arab neighbors. The Council would be most likely to be effective if its members acted together, but during the Cold War such common action was difficult and rare. Before, during and after the war, the UN handled the crisis poorly or not at all. This made the unanimous decision of November 22, 1967 a dramatic achievement.

Weeks before the June war, UN Secretary-General U Thant had called the situation in the Middle East extremely threatening, but neither the General Assembly nor the Security Council had convened to discuss it. During the Six-Day War, the Security Council several times called for a ceasefire, but when the fighting indeed stopped, this was not thanks to the UN, but because Israel had achieved its war goals. A few weeks after the war, the UN General Assembly met in an emergency session, and the two superpowers managed to agree on a formula for peace, but it was rejected by both sides in the conflict. The Arabs considered it a victory for Israel, and Israel feared that it could be interpreted as an obligation to withdraw to the borders drawn by the Armistice Agreements of 1949, which it considered indefensible. However, this common formula is believed to have paved the way for Resolution 242. It was now clear that the Arab-Soviet demand for full Israeli withdrawal would not get the backing of the West unless the Arabs committed themselves to real peace with Israel.

The regular session of the General Assembly subsequently took up the issue, but achieved nothing. At no time did the Security Council use Chapter VII of the UN Charter to impose measures to restore, or counter a threat to, international peace and security. This was characteristic of the paralysis that the Security Council suffered from during the Cold War.

In October, the mercurial Soviet ambassador to the UN was replaced by the deputy minister of foreign affairs Vasiliy Kuznetsov, who would play a key role in the passing of Resolution 242. Kuznetsov, the US ambassador Arthur Goldberg and the British ambassador Hugh Foot began working together closely on the Middle East dossier. In 1964, Foot had been granted a lifetime peerage which made him Lord Caradon.

2.1. A RESOLUTION THAT "BELONGS TO US ALL"

There were five drafts for a Security Council resolution. The oldest was a Latin American and Caribbean draft submitted to the emergency session of the General Assembly in July. Another was submitted by India, Mali, and Nigeria. It was known as the three-power proposal and drew on the Latin American and Caribbean draft. It was later withdrawn so as not to jeopardize the success of the UK submission. Then there was a US draft, followed by a British draft, which built on the previous texts, a debt that Foot was more than happy to acknowledge, and at a late stage a more extreme Soviet draft.

The preamble to the British draft began with the two elements that were central to the resolution as a whole: the obligation to withdraw from occupied land and the need for all states in the region to live in peace and security. Resolution 242 does not present these requirements as an exchange, but politicians would soon link them. In fact, from now on, the principle of exchanging land for peace would be the basis for most efforts to resolve the Arab-Israeli conflict. The first sentence of Resolution 242 says:

> Emphasizing the inadmissibility of the acquisition of territory by war and the need to work for a just and lasting peace in which every State in the area can live in security ...

Here we have, first, the obligation to withdraw from occupied land; second, the need for durable peace; and, third, the implied need for recognized borders and freedom from threats and the use of force. In his speeches and writings, Foot always said that in his understanding, 242 required Israel to withdraw from *all* territories occupied in June 1967, and it obliged the Arabs to make peace with Israel and peacefully negotiate border corrections that would enable Israel to defend its territory effectively (Caradon, 1981).

The resolution continued with another powerful statement in the first sentence of operational article 1:

> Affirms that the fulfilment of Charter principles requires the establishment of a just and lasting peace in the Middle East which should include the application of the following principles: (i) Withdrawal of Israeli armed forces from territories occupied in the recent conflict; (ii) Termination of all claims or states of belligerency and respect for and acknowledgement of the sovereignty, territorial integrity and political independence of every State in the area

and their right to live in peace within secure and recognized boundaries free from threats or acts of force; …

The sentence starting with "affirms" sounds compelling. The Council posits that if states do not comply with the principles stated here, they will have failed to live up to their obligations under the UN Charter. In effect, they will have violated international law. A Security Council resolution can hardly express itself more forcefully without invoking supranational powers. Any Security Council resolution containing a decision (as opposed to a call, appeal or request) is binding on Member States, even if Chapter VII of the UN Charter is not explicitly invoked.

In the event, Resolution 242 did not explicitly "decide" anything. Some years later, after the war of October 1973, the UN Security Council would pass Resolution 338, which "decides" that parties will start negotiations to establish a fair and durable peace, and also calls on states to implement Resolution 242 of 1967. This use of the word "decides" requires the parties in the 1973 conflict to start peace talks, but it does not retroactively confer mandatory power on Resolution 242.

2.2. A CHAIN WITH STRONG AND WEAK LINKS

Article 1.i, quoted above, contains – in English – a phrase that can be taken to mean that Israel is not obliged to withdraw from *all* territories occupied in June 1967. It looks like a nod to Israel, which immediately after the Six-Day War said it would never return to the borders drawn by the Armistice Agreements of 1949, which it considered indefensible. The French version of 1.i says "*retrait … des territoires occupés*", which is a correct translation of the English text but sounds like "withdrawal … from *the* occupied territories." The Spanish version is unequivocally different from the English: "*retiro … de los territorios*". All three versions are equally valid in international law, but the difference between them is perceived by most people as ambiguous.

Is this merely a matter of perception, or is the resolution inherently ambiguous? The quoted passages in the English, French and Spanish versions of 242 regarding Israeli withdrawal clearly permit – indeed they invite – diverging interpretations. There can be no doubt that they give rise to ambiguity. But this does not necessarily mean that the resolution as a whole is ambiguous. The UK government has always claimed it is not.

According to the British ambassador Hugh Foot and his Foreign Secretary George Brown, the resolution requires Israel to withdraw from all the lands it had occupied in June 1967. This, they asserted, was the only interpretation that was consistent with "the inadmissibility of the acquisition of territory by war". The preamble of 242 emphasizes this inadmissibility and gives equal emphasis to "the need to work for a just and lasting peace in which every State in the area can live in security".

When Lord Caradon submitted the draft resolution for voting, he explained:

> The Arab countries insist that we must direct our special attention to the recovery of their territories. The Israelis tell us that withdrawal must never be to the old precarious peace but to secure boundaries. Both are right. The aims of the two sides do not conflict. To imagine that one can be secured without the other is a delusion. They are of equal validity and equal necessity. We want not a victory in New York but a success in the Middle East. (Caradon, 1981, p. 5)

So the British were adamant that 242 was not ambiguous. In fact, by saying that the resolution was not really British, but "belongs to us all", Foot was suggesting that other members of the Council shared his interpretation, and this may have been true. But once the Council had passed 242, the text no longer belonged to the people who had drafted it and the states that had voted for it. It now led a life of its own. Israel, the Arab states, and everyone else took from it what suited their purpose, citing whichever official version they liked best, and ignoring or playing down what was not to their liking. Resolution 242 had become a political football. Despite Caradon's passionate and plausible insistence on the contrary, it was in effect ambiguous because parties were able to plausibly maintain contradictory interpretations of its clause on Israeli withdrawal.

There was another weak link in the resolution. It makes no mention of the Palestinians and the loss of their homeland, and only refers to "a just settlement of the refugee problem". In the mid-1960s, the Palestinians counted for little in the Security Council: the terrorist violence that would draw the world's attention to the plight of the Palestinians, the various ill-fortuned peace processes involving the Palestinians, and the establishment of limited Palestinian autonomy on the West Bank and in the Gaza Strip all lay in the future.

3.   SOURCES AND EXAMPLES OF AMBIGUITY

According to the Oxford English Dictionary, ambiguity is the quality of being open to more than one interpretation, or inexact. Let us first consider the quality of being inexact or vague. It is common for agreements, contracts, treaties and political resolutions to contain vague language like "reasonable effort", "in good faith", or "at an appropriate time". Such terms are not defined because it suits the parties to leave them open to further negotiation, or to interpretation by a court of law. This is inexactitude or vagueness. Ambiguity is a special kind of inexactitude. It suggests alternative and competing meanings. It offers the possibility of interpreting something in distinct and often incompatible ways.

Linguists distinguish various forms of ambiguity. Good negotiators are aware of the many meanings that words like "control", "integration", "coordination", and countless others have, and will take care to avoid misunderstanding. Ambiguity can be accidental, but poets, politicians and diplomats often use it deliberately.

In "Ambiguity: Language and Communication", Susanne Winkler distinguishes ambiguity that originates in the production of a statement (P) or its reception (R). Furthermore, ambiguity may be deliberate, that is to say strategic (S+), or not (S−). This results in a matrix that she calls her Ambiguity Model. She provides illustrations of each of the four types of ambiguity (Winkler, 2015, pp. 21ff).

Now let us look beyond Resolution 242 and consider other diplomatic uses of ambiguity. In 1972, US Special Envoy Henry Kissinger negotiated the Shanghai Communiqué with the People's Republic of China. In article 12 the communiqué says: "The United States acknowledges that all Chinese on either side of the Taiwan Strait maintain there is but one China and that Taiwan is a part of China."[2] This wording neatly avoids the issue of who legitimately represents China, the government in Beijing or the one in Taipei. This fudge allowed both governments to maintain their incompatible claims, and enabled the United States to do business with both. Winkler would classify this ambiguity as PS+.

When West Germany and the USSR were negotiating the Treaty of Moscow in 1970, the issue of borders was critically important, and the willingness of Willy Brandt's negotiators to be flexible on this issue contributed to the success of his *Ostpolitik*. To facilitate agreement, they wrote a confidential letter to the Soviet government saying: "The Federal Republic of Germany and the Soviet Union agree on the realization that the peace in Europe can only be maintained if no one violates today's borders." At the insistence of the Soviets, the Bonn government allowed

---

[2]   <http://www.taiwandocuments.org/communique01.htm>.

the Russian text to use the stronger word "recognition" instead of "realization". However, the FRG only tolerated it in the Russian version, not the German one. The West Germans also refused to allow the phrase "recognition of borders" (Link, 2001, p. 308). As in the case of Resolution 242, we see here a deliberate ambiguity between two official versions of the same document, allowing each side to put a different shine on the agreement. This is also a PS+ ambiguity.

Can omission also lead to ambiguity? The Treaty of Breda of 1667 does not explicitly deal with two important issues. The English had recently seized New Amsterdam and surrounding areas in North America from the Dutch, and the Dutch had captured Suriname in South America from the English. In the Treaty, the Dutch and the English agreed that each would keep the lands currently under their control, but the Dutch did not want these territories to be mentioned. This may have fueled doubts about the willingness of the Dutch to maintain the status quo. Indeed, in 1673, they briefly recaptured what was now called New York.[3]

Was the use of ambiguity successful in the cases described here? To the best of our knowledge, the answer is yes in the cases of the Shanghai Communiqué and the Treaty of Moscow. It is hard to say whether the same applies to Treaty of Breda. In all three cases, fudging difficult issues made it easier to sign the agreements. And in the first two cases – perhaps not in the third – it hardly reduced the usefulness of the agreements in the longer term.

Kissinger's constructive ambiguity was more than only a tactical compromise to get the document signed. It formed an essential part of the formula that allowed the United States to proclaim a One China policy and engage in trade and cooperation with the People's Republic while maintaining close relations with Taiwan.

4. HOW DID AMBIGUITY AFFECT THE IMPACT OF RESOLUTION 242?

UN Security Council Resolution 242 of 1967 would not have been passed unanimously – it may not have passed at all – without the ambiguity arising

---

3   <https://www.geheugenvannederland.nl/en/geheugen/pages/collectie/Nederland+en
     +Engeland:+de+band+tussen+twee+naties/De+Engels-Nederlandse+oorlogen>.

from differences between its English and other versions. There can be no doubt that in this case ambiguity helped the Security Council to reach agreement. That was its first and most obvious benefit. The interpretation offered by Hugh Foot to explain away the ambiguity, however plausible and fair it may have been, counted for little once the resolution had been adopted. It was embraced by those who liked it and ignored by those who did not. The question that now remains is how the perceived ambiguity about "withdrawal of Israeli armed forces from territories occupied in the recent conflict" affected the subsequent impact and use of Resolution 242.

There seems to be general agreement that "withdrawal of Israeli armed forces" means an end to all Israeli control over the territory concerned, and not merely military disengagement. When Israel finished its withdrawal from the Sinai in 1982, having signed a peace treaty with Egypt in 1979, it relinquished all control of the area. Egyptian sovereignty was restored, although Egypt had to agree to a limit on the armed forces it was allowed to station on the peninsula. But when Israel disengaged militarily from the Gaza Strip in 2005, the United Nations did not regard this as an end to military occupation, because Israel continues to control Gaza from the outside.

Resolution 242 of 1967 can be regarded as a basis for peace agreements such as the 1979 treaty between Egypt and Israel, the Oslo Accords of 1993 and 1995 between the Palestinian Liberation Organization and Israel, and the 1994 peace treaty between Jordan and Israel. In all these agreements, the principle of an exchange of land for peace was fundamental. Under the 1994 treaty, Israel did not return any land to Jordan, which had reversed its annexation of the West Bank in 1988. But the granting of some autonomy to the PLO on the West Bank was, in a way, a reward for Jordan's decision to make peace with Israel. The principle of such exchanges is another fruit of the resolution.

Despite its perceived ambiguity, Resolution 242 offers a rough framework for peace and reconciliation between the Arabs and Israel. If there is insufficient political will to make peace, this framework cannot be used for its intended purpose, but under more favorable conditions, it has been used to good effect and may prove beneficial. It helped to facilitate Egypt's peace with Israel, was also instrumental in the case of Jordan's peace treaty and had less of an impact in the case of the Palestinians. In the absence of favorable political conditions, it seems to have achieved nothing in the case of Syria. This suggests that when political conditions allow, there is a chance for Resolution 242 to fulfil its potential. It keeps the formula of exchanging occupied land for peace and security alive and enables it to be applied, if and when political conditions allow.

5. BENEFITS OF AMBIGUITY IN NEGOTIATED AGREEMENTS

Eighty years ago, Harold Nicolson defined the qualities of the "ideal diplomatist", putting truthfulness and precision at the top of his list (Nicolson, 1942, Chapter V). In the process of negotiation, it is indeed essential for the parties to understand each other correctly if they are to find common ground and sign a durable agreement. Truthfulness, precision and transparency are of great importance, even if they have their limits. However, as the time for signing approaches, negotiators will find that areas of disagreement or uncertainty remain.

The signed document, which for better or for worse is destined to lead a political life of its own, can deal with these disagreements or uncertainties in various ways. First, it can spell out the unresolved differences and problems: here are some things we could not settle. Second, it can leave out any mention of them, as the Treaty of Breda did. Third, it can use vagueness or ambiguity to evade, disguise, obfuscate, or minimize the remaining problems. This may seem deceptive, unprofessional, and myopic. Diplomats and scholars have for good reason warned of the destructive potential of ambiguity (Fischhendler, 2008). But sometimes, used with care, it is a useful way to deal with issues that negotiators were unable to resolve.

Constructive ambiguity potentially offers peace negotiators several benefits. In the short term, it may be decisive in allowing an agreement to be signed. It may defuse an issue that could otherwise cause the talks to break down. In the medium term, it can provide a formula, or the outlines of a formula for making peace, which parties can interpret in various ways. This may allow parties to manage the conflict. For instance, they may be better able to limit or avoid armed violence.[4]

In the long term, when political conditions become more favorable, parties may reach wider agreement on a formula for peace that was

---

[4]   Also see the discussion of pros and cons in Pehar (2001).

once interpreted in divergent ways. With a shared understanding of the formula, they will be more likely to achieve sustainable progress. Ambiguity can be said to keep the discussion alive on what an eventual agreement might look like.

REFERENCES

BAILEY, S.D. (1985), *The Making of Resolution 242*, The Hague; Boston, M. Nijhoff.

CARADON, H.F. (1981), *U.N. Security Council Resolution 242, a case study in diplomatic ambiguity*. Washington, D.C., Institute for the Study of Diplomacy, Edmund A. Walsh School of Foreign Service, Georgetown University.

FISCHHENDLER, I. (2008), "When Ambiguity in Treaty Design Becomes Destructive: A Study of Transboundary Water", *Global Environmental Politics* 8(1): 111–136.

LINK, W. (2001), "Die Entstehung des Moskauer Vertrags im Lichte neuer Archivalien", *Vierteljahreshefte für Zeitgeschichte* 49(2): 295–315.

NICOLSON, H. (1942), *Diplomacy*, London, New York, Toronto, Oxford University Press.

PEHAR, D. (2001), "Use of Ambiguities in Peace Agreements" in J. KURBALIJA and H. SLAVIK (eds.), *Language and Diplomacy*, Malta, Diplo.

WINKLER, S. (ed.) (2015), *Ambiguity: Language and Communication*, Berlin, De Gruyter.

THE IRAN NUCLEAR ISSUE (2003–2005)

Choosing to Negotiate

Stanislas DE LABOULAYE*

On August 4, 2003, the French, German and British Foreign Ministers sent a joint letter to their Iranian counterpart, Kamal Kharrazi, with regard to Iran's nuclear program, calling on his country "to cease its development of facilities which would give it the capacity to produce fissile material, including any enrichment or reprocessing capability".[1] Their proposal opened a timeframe during which efforts on both sides were made to address the international community's concern over Iran's nuclear program without referring the matter to the United Nations Security Council (UNSC).

---

* Former French diplomat, former Under Secretary of State for political affairs, chief negotiator for France in the EU3/Iran negotiation 2003–2006.
[1] Extract from the EU3 August 4, 2003 letter.

1. 2003–2005: A POSSIBLE AGREEMENT WITH IRAN

The ambition of the three European Ministers stemmed from an effort to try to avoid a new international crisis. Indeed, the initiative came five months after the American invasion of Iraq in March 2003 and one year after serious revelations had been made on clandestine nuclear activities conducted by Iran without informing the International Atomic Energy Agency (IAEA).[2] Following those revelations President Bush, in his January 2002 State of the Union Address, had accused Iran, along with Iraq and North Korea, of being part of "an axis of evil, aiming to threaten the peace of the world".[3]

1.1. 2003–2004: HOPE FOR A NEGOTIATED SOLUTION

On October 21, 2003, in Tehran, the three European Foreign Ministers, Dominique de Villepin, Joschka Fischer, and Jack Straw, after a day of intense negotiations, agreed with Hassan Rouhani, Secretary of the Supreme National Security Council of Iran, on a declaration according to which Iran "decided voluntarily to suspend all enrichment and reprocessing activities as defined by the IAEA".[4] In exchange, the Ministers of France, Germany, and the UK (the so-called "EU3") recognized Iran's right to the peaceful use of nuclear energy and paved the way for long-term cooperation.

Contrasting with the sanctions recommended by the United States, the Europeans favored a negotiated solution based on a mutual confidence-building process: the Iranians would suspend uranium enrichment and reprocessing activities, and the Europeans would endeavor to keep the matter within the scope of the IAEA, thus avoiding its transfer to the UN Security Council in New York for sanctions.

Throughout 2004, difficult talks were held to agree on the terms of the Tehran Declaration, especially on the definition and scope of "enrichment activities". A team of high-ranking diplomats led by Hassan Rouhani negotiated for Iran; the European side was represented by

---

2   An international organization linked to the UN, in charge of promoting peaceful use of atomic energy.
3   President George W. Bush, State of the Union Address, January 29, 2002.
4   Excerpt from the Tehran Declaration, October 21, 2003.

the three Political Directors,[5] working in close cooperation under the authority of their respective Ministers, who also met frequently on the issue. Soon Javier Solana, the High Representative and Secretary General of the EU Council, joined the discussions with a dedicated team.

These talks led to the Paris Agreement, signed on November 15, 2004. In the context of this agreement, Iran declared that it had no intention of developing nuclear weapons either now or in the future, but that as a confidence-building measure, it was willing to significantly expand the scope of the suspension of activities defined as enrichment and reprocessing. The suspension of such activities would last until "a long-term agreement" providing "objective guarantees" as to the exclusively peaceful nature of Iran's nuclear program was reached.

1.2.   2005: FROM AGREEMENT TO DISAPPOINTMENT

Despite the results obtained in Paris after two days of intense negotiations which clarified a number of issues which had been left open in 2003 (e.g., the scope and duration of the suspension), the process progressively ground to a halt in early 2005, with each side accusing the other of breaching the terms of the freshly signed agreement.

In Tehran, the Iranian negotiation team had likely been strongly criticized for the concessions they had made. They had also most probably lost the support of the Supreme Leader, Ayatollah Khamenei, who objected to prolonging the suspension. Meanwhile the EU3 had to deal with the United States' serious reservations about the political, economic and technical incentives they were intending to offer the Iranians.

In Iran, the radical hard-line mayor of Tehran, Mahmoud Ahmadinejad, elected in June 2005 as President of the Islamic Republic, took office in August. Siding with the members of Parliament who had voiced their concern about the agreement, he dismissed Hassan Rouhani and his team and resumed uranium conversion activities, the first step to enrichment. It was a deliberate breach of the Paris agreement. What followed was foreseeable: in February 2006, the IAEA's Board of

---

[5]   In European diplomacy, the Political Directors are in charge of coordinating all major issues handled by their departments under the authority of their Ministers. The equivalent position in the US is held by the Under Secretary of State for Political Affairs, and in Russia by the Deputy Minister of Foreign Affairs.

Governors,[6] noting Iran's failure to cooperate, referred the matter to the UNSC, which approved Resolution 1737 in December 2006, the first of a series of resolutions imposing sanctions on Iran. These are described by Tobias Langenegger in his chapter, "The Iran Nuclear Negotiations (2005–2015)", in this volume.

The UN resolution vote did not end the talks between the Iranians and the Europeans; however, it marked the end of a phase. Three years earlier, in exchange for Iran's voluntary suspension of enrichment activities, the EU3 had committed themselves to preventing the matter from being referred to the UNSC. Since uranium conversion had resumed, the EU3 considered that the terms of the agreement had been broken.

2. LESSONS LEARNED FROM A FAILURE: THE IRAN NEGOTIATION'S THREE INHERENT WEAKNESSES

In light of its initial ambitions, the first three-year phase of the negotiations on Iran's nuclear program may seem to have produced fairly limited results. The truth is that, from the beginning, the talks had run into strong opposition from the United States: negotiating with Iran was considered counterproductive, and even dangerous, as it would restore credibility to a government guilty of a threatening posture on the international scene. But others claim that the road was paved for a historical agreement between the EU3 and Iran, had it not been for the blindness of some of those involved in the talks. Such was obviously the opinion of the Iranian negotiators, and also, to a certain extent, of Mohamed ElBaradei, the Director General of the IAEA.

Wherever the truth lies, the time-frame opened by the EU3 in 2003 was closed by Iran's resumption of its enrichment activities and the following consequences in New York, leaving a sense of failure. Ten years later, what lessons can be drawn from this first phase of negotiations as talks, in a wider format, resume in the wake of Hassan Rouhani's election as President of the Islamic Republic?[7]

---

[6]   The Board of Governors (BOG) is the IAEA governing body composed of a selection of Member States.

[7]   This chapter was written in September 2013, two years before the signature, on July 14, 2015, of the agreement between the United States, Russia, China, the EU3 and Iran (Joint Comprehensive Plan of Action).

Among the many variables involved in this complex negotiation, three basic factors are probably worth reflecting on today, keeping in mind the exceptional circumstances of the specific timeframe and context:

- Did the parties agree on a common goal?
- Did the negotiators have legitimate standing?
- Was the political and security environment stable enough to allow the negotiators to uphold their respective positions?

2.1. FIRST WEAKNESS: SCANT CONVERGING MUTUAL INTERESTS

When the negotiations began, both the EU3 and the Iranians were determined to avoid a new armed conflict. This was a shared goal for the two parties. Between Afghanistan and Iraq, in which the Americans were involved, Iran was wary of another US intervention. Meanwhile the EU3, by emphasizing multilateralism, were anxious to offer a counterexample to the US handling of the Iraq crisis.

Originally the French and Germans had tried to get the Russians on board, thus restoring the trio that had opposed the American invasion of Iraq. But Russia declined[8] and was replaced by the UK, likely due to the fact that the British Foreign Secretary, Jack Straw, had not shared his Prime Minister's[9] enthusiasm for supporting the Americans in Iraq and favored other ways of dealing with such a crisis. In any case, his participation reconciled the three major European powers, which had been divided on Iraq a few months earlier, and provided a credible way forward to respond to the threat of weapons of mass destruction (WMDs) without resorting to military strikes. The EU3 offered to solve the crisis through negotiations and multilateral channels (in this case, the IAEA); Iran seemed to fully agree with this approach.

But beyond this starting point, what were the parties actually aiming for? On the EU3 side, it was nothing short of imposing *total cessation* of Iran's enrichment-related activities, contrary to what the parties had

---

[8]   After reflecting on it for a few days, the Russians decided not to sign the draft letter, considering it was pointless to expect the Iranians to *cease* all enrichment activities; they were also uncertain about the legality of such a demand. Nonetheless the Russian Minister, Igor Ivanov, informed his colleagues he would send Kharrazi a letter along the same lines. The content of the letter was never disclosed.

[9]   Tony Blair (UK Prime Minister from 1997 to 2007).

agreed on in both the Tehran Declaration and the Paris Agreement, which was a *temporary suspension.* By conditioning Iran's ending of suspension on "objective guarantees" that its nuclear program served civilian uses only, the EU3 were convinced that suspension would remain indefinite since Iran would never succeed in providing such guarantees. Hence, in their view, Iran would be forced to give up its "dual use"[10] activities, as Libya had done in December 2003 under international pressure.

Why were the EU3 so uncompromising? Given the Iranian's decades-long concealment of their activities, the Europeans inherited a profound lack of trust towards Iran: progressive disclosure of different aspects of Iran's clandestine program; the links with the criminal network of A.Q. Khan, the "father" of Pakistan's bomb; the continuation of a ballistic program based on North Korean technology, etc. all factored into the EU3's difficulty in giving the slightest credit to the Iranians' claims of transparency.

On Iran's side, suspension of enrichment activities, which had been agreed on in Tehran in October 2003, was never a goal in itself. For Hassan Rouhani, as he explicitly stated in later interventions, it was only a temporary confidence-building move, one of various cooperative gestures towards the IAEA intended to normalize Iran's relationship with the international community: – the final aim being to regain its status as a "normal" country enjoying the full range of its sovereign rights, including uranium enrichment and reprocessing.

2.2. SECOND WEAKNESS: THE NEGOTIATORS' LACK OF LEGITIMACY

The joint initiative of the French, German, and British ministers followed several trips they each had made to Tehran, separately, for bilateral talks in the first half of 2003 (none of which had achieved concrete results), as well as visits by EU representatives (Chris Patten for the EU Commission; Javier Solana for the EU Council). However, in a context of a seemingly unequivocal American military success in Iraq, the international community, quite unanimously, had put considerable pressure on Iran in various forums (G8, IAEA, European Council), and hence made it more amenable to negotiations with the Europeans.

---

[10] Civilian and military uses: low enriched uranium can be used as fuel; high enriched uranium can be used to make bombs. The issue is to control enrichment technology.

If, for the Iranian side, it seemed normal (and preferable) to deal with the three major European powers, such was not the opinion of the other EU Member States: they felt slighted by the EU3, whom they considered were showing disregard for the fledgling European Security and Defense Policy (ESDP). Italy and the Netherlands were particularly outraged at the self-attributed role of the three countries. It was not until the EU High Representative Javier Solana, whose portfolio included ESDP, was associated with the negotiations in late 2004 that the role assumed by the EU3 grudgingly gained legitimacy in Brussels.

The same difficulty for the EU3 was seen in Vienna: the IAEA Board of Governors had appointed the Agency's director, Mohammed ElBaradei, to negotiate with Iran and he at first had strong reservations about seeing his leeway limited by the intrusion of the EU3. But relations improved later on when the IAEA found it increasingly expedient to refer in its resolutions to the terms agreed on by the EU3 and Iran, therefore offering international support to the European negotiators. Still, many in Vienna continued to believe that the EU3's initiative was superfluous given the Agency's role.

Most importantly, however, and despite the fact that the initiative was meant to be a European one, the EU3 acknowledged that they had little chance of succeeding should the US not back it. Many of the offers they were planning to make were vetoed by the Americans, be they Iran's accession to the World Trade Organization (WTO), the supply of spare parts for its aircraft, or civilian nuclear cooperation. As a result, in addition to negotiating with the Iranians, the EU3 were also engaged in tedious discussions with a suspicious and reluctant US administration. The Iranians were fully aware of this and doubted that the EU3 could get Washington to budge; while the EU3 had no illusions and knew that the Iranians dealt with them short of being able to negotiate directly with the US.

On the Iranian side, the legitimacy of the negotiating team was less precarious. In October 2003 Ayatollah Khamenei had put Hassan Rouhani in charge of the interdepartmental coordination in view of the negotiations. His position in the system, his proximity to both the Supreme Leader and to President Khatami as well as to former President Rafsandjani, along with his role as Secretary of the Supreme National Security Council, gave him institutional authority to fill this role. He put together a team of skilled diplomats (including Mohammad Javad Zarif, the current Foreign Minister) to be the permanent interlocutors of the EU3 Political Directors in charge of the negotiation on a day-to-day basis.

It was undeniably Rouhani who, in Tehran on October 21, 2003, convinced Ayatollah Khamenei to agree on suspending enrichment activities. But from the very start this major concession had been objected to by radical political circles and the powerful Iranian nuclear lobby.

Rouhani managed to maintain his position throughout 2004. But the new concessions made in November 2004 for the Paris Agreement elicited a very negative reaction in Tehran and the negotiation team had to explain themselves in an openly hostile climate. The Supreme Leader may have considered that they had twisted his arm on prolonging the suspension. Debates in the Majlis[11] became increasingly critical of Rouhani's position: members of Parliament demanded that Iran withdraw from its commitments to the IAEA and resume its enrichment program, which was deemed to be an "inalienable right". The hard-liners eventually won the day when Mahmoud Ahmadinejad was elected President in June 2005 and took office in August. His first move was to replace Rouhani with a much less flexible negotiator, Ali Larijani.

The new President set the tone at the UN General Assembly in September 2005, stating that Iran would invoke its "rights." The time for concessions was over. From thereon, there was no more talk of confidence-building. The initial deal was broken: the rationale was now to refer the matter to the UNSC in New York for a vote on sanctions.

2.3. THIRD WEAKNESS: A HIGHLY UNSTABLE CONTEXT FOR NEGOTIATIONS

At the beginning, the EU3/Iran negotiations were seen as a spin-off of the American intervention in Iraq, as was the dismantling of Libya's nuclear program a few months later. At the G8 meeting in Evian, France in June 2003, countries which had recently opposed each other on the war in Iraq agreed on a statement denouncing Iran and North Korea as guilty of nuclear proliferation. Even at the IAEA Board of Governors, where positions were usually split between non-aligned countries and the West, consensus was reached on Iran with the US and the Europeans on the one hand and Russia and China on the other, as well as with emerging countries possessing nuclear programs, like South Africa, India, and Brazil. Inflexibility with regard to Iran was widely shared.

---

[11]   The Iranian Parliament.

As early as 2004 however, the situation in Iraq made the US position much less enviable. The proven absence of WMDs in Iraq was a further blow to the legitimacy of the Anglo-American military intervention. The situation on the ground was rapidly deteriorating, as the occupation forces faced a violent insurrection which was ripping the country apart. President Bush took this into account by progressively replacing the most hawkish members of his administration and starting to mend fences with the EU. In early 2005, the new Secretary of State, Condoleeza Rice, took some steps in the EU3's direction and showed wary openness to the proposals they intended to make to the Iranians.

But the new flexibility showed by the Americans occurred precisely when the Iranians were feeling less inclined to negotiate. Radical circles were strengthening their position in Tehran. They interpreted the American overtures as an admission of weakness, to be exploited by demanding that suspension of enrichment and other commitments made to the IAEA be terminated. President Ahmadinejad endorsed their views as soon as he took office, and progressively resumed enrichment activities, accompanying each new phase with inflammatory rhetoric. The initial negotiations with the EU3 were therefore doomed.

Since then, discussions with Tehran, punctuated by the UNSC's adoption of sanctions, have led nowhere. Although increasingly penalizing for the Iranian economy, these sanctions have not prevented Iran from pursuing its nuclear program and installing more powerful centrifuges.

3. CONCLUSION: A NEGOTIATION WHICH WAS NOT RIPE

The short timeframe between summer 2003 and summer 2005 was undoubtedly a time when hope, however slim, was permitted: the Europeans were intent on improving their relations with Iran while the Iranians were aspiring to break their isolation and build a new relationship with the West (primarily, through the Europeans, with the US). The EU3, with support from Russia, had begun negotiations that seemed to achieve what they had aimed for, i.e., Iran's voluntary and lasting suspension of its potentially dangerous nuclear activities.

But the EU3 initiative lacked an ingredient essential to all successful negotiations: a minimum amount of trust. Had trust been established from the start, it may have been possible to agree (albeit implicitly at first) on the major bone of contention: the temporary nature of the suspension.

But neither party was able to reach that point. The diplomacy of both the EU3, and Iran with Rouhani's team, undoubtedly fell victim to those who did not want the discussions to succeed.

In Tehran, there were those who were determined to continue the fight against the Great Satan and his henchmen. Those hard-liners were the ones who relentlessly protested against Iran's surrender of its "inalienable rights" and refused to admit to the breaches of their country's commitments to the IAEA. Those were the ones who ostensibly carried out an aggressive ballistic program throughout the negotiations, placing Rouhani's team more than once in an awkward position.

And on the European side, there were those who were convinced that it was impossible to trust a country that had had recourse to state terrorism and hostage-taking on the international scene, and become a master of deceit and dishonesty. Their attitude, shared by the Americans (and the Israelis), led them to believe that no deal was possible with the Iranians without first witnessing a regime change in Tehran.

REFERENCES

DE LABOULAYE, Stanislas, "Iran: la détermination de Rouhani", *Le Figaro*, July 4, 2013.

DE LABOULAYE, Stanislas, "Nucléaire iranien: revenir à l'esprit de compromis de 2003 est-il possible?", *Le Monde*, August 3, 2013.

ELBARADEI, Mohamed, *The Age of Deception; Nuclear Diplomacy in Treacherous Times*, Picador, 2011.

MOUSAVIAN, Seyed Hossein, *The Iranian Nuclear Crisis: a Memoir*, Carnegie Endowment for International Peace, 2012.

STRAW, Jack, *Last Man Standing: Memoirs of a Political Survivor*, Pan Macmillan, 2013.

THE IRAN NUCLEAR NEGOTIATIONS (2005–2015)

Tumbling in the Escalation Trap

Tobias W. LANGENEGGER*

When a comprehensive plan was finally agreed upon in the summer of 2015 to settle the long-standing dispute with Iran about its nuclear activities, it was perceived as a victory of international diplomacy and a contribution to a more secure world. But it was no easy path that led to this agreement. It had been preceded by intense confrontations and many years of extensive negotiations. These developments can be seen as an example of the nexus between the seemingly inexorable escalation of a conflict and the difficult quest for a possible agreement.

1. A HISTORY OF LOST TRUST (1941–1988)

Iran's tumultuous modern history is one reason for its complicated relations with the West – and with the United States in particular. In 1941, during the Second World War, an Anglo-Soviet invasion of Iran forced the ruling Shah to abdicate to secure the interests of the Allies in the region. He was replaced by his son, who established good relations with Western countries

*   Lecturer and Researcher, ETH Zurich.

and who initially gave a lot of power to the parliament. In 1951, after a series of unstable administrations, Mohammad Mosaddegh was appointed as prime minister. Mosaddegh introduced a wide range of social and political reforms, including further nationalization of the British-owned Anglo-Iranian Oil Company, which controlled the Iranian oil industry. These new policies led to a disturbance in relations with Iran's Western allies. In 1953, a successful coup d'état organized by the American Central Intelligence Agency (CIA) and the British MI6 forced Mosaddegh from office (USGPO, 2017), resulting in a substantial interruption of Iranian future political development (Gasiorowski, 1987). From then on, the Shah ruled Iran as an autocracy that was supported by the US.

In 1979, growing dissent against political repression, mismanagement, and resentments against foreign influence led to the Iranian Revolution and forced the Shah to flee the country. The revolution transformed Iran from an absolute monarchy to an Islamic republic with a theocratic constitution and a supreme leader. The capitalist economy was replaced, many industries were nationalized, laws were changed, and Western influence was banned.

The Iran hostage crisis, a pivotal event with a long-lasting impact, further deteriorated Iran's relationship with the West. In the aftermath of the revolution, a group of Iranian students took over the US embassy in Tehran. The crisis caused the US and Iran to break off formal diplomatic relations that have never been reestablished. The hostage crisis and a failed military rescue attempt remain traumatic experiences for the US.

In 1980, Iraqi leader Saddam Hussein sought to take advantage of the political and social tumult in neighboring Iran and ordered the Iraqi army to invade Iran. The Iran-Iraq War lasted for eight years, included the use of chemical weapons by Iraqi forces, and led to hundreds of thousands of casualties on both sides. The war still influences many Iranian decision-makers who became highly suspicious of Western involvement in the Middle East, partly because of military, financial, and political support to Iraq during the war and also because the use of chemical weapons by Iraqi forces seemingly occurred under the rather indifferent eyes of the international community.

2. NUCLEAR AMBITIONS

Iran's nuclear ambitions began in 1957, when the foundation of its nuclear program was laid through an agreement with the US regarding the peaceful uses of atomic energy. This act was part of the "Atoms for Peace" program, intended to spread nuclear technology for civilian use to countries that were politically close to the US. In 1960, Iran purchased its first research reactor, and in 1970, Iran ratified the Nuclear Non-Proliferation Treaty (NPT). In so doing, it agreed not to become a nuclear weapon state and made its nuclear program subject to verification by the International Atomic Energy Agency (IAEA). During the 1970s, Iran devised various plans to purchase nuclear technology from the US, France and West Germany with the intention to establish a complete nuclear fuel cycle. This would include the enrichment of uranium and the reprocessing of spent fuels, both of which are dual-use activities that can also be used for a military program to develop nuclear weapons.

Most international cooperation regarding the nuclear program ceased after the Iranian Revolution, and the resumption of the program was initially not prioritized. But from the mid-1980s on, under the pressure of the war and a developing Iraqi nuclear program, the belief – already present under the Shah – that Iran would need some potential of deterrence to balance its neighbor strengthened (Gaietta, 2015). Ongoing international isolation further reinforced Iran's attempts to establish a complete nuclear fuel cycle that would provide self-sufficiency in the energy sector and reduce dependency on foreign suppliers. As nuclear cooperation with the West was mostly severed, Iran oriented itself toward other actors with nuclear know-how such as Argentina, China, Pakistan, and Russia. When the Iran-Iraq war ended in 1988, Iran's nuclear cooperation with Pakistan[1] began to increase. Iran started to plan its enrichment program according to the Pakistani design of gaseous centrifuges technology, and there were further deals with Russia for the completion of a nuclear power plant. From the end of the 1990s to the beginning of the 2000s, Iran planned and built the majority of its now existing nuclear plants (e.g., conversion, enrichment, and production plants).

In 2002, an Iranian dissident group that opposed the Islamic regime publicly revealed the existence of secret nuclear plants under construction. This revelation raised serious concerns about a possible military dimension of Iran's nuclear program and a possible aim of obtaining nuclear weapons. The IAEA requested further information and access to these facilities, insisting on the Iranian government's full cooperation regarding its commitments under the NPT. Iran denied a military aspect of its nuclear

---

[1]   In particular through the network of A.Q. Kahn, the founder of Pakistan's uranium enrichment program for its atomic bomb project.

program and reaffirmed its peaceful nature but postponed visits by the IAEA to inspect the sites. The IAEA later concluded that Iran had carried out activities aimed at developing nuclear weapons prior to 2003. These activities were part of a structured program that ended in 2003, but some activities might have continued until 2009 (IAEA, 2015).[2] Iran however insisted on its right under the NPT for the civil use of nuclear technology, including the dual use aspects such as the enrichment of uranium. It continuously expanded its nuclear program and increased its enrichment capacities – especially the number of centrifuges[3] – to a maximum of around 20,000 centrifuges in 2013.

3. INCREASING PRESSURE THROUGH COERCIVE MEASURES

Following the 2002 revelation of Iran's uranium enrichment program, serious questions were raised regarding its potential non-peaceful purpose. Concerns were high that Iran would secretly work on the development of nuclear weapons. To disincentivize Iran's nuclear activities and ensure adherence to the NPT, the US, the United Nations Security Council (UNSC), and the European Union (EU) imposed numerous sanctions against Iran.[4] These sanctions have been a key element in the relation between Iran and the international community for more than 10 years.

The history of US sanctions against Iran goes back to the Iran hostage crisis, with additional restrictions set in place in the following decades. Some were eased after the election of reformist President Khatami in 1997, but the relationship between the US and Iran remained tense. From 2005 to 2014, beginning with the election of President Ahmadinejad and in response to the advancement of the Iranian enrichment program, the US issued multiple new sanction provisions every year. This led to an intense and comprehensive sanction regime that further affected foreign companies doing business with Iran.

---

2   According to the IAEA's assessments, "these activities did not advance beyond feasibility and scientific studies, and the acquisition of certain relevant technical competences and capabilities" (IAEA, 2015, p.14).

3   Centrifuges are used to enrich uranium-235. Low-enriched uranium (2 to 5%) is used in nuclear power plants and highly enriched uranium (85% or more) is used for the construction of nuclear weapons.

4   Additional sanctions have been issued against Iran by other countries, such as Australia, Canada, India, Israel, Japan, South Korea, and Switzerland. However, sanctions by the US, the UNSC, and the EU have been by far the most significant.

The EU, for its part, first issued its own sanctions against Iran in 2010 because of Iran's suspect nuclear program and the failure to negotiate over it. It introduced the freezing of funds, prohibited the sale of weapons and dual-use technologies, and targeted the oil and gas sector. In 2012, it announced an embargo on Iranian oil exports and added extensive restrictions on foreign trade and the financial sector. As a result, the Society of Worldwide Interbank Financial Telecommunication (SWIFT) expelled Iranian financial institutions, including the Central Bank of Iran, from its system and thereby extensively constrained the institutions' ability to conduct international business. The EU continually increased pressure on Iran until the end of 2014, which strongly reduced the economic relationship between the two sides.

The UNSC, finally, passed several resolutions as part of international efforts to address Iran's nuclear program. These resolutions came after the IAEA's report about Iran's noncompliance and the lack of clarity about its nuclear program. The UNSC adopted the first resolution in 2006 and demanded that Iran suspend its enrichment activities. The resolution was followed by a second in the same year that imposed sanctions under Article 41 of Chapter VII of the Charter of the United Nations, which was legally binding for all UN Member States. These restrictions were extended in further resolutions over the following years.

4. DIPLOMATIC EFFORTS AND COMPREHENSIVE NEGOTIATIONS

In addition to unilateral and multilateral sanctions intended to prevent the nuclearization of Iran, multiple diplomatic initiatives have been put in place to find a solution to the conflict. One of the first attempts was in 2003, when Iran issued a proposal to the US through the Swiss embassy[5] that called for direct talks between the two countries. Iran proposed negotiations on various contentious issues including disarmament, terrorism, regional security, and economic cooperation that would result in the relief of all US sanctions,[6] but the Bush administration dismissed the proposal.

---

[5]   Since the break-off of diplomatic relations after the Iranian Revolution, Switzerland represents US interests in Iran.

[6]   The document as well as other proposals have been collected by the Arms Control Association (2015).

It has been primarily the EU that has looked for a diplomatic solution to the crisis. Under the onus of the problematic US-led invasions of Iran's neighboring countries, Afghanistan (2001) and Iraq (2003), the EU was striving for a diplomatic solution and was trying to prevent military escalation and a possible war in Iran. Therefore, France, Germany, and the United Kingdom (the so-called EU3) started negotiations later in 2003, as described by Stanislas de Laboulaye in "The Iran Nuclear Issue" in this volume, to ensure that Iran complied with its obligations under the NPT and would not develop nuclear weapons. These negotiations continued in the following year and resulted in the signing of the Paris Agreement on November 15, 2004, which was intended to provide a basis for a long-term solution. The EU3 recognized Iran's right to the peaceful use of nuclear technology under the NPT, and Iran agreed to suspend all enrichment- and reprocessing-related activities, including the installation of centrifuges, for the time during which negotiations on a long-term agreement proceeded. The Paris Agreement had positive initial effects. For some months, expectations were high that the negotiations would lead to an overall diplomatic solution. However, the negotiations failed in 2005 after the two parties were unable to agree to a lasting solution[7] and both sides accused each other of breaching the agreement. Shortly after the election of Mahmoud Ahmadinejad, Iran communicated that it would not continue with full suspension (IAEA, 2005). Enrichment activities resumed, and the EU3 stopped negotiations.

Subsequently, the IAEA adopted a resolution in which it found Iran in noncompliance with its safeguard agreements and referred the Iranian case to the UNSC. In response, Iran announced that it would cease the voluntary implementation of additional measures and would end all cooperation with the IAEA beyond the legally binding agreements. The gulf between Iran and the West widened; the next years were to witness a series of sanctions mixed with negotiations.

It had become obvious that the US, as a key stakeholder in this dispute, would have to be included in future negotiations with Iran. With the referral of the case to the UNSC, the negotiation format changed from the EU3 to the P5+1[8] to include China, Russia, and the US. In June 2006, the P5+1 and the EU offered a proposal for comprehensive negotiations with Iran that included some of the same elements as previous proposals

---

7   This was partially also due to pressure from the US, which insisted on halting the Iranian nuclear program permanently and not accepting any enrichment activities at all.

8   The five permanent members of the UNSC plus Germany, also referred to as EU3+3.

as well as additional incentives. Iran asked for more time to respond while continuously increasing the number of installed centrifuges. The request for more time was viewed critically and some countries suspected that Iran would use this time to increase its enrichment capacity. In late July 2006, the UNSC passed its first resolution against Iran. Iran ultimately rejected the P5+1 proposal, announcing that it would never agree to a complete suspension of enrichment activities. Negotiations seemed completely blocked.

Only two years later, after further increase of sanctions and centrifuges, the P5+1 presented a revised package of the earlier proposal in June 2008. One month later, the first rounds of Geneva Talks were held between Iran and the P5+1 in Switzerland. It was the first high-level meeting between the U.S. and Iran since their termination of diplomatic relations in 1979. Despite the success of direct negotiations, the talks remained inconclusive. In 2009, however, the new US administration under President Obama announced that it would fully participate in the P5+1 talks with Iran without preconditions.

Throughout this time, and especially in 2010, the pressure increased from both sides. While Iran was expanding its nuclear activities, the UNSC significantly increased its sanctions, the US Congress adopted the "Comprehensive Iran Sanctions, Accountability, and Divestment Act", and the EU issued its own sanctions against Iran for the first time.

There were multiple proposals and talks during 2011 and 2012, but the situation remained tense. After two rounds of talks in 2013, the two sides announced that they remained far apart and that no further meetings were scheduled. But shortly after his election as the new president of Iran in mid-2013, Hassan Rouhani called for the serious renewal of negotiations.

After multiple rounds of negotiations, the two sides signed the Geneva interim agreement, known as the Joint Plan of Action (JPoA), at the end of 2013. This agreement consisted of a short-term freeze on escalation as the parties worked toward a long-term agreement. It defined specific steps for a six-month period (which could be extended) and a broad framework to guide the negotiations for a comprehensive solution. During this time, Iran would fully cooperate with the IAEA, halt the installation of new centrifuges, and reduce its stockpile of enriched uranium. On their side, the P5+1 would not issue any new nuclear-related sanction. They would even suspend sanctions on petrochemical exports, ease other restrictions, and facilitate humanitarian trade.

Early in 2014, Iran and the P5+1 met multiple times under the framework of the JPoA. Negotiations were extremely difficult, and the gaps in their positions remained wide. They failed to cut a deal and had to extend the deadline multiple times. The parties met again under the new extension in Geneva for three additional rounds of negotiations. Finally, after a series of intensive talks from March to April 2014 in Lausanne, they announced that the parties had reached an agreement on a framework deal for Iran's nuclear activities. This would serve as a precursor for a final agreement that was to be completed by the end of June.

The talks were resumed in Vienna, but the deadline passed again without an agreement. Nevertheless, negotiations continued and the parties extended the deadline several times. Finally, the Joint Comprehensive Plan of Action (JCPoA) was signed on July 14, 2015, formally adopted in October 2015, and implemented in January 2016. The agreement comprises 159 pages (including all annexes) that regulate in detail the development of the Iran nuclear program,[9] monitoring and verification, dispute resolution mechanisms, and relief of sanctions. Thereby, it substantially reduced the danger of a nuclear armed Iran and a military escalation of the conflict.

5. THE MECHANISM OF ESCALATION AND AGREEMENT

Studying the Iran nuclear dispute shows a case where a deal was found after many years of negotiations accompanied by intense sanctions. However, did these coercive measures help? At the same time as the sanction pressure was increased, Iran's nuclear program was substantially expanded. In the end, a deal was possible and sanctions may have contributed to that. But it seems that they contributed more to an escalation[10] than to unilateral concessions. Eventually, this development led to the conclusion that a negotiated solution was the only reasonable way forward and was the preferred alternative to a further, potentially also military, escalation. But the ongoing escalation delayed the deal and increased the costs of an agreement for both sides.

---

[9] It limits, for example, Iran's installed centrifuges for the following 10 years to 6,104, with 5,060 being allowed to operate.

[10] Escalation is the process of an increase or rise in intensity. With respect to conflicts, escalation describes an ongoing increase in conflict intensity, leading to a change in conflict relations. For a further discussion of the concept and its relation to negotiations see also Zartman and Faure (2005).

The usefulness of economic sanctions is not always clear. International Relations literature shows that such measures often only have a limited success rate in reaching unilateral concessions (e.g., Hufbauer, Schott, Elliott, 1990, Pape, 1997). The Iran case even illustrates that sanctions can contribute towards an escalation of the conflict.[11] Reasons for such a development are manifold and can be found in mistaken beliefs about the other side's reaction, possible domestic motivations for the policy decision, or perception biases such as sunk costs. If such escalation occurs, at a certain point a cooperative solution can become the preferred alternative to a further confrontation. Therefore, it seems as if economic sanctions can help to bring the other side to the negotiation table. However, at the same time, an escalation often makes the final negotiated solution more expensive than earlier (not accepted) offers.[12]

This result can be seen in the Iran case when considering the number of centrifuges as a measure for Iranian enrichment activities. Earlier proposals that would have given Iran the right to have fewer than 1,000 centrifuges were consistently dismissed, while insisting on a total stop of all enrichment activities. Sanction pressure was increased instead. At the same time, Iran refused to accept a complete cessation of its nuclear program. Rather, it increased the number of installed centrifuges to 20,000, despite the severe economic drawbacks. Pressure increased for both sides, and the ongoing escalation even threatened a possible military intervention. In the end, the two sides agreed on 5,060 operating Iranian centrifuges – a number substantially below the maximum number of centrifuges Iran had installed but also higher than initial offers 10 years earlier.

It appears that if it had been possible to reach an agreement earlier, this may have been more beneficial for both sides. One side would only have had to accept a reduced number of centrifuges compared to the final outcome, and the other side would not have endured a period of harmful economic sanctions. Only over time did the disadvantages of an escalation became visible and a negotiated solution become more attractive. Changes in both administrations may have even been needed to reassess this dynamic.

Even though it would generally be better to skip the escalation and begin negotiations early, this remains a difficult challenge, as the mechanisms that

---

[11] There can be seen some similarities to the security dilemma (Herz, 1951), where actions intended to heighten the security of a state can lead other states to respond similarly and thereby increase the tensions.

[12] This mechanism of escalation and agreement is quantitatively analyzed in Langenegger (2018).

lead to conflict escalation are often only recognized in retrospect and the possible advantages of a compromise are only seen when the escalation has already taken place. The use of sanctions therefore remains challenging, as it can bring the other side to the negotiation table but can also fuel the escalation process that can lead to more expensive negotiated agreements in the end. It remains to be seen whether the withdrawal of the US from the JCPoA in May 2018 and the reinstatement and expansion of sanctions will start a new escalation process – and how this may influence a future settlement of the conflict.

REFERENCES

ARMS CONTROL ASSOCIATION, *Official proposals on the Iranian nuclear issue, 2003-2013*, 2015, <https://www.armscontrol.org/factsheets/Iran_Nuclear_Proposals>.

GAIETTA, M., *The Trajectory of Iran's Nuclear Program*, 2015, New York, NY: Palgrave Macmillan.

GASIOROWSKI, M. J., The 1953 Coup D'Etat in Iran, *International Journal of Middle East Studies*, 1987, 19(3), 261–286.

HERZ, J.H., *Political Realism and Political Idealism: A Study in Theories and Realities*, 1951, Chicago: University of Chicago Press.

HUFBAUER, G.C., SCHOTT, J.J., ELLIOTT, K.A., and OEGG, B. *Economic Sanctions Reconsidered*, 1990, Washington, DC: Peterson Institute.

IAEA, *Iran Starts Feeding Uranium Ore Concentrate at Uranium Conversion Facility*, Press Release, 2005.

IAEA, *Final Assessment on Past and Present Outstanding Issues regarding Iran's Nuclear Programme*, 2015.

LANGENEGGER, T.W., *A Simulation Model of Sanctions and Negotiations: The Example of the Iran Nuclear Dispute*, 2018, ETH Zurich.

PAPE, R.A., Why economic sanctions do not work, *International Security*, 1997, 22(2), 90–136.

UNITED STATES GOVERNMENT PUBLISHING OFFICE (USGPO), Foreign Relations of the United States, 1952–1954, Iran, 1951–1954, 2017, James C. VAN HOOK (ed.), Washington D.C.

ZARTMAN, I.W., and FAURE, G.O. (eds.), *Escalation and Negotiation in International Conflict*, 2005, New York, NY: Cambridge University Press.

PART VI
MEDIATIONS

RAOUL NORDLING AND THE 1944 LIBERATION OF PARIS

A Mediator Saves Paris

Arnaud STIMEC*

"*Paris brûle-t'il* [Is Paris burning]?" Supposedly asked by Hitler, this question is the title of both a French historical novel by Dominique Lapierre and Larry Collins[1] and a film directed by René Clément[2] based on that book. After landing on the Normandy coast on July 6, 1994, Allied forces advanced quickly, cutting Paris off from other German-occupied territory as it went. General de Gaulle wanted the Allied armies to liberate Paris as soon as possible for symbolic reasons at the very least, but the American Command saw things differently. Paris and its inhabitants posed a complex logistics problem (resupply), and there was a danger of losing time and opportunity without gaining any noticeable military

---

*   Professor, Sciences Po Rennes, France.
[1]   Published by Robert Laffont, 1964.
[2]   *Is Paris Burning?* (French: *Paris brûle-t-il?*), a 1966 French film.

advantage (20,000 German soldiers were stationed in Paris and, according to General von Choltitz, three divisions would be needed to take control of the metro system). With de Gaulle's consent, General Leclerc's armored division forced the Command's hand by deciding to go to Paris anyway (after deliberately stocking up on fuel and munitions). The Allied forces had no choice but to support them: failure would be an embarrassment. Faced with a military rout, Hitler adopted a scorched-earth policy, relying mainly on Germany's secretly developed rockets (the infamous V1 and V2). This is where Raoul Nordling played a decisive, albeit little-known role (his diaries were not found until 1995). The pair he formed with von Choltitz provided the basis for Cyril Gély's play, *Diplomacy*, which premiered at Paris's Théâtre de la Madeleine in January 2011, with André Dussollier in the role of Nordling and Niels Arestrup playing General von Choltitz. The play takes a number of liberties with the historical facts, however: Nordling was much more of a spokesperson and catalyst than he was a master of the art of argument.

1. AN EXPLOSIVE LIBERATION

Raoul Nordling[3] was the Swedish consul-general in Paris, a peculiar position at the time that he seems to have inherited from his father and which required him, like many Scandinavian diplomats, to hold another job to earn his living (he held a management position at a Swedish ball-bearing company). Another peculiarity is that Nordling had always lived in France (he attended Janson de Sailly high school) except during his military service. He was thus very much a Francophile, even though Sweden chose to remain neutral (and agreed to sell ore to Germany throughout the war).

General von Choltitz, a German officer who saw the worst of the fighting on the Russian front, was appointed on August 7, 1944 by Hitler himself, who commented from his bunker that "I am appointing you commander-in-chief of the Wehrmacht troops. You are being given power that is as absolute as a general can have. You have the rights of a commander of a location under heavy siege" (Von Choltitz, 1964, p. 206).

---

[3] The other parties involved will be introduced later in this chapter. Otto Abbetz, Pierre Taittinger, and Dietrich von Choltitz have been denounced for their actions during the Second World War. Highlighting the roles they played in saving Paris and its inhabitants in mid- to late-August 1994 does not imply any judgment as to their conduct in general.

Hitler does not doubt that this faithful, courageous officer will carry out his orders promptly. And yet, the soldier in General von Choltitz could not destroy Paris without a good reason (he indicated in his memoir, however, that he would have done so without hesitation if that would have changed the outcome of the war). Nor could he disobey and fail to do what he believed to be his duty. He therefore had to negotiate with the Allied forces, and get them to agree not to do anything that would provoke him to do what could not be undone.

2. WARM-UP EXERCISES: NEGOTIATING THE RELEASE OF PRISONERS

This was Nordling's idea, but it was inspired by his contacts with the Resistance through Alexandre de Saint-Phalle.[4] After obtaining assurances that de Saint-Phalle could act as a go-between between him and the Resistance, Nordling refused to meet with official Resistance representatives so that when the time came, he could talk to the Germans and be able to "flatly deny any contact with the French provisional government's emissaries". He wrote a memo logically setting out "the opinions from very different spheres" and highlighting how the Germans' reputation would suffer if they mistreated prisoners. It quickly became apparent, however, that following the chain of command (which meant going through the SS officer Carl Oberg and getting Himmler's approval) was not only slow, but more importantly, highly uncertain.

On August 15, Nordling managed to meet with Pierre Laval, then Otto Abetz.[5] Abetz tried to downplay the problem, especially because the Red Cross had been authorized to give the prisoners food before they were deported and the number of prisoners per train car had been reduced. But Nordling's goal was to stop prisoners from being deported and suggested that the camps be placed "under the protection and authority of the Red Cross". Anticipating Abetz's fears for the camp's German guards, he added that they would be granted safe conduct, saying: "I'm making this commitment in the name of the French government." Although Laval was aware that the end of his government was imminent (he was taken to

---

[4] A Parisian banker involved in the Resistance. He was the first go-between between Nordling and the Resistance.

[5] He was the German ambassador during the occupation and worked to secure Franco-German collaboration.

Germany on August 19), he reacted harshly: "You seem to be forgetting that I am the one who represents the French government." Negotiations were cut short and Nordling's counterparts got up from their chairs several times to signal the end of the meeting. He decided to risk everything and emphasized Germany's desperate situation and future honor.

The next day he met with Alexandre Parodi,[6] who assured him the Allies could make good on his promise of safe conduct for the German guards. The Allies were happier with Nordling's involvement at this point because taking the prisons by force involved a number of dangers, in particular the risk that an asphyxiant gas would be used against the prisoners. The situation was urgent because a train with 2,400 prisoners was about to leave. Fortunately, Resistance sabotage efforts bought them some time.

Nordling then enlisted the help of Emile Bender, a German army reserve officer with whom he had had business dealings. "Bender was also one of the countless, mysterious individuals who gravitated around Occupation authorities" but he had been the German counter-espionage chief's right-hand man. Bender used the same technique children everywhere use: he asked each person privately whether they would agree if the other person also agreed (playing on the ambiguity of whether agreement had already been secured or not). On August 17 in Nordling's presence, he asked the director of the Fresnes prison if he would object to evacuating the prisoners. After receiving explicit consent to evacuate them, Bender and Nordling went to the Hotel Meurice to meet with von Choltitz (but Nordling did not meet with him directly). Once reassured that the prisoners in question were not prisoners of war or irregular armed forces, von Choltitz gave his support but indicated that Major Huhm's approval would be required – and Huhm had to leave Paris before noon. Nordling raced across Paris and tough negotiations ensued. Huhm started high, demanding 25 German prisoners for each French prisoner. Nordling reframed the situation as "I don't have any German prisoners and I don't have the slightest reason to capture any" but Huhm stayed camped on his position until finally intimating that it was merely a formality (i.e., the figure he had given did not have to be met – their most important concern was to cover themselves). Agreement was finally reached on a ratio of one to five, which Oberg approved (Oberg had gone to von Choltitz's office that morning while Bender was negotiating).

---

6   Alexandre Parodi (Cérat) took over after the tragic death of Jean Moulin.

That is how Nordling, along with the Red Cross, became superintendent of the prisons for a few days and organized the prisoners' progressive release, taking care to avoid any unrest that would cost human lives.

3.   SAVING PARIS AND ITS INHABITANTS

Nordling's other major mediation took place partly at the same time. On August 14, von Choltitz was ordered to destroy Paris's bridges. Although he did not officially object to it, von Choltitz found the order absurd (destroying the bridges could hurt the German troops just as much as it did the Allies, and they would not be able to build temporary bridges while leaving the area) and played for time. He asked for additional explosives and infantrymen, and organized reconnaissance missions. When he was finally ready to have the explosives put in place, he was careful to demand that he be the only one to be able to give the order to set them off. That is when he had his first, brief meeting with Nordling, who had just informed him of an important fact: von Choltitz's orders had been intercepted by other sections and various measures had been taken, such that von Choltitz could lose control of the situation at any time. Nordling thus carried out one of a mediator's key functions: to address his counterpart's major concerns (in this case, maintaining control over the situation).

Saturday, August 19 was the beginning of the Paris uprising, during which the French Forces of the Interior (FFI) took control of the prefecture. Although extremely powerful symbolically, such events ran the risk of escalating the fighting, as the German army still controlled most of Paris. Nordling therefore focused on the taking of the prefecture and, after briefly meeting with the new Gaullist prefect, had a first meeting with von Choltitz about it. Von Choltitz was at that very moment fulminating against the FFI, whom he considered to have no discipline and to constitute irregular forces. He was considering reprisals. There followed a vociferous discussion during which Nordling tried to persuade him that "the French people were all behind de Gaulle and the Resistance" (Nordling, 2002), and that the rebellion was directed more at the despised Vichy regime than at the Germans (in his memoir Nordling admitted that this was a risky argument). As proof, he insisted that those ousted from the prefecture were Vichy supporters.

Von Choltitz protested vehemently, getting carried away while talking about the German soldiers that had been killed, then suddenly stopped. A young woman had just ridden by on a bike, oblivious as the breeze gently lifted her skirt to reveal her legs while the Tuileries shimmered in the summer light behind her. "We have no right to shoot at her or young women like her!" exclaimed von Choltitz (Nordling, 2002, p. 115). "Paris is a beautiful city." They started listing Paris's charms, and von Choltitz told Nordling of his frustration at not having joined the retreats from Stalingrad and his doubts about the future. Nordling followed up by speculating on what historians would write if the Germans destroyed Paris. "If the enemy had leaders we could negotiate with," replied von Choltitz, "perhaps we could reach an agreement" (Nordling, 2002, p. 116), thus implicitly authorizing Nordling to act as go-between.

That evening, German troops assembled in front of the prefecture. After a call from the forces occupying the prefecture, Nordling, again assisted by Emile Bender, tried to persuade the German commander that the attack was likely to seriously compromise all chances of negotiation and might even spark a general uprising. But it was the reality of their situation (with few weapons or resources) that led those inside the prefecture to negotiate. Von Choltitz was contacted, and the ensuing discussions resulted in the occupiers of the prefecture being recognized as representatives of the French Provisional Government and a cease fire being progressively instituted. Nordling was also called on to prevent the captured FFI fighters from being shot after the Neuilly city hall was taken.

Nordling's actions eventually led the representatives of the Resistance Council to seek him out, as it was both symbolically and practically difficult for them to negotiate directly. The goal was to gain time for the French and to avoid useless casualties or a dishonorable end for the Germans (to be placed in the context of the danger to soldiers' families who were still in Germany). The French wanted to fight but were much weaker at that time. The Germans preferred to avoid fighting, provided they were not pressured into it. An agreement was finally reached on the following text:

> Due to the promises made by the German Command not to attack the public buildings occupied by French troops and to treat all French prisoners in accordance with the laws of war, the French Provisional Government and the National Resistance Council ask you to hold your fire against the occupiers until Paris has been completely evacuated. The population has been advised to maintain the utmost calm. We have been asked not to loiter in the streets.

Every word was weighed so the agreement could not be considered proof of treason if it was reported to Berlin.

The means for disseminating the text (by French and German cars equipped with loud-speakers) was subject to negotiation and last-minute changes, and some members of the Resistance, first and foremost Colonel Rol-Tanguy, objected to the truce and set about circumventing it. The cars were scheduled to broadcast the message at 4 pm on Sunday, August 20.

There were a number of incidents, about-faces, and unforeseen events before General Leclerc rolled in with his tanks on Thursday, August 24 (e.g., three eminent members of the Resistance were unexpectedly arrested and Nordling negotiated their release;[7] a column of German soldiers unexpectedly passed through then withdrew and created a major incident; etc.), as well as some unexpected help from the Germans in the hour of defeat (in particular, the disobedience of Major Hans Speidel, who refused to launch the V1 and V2 missiles on Paris and paid very dearly for it; and Otto Abbetz's promising von Choltitz, as he was leaving Paris, that he would complain to Hitler of von Choltitz's brutality, thus giving him a few additional days' respite). But the goal had been achieved: to save as many prisoners as possible, keep deaths to a minimum, and save the city.

4. THE MEDIATOR AS ORCHESTRATOR: WAIT UNTIL THE TIME IS RIPE AND TAKE ADVANTAGE OF TURNING POINTS

The two episodes discussed here highlight two roles a third party can play in a negotiation. In a situation like the first (the release of prisoners), the third party plays an active role, taking initiative and acting as an intermediary or even more. In the second (the truce), they are mainly there to facilitate a conversation that would not take place without a go-between but that the stakeholders are ready to have. In both cases, for negotiations to succeed, the time must be ripe for each party.

4.1. STAKEHOLDER READINESS: A PREREQUISITE TO SUCCESSFUL MEDIATION

Nothing would have been possible if the parties had not been ready – in particular von Choltitz, who could have destroyed Paris. Ripeness is a prerequisite to most successful mediations. I. William Zartman (2008)

---

[7]   One of them, Parodi, refused to shake hands with von Choltitz, who was about to release them and suggested that a handshake between officers was not unthinkable. This almost compromised their release and subsequent events.

identified two requirements for ripeness: a "mutually hurting stalemate" and a way out. The first implies that the stakeholders feel that anything other than a negotiated solution constitutes a stalemate. Von Choltitz progressively became convinced that the war was lost and that Hitler no longer knew what he was doing. The August 7, 1944 meeting (which followed the July 20 assassination attempt, which Hitler barely survived) brought him face to face with a sick, delirious man. Hitler claimed that he had a fail-proof plan to throw the Allies back into the sea, but at the same time asked von Choltitz to arrange for the retreat of most of the Parisian administration and able-bodied troops. Such inconsistency is the fruit that will progressively ripen. In addition, this stalemate was painful to contemplate, because the military was making precise plans to cause damage that is pointless in this type of situation.

Because the stakeholders eventually found themselves in the tight grip of a hurting stalemate, a way out had to be found. While the general was reluctant to carry out absurd orders, his family's safety and his honor as an officer made negotiating with the Allies – which would have been blatant treason – impossible. The Allies were not really ready to negotiate either, and especially not directly. Nordling therefore had to facilitate the negotiation of an honorable exit for von Choltitz while the Allies stood by with flowers in their rifles, understanding that a false step could lead to the destruction of Paris, a general panic, or the death of numerous prisoners. Various factors were at play here: not only the artificial agreement to exchange prisoners (one for five) and false assurances that none of them were irregular soldiers, but also the lack of direct negotiations with the enemy. As a Frenchman at heart but consul of a neutral country (that had maintained ties with Germany), Nordling could embody an honorable way out.

4.2. TURNING POINTS IN THE NEGOTIATION

Ripe fruit does not always fall by itself. Sometimes it needs something to make it fall, or it may rot. That is the concept of turning points developed by Druckman (2001): they are moments when things shift and change the flow of events. Turning points are sometimes voluntarily triggered, but they usually arise by chance and their effects must therefore be understood. There are at least two in the case under discussion. The first was when von Choltitz learned by chance from an SS officer that Hitler had just instituted a rule of reprisals against the families of German officers (i.e., that "innocent children and women [were] in danger of being killed to give the orders more force"). Like Stalin, Hitler had thus decided to put the lives of officers' families at stake to obtain blind obedience. While this could have been an obstacle to negotiations, it triggered deep disgust in von Choltitz, who then obtained protection for his family before it was too late.

The second turning point came when the young woman rode by in the summer sunshine with the Tuileries in the background, just as the conversation between von Choltitz and Nordling was beginning to heat up. This story is confirmed by Lapierre and Collins as well as, oddly, Pierre Taittinger. He seems to have experienced a similar event when he came to plead the cause of Paris on August 17, which confirms that von Choltitz had a certain mindset. Taittinger writes, "he was at the window. And the German governor, extending his hand, showed me two young cyclists whose skirts were joyfully flapping in the breeze" (Taittinger, 1948, p. 165). And if the fact that that particular young woman rode by was not the turning point, it was perhaps simply that von Choltitz was moved by the neighborhood's summer beauty and the sight of several young women riding by.

5. CONCLUSION: THE RIGHT PERSON AT THE RIGHT MOMENT

The mediation discussed here contains no heroic deeds, no sophisticated technique: the mediator simply harvested ripe fruit. But this does not diminish the value of what he did. One has to know how to seize the moment, choose the right approach and place, and be willing to invest the effort to achieve the desired outcome. An important point in Raoul Nordling's favor was that he was a neutral third party, which was not a simple matter. It was not easy for him or Sweden to be neutral, as the study of war clearly shows. Julien Freund (1983) sums it up this way: conflict eliminates third parties. Everything pushes people to take sides and form alliances. But without a third party, these all-important negotiations would not have taken place.

REFERENCES

DRUCKMAN, D., 2001, "Turning Points in International Negotiation: A Comparative Analysis," *Journal of Conflict Resolution*, vol. 45(4): 519–544.
FREUND, J., 1983, *Sociologie du Conflit*, PUF, Paris.

NORDLING, R., 2002, *Sauver Paris: Mémoires du Consul de Suède (1905–1944)*, Editions Complexe/CNRS, edited and annotated Fabrice Virigili.

TAITTINGER, P., 1948, *Et Paris ne Fut pas Détruit*, L'élan.

VON CHOLTITZ, 1964, *De Sébastopol à Paris*, J'ai lu.

ZARTMAN, I. W., 2008, *Negotiation and Conflict Management: Essays on Theory and Practice*, Routledge, New York.

THE PEACE PROCESS IN NORTHERN IRELAND (1997–2007)

From Hatred to Reason

Marc Beretta[*]

Behind the picture-perfect Ireland seen on postcards, famous for its friendly people and beautiful countryside, hides a population torn apart by centuries of war between Catholics and Protestants, and between the Irish and the British Crown. The deep historical roots of resentment made it seem that it would take two or three generations before peace would be achieved, but after four centuries of struggles of varying degrees, the 10 years between 1997 and 2007 saw women and men of courage take action to put an end to the cycle of violence. The Good Friday Agreement (1998)

---

[*]   President of Inis Alga Inc.

and the institution of a mixed government in Northern Ireland (2007) stand as bookends to a remarkable period of convergence between the parties. These 10 years of negotiations constitute the history of a successful peace process. An analysis of the conditions for the success of the process in Northern Ireland may serve, at least in part, as the example of a well-led process to end other conflicts currently raging in the world.

1. SECULAR WARS IN IRELAND

For 19 centuries, the island of Ireland was peopled by successive flows of migrants who generally became well integrated. The Celts arrived from Central Europe roughly 600 years before our era, and were Christianized by Saint Patrick in the fifth century. The Vikings arrived from what is now Denmark in the eighth century and founded the city of Dublin. The Normans based in Wales were invited in the 12th century by an unfortunate pretender to one of Ireland's thrones. While assimilating the Normans (through marriage and adoption of the Irish language) originally fit into the English plan of developing an independent country, it eventually became a problem as it meant a loss of power. In 1366, the British Parliament based in Ireland ordered the cultural and ethnic separation between locals and settlers: new arrivals were prohibited from speaking Irish, using Irish names, and marrying the Irish. This attempt at separation failed, however, and two centuries later the Normans were fully assimilated except in the fortified area around Dublin.

The English then colonized the island and imposed their law. To better control the country, Henry VIII decided in the 16th century to appoint a representative from the Irish territory to London and tried in vain to impose Protestantism. The Irish rebelled but were beaten at the battle of Kinsale in 1601. The Irish leaders went into exile, leaving behind them land for the taking. Scottish Presbyterians then colonized a portion of Ulster (a northern territory) to civilize the island. An English government was established in Dublin and English garrisons occupied Ireland. In the 17th century, 3000 Protestant colonists were exterminated during a siege by Catholics. Oliver Cromwell's response was bloody, and fertile lands were distributed on a large scale to Protestant settlers. Criminal laws were then passed that left the island's Catholic majority with little to no rights. On July 1, 1690, James II, the deposed Catholic King of England who was seeking to regain the throne, lost the Battle of the Boyne to his Protestant rival, William of Orange. To this day, the Orange Order celebrates William's victory on July 12 (due to the change to the Gregorian calendar).

At the close of the 18th century, Republican winds began to blow across Ireland. The Protestant Wolfe Tone managed to bring Presbyterians and Catholics together against the king of England and in favor of a Republic, but in vain. Westminster, sensing the Republican threat, once more imposed direct control from London: in 1800 the parliament in Dublin was dissolved and London passed The Acts of Union, merging Ireland into the United Kingdom. The British deliberately mismanaged the consequences of the great famine (1845–1849), which decimated the Irish population, killing one million people and causing another million to emigrate. This led to the founding of the Irish Republican Brotherhood, the ancestor of the Irish Republican Army (IRA), composed of "Volunteers" who favored armed struggle to establish a republic and Irish independence. In the late 19th century, two Protestants, Charles Stewart Parnell, a landowner and member of the House of Commons, and the British Prime Minister William Gladstone, started the Gaelic revival, a movement that promoted the Irish language and the redistribution of Anglo-Irish lands to Gaelic Irish. This movement eventually led to the Home Rule Act (1914), which instituted more decentralized management of Ireland. Once again feeling that they were under siege, northern Irish Protestants mobilized their own Volunteers in a paramilitary movement called the Ulster Volunteer Force (UVF).

The time for Republican emancipation had come: on Easter Monday 1916, Republicans in Dublin rebelled against the sitting government, established a provisional government and declared a Republic. The rebellion was put down, the leaders executed, and the population punished, causing a swell of support for Republicanism and Sinn Féin, the political branch of the Irish Republican Volunteers. As a result, the 1918 election was an overwhelming victory for Sinn Féin. Campaigning on an independence platform, they won 73 of the 105 seats for Irish deputies in the House of Commons. But instead of going to London in 1919 to take those seats, the Sinn Féin deputies set up their own parliament in Dublin, the *Dáil Éireann*, and proclaimed the Irish Republic. The British government immediately outlawed the Dáil, setting off a two-year war of independence to defend the results of the 1918 election. The Republican Volunteers became the IRA. In the context of this struggle and to preserve the Protestant majority in the northern part of the island, the British government, pressured by Unionists, partitioned Ireland between the province of Ulster in the north, which remained subject to the crown, and the rest of the island. In 1920 a decree then partitioned Ulster, excluding three of its nine counties because they had a Catholic majority. In 1921 Michael Collins, an IRA leader, went to 10 Downing Street in London to negotiate, and eventually signed the Anglo-Irish Treaty with Lloyd George. The treaty provided for an Irish Free State, which the British government would recognize as a Dominion in exchange for an oath of allegiance to the king. When Collins returned to Ireland, the treaty was rejected by Sinn Féin hardliners led by Collins's rival, Éamon de Valera, and the 1922–1923 civil war began between the pro- and anti-Treaty factions. The Free State won, and in 1937 de Valera had the Republic of Ireland's claim to Northern Ireland included in the Irish Constitution (articles 2 and 3).

The history of Ireland is thus the history of repressed nationalism against a background of *de facto* apartheid between Protestant settlers and Irish Catholics. In the 1960s, Catholics in Northern Ireland were in a position of complete inequality: the police were 90 per cent Protestant, judges were 100 per cent Protestant, priority was given to Protestants for housing and jobs, and the unemployment rate was twice as high for Catholics as it was for Protestants. The proportional representation law was even amended to guarantee a Protestant majority in cities that had a Catholic majority, such as Derry (renamed Londonderry). In 1967, the Northern Ireland Civil Rights Alliance began a "one man, one vote" campaign that, in 1969, met with violent repression by Unionists, who beat demonstrators with clubs while the local police stood by. This event marked the beginning of the Troubles in Northern Ireland. Stretched thin by the incessant violence, the Royal Ulster Constabulary asked the British Army for reinforcements. While the northern Irish Catholics were initially relieved to see them arrive, they were quickly disenchanted: on January 30, 1972 the British Army killed 13 people in Derry. The images of what became known as "Bloody Sunday" were seen around the world, strengthening support for the IRA abroad and causing an influx of money, arms, and new recruits. Reprisals and counter-reprisals succeeded one another.

In 1980 Bobby Sands, elected as a nationalist deputy while in prison, died following the hunger strike he had begun to protest the harsh treatment of Republican prisoners in British prisons. Ten other prisoners died under the government of Margaret Thatcher ("the Iron Lady"), and the world again expressed massive support for the IRA. The pressure led to the start of talks in 1993 at the instigation of John Major, who had succeeded Thatcher as UK Prime Minister in 1990. The Irish government announced that it might give up its quest for the Northern Territory written into its constitution. A framework for the future, a simple statement of intent, but a first essential step, was put on paper, but there was also distrust: in 1996 Sinn Féin claimed the English wanted a victory, not a ceasefire.

2. TEN YEARS TO BRING AN END TO SECULAR STRUGGLES

As soon as he arrived at 10 Downing Street in 1997, Tony Blair made the Irish problem one of his priorities and informed his Irish counterpart, Bertie Ahern, of his desire to bring an end to the violence. Negotiations with the main parties were begun, and eventually culminated in the 1998 Good Friday Agreement. This Agreement, which takes the form of what I. William Zartman would call a formula that precedes the subsequently negotiated details, provided for:

- keeping Northern Ireland in the United Kingdom;
- British recognition of the Republic of Ireland's full sovereignty over its own territory;
- removal of articles 2 and 3, related to the Republic's claim over the northern territories, from the Constitution of the Republic of Ireland;
- the nomination of an Assembly with a Northern Irish Executive, so power would be shared between Protestants and Catholics;
- a North/South council composed of ministers of both the Republic of Ireland and Northern Ireland, with a veto right for each party.

For the first time, the Republicans publicly agreed to negotiations that would not move in the direction of a reunified Ireland, and the Unionists agreed to share power with the Catholics. Off-camera, their leaders met for the first time since 1920 and in 1998, the Assembly met. Bill Clinton's visit and the award of the Nobel Peace Prize to John Hume and David Trimble, the moderate leaders, respectively, of Northern Ireland's Social Democratic and Labor Party (SDLP) and Ulster Unionist Party (UUP), provided support for the peace process.

Even though the peace process had begun, however, on Saturday August 15, 1998 a bomb exploded shortly after 3 pm in the shopping center of the peaceful town of Omagh. The hardline Real IRA (RIRA) claimed credit for the action, which killed 29 people (including a woman pregnant with twins) and injured hundreds. Tony Blair saw this bomb not as a return to the past, but as confirmation that the political process had to move forward. Isolated, the RIRA ceased all violent operations three weeks later, though this did not keep Sinn Féin from declaring later that year that they would never disarm.

Disarmament nonetheless progressed in tandem with political emancipation. After various options had been considered, it was decided that both sides' paramilitary organizations would turn in their arms and John de Chastelain, a neutral observer, would supervise the decommissioning until the arms were destroyed. A first deadline was set in 1999 to coincide with the institutional process: meeting of the Assembly; first meeting of the Executive; and the first official handshake between Unionists and Republicans. From then on, neither party would want to be responsible for the failure of negotiations. The peace process had started. It would last another eight years.

The decommissioning schedule was not followed, and the institutional process was interrupted for the first time in 2000. After obtaining relaxed police inspections in Northern Ireland, the IRA declared that it agreed to disarm the movement in a context where the conflict's causes were removed. This was a turning point. The northern Irish Assembly and Executive began meeting again, even though violence persisted.

The process was interrupted a second time in 2002, as a result of the terrorist attack in New York on September 11, 2001, and arms talks. The IRA quickly claimed that its arsenal had been destroyed and Tony Blair made a televised statement welcoming the news, which he said was not an act of weakness but a sign that politics was working. However, evidence of arms trafficking on both sides was brought to light in 2001–2002, which in 2002 led to the second suspension of the northern Irish institutions.

Despite some reluctance, negotiations began again in 2003 on the issue of creating a disarmament commission (the Independent Monitoring Commission, or IMC) composed of three members – one Irish, one English, and one American – to supervise the decommissioning process on both sides by carrying out inspections and imposing penalties. The institutional process was also able to start up again, and saw electoral wins by the two extremist parties: Sinn Féin and the Unionist DUP led by Ian Paisley, known as "Mr. No". Paisley's arrival in the process worried those who wanted peace, but in 2004 he underwent surgery, coming back transformed and with a mission: to find a solution to the problem of Northern Ireland. While many former combatants were taking up politics one after the other, "proximity talks" were started in London.

The institutional process was halted a third time in late 2004, after 30 million pounds were stolen from the Northern Bank by movements close to the IRA. Martin McGuinness, a co-leader of Sinn Féin who did not want to leave all the power in Unionist hands, said that "the struggle can now be taken by other means … In the past, I have defended the right of the IRA to engage in armed struggle. I did so because there was no alternative for those who would not bend the knee or for those who wanted a national republic. Now, there is an alternative. That alternative is Sinn Féin."[1] This was another turning point.

In 2005, in the difficult context of a wave of Islamic terrorist attacks in London, de Chastelain announced on September 26 that all the arms of the Republican and Unionist paramilitary movements had been destroyed. The Executive was able to begin meeting again; Sinn Féin and the DUP were the two big winners in the March 2007 Northern Ireland Assembly elections; and Ian Paisley was ready to appoint his Executive cabinet members. In May 2007 an agreement was reached: Paisley would be prime minister, and Sinn Féin's McGuinness would be deputy prime minister. On May 8, 2007 they were sworn in in the presence of Tony Blair, Bertie Ahern, and a few individuals with a troubled past, but all united by the peace process. Tony Blair declared it was time "to escape the chains of history".[2] Violence finally gave way to political struggle.

3. A SUCCESSFUL PEACE PROCESS: DETERMINATION AS TO THE OBJECTIVES, FLEXIBILITY AS TO MEANS

3.1. BE STRONG BUT FLEXIBLE

In hindsight, it seems that the main feature of the peace process in Northern Ireland is that it benefited from the unfailing courage and commitment of the main players, starting with Tony Blair and Bertie Ahern. Their tenacity and ability to stay the course – to persevere with the search for peace despite frequent outbreaks of violence – was without a doubt a decisive factor. Blair restarted the process several times when it had reached an impasse. Faced with a "no", he asked his negotiators to try again and be creative. The process was also subject to deadlines, which guaranteed progress.

Despite their determination, both parties had to prove their openness. As soon as he took office in 1997, Blair issued an official apology to Ireland on behalf of the British government, for the government's role during the

---

[1]   POWELL (2008, p. 269), citing Mac Guinness.
[2]   POWELL (2008, p. 307), citing Blair.

great famine of 1845–1849. At the same time, he promised the United Kingdom's unswerving support to the Unionists. These concessions helped cool the debate. Republicans felt their pain was being heard and Unionists felt less under siege. Dialogue was finally possible. The clear recognition of each party's deepest aspirations, be it symbolic historical recognition or recognition of an immediate need for security, helped reassure them both with respect to the rest of the process.

In addition to recognizing these crucial needs, a certain amount of practical creativity came in handy. Concrete interests had to be defended and understood. Why was the IRA supported by the Catholic community? Because it defended that community's cause. Simple police measures could not put an end to the conflict. In the 1980s a new, independent government had been set up to guarantee a more equitable distribution of housing and jobs between Catholics and Protestants. The reform did not resolve the conflict, but it eased tensions. Then came the power sharing – incorporating each party's hopes and protecting minorities. Finally, the ambiguity promoted in the beginning to get the dialogue started progressively gave way to precision, especially in regard to neutralizing arms.

In short, an ability to put one's personal feelings aside and be patient, persevere, and get to know one's counterparts was essential.

3.2. MAKE THE PROCESS FORESEEABLE AND INCLUDE THIRD PARTIES

The parties were able to agree, at crucial times, to call on a mediator. Behind the disarmament issue lay the question of trust: once disarmed, a paramilitary movement can always buy more arms. Turning to a mediator like de Chastelain helped soften the edges, prevent discussions veering off track, and keep the process moving slowly but surely toward a common goal.

3.2.1. Sequence the Process

When a mediator tries to reconcile opposing parties, each avoids making the first gesture because there is always a fear the other will not reciprocate. This is why it is important to divide the process into small stages and maintain constant contact with those involved. For example, the sealed arms depots were regularly inspected by neutral observers, as was the case in Bosnia. The parties must not feel they are surrendering.

3.2.2. Six Principles of Non-Violence

Both parties eventually agreed to the six principles of non-violence that the US Senator George Mitchell proposed in 1996, which have been used to resolve a number of conflicts since then:

1. Favor peaceful, democratic means.
2. Completely disarm paramilitary organizations.
3. Have an independent commission supervise disarmament.
4. Renounce the use or threat of force.
5. Accept the agreement obtained without force or the threat of force.
6. Accept the end of repression and reprisals.

Practical arrangements made with these principles in mind can give full effect to symbolic connotations. In 2007 the bitter rivals Ian Paisley and Gerry Adams, a Sinn Féin co-leader, had to sit down at the negotiating table. Should they be seated across from each other like adversaries, as the Unionists advised, or next to each other like friends, as the Republicans suggested? In the end they chose a diamond-shaped table, so each could sit at the head and thus be both across from and next to each other, like partners.

3.3. SHIFT FROM NEGOTIATING POSITIONS TO NEGOTIATING INTERESTS

3.3.1. Find the Shared Interest in the Parties' Individual Interests

For the Republicans, the important issue was not necessarily a reunified Ireland, but the defense of their rights over the northern Irish territory and access to power over Ireland's affairs. For the Unionists, the real issue was not to be part of the United Kingdom but to be recognized by the British crown and to have a say in the management of Northern Ireland, where most of them had lived for 400 years. Their shared interest was peace.

3.3.2. Leave a Door Open

Unlike in previous Northern Ireland negotiations, disarmament was not a prerequisite to talks but led simultaneously to political emancipation. This left time to think and prevented the risk of hitting an impasse, which would have caused the parties to camp on their positions: union with the

United Kingdom or not. We can observe that disarmament was also not a prerequisite in other peace processes described in this book, notably in Columbia (see Frans Schram's chapter, "Negotiating Peace with the FARC (2010-2016)", in this volume) and in the Philippines (see Ariel Macaspac Hernandez's chapter, "Four Decades in the Southern Philippines (1971–2008)", in this volume).

4. PEACE FOR NORTHERN IRELAND

The source of the conflict in Northern Ireland was not ethnic or religious, it was above all nationalist: it involved sovereignty over territory and the rights of peoples. The key to resolving it lay essentially in managing the process in a European context.

The peace is, of course, fragile: the Government worked until December 2016, but since January 2017, there has been no government, and no leadership to maintain the governance. At the time of writing (at the end of 2018), it is expected that a new government should be formed in the near future. Meanwhile, the Brexit process has also developed in a way that could have severe repercussions on Northern Ireland.

No one would like to go back to the old times again, and this peace process is considered a success; while no negotiations can be transferred wholesale, this process could be a source of inspiration in the search for ways to reduce differences in armed conflicts, such as in the Palestinian territories or the Kashmir.

It is also a source of hope for all of us, because what happened there is also what is happening here and now for each of us: can I lower my weapon, question my initial position and look instead for shared interests? The peace process in Northern Ireland shows that it is possible.

REFERENCES

HIBBERT, Christopher, *The Story of England*, Phaidon, 2004.

KILLEEN, Richard, *A Short History of Ireland*, Gill & Macmillan, 2009.

O HEITHIR, Breandan, *A Pocket History of Ireland*, The O'Brien Press, 2006.

POWELL, Jonathan, *Great Hatred, Little Room: Making Peace in Northern Ireland*, The Bodley Head, 2008.

ZARTMAN, I. William, *Elusive Peace: Negotiating an End to Civil Wars*, Brookings Institution, 1995.

FOUR DECADES IN THE SOUTHERN PHILIPPINES (1971–2008)

Can "Biased" Mediators be Helpful?

Ariel Macaspac HERNANDEZ*

In the Southern Philippines, the final sprint of the half-a-century long peace process, known as the Bangsamoro peace process, reminds us that the "devil is in the details". After more than four decades of talks, despite numerous mediated negotiations, framework agreements, final agreements, plebiscites/referendums, creation of autonomous governance bodies and implementation of peace agreements, the closure of the Bangsamoro peace process is still yet to come. Very recently, the current efforts to create the Bangsamoro Autonomous Region in Muslim Mindanao after the passage of the Bangsamoro Organic Law in July 2018 and the plebiscite in 2019 that replaced the Autonomous Region in Muslim Mindanao (ARMM) is yet another culmination of both international and local efforts to end the intractable armed conflict between the Government of the Republic of the

---

* German Development Institute.

Philippines (GRP) and the two main insurgent groups: the Moro National Liberation Front (MNLF) and the Moro Islamic Liberation Front (MILF).

The Bangsamoro peace process is a mediated negotiation process which was helped by Libya and Malaysia, both holding a political mandate from the Organisation of Islamic Conference (OIC). These two countries were useful at creating channels of negotiations between the GRP and the Moro rebel groups. However, the Libyan and Malaysian mediation efforts contradict the dominant literature on mediation with regards to neutrality and impartiality, as these are considered as necessary elements of successful third-party mediation.[1] Neutrality in mediation refers to the absence of or at least transparency on bias (Milne, 1985). On the other hand, impartiality pertains to the mediators not being stakeholders to the process and not benefitting directly or indirectly from any of its outcome. The analysis of the mediation efforts of Libya and Malaysia between 1971 and 2008 suggests that biased mediators can still be successful in helping parties to elusive conflicts reach agreements. In the case of the Bangsamoro peace process, it can even be argued that the bias of mediators was instrumental in pushing forward the process. In addition, the Bangsamoro case tends to show that under certain conditions, biased mediators need to be omni-partial,[2] that is, that they are willing to take either side depending on issues. Moreover, biased mediators can tap additional leverage that can help to achieve agreements because conflicting parties are to some extent dependent on the mediators that play other important roles in a different context.

1. THE INTRACTABLE MORO CONFLICT AND MEDIATION EFFORTS

The conflict between the GRP and armed Muslim separatist groups that spans more than 50 years has witnessed multiple agreements. It is an example of an elusive conflict whose achieved agreements have also encouraged the mobilization of splitter rebel groups, which initially waged a new series of armed confrontations with the GRP before agreeing to sit at the negotiation table.

---

[1] Christopher Moore (1996, p. 6) defines mediation as "the intervention of an acceptable impartial and neutral third party who has no authoritative decision-making power […]".

[2] Omni-partiality refers to the German concept of "Allparteilichkeit", in which mediators assume neutrality in the "content" but are also willing to influence relevant persons if this serves the purpose of achieving agreements (von Hertel, 2009, p. 31).

The Bangsamoro, originally an exonym, is an "identity" group that aggregates 14 Philippine ethnic groups in the Southern Philippines. It comprises about 11 per cent of the total Philippine population, so around 11 million people. Thus, classifying the conflict in the Southern Philippines as merely ethnic or religious would be misleading. It is rather an expression of the structural imbalance in the functional interactions between the "centre" and the "periphery" as well as the lack of retributive and compensatory mechanisms to "correct" historical errors following 400 years of colonial experience (Hernandez, 2014). The mobilization of the Bangsamoro is the result of center-periphery constitution of societal relations.

Two "biased" mediations have occurred: on one hand, Libyan-led mediation efforts that started in 1975, leading to the 1976 Tripoli Agreement and the 1996 Final Peace Agreement between the GRP and the MNLF; and on the other hand, a Malaysian-led mediation from 1996 leading to the 2008 Memorandum of Agreement on Ancestral Domains (MOA-AD) between the GRP and the MILF. The fact that in 2008, the Philippine Supreme Court declared the MOA-AD as unconstitutional, leading to an impasse and to subsequent new rounds of negotiations between the MILF and the GRP, which are continuing now, with support from Malaysia, is not analyzed in this chapter.

The acceptance of Libyan-biased mediators by the GRP was initially a strategic approach in the peace negotiations with the MNLF due to the looming oil embargo of the oil-producing members of the Organisation of Islamic Conference (OIC) against the Philippines. Later, the GRP's acceptance of the Malaysian negotiators was more pragmatic and was motivated by the change of tune in Malaysia's foreign policy with regards to supporting independence movements abroad. All in all, the GRP had seemed to realize that the best way to integrate "patronage" states that were serving as diplomatic, financial and moral supporters of the Moro insurgency, and to limit their influence, was to involve them as mediators.

1.1. THE LIBYAN MEDIATION BETWEEN THE GOVERNMENT OF THE PHILIPPINES AND MNLF: 1971–1996

The involvement of Libya started in 1971 when Muammar Qaddafi heard on BBC Radio that 70 Filipino Muslims had been killed by Christian vigilantes inside a mosque in Cotobato (Vitug and Gloria, 2000: 60). Qaddafi, advocating his role as revolution leader, wanted Libya to serve as agency for the empowerment of Muslim communities in many parts of the world against oppression. Furthermore, the founder of the MNLF Nur Misuari was a known communist. The involvement of Libya in the Philippines can therefore be classified as cultural and ideological.

Libya first intervened in the conflict in the Southern Philippines by providing arms to the MNLF. It also provided safe haven and training for Muslim rebels in Tripoli. Libya used its convening power and included the Philippines as an agenda item in OIC meetings. Libya initiated the formulation of the socio-linguistic narrative that justified intervention in the Philippines: "In the spirit of ummah, Muslims overseas were called to support their beleaguered brothers in the Philippines" (Vitug and Gloria, 2000, p. 60). In 1973, at the Fourth Islamic Conference in Tripoli, Libya pushed for the adoption of a resolution expressing "deep concern over the reported repression and mass extermination of Muslims in Southern Philippines and [urging] the Philippine government to halt these operations immediately" (OIC, 1974).

Libya's efforts expanded the audience of the GRP's strategies in addressing the Muslim insurgency. The Marcos government was coerced to address the conflict, which inevitably gave the separatist groups "belligerent status" and gave political legitimacy to the MNLF in front of the general Muslim audience. The GRP could not ignore the concerns of Muslim countries particularly because of its dependence on oil imports from the Middle East. In addition, the OIC resolution of 1973 imposed a mandate on OIC states to pressure the GRP. After trips of GRP officials to the Middle East in January 14 to 20, 1975, Marcos accepted that any attempt to improve the Philippines' diplomatic ties with the Middle East countries was dependent on a settlement with the MNLF (Vitug and Gloria, 2000, p. 62), and the Philippines experienced a series of oil embargos until the 1980s.

While launching military offensives against the MNLF, the Marcos government accepted the OIC's involvement in the negotiations with the MNLF after the 1974 Fifth Islamic Conference of Foreign Ministers in Malaysia formally recognized the national sovereignty and territorial integrity of the Philippines, assuring the Philippine government that the OIC was not supporting independence of Muslims in Southern Philippines. Libya assumed de facto leadership of the OIC's Committee of the Four (Libya, Saudi Arabia, Senegal, and Somalia) that guided the OIC's involvement in the Philippines. In the next few years, talks between the GRP and the MNLF were held. In November 1976, President Marcos sent First Lady Imelda Marcos to the Middle East, where she was sent to ask Qaddafi to convince the MNLF to agree to sign a peace agreement.

This meeting led to the final stage of the negotiations which culminated in December 1976. Towards the end, the GRP panel vigorously objected to provision 15 which called for the establishment of a "provisional government" in the areas covered by the autonomy pact. Libya called Marcos to convince the head of the GRP panel to sign the agreement. Marcos instructed the panel to sign the agreement on one condition that an additional provision be added in the final draft (Vitug and Gloria, 2000, p. 34). This provision is referred to as Paragraph 16 of the Tripoli Agreement; it says that "the Philippine government shall undertake all the necessary constitutional process to implement the entire agreement" (Tripoli Agreement, 1976). Clearly, it can be considered as a loophole in the agreement, because it gave the GRP scope to delay implementation.

The 1976 Tripoli Agreement was eventually signed in the presence of the Secretary-General and the members of the Quadripartite Ministerial Commission of the OIC. The implementation of the 1976 Agreement was, however, stalled by political instability in the Philippines including the popular uprising to support the coups led by Juan Ponce Enrile and General Fidel Ramos in February 1986. The end of Marcos' regime in 1986 and the resulting political vacuum further delayed the negotiation process. The "revolutionary" government of Corazon Aquino, which was confronted with nine coup attempts between 1986 and 1990, focused on stabilizing the country rather than on the agreement, even though attempts were made to continue the peace process. At the same time, the Bangsamoro movement started to become fragmented: three power centers (Nur Misuari of the MNLF; Hashim Salamat of the MILF; and Pundato Dimasangkay of the MNLF Reformist Group) within the MNLF emerged following some factions' dissatisfaction with the 1976 Tripoli Agreement. The stalemate lasted for 16 years until presidential candidate Fidel Ramos met with Qaddafi in Tripoli in 1992.

In the meantime, Libya had eventually had changed its position and strategy. With the UN sanctions against Libya, it had opted more for the role of a peace broker. So in October 1992, when the newly elected President Ramos dispatched to Tripoli a team to follow-up the earlier meeting with Qaddafi, Libya was in a position to play a decisive role. Confronted with the refusal of Nur Misuari's to be in the same room as one of the members of the GRP panel, Representative Eduardo Ermita, Qaddafi ordered the MNLF to sit down with Ermita (Vitug and Gloria, 2000, p. 29). The meeting was concluded with an agreement to hold the second round of exploratory talks.

In 1994, several agreements including the interim ceasefire agreement were reached. The Final Agreement on the Implementation of the 1976

Tripoli Agreement between the GRP and the MNLF was finally achieved in Manila in 1996, 20 years after the signing of the Tripoli agreement. Libya eventually witnessed the formal end of its intervention in the Philippines.

Without the formal involvement of Libya, the peace process in Mindanao would not have been able to develop. Although Libya was biased, its involvement as mediator: (1) coerced the GRP to recognize the sentiments of the Muslim population; (2) coerced the MNLF to drop off its demand for independence paving way for negotiations; (3) limited its own financial and military support to the MNLF; and (4) led to the 1976 and 1996 Peace Agreements.

Some could argue, however, that the involvement of Libya may have also contributed to the intractability of the conflict. Yet a contrary argument is that without its involvement as mediator, Libya would have most probably continued supporting MNLF with weapons, further protracting the conflict. This role as mediator structurally limited Libya's "bias" and ensured "omni-partiality", as shown in the cases where Libya coerced the MNLF to accept contested terms of the 1976 agreement. Finally, the mediation gave Libya an exit opportunity and the option to shift its strategy from supporting armed violence to assuming the role of a genuine peace broker.

1.2. THE MALAYSIAN MEDIATION BETWEEN THE GOVERNMENT OF THE PHILIPPINES AND MILF: 2001–2008

The MILF is a break-away faction of the MNLF that emerged after Nur Misuari's accepted of the 1976 Peace Agreement, whereby claims for independence were dropped. At this point in time, the MILF refused to recognize the establishment of the Autonomous Region of Muslim Mindanao in 1990 and decided to continue armed operations. Following the 1996 agreement with the MNLF, a general cessation of hostilities agreement was eventually signed between the GRP and MILF in 1997. However, the newly elected President Estrada (1998) soon terminated this agreement and declared an "all-out-war" against the MILF. After a popular revolt deposed President Estrada in 2001, the new President Gloria Arroyo concluded a ceasefire agreement with the MILF and resumed the peace talks (2001).

This is where President Arroyo requested Malaysia to help in the Mindanao peace process. Malaysia agreed and sent peacekeeping missions in Southern Philippines. Kuala Lumpur then hosted several rounds of peace talks. A new ceasefire agreement was reached in 2003. Malaysia sent police and military personnel to lead the 80-strong International Monitoring Team that helped monitor the proper and effective implementation of the agreement on the cessation of hostilities in Mindanao. Both the Philippine military and the MILF credited the presence of Malaysia and the International Monitoring Team for the dramatic reduction of armed confrontations in the region. In July 2008, however, attacks by MILF renegades on civilian communities prompted the end of the ceasefire. Eventually, the peace negotiations between the GRP and the MILF reached in a stalemate in 2008 after the Malaysia-brokered Memorandum of Agreement on Ancestral Domains was declared unconstitutional by the Philippine Supreme Court.

In these events, we can see that Malaysia assumed the role of the mediator upon request of the MILF and the GRP. Yet as a patronage state of the Bangsamoro, Malaysia can to be classified as a biased mediator. At the climax of the Mindanao war in the 1970s, MNLF combatants underwent training from 1969 to 1974 in Sabah (Vitug and Gloria, 2000, p. 175). In addition, Malaysia was initially supportive of the initiatives made by Libya in OIC meetings. However, Malaysia's position changed due to pressure from its domestic audience. Malaysia could not contradict itself by fostering pragmatic domestic institutional arrangements to accommodate its multi-ethnic and multi-religious composition while at the same time supporting insurgent movements abroad against governments that were seeking similar institutional arrangements. Unable to politically afford any further military support for the Muslim rebel groups, and yet very close to the Philippines because of its historical ties to the conflict, Kuala Lumpur saw mediation as a legitimate intervention in order to maintain involvement without jeopardizing domestic policies.

2. NEUTRALITY, PROCESS NEUTRALITY AND THE IMPARTIALITY OF STATES

2.1. MEDIATION THEORY AND NEUTRALITY

Critical to any successful mediation of elusive peace negotiations is the perception by conflicting parties that the intervening actor has no direct interests at stake. Neutrality or impartiality of mediators is theoretically a necessary condition not only to ensure that conflicting parties will accept their intervention in tedious peace negotiations, but also that the achievement of potential agreements will not be inhibited by vested interests of mediators (Agusti-Panareda, 2004; Bercovitch, 2009). Conversely, if the prospective state mediator is too closely aligned with one party or too directly involved in the conflict, it will not be capable of meeting the minimum conditions of a balanced agreement.

However, finding states without vested interests is in practical terms a myth. Any engagement of a state requires the approval of a domestic audience, which often demands normative justification of (and therefore value-laden) commitments. States when assuming a mediator role, particularly in elusive conflicts, become "change agents" as they seek to alter existing procedural structures and functional interactions among conflicting actors that debar direct negotiations.

In the academic literature, the success of mediation is often attributed to neutrality of mediators. For example, Jacob Bercovitch (2009), suggests that the success of mediation is indicated by the equitability of the procedures and outcome achieved through mediated negotiations. For Bercovitch, this equitability requires levels of process neutrality, i.e., that mediators do not alter values and norms used in the process. However, process neutrality does not suggest that the intervening actor needs to be completely indifferent to the outcome nor that a biased actor cannot be capable of prioritizing the interests of conflicting parties over his own interests. Some negotiation scholars even argue that a biased mediation can avoid mediation being ineffective and can facilitate the negotiation process (Touval and Zartman, 1985; Crocker et al., 2009). In addition, particularly when governments of mediating countries need to legitimize their engagement in front of an international and domestic audience, the claim of neutrality or impartiality is undermined. The constant pressure of achieving an agreement to satisfy the audience can influence the mediating state to direct or even manipulate the process for the sake of having any outcome.

2.2. CONDITIONS FOR ACCEPTABILITY AND EFFECTIVENESS OF A BIASED MEDIATION

In the present case, the historical and cultural bias of Malaysia for the benefit of the Muslim population was balanced by Malaysia's political bias for the benefit of the GRP as demanded by its global and domestic audience. Moreover, as a founding member of the ASEAN, Malaysia could not but support the ASEAN's principle of non-interference in domestic issues, and it is now making clear that the Moro insurgency is an internal issue. In doing so, it obviously preferred to resolve the Philippine conflict without undermining itself. As we see, it seems that biased mediation can be successful when mediators have stakes in being impartial, or omni-partial (von Hertel, 2009).

It could be added that one possible condition for biased mediation to succeed is that the biased mediator should not be a superpower. Small and medium powers such as Libya and Malaysia were accepted as mediators, because these countries were not seen as capable of coercing the Philippines.

In addition, as shown by this chapter, the fact that Libya's and Malaysia's mediation efforts were constituted within the political framework of the OIC, which is an international institution that promotes sovereignty and territorial integrity of other states, constrained the claims for independence of territories within existing the Philippines. The GRP rightly anticipated that the mediators deriving their mandate from the OIC would not perpetually support demands for independence of Muslim separatists. The Indonesian government, a traditional ally of the GRP, also pushed in this direction. During the mediation, Indonesia had expressed its interest in preserving the sovereignty and territorial integrity of the Philippines in the series of meetings of the OIC and this kind of action was a solid guarantee that the biased Libyan and Malaysian supports for independence could be contained. Finally, the fact that Libya and Malaysia had derived their mandate from the OIC made it possible for Indonesia to use its "convening power" to block Libya's and Malaysia's efforts to support independence.

The Mindanao conflict took more than 150,000 lives. After two decades of talks with the MILF and more than two decades with the MILF, the Filipino president eventually met the MILF leader in person in 2011, and talks resumed again, this time with higher chances of success. A framework agreement could be signed in 2012, confirmed in March 2014 with the signature of the *Comprehensive Agreement on the Bangsomoro*, at which the Malaysian Prime Minister was present. Sad new twists and armed confrontations continued to occur in-between, but the peace process, its institutional arrangements (the autonomous region) and the attached plebiscites have been giving true hope since then. Peace, albeit fragile, is moving on in the Southern Philippines.

REFERENCES

AGUSTI-PANAREDA, J., "Power Imbalances in Mediation: Questioning Some Common Assumptions", *Dispute Resolution Journal* 59, 2, 2004, 24–31.

BERCOVITCH, J., "Mediation and Conflict Resolution" in BERCOVITCH, J., KREMENYUK, V. and ZARTMAN, I.W., eds., *The SAGE Handbook of Conflict Resolution* (2009), London, pp. 340–357.

CROCKER, C., HAMPSON, F.O. and AALL, P., "Why Mediation Matters: Ending Intractable Conflicts" in BERCOVITCH, J., KREMENYUK, V. and ZARTMAN, I.W., eds., *The SAGE Handbook of Conflict Resolution* (2009), London, pp. 492–505.

HERNANDEZ, A., *Nation-building and Identity Conflicts* (2014), Wiesbaden, Germany.

MILNE, A., "Model Standards of Practice for Family and Divorce Mediation", *Conflict Resolution Quarterly* 8, 1985, 73–81.

MOORE, C., *The Mediation Process* (1996), San Francisco.

OIC (1974): Resolution No. 474: The problem of Muslims in the Philippines, Organisation of Islamic Conference.

TOUVAL, S. and ZARTMAN, I.W., *International Mediation in Theory and Practice* (1985), Boulder, USA.

TRIPOLI AGREEMENT, December 23, 1976, Tripoli, Libya, signed by Carmelo Barbero, Nur Misuari, Ali Abdusaalam Treki and Amadou Karim Gaye, https://www.hdcentre.org/wp-content/uploads/.../The-Tripoli-Agreement-1976.pdf.

VITUG, M. and GLORIA, G., *Under the Crescent Moon. Rebellion in Mindanao* (2000), Quezon City, Philippines.

VON HERTEL, A., *Professionelle Konfliktlösung. Führen mit Mediationskompetenzen* (2009), Frankfurt am Main.

CONCLUSION

Lessons for Modern Diplomacy

Emmanuel V IVET*

What do these 30 historical accounts teach us that might be useful for today's diplomats?

Naturally we have to be careful about how to draw lessons from the past. As I. William Zartman says in the introduction, historical cases may well be "intriguing tales with meaning for the train of events of the times", but they also "tend to come from past eras and any possible lessons for later eras is hidden in the idiosyncrasies of the times". Even landmark negotiations of the past therefore cannot provide lessons unless the analytical tool is sharp enough. It must allow for filtering and comparing to bring isolated events from the past into focus: "One has to establish the causative relations or terms of analysis that explain the relations or regularities illustrated in this particular case that the analyst seeks to convey. It is the move from proper to common nouns ... that turns the data into knowledge."

I would note that historians of international relations come more or less to the same conclusion: it is not easy to draw lessons from history. Some historians believe in trying, however. Hedley Bull, for example, sees history as a source of inspiration and a useful theoretical guide for today. Others, such as Herbert Butterfield (another member of the English School of International Relations Theory), are critical of such attempts and prefer to try to understand history for what it is; we should avoid making judgments based on hindsight. In addressing this dilemma, William Bain suggests that we turn to Michael Oakeshott's conceptions, whereby historical inquiry must be distinguished from normative inquiry. Lessons of history are not what a neutral past or history provides us, but rather they are instances or prescriptions of normative theory that are dressed in the clothes of neutral history. When people read the past for didactic purposes, they are

---

* ESSEC IRENE, France.

no longer making an historical argument but rather a normative argument: "If we seek guidance on how we should act in response to the circumstances of our world, we require a normative theory that is appropriate to the intelligent, thinking, choosing world of human conduct. ... [I]t is normative theory that endows the so-called lessons of history."[1]

Here we are. Couldn't this theory or these theories, in our particular research attempt, be that of negotiations? Because, according to Bain, without such a theory or normative orientation the lesson and its point are lost to us. And that is precisely how this book is made: it includes, with each historical account, an analysis based on the latest conceptual tools developed in the field of negotiation studies. The proposal here is that our theoretical framework might be the theory or theories of negotiation.

This being said, another reason for caution is that each chapter contains more than one lesson (one about process and another about cognitive bias, for example). Just as historical events have several causes, the *post hoc* assessment of an event may lead to several conclusions, precisely because of the theory guiding the analysis. Some conclusions are obvious, but others may still be obscured. In each chapter the authors focus on the most meaningful conclusions of the case study. However, any given account may be studied from various angles and the following categorizations are simply a choice.

One of this book's first lessons for contemporary diplomacy may be found in the discussions of successful multilateral negotiations and how they were achieved. The Philadelphia Convention (1787) that led to the drafting of the US Constitution, the European Convention (2005) that produced a draft European constitution (even if it was ultimately rejected), the Congress of Vienna (1815) that established the post-Napoleonic European order, and the Treaty of Paris (1856) bringing the Crimean War to a peaceful end – they all confirm that the success of a multilateral conference lies in its management: the process must be balanced and at least as much thought has to be given to organizing the negotiations as to the content. There must be a balance between the plenary sessions and informal discussions; all parties must be included; small groups of states must be able to make decisions; the amendment process must be managed; etc. While the theme is always the same, the lessons vary from one chapter to another. For example, the case study about negotiating UN Security

---

[1]   BAIN, William (2007). "Are There Lessons of History? The English School and the Activity of Being a Historian", *International Politics*, 2007, 44: 527.

Council Resolution 242 of 1967 provides an innovative, productive analysis of the advantages and disadvantages of ambiguous drafting.

Additional studies will be useful for delving more deeply into multilateral failures. The chapter on the Constantinople Conference of 1877 shows that there were clearly multiple contributing factors to that conference's failure. Other cases which were ultimately unsuccessful, such as the World Trade Organization negotiations in Seattle in 1999 or the climate conference in Copenhagen in 2009, were not analyzed here but could be examined in the future to supplement our work and highlight the process-related factor or factors that were missing.

This book also contains lessons for today's negotiators about press management and appropriate levels of transparency. What balance should they strike between diplomatic secrecy and transparency? In Philadelphia, Benjamin Franklin shut the press out entirely. Seventy years later, the plenipotentiaries who met in Paris kept the press at a respectful distance. Another 20 years later, in 1877, delegates to the Constantinople Conference learned that an uninformed press could make their task more difficult. But in 1914, the disadvantages of being overly close-mouthed became crystal clear: the embassies' convoluted secret diplomacy led to misunderstandings and is one of the factors that triggered World War I. In 1919, Woodrow Wilson made the pendulum swing back the other way and promoted "transparent diplomacy", but it proved impossible to put into practice and Wilson was the first to ignore his own advice. Nearly a century later, in 2005, the press was given regular updates during the Security Council negotiations on Darfur, and the delegates to the Brussels convention found a way to work with the press. Finally, in 1998 at St Malo, the useful deal struck between the UK and France came out absolutely unexpectedly, and did bear fruit. What conclusions can we reach? A certain amount of secrecy is clearly necessary for interesting options to be proposed and to bring sensitive negotiations to a successful end. But the balance between transparency and secrecy must be carefully managed as a topic in itself, with alternating phases of both.

This book also provides lessons on commercial negotiations. The first date from 960 BCE, with the Phoenicians and their strange but effective art of silent bargaining, and their insistence on maintaining a long-term trustful relationship. Three thousand years later, our contemporary free trade agreements are far more complex. Here, the negotiation linkage theory used to analyze the United States-Chile agreement of 2003 provides extremely useful tools for understanding the complexity of those agreements, minimizing risks, and increasing the chances of success.

In 1868 in Japan, the issues were simpler and the Scottish merchant Thomas Blake Glover already had a strong market position, but that did not prevent him from getting mired in details despite what had seemed to be successful and creative negotiations. As for Christopher Columbus, he was clearly a better navigator than negotiator – it took him seven years to obtain the funds for his "small maritime expedition", which almost nobody was interested in.

Negotiating peace treaties is of course one of the crucial aspects, and one of the high points, of all diplomacy. It is hoped that this book may point to ways to do so successfully. The negotiations of 1659, 1815, 1856, and 1877 are described in terms of managing a process between sovereign states that negotiate in good faith. But that is not the case when the parties are still fighting, such as in Colombia, the Philippines, and Northern Ireland. How do we find our way "out of the woods", to quote the subtitle of the chapter on the FARC-Colombia negotiations? How slowly negotiators and mediators must go! What patience and perseverance they need to "ripen" a peace that is always having to be saved! Each of these three chapters reveals the key factors in sequentially managing the various steps toward peace.

What lessons can be learned from these three cases, where the parties came to the table without a ceasefire? In Colombia and the Philippines, negotiations took place while fighting continued, and mediation had begun in Northern Ireland before the armed struggle had come to an end. Did the absence of a ceasefire help to ripen the negotiations?

The Philippine case is also a surprising example of another, fairly counterintuitive phenomenon: mediation that, despite being conducted by partisan, non-neutral mediators (first Libya then Malaysia), is productive and moves the parties closer to peace.

Another approach, through game theory, is used to analyze the 2018 meeting between Kim Jong-un and Donald Trump. Both parties moved slowly toward each other through a mix of positive and negative signals that had to be subtly managed. This analytical framework is very interesting. Game theory will probably be productive for analyzing other instances where two parties in a very tense relationship send signals that gradually create a more cooperative working environment.

This book also led us to borderline cases. Sometimes, for various reasons, the parties simply do not plan to negotiate. Some have moral objections: in 200 BCE, Roman diplomats under the Republic believed that negotiating was contrary to the notion of justice and to Rome's image itself. For as long as its BATNA allowed, Rome negotiated as little as possible. The case of Germany in 1917, a year before the end of World War I, is more tragic: it voluntarily lost an opportunity to negotiate in good conditions because of the mistaken worldview of commanding general, Ludendorff, who was a victim of groupthink. From an analytical point of view, the ripeness and readiness theories are particularly relevant for understanding a certain number of such refusals to negotiate. The good faith negotiations conducted with Iran in 2003 that eventually failed in 2005 fit within this analytical framework. The reason why parties decide to negotiate, or not, remains a formidable theoretical question, and open for further research.

When the parties are not acting rationally, how should the situation be analyzed? Here, cognitive bias analysis provides effective tools, as shown in the chapter on the start of the Korean conflict in 1950. Surprise, anger, the desire not to back down, and emotions in general all played a role. It is very important to have conceptual tools to analyze such situations where the causes are not entirely rational. The same can be said for the symbolic issues that set off hostilities in Syria in 1920. Symbolic issues also played a role in 1659 between France and Spain: the code of honor, and more broadly the Spanish ministers' chivalric conception of the world, almost caused the peace to fail. It took all the skill France's (Italian) prime minister had to get the issue of honor set aside and to focus the negotiations on interests while not ignoring identity issues. The importance of combining interests with value-related considerations and emotions, which are understandable if not legitimate, is one of this book's lessons.

Not negotiating often means taking the risk of seeing costs increase. Several chapters deal with escalation: in Korea in 1950; between Kim and Trump in 2018; and in Europe in 1914. A detailed analysis of the escalation between Iran and the West between 2005 and 2015 shows that both parties may ultimately pay a higher price than they thought they would.

Conversely, some negotiators take initiative. International negotiations involve risk and courage. The most striking case is perhaps that of the governor of Burgundy who, in 1513, took the risk of negotiating a separate peace with the invading Swiss army, alone and without instructions from his king. He negotiated without a mandate, which negotiation manuals generally advise against. He was inventive and was disavowed, but the surprising thing is that in the end, he successfully defended the interests of the kingdom. That is also one of this book's takeaways: practice is always a little surprising, and sometimes goes beyond theory.

INDEX

CPSIA information can be obtained
at www.ICGtesting.com
Printed in the USA
FFHW012024181119
56068665-62068FF